BANANA CULTURES

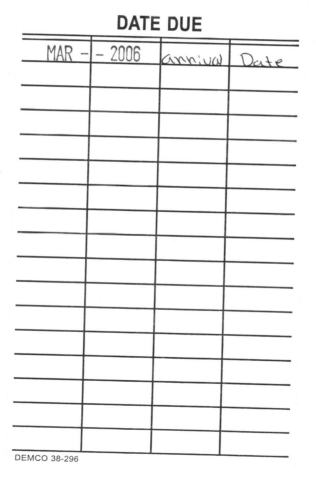

DATE DUE

MAR – – 2006		annival	Date

DEMCO 38-296

Banana Cultures

Agriculture, Consumption, and Environmental Change in Honduras and the United States

JOHN SOLURI

University of Texas Press   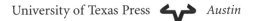   *Austin*

Requests for permission to reproduce material from this work should be sent to:
Permissions
University of Texas Press
P.O. Box 7819
Austin, TX 78713-7819
www.utexas.edu/utpress/about/bpermission.html

♾ The paper used in this book meets the minimum requirements of
ANSI/NISO Z39.48-1992 (R1997) (Permanence of Paper).

LIBRARY OF CONGRESS CATALOGING-IN-PUBLICATION DATA

Soluri, John.
Banana cultures : agriculture, consumption, and environmental change in
Honduras and the United States / John Soluri. — 1st ed.
    p.   cm.
Includes bibliographical references and index.
ISBN 0-292-70957-9 (cloth : alk. paper) — ISBN 0-292-71256-1 (pbk. : alk. paper)
1. Banana trade—Honduras.   2. Banana trade—Social aspects—Honduras.
3. Banana trade—Environmental aspects—Honduras.   4. Banana trade—United
States.   5. Banana trade—Social aspects—United States.   I. Title.
HD9259.B3H678   2005
306.3′49′097283—dc22   2005015808

For Amalia

Contents

Preface

This book began as a research question focused on the relationship between social and environmental change in Honduras. Over many years, it has evolved into a study of the mass production and mass consumption of bananas — the most frequently consumed fresh fruit in the United States. The title refers both to the tropical places where export bananas grew and the cultural spaces where bananas were consumed. When I first became interested in the topic as an undergraduate in the late 1980s, events taking place in Honduras and Central America routinely made headlines in the United States. Today, the U.S. government's latest effort to "install democracy" has shifted public attention to other places and commodities. In Honduras, the value of exports of apparel now dwarfs that of banana exports. However, this ought not to discourage serious reflection on the history of bananas — an important internationally traded commodity that gave rise to, among other things, the United Fruit Company, one of the first and most powerful transnational corporations of the past century. Living in an era when many people seem at a loss to imagine a world not dominated by corporations and mass markets, it strikes me as imperative to reexamine the historical processes that have shaped places where commodities are produced and consumed.

If this book has an overriding message, it is the need for people to think and act in ways that acknowledge the dynamic relationships between production and consumption, between people and nonhuman forms of life, and between cultures and economies. Ultimately, I believe that many twentieth-century models and ideologies of development and conservation are flawed because they share underlying (and unexamined) assumptions that nature and culture are either static or change in predictable ways. However, there is little that is timeless about nature — human or otherwise.

On a less lofty level, this book seeks to answer (finally) a question that friends, family members, and acquaintances frequently ask: "Do you eat bananas?" The simple answer, for me, is "yes" (organic when available). But the question itself is somewhat misguided. In the contemporary United States, food and eating have produced both high anxieties and great denials. One result is a tendency to inscribe moral judgments upon particular foods, such as bananas, veal, grapes, or the most recent (and sweeping) evil: carbohydrates. An alternative approach might be to rephrase the question as "What does it mean to eat bananas?" This question compels us to think about people in the United States who consume inexpensive, identical looking and tasting bananas on an everyday basis while symbolically distancing themselves from the "banana republics" where people live and labor to produce inexpensive, identical looking and tasting bananas. In other words, the question forces us to ponder consumption, work, power, history, and the nature of banana cultures.

Acknowledgments

Any project that is ten years in the making accumulates a long list of people and institutions to thank. My journey into the lowland tropical regions of Honduras began in Oswego, New York, a place better known for its blizzards than bananas. I have had the good fortune to be part of a family that has continually supported me and encouraged my intellectual pursuits even when they have led to odd destinations. Although not readily apparent from its subject matter, this book bears the lasting influence of James and Sally Soluri.

I am also grateful to a number of individuals who mentored me at the University of Michigan, including Rebecca Scott, Richard Tucker, Ivette Perfecto, John Vandermeer, Frederick Cooper, and Sueann Caulfield. Their creative and rigorous scholarship has served as both an inspiration and a challenge. I am equally grateful to the Rackham School of Graduate Studies for providing me with outstanding financial support throughout my graduate career, including a grant (funded by the Andrew Mellon Foundation) for the dissertation research from which much of this book is derived. A very special acknowledgment is extended to Darío Euraque, who in addition to reading multiple versions (in English and Spanish) of this project has served as an invaluable bridge between the often very different worlds of "gringos" and "catrachos."

I can only begin to thank all of the people in Honduras who made this book possible. In Tegucigalpa, Mario Argueta of the National Autonomous University of Honduras (UNAH), and the present director of the Honduran National Archive, Carlos Maldonado, set high standards for professionalism while working under challenging circumstances. I also am indebted to the staffers of the National Archive and former director Fredy Flores. My research assistant and friend Lenin Valenzuela risked his health to help me clean, sort, and transcribe documents for several weeks in 1995. On the North Coast, the staffs of the municipal secretaries of El Progreso, La Ceiba, Olanchito, Sonaguera, and Tela demonstrated tremendous patience and humor while I sifted through their archival holdings. I have spent many productive hours consulting the library and human resources of the Fundación Hondureña de Investigación Agrícola (FHIA) in La Lima. I extend my sincere gratitude to FHIA director Dr. Adolfo Martínez and Lic. Emily de Alvarado, whose intelligence is only surpassed by her warmth.

The late Dr. Robert Stover, truly a world expert on banana pathogens, shared his collection of unpublished research reports, and his longtime assistant Jorge Romero helped me to interpret them. I am forever indebted to both of them. I also thank Dr. Eugene Ostmark and J. P. Sánchez for providing me with unpublished manuscripts related to the history of the fruit companies' research departments. My deepest gratitude is to the many men and women who took the time to share with me their memories and impressions of bygone days on the North Coast. On more than one occasion, I arrived with little warning; more often than not I was treated with a hospitality that most people in the United States only reserve for their closest friends. If I am able to convey a sense of the complex world in which they live — a reality that cannot be captured by the word "underdeveloped" — I will be content.

In the United States, staff members at the National Archives in College Park, Maryland, and the Library of Congress helped me to navigate through a wide range of primary source materials. I am similarly indebted to the staff of Harvard University's Baker Library. In particular I thank Laura Linard for her support over several years. Thanks also to the staff of Tulane University's Howard-Tilton Library in New Orleans and Mary Sicchio, archivist of the W. B. Nickerson Room at Cape Cod Community College in Barnstable, Massachusetts.

Since 1999, I have been a member of the Carnegie Mellon University History Department. It is hard to envision a more supportive environment for junior faculty. Not only has Carnegie Mellon provided funds for follow-up research trips to Honduras and Washington, D.C., but a number of my colleagues there have taken the time to comment on portions of this book. I thank Paul Eiss, Caroline Acker, Scott Sandage, David Miller, Mary Lindemann, Kate Lynch, and Edward Constant.

In addition, Steve Striffler, Stuart McCook, and George Reid Andrews commented on the entire manuscript. All three deserve special acknowledgment for setting high standards with their own work and pushing me to clarify my arguments in earlier versions of this book. Christian Brannstrom, Reinaldo Funes, Stefania Gallini, Lowell Gudmundson, George Lovell, Michael Miller, Lara Putnam, Adam Rome, Doug Sackman, Susan

Strasser, Allen Wells, and Ronny Viales offered feedback on portions of the manuscript. In addition, the superb research of scholar-activist Steve Marquardt has helped to reassure me that fungi, indeed, matter. Geographer Michael Pacey produced the excellent "representations of space" (i.e., maps). Finally, I am grateful to the following individuals for helping me to locate sources: Bernadette Callery, Carnegie Museum of Natural History; John A. Collins, Lamont Library; Angela Krulc, Harvard Botany Libraries; Jim Longhurst; and Marnie Hampton.

University of Texas Press Sponsoring Editor William Bishel was willing to take a chance on a book about Honduras. My gratitude to Bill and his colleagues at the University of Texas Press, including Lynne Chapman and Teri Sperry, who brought their considerable talents, patience, and enthusiasm to bear on this sometimes complicated project.

Since I began this project, Amy Crosson has been my *compañera* in the truest sense of the word. She has worked in archives, conducted interviews, formatted bibliographies, and driven death-defying Honduran highways—all while pursuing her own interests in human rights, early childhood education, and scholarly research. She is, without doubt, my top banana.

Introduction

Linking Places of Production and Consumption

The first sweetened cup of hot tea to be drunk by an English worker was a significant historical event, because it prefigured the transformation of an entire society, a total remaking of its economic and social basis. We must struggle to understand fully the consequences of that and kindred events, for upon them was erected an entirely different conception of the relationship between producers and consumers, of the meaning of work, of the definition of self, of the nature of things.

SIDNEY MINTZ, 1985

Once they fell into United Fruit hands, tropical swamps and jungles soon blossomed into immense plots of luscious green banana plants, set out in rows, on well-drained, properly fertilized, and irrigated soil. Progressive agriculture practices never heard of before, in connection with silting, flooding, and spraying in a never-ending fight against plant disease, produced millions of stems of the golden fruit for export.

STACY MAY AND GALO PLAZA, 1958

Chances are good that most U.S. readers who pick up this book will have eaten a banana in the recent past. Chances are equally good that they will not remember the experience because banana eating in the United States has become rather banal. But this was not always the case. Prior to the mid-nineteenth century, few residents of the United States had tasted a banana and fewer still ate them on a regular basis. However, the last quarter of the nineteenth century witnessed a sharp rise in banana consumption in the United States that transcended lines of gender, class, race, and region.

Entering the 1920s, the only fresh fruit eaten in greater quantities in the nation was the apple. By that time, the banana had acquired important symbolic meanings too, slipping into anglophone street slang, popular music, comedy, literature, and poetry. The slender, yellow fruit was one of a growing number of tropical commodities that helped to define everyday consumer culture in the United States.

If bananas had shed most of their exoticism by the early twentieth century, the same cannot be said of their tropical places of origin. Yankee writers, merchants, diplomats, and cartoonists tended to view the tropics as a world apart, filled with dark, sensual, and slothful people who survived largely due to the natural fecundity of the sun- and rain-drenched landscapes that they inhabited. This perception of tropical lands and peoples was captured by the phrase "banana republic," coined in a 1904 novel by O. Henry, the pseudonym of U.S. writer William Sydney Porter. The tragically powerful metaphor has served as both an explanation of and a justification for the political conflicts, poverty, and U.S. interventions that were at the center of twentieth-century Central American history. Paradoxically, many people in the United States have distanced themselves from Central America by using bananas — the very commodity that has linked the two regions for more than a century — as a symbol for "corrupt," "backward," and "underdeveloped" societies.

Honduras, one of the world's leading exporters of bananas between the 1870s and 1970s, has been considered by many observers in the United States to be the "banana republic" par excellence. To be sure, Hondurans have faced more than their share of political instability, poverty, and U.S. strong-arming during the past century. Nevertheless, they have their own set of meanings for bananas. Even more so than in the United States, bananas and plantains have formed a central part of Honduran diets. Most Honduran home gardens — be they cultivated by Pech Indians in Mosquitia or urban professionals in Tegucigalpa — include at least a couple of varieties of bananas and plantains. The expansion of export production in the late nineteenth century transformed the banana from a mundane dietary staple into "green gold" (oro verde). The fruit symbolized the material riches that filled the dreams of many working people in Honduras and elsewhere in Central America. Export production gave rise to the North Coast (la costa norte), a region filled with the wonders of Yankee-style modernization: hospitals, electricity, ice factories, railroads, airplanes, radios, and imported foods, clothing, and music. The region's dynamic economy attracted a heterogeneous group of immigrants who helped to create powerful social and political movements in the twentieth century. Many Honduran writers portrayed banana workers as icons of resistance to U.S. hegemony and capitalist exploitation. In Honduras, then, the banana is an ambivalent symbol whose complexity stands in sharp contrast to the fruit's trivial status in U.S. popular culture.

The banana's late-nineteenth-century transition from an exotic novelty to a commodity of mass consumption in the United States produced much more than new symbolic meanings for the fruit. A dramatic increase in production transformed lowland tropical landscapes and livelihoods from Mexico to Ecuador. Over the span of a century, workers felled forests and drained wetlands; planted, cultivated, and harvested bananas; built railroad tracks and entire towns; and prepared meals, laundered clothes, and raised children. This was not the first time that human initiative had transformed these regions, but the rate and scale of resource use were without historical precedent. These environmental changes in turn helped to transform a low-input production process into one that was, and continues to be, both capital and labor intensive.

This book traces the entwined environmental and social transformations that shaped the North Coast of Honduras between roughly 1870 and 1975. The story takes place primarily in and around banana farms, but the setting periodically shifts to the United States, where millions of people consumed bananas physically and symbolically. I follow the banana from farm to market in order to explore the dynamic relationship between mass production and mass consumption that drove, both directly and indirectly, environmental and social change on the North Coast. This transnational perspective also reveals that the fruit companies' economic power derived from both their railroad and land monopolies in Central America *and* their control over mass markets in the United States. The discursive power of the "banana republic" metaphor makes it easy to overlook the ways in which monopoly capitalism in the United States shaped the twentieth-century history of the banana trade. In following the banana on its international journey, I cross the boundaries of several academic fields in order to write a history that is cross-fertilized by the perspectives of biologists and geographers in addition to those of cultural, environmental, and social historians. The study incorporates a wide range of sources, including manuscript census data from Honduras, fruit company records, published scientific papers, Honduran and U.S. government correspondence, oral testimonies, and ephemera (e.g., song lyrics, recipes, and advertisements) from U.S. mass culture. Some recent studies on bananas have worked with a subset of these sources, but few have sought to integrate them.[1]

The "banana lands" or "enclaves" of Latin America and the Caribbean have drawn the attention of both English- and Spanish-language writers over the years, including Nobel Laureates Miguel Ángel Asturias, Gabriel García Márquez, and Pablo Neruda, in addition to journalists, travelers, and scholars. Few multinational corporations operating in Latin America have generated as much controversy as the U.S. companies that dominated the twentieth-century banana trade. The companies' defenders upheld them as pillars of modernity and prosperity, pointing out that they created tens of thousands of jobs, constructed transportation infrastructure, and introduced scientific approaches to tropical agriculture and medicine.[2] Critics countered by citing the companies' land and transportation monopolies, repression of labor movements, and tax subsidies as evidence that the companies' profits resulted from the exploitation of Latin American people. During the 1960s and 1970s, the banana companies were often at the center of debates between modernization theorists on one side, who saw the infusion of capital and technology as necessary to help Latin Americans shed their "traditional" livelihoods and ways of thinking, and their dependency school critics on the other, who claimed that foreign capital was "underdeveloping" Latin America.[3]

The polemical debates often obscured the fact that the opposing sides shared some key assumptions. As historian Catherine LeGrand has observed, "scholars working from modernization and dependency perspectives have tended to agree that foreign companies held the power and did what they wished, while locals were passive, acted upon."[4] LeGrand and several other scholars have successfully challenged images of omnipotent U.S. banana companies manipulating "comprador" elites and hapless peasants by showing how national banana growers in Colombia, merchants in Honduras, labor union activists in Guatemala, West Indian migrants in Costa Rica, and worker-cultivators in Ecuador challenged and at times redirected the policies pursued by government authorities and fruit company managers.[5] This body of research has identified the agency of a wide range of actors while providing historical content to a topic long-dominated by rigid typologies such as "enclave," "proletariat," and "boom and bust" economy.

Recent scholarship on export banana production has devoted less attention to the shared assumptions held by modernization and dependency theorists about lowland tropical landscapes. With few exceptions, writers from both theoretical camps have placed great faith in the capacity of science and technology to enable the efficient utilization of natural resources. Both Spanish- and English-language sources from the early twentieth century frequently praised foreign capital and technologies for turning unhealthy "wastelands" into productive gardens. Modernizationists and *dependentistas* considered the transformation of tropical landscapes as progress toward different imagined ends (a stable middle class for the former, and a revolutionary proletariat in the case of the latter). Once again, the shared assumption is that tropical landscapes, not unlike their inhabitants, are essentially passive, acted upon.

The story that follows challenges this assumption by exploring the interactions among diverse and often divided people, not-so-diverse banana plants, and persistent yet unpredictable pathogens that formed and reformed tropical landscapes and livelihoods in export banana zones. In other words, I try to put the agriculture back into banana plantation history in order to pay critical attention to both scientific ideas about tropical landscapes and the everyday cultivation practices that absorbed so much of working people's time and energy. I am less interested in arguing for the primacy of cultural or biological processes than in demonstrating their historical entanglement. In order to do so, I borrow concepts from agroecology, an emerging field of research that studies interactions between cropping systems and their surrounding environments. Agroecosystems are places created and transformed by fluid processes that are subject to change over time and space and therefore possess both dynamic pasts and uncertain futures rooted in an ecosocial realm of possibilities. In emphasizing the role of contingency, or the historicity of agroecological systems, I am not suggesting that people-plant interactions take place in an "anything goes" world without limits. The qualitative differences between a banana plantation and a lowland tropical forest cannot be denied; indeed, their disparate qualities are central to this book's overarching argument. Nevertheless, attempts to draw well-defined borders between natural spaces and cultural places run the peril of ignoring all-important interactions between fields, forests, and waterways; and between cultivated, wild, and hybrid organisms.[6]

Banana plants, like most crop plants, are at once biological organisms and cultural artifacts—products of both evolutionary contingencies and human agency. Early cultivators in Southeast Asia first domesticated bananas several thousand years ago. Dozens of varieties subsequently diffused throughout South Asia, the Pacific, and Africa. How and when banana cultivars reached the Americas is subject to debate, but they have been widely cultivated in the hemisphere for at least 400 years.[7] Between 1500 and 1850, their consumption was largely confined to the tropics; in the sugarcane-growing regions of Brazil and the Caribbean, slaves routinely grew bananas and plantains on provision grounds. The self-propagating, high-yielding herbaceous plants were well suited to meet the needs of slaves because they required little labor to cultivate and transform into food. In addition, the fast-growing, tall and leafy plants provided shade for ground crops.[8] The dynamics of the post-emancipation period in the Caribbean helped to set the stage for export banana growing in the region. In the struggle to find dignified livelihoods, the descendants of slaves would be among the first to sell bananas to itinerant North American schooner captains in the mid-nineteenth century.

The export banana trade formed around a single variety: Gros Michel. The variety apparently did not reach the Americas until the early nineteenth century. In 1837, Jean Pouyat, a coffee planter in Jamaica, introduced a Gros Michel rhizome that he had acquired in Martinique. The variety soon flourished in Jamaica and later spread throughout Central America. Although this "creation story" may be apocryphal, it suggests that the variety's genetic base was exceedingly narrow, a condition that would shape export production in crucial ways. As both small- and large-scale Gros Michel monocultures replaced lowland forests and wetlands, a qualitatively different agroecosystem took form that "invite[d] the development of disease epidemics by providing high densities of genetically uniform hosts."[9] In addition, the railroads and shipping lines that linked production zones facilitated the movement of pathogens across localities and regions.

Two plant pathogens—popularly known as Panama and Sigatoka diseases—have played leading roles in the history of export banana growing in the Caribbean and Latin America. The significance of the two diseases varied over time and space. In the early twentieth century, the fruit companies responded to Panama disease, a soil-borne pathogen, by practicing what I call "shifting plantation agriculture," abandoning infected soils and removing infrastructure for reuse in areas where the disease was not present. When Sigatoka appeared in the 1930s, banana producers did not have time to run from the air-borne fungal pathogen. Instead, United Fruit Company scientists in Honduras devised a capital- and labor-intensive control system based on high-volume Bordeaux spray (copper sulfate), the costs of which forced many small-scale growers to abandon the trade. For farmworkers and other North Coast residents, the fruit companies' efforts to control the two plant disease epidemics shaped livelihoods in important and long-lasting ways. Although human diseases such as malaria have received more scholarly attention, the fungal pathogens that invaded Gros Michel banana plantations have arguably played a larger, albeit indirect role in shaping the daily lives of people in the North Coast's *zonas bananeras.*

The historical significance of Panama and Sigatoka diseases cannot be explained entirely in terms of regional agroecological dynamics. Complex interactions between pathogen, plant host, and agroecosystem shaped the epidemics, but so too did the cultural, economic, and social processes that gave rise to mass markets for bananas in the United States. Economic historians have written extensively about the "boom and bust" cycles that characterized Latin American export production during the past 150 years, but they have devoted little attention to understanding how mass markets affected the agroecological resources upon which export economies have been based.[10] I describe the formation and evolution of U.S. mass markets for bananas in both socioeconomic and cultural terms in order to shed light on both who could afford to eat bananas and why people chose to eat them in the first place. In other words, this book examines the transformation of a tropical plant into a food commodity. Taking an excursion into banana cuisine is pleasurable and at times amusing, but my primary reason for paying critical attention to mass markets and consumer culture is to explain the transformation of export banana agriculture in the tropics.[11]

If this study aspires to operate on a transnational level, it also seeks to shed light on the history of a specific region: the North Coast of Honduras. Approaching the region from the Caribbean Sea, a nineteenth-century traveler first encountered miles of sandy beaches, mangrove swamps, and stands of coconut palms cultivated primarily by the Garífuna people, who had inhabited the coastline since the late eighteenth century. Beyond the littoral zone lay a narrow plain that quickly gave way to foothills and mountain ranges whose highest peaks exceeded 2,500 meters. Xicaque Indians and mestizo cattle ranchers inhabited the sparsely populated lowlands. Numerous rivers descended from the highlands and meandered toward the sea. The alluvial valleys carved by the largest rivers — the Aguán and the Ulúa — were the sites of pre-Columbian settlements. The region appears to have been a dividing line of sorts between Mayan and Xicaque indigenous groups. Important crops included cacao, cassava and other tubers, and seed crops such as maize and beans. The drastic demographic decline among indigenous populations following sustained contact with Europeans and Africans contributed to an expansion of forest cover in lowland areas. By the late 1800s, all that remained of the region's pre-Columbian settlements were the ceramic artifacts that export banana growers frequently unearthed when planting their farms.[12]

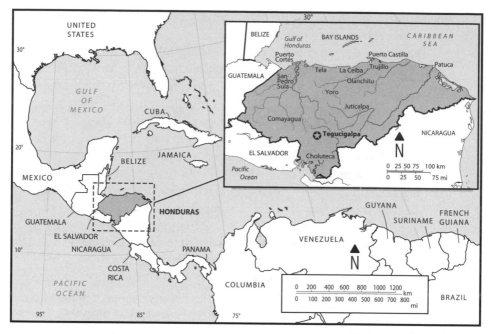

MAP I.1. *Honduras*

Unfortunately, exceedingly few scholarly histories on this region have been published in English. With the notable exception of Darío Euraque, historians working in the United States have focused their attention on banana enclaves located elsewhere in Central America, notably Costa Rica and Guatemala.[13] Honduran researchers, often working with limited financial and archival resources, have produced a small number of valuable studies that have not circulated widely.[14] As a result, scholarly analyses of the export banana trade have been formulated with limited knowledge of the region that probably shipped more export bananas between 1870 and 1950 than any other place in the world. In 1929, Honduran exports far exceeded the combined exports from Costa Rica, Guatemala, Nicaragua, and Panama. Honduras remained the leading Central American exporter of bananas through 1970.[15]

But the importance of the North Coast of Honduras extends beyond the sheer volume of bananas that left its shores; the region's history sheds light on a number of issues central to understanding the banana trade's trajectory. For example, many studies on export banana production tend to conflate the formation of the United Fruit Company in 1899 with the beginning of "modern" export banana production. This periodization overlooks the fact that a heterogeneous group of growers along the Caribbean coast of Honduras and elsewhere in Central America and the Caribbean began selling bananas for export no later than the early 1870s. These seldom-acknowledged cultivators helped to set the export trade in motion some twenty-five years before the incorporation of the United Fruit Company. In fact, United Fruit did not secure its first railroad concession in Honduras until 1913, approximately forty years after individuals in Honduras began growing bananas for U.S. markets. The cursory accounts of the late-nineteenth-century banana trade generally portray the period as either a "golden age" for growers or a "chaotic" period characterized by unsophisticated production and shipping practices. Both views oversimplify a complex dynamic between growers, shippers, and the Honduran state. They also downplay the continuities in the nineteenth- and twentieth-century trades. Although the early twentieth century witnessed a dramatic increase in the scale of production, cultivation practices remained relatively unchanged during the first half-century of trade.

Scholars have also underestimated the persistence of non-company growers in Honduras during the years when the U.S. fruit companies began to integrate vertically. For writers who have portrayed the fruit companies as introducing advances in agriculture, medicine, education, and economic organization, small-scale cultivators and their low-input agricultural methods have often symbolized the non-modern "other" with which the virtues of the banana companies' modernizing projects are contrasted.[16] On the other hand, many Marxist critiques, endeavoring to fit the banana industry's history into linear models of proletarianization, have focused on the emergence of a class-conscious proletariat disposed to organizing strikes, trade unions, and communist movements.[17] Both of these approaches generally fail to account for the dynamic presence of small-scale cultivators whose initiative, persistence, and unpredictability undermine both liberal and Marxist visions of modernity.

In some instances, the extension of company railroads actually stimulated small-scale production by providing cultivators with vital links to seaports. Non-company growers continued to produce and sell significant quantities of bananas through the 1930s. Both the scope and persistence of non-company production on the North Coast call into question the distinctions often drawn between Honduras and export banana zones in Colombia, Costa Rica, and Jamaica, where the presence of non-company growers has been widely acknowledged. For example, banana exports from Honduras and Costa Rica were on a par around 1900. By the 1930s, non-company production in Costa Rica accounted for a much larger proportion of that nation's banana exports (75 percent) than non-company exports accounted for in Honduras (30 percent), but the quantity of bananas sold by non-company growers in the latter country exceeded the quantity sold by non-company producers in the former. The point is not to diminish the significance of non-company growers in Costa Rica but rather to suggest that scholars working within national frameworks have made cases for "exceptionalism" by assuming that somewhere (and Honduras is often that place) an archetype enclave existed consisting of company-controlled plantations and proletariat.

In fact, not one but three major U.S. fruit companies (United, Standard, and Cuyamel) operated in Honduras between 1900 and 1930. On the one hand, this fact can be used to lend support to that nation's status as the ultimate banana republic. On the other hand, it suggests that the United Fruit Company was unable to establish an absolute monopoly in Honduras such as it enjoyed in Guatemala and Costa Rica during the first half of the twentieth century. Indeed, evidence suggests that North Coast elites were able to leverage power by playing the fruit companies against one another. This ability diminished considerably following United Fruit's purchase of Samuel Zemurray's Cuyamel Fruit Company in 1929. However, Zemurray would wrest control of United Fruit in 1933, using his enormous stock holdings to force the board of directors to recognize him as a de facto chief executive officer. He remained a powerful figure in the company until he resigned from the board in 1957. If banana men in Costa Rica (Minor Keith) and Jamaica (Lorenzo Dow Baker) played leading roles in founding United Fruit, Zemurray—who built his fortune primarily in Honduras— presided over the restoration of the company's economic power following the crisis of the early 1930s.[18]

All three U.S. fruit companies operating in Honduras made important innovations in both production and marketing processes that transformed the entire export banana industry. Between 1930 and 1984, Honduras was the home of United Fruit's tropical research department, which, along with British research programs in Jamaica and Trinidad, set the agenda for banana research for most of the twentieth century. Among the most significant innovations made by United Fruit scientists was the Bordeaux spray system devised in 1935 to control Sigatoka. The system diffused rapidly throughout export banana zones in the Caribbean and Latin America and set an important precedent for the large-scale use of chemical fungicides in tropical agriculture. Although the New Orleans– based Standard Fruit Company did not establish a research department in Honduras until the early 1950s, the company initiated one of the most important changes in the twentieth-century trade when it began shipping Panama disease–resistant Cavendish bananas in cardboard boxes in 1957. Within ten years, virtually all bananas bound for the United States traveled in boxes, an innovation that would alter both the production and marketing of the fruit.

The North Coast was also the site of numerous challenges to the fruit companies' power. People living in banana zones struggled to establish and maintain livelihoods by forming grower associations, challenging the fruit companies' claims to the region's resources, and by "voting with their feet" when plantation working conditions became intolerable. In the 1920s, a dramatic expansion of banana exports coincided with rising labor militancy: dozens of strikes took place over a range of issues, including wages and the companies' use of Caribbean laborers. In 1932, banana company workers went on strike in response to wage cuts. In the case of the Truxillo Railroad Company (a United Fruit subsidiary), a two-month-long strike involving some 3,000 laborers did not end until government and company officials cooperated in the arrest and temporary removal of the strike leaders.[19] That same year, National Party candidate Tiburcio Carías Andino was elected president, initiating sixteen years of authoritarian rule. When Carías finally stepped down from power in 1948, labor organizers wasted little time in pushing for reforms. Then in 1954, United Fruit workers walked off the job en masse. The strike quickly spread to Standard Fruit's operations and eventually to other sectors of the economy. The *Gran huelga* of 1954 gave rise to powerful union and campesino movements that, in alliance with liberal North Coast merchants, succeeded in reforming Honduran labor codes, agrarian laws, social welfare, and tax structures.[20] The fruit companies responded to the rising power of Honduran workers by cutting jobs. They closed farms, mechanized Sigatoka control, and contracted out labor-intensive production processes via "associate grower" programs. These changes accelerated an industrywide shift to a heavy reliance on both agrochemicals and contract farming.[21] In sum, many of the environmental and social transformations that took place on the North Coast of Honduras affected the trajectory of the entire export banana trade during the twentieth century.

Finally, the North Coast is important not only because of its relationship to the rest of Honduras, but also because of its close historical ties to the United States. Although far greater attention has been given to the role played by the United States elsewhere in Central America, the North Coast was the site of at least seven military interventions during the early twentieth century.[22] In 1928, U.S. President-elect Herbert Hoover visited

Amapala, Honduras, where he gave a speech calling for cooperation and understanding among the nations of the Western Hemisphere. The U.S. government under President Franklin Delano Roosevelt supported Honduran President Tiburcio Carías Andino through World War II, less for his commitment to democracy than for his ability to bring "stability" during a period when the United States sought to create a hemispheric alliance of "good neighbors" against Nazi Germany. Following 1945, the defeat of fascist governments, combined with rising fears about the spread of communism, led the United States to play a much more active role in the Caribbean and Central America. This took many forms on the North Coast, ranging from seminars for union leaders on how to build anticommunist labor movements to covert activities including "Operation PB Success," the CIA-planned overthrow of the Arbenz government in Guatemala that used Honduras as a staging ground. More recently, the U.S. State Department pressured Honduran leaders into providing assistance for its covert operations carried out against the Sandinista government in Nicaragua and the FMLN guerrillas in El Salvador.[23]

But interactions between the United States and the North Coast of Honduras have not been restricted to diplomats and military officials. This book reveals some of the "everyday" encounters between people in Honduras and the United States that resulted from the mass production and mass consumption of an agricultural commodity. These routine — even mundane — exchanges were seldom as dramatic as a CIA-financed coup d'état, but they nevertheless changed life in *zonas bananeras* in lasting ways.

Before outlining the organization of the book, I offer some final remarks on the unconventional cast of characters awaiting the reader. Political leaders, customarily assigned leading roles in historical drama, are here upstaged by banana plants, pathogens, and working people. My decision to move politics off center stage is not to deny its importance to the story of export banana production. As many scholars have demonstrated, the profits made by U.S. fruit companies operating in Honduras resulted largely from their ability to secure generous concessions that provided them monopoly privileges over regional transportation networks, access to subsidized soil and water resources, and the ability to import workers. However, images of "banana men" cutting backroom deals with corrupt politicians obscure the fact that bananas grow in soil, not on paper; the concessions provided the banana companies with crucial advantages over potential competitors, but they did not make banana production a fait accompli. The biophysical resources needed to grow bananas were not infinitely malleable "raw materials," but components of dynamic agroecosystems. Ultimately, the fruit companies had an easier time manipulating politicians than they did controlling the people, plants, and pathogens whose daily interactions largely shaped landscapes and livelihoods on the North Coast.

The work of cultivating and processing plants has been a central endeavor—if not a defining act—of human societies for millennia. Even today, when a majority of the world's population engages in non-agrarian livelihoods, manipulating plants—be it at the cellular or landscape level—continues to occupy a central place in the material and symbolic realms of daily life. This book calls attention to the continued importance of agriculture in a postmodern age. My intent is to restore dynamism to agriculture and to recover the livelihoods of worker/cultivators in export banana zones without romanticizing their often arduous and uncertain work, over-simplifying their lives, or inscribing political tendencies upon them. Finally, I seek to identify the human agents who collectively formed the mass market "structures" that played a central role in shaping production. These are not always easy tasks, yet they are important ones for historians (and others) seeking to interrupt discourses on development that equate progress with rising rates of consumption and technological innovation while displaying little concern for those who bear the brunt of the risks that accompany changing landscapes and livelihoods.

I have organized this rather unconventional history in a very conventional way: the chapters proceed roughly in chronological order, beginning in the nineteenth century and ending in the late twentieth century. In so doing, I intend not only to engage readers but also to place emphasis on the explanatory power of historical narrative. Quite simply, I hope to offer a new perspective on change over time in an export banana zone. That said, this project has no intentions of turning back the clock on the important exchanges that have taken place in recent years between history and other fields of study, including anthropology, literary studies, and cultural geography, which have emphasized the complex and contested nature of historical memories and meanings. I have attempted to craft a story in which both explanation and meaning exist in creative tension.

The first chapter attempts to establish an agroecological baseline for the North Coast circa 1875 from which to chart changes in production processes over time. The interactions of banana growers, exporters, consumers, and the state during this pre–United Fruit era shaped the trajectory of the trade in important and enduring ways, not the least of which was a preference for Gros Michel bananas. Expanding markets provided a heterogeneous group of cultivators with an opportunity to accumulate capital, but incessant struggles between growers and exporters over shipping schedules, purchase prices, and definitions of quality undermine images of the era as a "golden age." The chapter also argues that the expansion of export banana production cannot be attributed entirely to market forces. The Honduran state, anxious to control the people and resources of the North Coast, created liberal land and tax policies in order to stimulate export agriculture. Paradoxically, the resource-strapped state sought to achieve hegemony (and economic expansion) by granting concessions to non-nationals whose projects more closely conformed to liberal visions of *fomento,* or development, than did the livelihoods of many of the North Coast's resident peoples. The U.S. banana companies did not single-handedly modernize Honduras; modernity — as a set of ideas about agriculture, economic trade, and nationalism — preceded their arrival.

Chapter 2 examines the profound agroecological transformations that took place between 1910 and 1940, a period when people, Gros Michel bananas, and fungal pathogens "invaded" the North Coast. At the same time, Gros Michel bananas "invaded" the United States on an unprecedented scale, triggering congressional debates over taxes, inspiring dance crazes, and nourishing tens of millions of people. I link these simultaneous invasions by examining early efforts to find a Panama disease–resistant export banana, a goal that would frustrate a generation of banana breeders who faced constraints imposed by the banana's biology, the organization of production, and the structures and aesthetics of mass markets. Unwilling to export a banana that did not closely resemble Gros Michel, the banana companies abandoned diseased farms and relocated to pathogen-free soils. In order to sustain this strategy of "shifting plantation agriculture," the companies had to secure access to large quantities of land, a need that would bring them into conflict with one another as they tried to position themselves to win additional concessions from the Honduran government.

Chapter 3 explores the effects and meanings of the agroecological changes associated with the expansion of banana production from the perspective of non-company cultivators and local communities. After documenting the persistence of non-company banana growers and the changing conditions under which they marketed their fruit during the 1920s and early 1930s, I describe struggles for resources that took place in four localities scattered across the North Coast: Cuyamel, Cortés; Mezapa, Atlántida; Sonaguera, Colón; and La Paz, Colón. These four places cannot be taken as representative of the entire region, but their linked histories reveal the cross-cutting effects of the fruit companies' shifting cultivation strategy. The practice had a devastating economic impact on local economies. But one community's bane was another's boon: the extension of railroads into places where none had previously existed created opportunities for new livelihoods.[24] People contested the fruit companies' control over local resources in a variety of ways. In some places, they staged public protests; more often, challenges materialized in the form of individuals and small groups of people who drafted petitions and set up squatter settlements. Working people often articulated their claims to resources in terms of nationalism and social justice, creating discourses that invoked a racialized view of citizenship that excluded immigrant West Indians and others from having a claim to the North Coast's resources.

The fourth chapter focuses on the science and work of Sigatoka control following the pathogen's appearance and subsequent spread in the Sula valley in 1935. Less than one year after the initial outbreak of Sigatoka, United Fruit scientist Vining Dunlap devised a means to control the disease through the use of Bordeaux spray (copper sulfate and lime). Dunlap's innovation has been credited with saving the export banana industry in Central America, but the capital- and labor-intensive control system was not a viable option for most non-company growers, whose production collapsed in the late 1930s. Those who continued to grow and sell export bananas relinquished virtually all of their autonomy to the fruit companies in return for loans and technical assistance. Sigatoka control also changed daily work for field hands, creating hundreds of relatively high paying jobs that involved applying an aqueous solution of copper sulfate. Indirect evidence strongly suggests that prolonged exposure to Bordeaux spray caused respiratory problems. Sigatoka control, then, anticipated a trend in twentieth-century agriculture toward a greater reliance upon chemical compounds to control agroecological processes that diminished yields of export-quality fruit.

Chapter 5 revisits the plantations portrayed in Honduran writer and Communist Party organizer Ramón Amaya Amador's novel *Prisión verde*. First published in 1950, the novel portrayed working-class life on the North Coast during the regime of Tiburcio Carías Andino (1932–1948), a period marked by severe repression of opposition political parties and labor organizers.[25] In fact, labor histories of Honduras tend to jump from the widespread labor unrest of 1932 to the Great Strike of 1954 because formal worker organizations were all but nonexistent during the *Cariato*.

At times, the oral histories told to me by former fruit company employees resonated so forcefully with Amaya Amador's description of plantation life that I was left wondering to what extent the novel's characters and events had interpenetrated individual and collective memories about the past. The recollections of ex-*campeños,* former field hands, also diverged from Amaya Amador's account in important ways. Workers found ways to survive the often harsh conditions of plantation life by taking advantage of decentralized management structures and isolated work places to negotiate and deflect the power of their bosses. However, rather than catalog a "weapons of the weak," the chapter tries to portray *campeño* livelihoods as a near-constant challenge to the same structures of inequality that circumscribed worker freedoms. I also highlight the daily work with plants, soils, and mules that absorbed so much of *campeños'* energy and time. The chapter incorporates a handful of women's voices in order to shed light on women's work experiences. Evidence suggests that female cooks, laundresses, venders, and prostitutes forged livelihoods that generated significant incomes for women and their families, creating "micro" backward linkages in the plantation economy.[26]

The sixth chapter examines the lives and time of Miss Chiquita, one of the most recognizable U.S. consumer product icons of the twentieth century. "Born" in 1944, Miss Chiquita faded from public view in the 1950s before resurfacing in the 1960s as a brand name for United Fruit's boxed Cavendish bananas. The period in between Miss Chiquita's debut and revival witnessed important transitions in the production and marketing of bananas. In Honduras, the rapid spread of Panama disease, the 1954 strike, and political changes compelled the fruit companies to replace Gros Michel plants with resistant varieties. This change, initiated by the Standard Fruit Company, brought an end to both the era of shifting plantation agriculture and the practice of exporting unprocessed bunches of bananas. The companies built packing plants where Cavendish fruit was cut from the stem, washed, selected, and packed into cardboard boxes prior to being shipped. The decision to box bananas resulted from a need to protect the delicate peel of Cavendish varieties, but it also reflected the post–World War II rise of self-serve supermarkets in the United States. By shipping bananas in branded, "consumer-sized" units from production zones, the fruit companies caught up with twentieth-century marketing trends. In Honduras, Miss Chiquita's rebirth as a brand name altered the lives of real women by creating hundreds of jobs in *empacadoras,* packing plants.

The conversion to Cavendish bananas helped to stabilize banana production, but it did not eliminate the problem of plant pathogens. Chapter 7 traces changes in production processes and their effects on workers between roughly 1945 and 1975, a period when the fruit companies turned increasingly to agrochemicals both to reduce labor costs and to control diseases and pests perceived to lower yields of high-quality fruit. For field hands, daily plantation work brought them into contact with a wide range of agrochemicals capable of producing acute and chronic health problems. The history of Nemagón (DBCP), a pesticide that produced both dramatic increases in fruit yields and reproductive health problems for hundreds of men and women in Honduras, clearly reveals the promise and perils of pesticide use. By situating the use of DBCP and other agrochemicals in the context of production-consumption dynamics, I reveal the historical and agroecological roots of practices that continue to shape the daily environments of farmworkers.

The concluding chapter places the history of the export banana trade between Honduras and the United States in comparative perspective by drawing upon scholarship on other agricultural export commodities, including coffee, deciduous fruits, and sugar. A comparative view reveals both the diversity of historical experiences spawned by the mass production and mass consumption of food commodities and some common themes upon which variations occur. Confronting the paradox of regional variation in a "global" world is central to the formulation of new explanatory models capable of informing discussions about agriculture, food, and environmental change — discussions in which I believe historians must struggle to make their voices heard.

Chapter 1

Going Bananas

George Bush, purser of the S.S. Chase *was arrested by an officer acting as* Comandante *in consequence of a dispute with some* negros *about the payment of some rejected fruit. Consul deposited the amount in dispute to get Bush out of prison.*

WILLIAM BURCHARD, U.S. CONSUL, ROATÁN, JULY 15, 1881

In the mid-1840s, Thomas Young, Deputy Superintendent of the British Central American Land Company, traveled along the Río Negro, one of many rivers that cut through the narrow coastal plain that stretches along Honduras's Caribbean coastline. Paddling upstream with a group of Miskito Indians, Young observed "thousands of banana trees growing spontaneously, the fruit of which is so much sought after by the natives, who come from very distant parts to Black River, to gather it." He noted the ease with which the plant could be cultivated and added that "the ripe fruit is highly esteemed, although it is apt to disagree with Europeans if eaten shortly before or after taking spirits. The green fruit is cut into slices by the Spaniards, and exposed to the sun, and when rubbed, forms a kind of flour of which they are fond."[1]

When Young visited the Río Negro region, bananas were a novelty item in Europe and the United States, and little export-oriented agriculture of any kind took place in the Caribbean lowlands of Honduras. Most of the region's nineteenth-century exports, including mahogany, fustic (a dyewood), deer skins, sarsaparilla, and rubber, were extracts from forested ecosystems and wetlands. As late as 1859, a traveler journeying by canoe from Omoa to Puerto Cortés described forests that extended from hillsides down to the edge of narrow sandy beaches along the coast. A large lagoon near Puerto Cortés featured an "incredible" number of sea nettles and "large shoals" of fish.[2] Most of the indigenous people in the region forged livelihoods based on forestry, fishing, foraging, hunting, and livestock raising, supplemented by small-scale production of corn, beans, and yuca.[3] Agriculture in the region can best be described as small-scale monocultures and polycultures. Extensive plantings of bananas, plantains, sugar cane, and pastureland were few and geographically dispersed.

This situation started to change in the 1870s, when schooners from U.S. ports began arriving with increasing frequency in order to purchase bananas and coconuts. Around the same time, the Honduran national government began to embrace export-oriented economic development models. The institutionalization of nineteenth-century liberalism took place during Marco Aurelio Soto's presidency (1876–1883). President Soto imagined a national landscape filled with productive citizens transforming tropical nature into wealth: "We will take advantage of what Nature has abundantly provided us. We will work so that the light of civilization reaches even the most remote forests and that through work, blessed work, the lands will be made productive so that all Hondurans may enjoy the benefits of universal progress."[4] Soto's government turned this vision into state policy via the Agrarian Law of 1877, which provided tax and other financial incentives for cultivators to grow crops for international markets. Surprisingly, the legislation did not make any specific reference to banana production, an activity already initiated by small-scale cultivators on the Bay Islands, a small archipelago lying to the north of Honduras's Caribbean coastline.

The abolition of slavery in Jamaica and elsewhere in the British Caribbean prompted both former slaveholders and ex-slaves to migrate to the Bay Islands. In 1861, Britain transferred sovereignty over the islands to Honduras. Shortly thereafter, schooners from New Orleans began arriving in Roatán and Utila, the two principal islands on which small-scale cultivators grew both bananas and coconuts.[5] "A large majority" of the approximately 6,000 inhabitants on Roatán were anglophone "Creoles," and most business transactions and other social activities took place in English. Island residents imported nearly all of their provisions, building materials, and general merchandise from the United States.[6] Ties to the Hispanic mainland were few and tenuous. When the Honduran government declared the island of Roatán to be the only official port of entry in 1879, disgruntled residents on the islands of Utila and Guanaja appealed to the British government. The British obliged the desires of their former colonial subjects by sending a warship to Roatán so that the matter could be "discussed" with local Honduran officials.[7] Three years later, in a measure largely aimed at the English-speaking population of the Bay Islands, the Honduran Congress declared Spanish the official language. Bay Islanders continued to challenge their Honduran citizenship as late as 1902.[8] The politics of the export banana trade, then, acquired an international dimension early on due to both the presence of imperial powers old (Great Britain) and new (United States), and the historical ties that linked Bay Island residents to Anglo-Caribbean culture.

By the mid-1870s, the Bay Island fruit trade was "brisk and constantly on the increase."[9] In 1877 the Oteri and Brothers Company initiated steamship service between their headquarters in New Orleans and the Bay Islands. Two years later, five additional U.S. steamships were regularly running bananas from the islands to various U.S. ports.[10] In the month of November 1880, three schooners and two steamships left Roatán bearing bananas and coconuts.[11] By 1881, the Honduran government promoted steamer traffic by waiving port entry fees for steamships, a policy that rankled schooner captains who did not enjoy the same exemptions.[12] One local official justified the policy by pointing out that steamships were larger and faster than schooners and therefore capable of moving larger volumes of fruit than wind-driven vessels. Demand for fruit soon began to outstrip supply on the Bay Islands, driving prices up and stimulating increases in production. A Honduran government official on Roatán could not contain his satisfaction with the booming economy: "It's no longer just a dream . . . thanks to the abundance of Peruvian *soles* and Mexican *pesos* everyone here is up at dawn and, with machete in hand, sets out to work."[13] The somewhat less hyperbolic reports of U.S. consular agents stationed on the Bay Islands also indicated that banana growing in the 1880s could be quite lucrative for small-scale growers with limited capital and labor resources. According to William Burchard, a 4-hectare banana farm (3,000 plants) cost about $250 in 1880 and provided "under favorable circumstances" $1,500 in revenue the first year and anywhere from $3,000 to $5,000 in subsequent years. He favorably compared banana farming to coconut cultivation, another important export crop, noting that coconuts required a significantly larger initial investment and much more time to generate returns than bananas.[14]

Growing export bananas in the late nineteenth century did not require large inputs of labor. Land clearing was accomplished by burning underbrush during the dry season (January–April). Later with the first rains in May, planting was done using "pointed sticks of hardwood." Cultivators spaced the young plants at a distance of some 3–4 meters. Weeding with machetes was the only task carried out during the ten to twelve months between planting and harvesting. Growers harvested bananas when the fruit bunches were green. Harvesters armed with machetes cut the tall stem of the plant so that the heavy fruit bunch would fall slowly to the ground. Harvested bunches, weighing anywhere from 40 to 80 pounds, were carried by pack animals to the shoreline, where they were loaded onto small boats that carried the fruit to larger, oceangoing vessels. After the harvest, the tall stalk was cut near its base in order to make room for the suckers or offshoots that would reproduce the cycle of fruit production.[15]

In the eyes of U.S. Consul Burchard, the Bay Islanders' cultivation techniques were "quite rude and primitive."[16] Remarking upon the large quantities of bananas that rotted on the stem during the months of limited demand, he noted that a "Northern farmer would utilize this surplus fruit by raising hogs for the Cuba market which could be made a profitable business. When this idea is suggested to a Creole, he will shrug his shoulders and tell you that it is too much work: 'me no want to bodder wi'd hog sar.'" Burchard's understanding of Caribbean tools and work habits as technologically backward is not surprising. Ironically, the relative simplicity of cultivation and minimal labor inputs were precisely what made export banana farming an attractive livelihood. The use of fire and wooden planting sticks reduced both labor requirements and the need for imported, forged implements. Weeding practices — chopping only the tops of the grasses once during each growing cycle — further indicates the relatively light labor demands that banana growing placed upon small-scale growers. The seedless banana's capacity to self-propagate or "clone" meant that annual replanting was not necessary. The banana's biology therefore made possible — but did not guarantee — a comparatively quick and steady return on both capital and labor investments. Of course, this same biology also presented some challenges: the giant herb's treelike stature rendered it very susceptible to wind damage, particularly when the plants were bearing heavy fruit bunches.

THE MAINLAND GROWERS

As late as 1874, the principal goods exported through the port of Omoa were forest extracts including tropical timber.[17] However, following the passage of the 1877 Agrarian Law, President Soto's vision of Hondurans working to transform forests into farms became a reality in the form of expanding export banana production on the mainland. By the early 1880s, the growing number of steamships visiting the coast in search of bananas stimulated cultivation along the narrow coastal plain that stretched from the Motagua River in the west to the Río Negro in the east.[18] For example, when the New Orleans–based steamship Margaret docked in Roatán in 1881, the captain reported that he was seeking to buy "green fruit [bananas] and coconuts" either on the islands or in the vicinity of the mainland ports of Trujillo and Omoa.[19] In 1884, Guillermo Melhado of Trujillo wrote that experiments with planting export bananas had given "very good results on this coast," and he predicted that they would become a leading export.[20] Five years later, in an attempt to strengthen banana exports, the national government exempted steamships servicing Puerto Cortés from port duties.[21] By the late 1880s, bananas were the leading export from Omoa and reports indicated a sharp rise in demand for fruit in La Ceiba.[22] U.S. consular agent William Burchard, apparently swayed by the profitability of growing bananas on the mainland, founded the Burchard-Honduras Fruit Company near the mouth of the Sangrelaya River in 1891.[23]

By 1899, banana production had achieved sufficient scale to prompt the Honduran government to authorize a survey of existing farms in order to "make known one of the great sources of wealth on our Atlantic Coast."[24] The survey team documented 1,032 banana farms covering some 10,300 hectares of land in seven municipalities. Five of these municipalities were situated along the coast where growers had access to both flat, fertile soils and the shippers who plied the coastal waters. The exceptions to this pattern—the municipalities of San Pedro Sula and Villanueva—lay along a stretch of the never-completed Interoceanic Railroad that ran from Puerto Cortés to a point several kilometers south of San Pedro Sula. The vast majority of the export banana farms recorded in 1899 were small: nearly 70 percent (716 of 1,032) were less than 7 hectares in size and 85 percent (880 of 1,032) did not exceed 14 hectares. However, the average size of banana farms varied among municipalities. For example, in San Luis 98% of the growers had fewer than 14 hectares of bananas and the largest plantings were only 21 hectares. In Puerto Cortés, where nearly 50% of the banana farms were smaller than 4 hectares, only 11% exceeded 14 hectares; the largest banana farm was around 40 hectares. Banana farms in El Porvenir, La Ceiba, and San Pedro Sula lay at the other end of the spectrum: only 25% of the La Ceiba cultivators and 33% of those in El Porvenir and San Pedro Sula held fewer than 4 hectares in bananas. The largest holdings (around 70 hectares and up) were concentrated in the neighboring municipalities of El Porvenir and La Ceiba.[25] The twenty-eight largest banana plantations listed in the 1899 survey—less than 3% of the total number of banana farms—occupied nearly 1,700 hectares (about 28%) of the total area planted in bananas. These data point to a significant degree of strati-

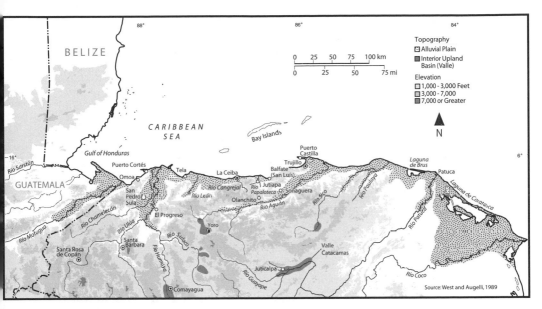

MAP 1.1. *Topography of North Coast of Honduras*

fication that took place in the late nineteenth century. On the other hand, the evidence indicates that large-scale farms did not dominate production to the extent that they would in the twentieth century.

Descriptions of mainland cultivation practices during the 1890s are rare, but there is little reason to believe that production processes varied significantly from those described for the Bay Islands. Average reported planting densities ranged from around 380 plants/hectare in La Ceiba to nearly 880 plants/hectare in San Luis, where many of those farming less than one hectare of land planted at densities greater than 1,200 *matas* per hectare. La Ceiba's and neighboring El Porvenir's considerably larger average farm size may partially explain their lower planting densities. Monthly yields also fluctuated widely, from a mere 23 bunches/month to 74 bunches/month. All told, the 1,000 odd farms produced approximately 272,500 bunches per month, or more than 3.3 million bunches in 1899, a level of production comparable to that of Costa Rica.[26] The amount of grower profits generated from banana sales is hard to pin down with precision. In smallholder-dominated San Luis, potential monthly sales ranged from $10 to $450, with an average of about $70/month. In El Porvenir, five of the largest cultivators potentially grossed more than $1,000/month from fruit sales, and fifteen others produced between $250 and $750 worth of bananas each month. These figures give an idea of the magnitude of the capital that potentially circulated in banana-growing areas, but shed little light on growers' ability to accumulate capital. The most convincing circumstantial evidence that the banana trade was perceived to be lucrative was the increase in the number of producers through the end of the nineteenth century.

Unfortunately, the 1899 survey did not record information about land tenure, but most of the farms were probably located on *ejidos,* municipal lands leased to local residents. Local governments promoted banana cultivation by revising zoning regulations in order to restrict the movement of free-ranging cattle that were capable of destroying crops. For example, in Tela, an 1887 ordinance established an "agricultural zone" in which livestock were not allowed to roam. The rule, which established monetary fines for violators, was strongly worded: "In order to avoid damage caused by livestock, it is necessary to impose serious measures and penalties given the experiences and cases that have been difficult to remedy due to the resistance of certain persons who respect neither the law nor property."[27] The municipal acts for subsequent years provide few clues as to how well the zoning code was honored or enforced in Tela, but the minutes from an 1895 council session suggest that local cultivators continued to push for, and receive, additional lands for crops.[28] Cattle ranchers also found themselves losing ground in El Progreso, Trujillo, and San Pedro Sula.[29] These policies — what we might think of as local expressions of liberal economic doctrines — helped to ensure that land was generally available for banana cultivation.

Labor may have been harder to come by than land in the late nineteenth century. An 1882 letter from US consul and investor William Burchard described four kinds of ethnic laborers, including Garífunas, two indigenous groups of Honduran Mosquitia, and "the common 'mozo' or peon of the interior," described as the "most numerous" of the laborers. Burchard indicated that mahogany loggers utilized forms of debt peonage with mixed results. He also noted that vagrancy laws compelling "tramps and idlers" to work could be invoked in times of labor shortage. Five years later, Burchard reported that a "want of reliable labor offers a serious drawback" to the development of agriculture. Unfortunately, his reports make no specific references to banana farms; whether export banana production was inhibited by an absence of labor or contributed to the labor shortage by providing lucrative livelihoods for small-scale cultivators is unclear.[30] In addition, frequent armed conflicts disrupted labor supplies by causing men to flee towns and farms in order to avoid impressment. Scattered concerns about labor shortages on the North Coast persisted into the early twentieth century. For example, in 1902 a U.S. citizen named Howard Reed complained about labor shortages due to the unwillingness of Hondurans living in the highlands to work on the coast. The Honduran government approved his request to introduce up to one thousand workers "suitable for agricultural work in the tropics excluding Chinese, Blacks and Coolies."[31]

Although men would dominate farmwork in the twentieth-century Honduran banana industry, there is some evidence that women participated in the early days of the trade. One traveler's 1890 description of Garífuna women selling bananas presented them as both skillful handlers of small boats and sharp negotiators.[32] The involvement of Garífuna women is hardly surprising given both the numerous Garífuna settlements along the Honduran Caribbean coastline and women's traditional role as caretakers of home gardens planted with yuca, yams, plantains, and bananas. In addition, a small number of Spanish-speaking women were founding members of some late nineteenth-century growers' associations. The extent to which these women participated in day-to-day farm work is unknown, but given the large number of small-scale farms and the relatively small amount of labor inputs needed at the time, I suspect that workforces often included multiple family members, even children.[33]

The late-nineteenth-century banana boom on the mainland appears to have come at the expense of Bay Island growers. As early as 1890, a Honduran official reported that "the banana of this island [Roatán] appears to be little-sought after, the buyers nearly always preferring that grown on the mainland."[34] The official speculated that the islands' soils were exhausted and that successful banana farming in the future would require fertilizer inputs. Four years later, more than two hundred residents of Roatán requested that the national government declare their island to be a *puerto libre*, or duty-free zone, in order to stimulate a moribund economy. The authors attributed the near-death of the trade to their inability to compete with the "rich soils" (*feracísimas tierras*) on the mainland, further suggesting that falling yields contributed to the demise of the Bay Island fruit trade.[35] In 1905, a U.S. consular agent declared that "the standing menace to the prosperity of the island is the impoverishment of the soil, cultivated for a half century, which impairs the quality and reduces the quantity of the bananas and plantain."[36]

Limited evidence indicates that the "largest and best" portion of the soils on Roatán were under cultivation by 1880. Banana plants require large amounts of nitrogen in order to yield large fruit, but there is no evidence that island growers used fertilizers or crop rotation schemes.

Therefore, there is a good chance that yields on the Bay Islands were in decline by the 1890s after ten, twenty, or even thirty years of continuous production. Contemporaries repeatedly linked assessments of soil fertility to economic conditions. Decades of cultivating the same crop in a relatively small area depleted soil nutrients and in turn lowered fruit weights, prompting shippers to purchase fruit from mainland growers whose young plantations yielded heavier fruit. Thus, the loss of soil nutrients did not render agricultural production impossible on the Bay Islands, but it lowered the economic viability of growing bananas in light of expanding production on the mainland.[37] By the turn of the century, banana exports from Roatán had all but ceased; a 1903 observer noted that "plantain and banana plantations are yielding to the encroachment of underbrush."[38] Less than 20 years after the boom, the Bay Islands' export banana production had crashed.

It is doubtful that many growers on the Honduran mainland paused long enough to consider the potential implications of the Bay Islands' decline. The banana trade continued to expand following the turn of the century. A 1901 report anticipated the creation of new banana farms in the Sula valley and on the León coast where "there still exist immense extensions of virgin land appropriate for banana cultivation."[39] The following year, nearly 17,250 hectares of bananas yielded some 3.2 million bunches[40] Some 8,600 hectares of bananas were planted in the department of Cortés. In the recently created department of Atlántida, growers had 5,520 hectares in production and new farms were "forming constantly" around Tela, swiftly becoming one of the region's most important banana ports. Exports from La Ceiba topped 2 million bunches in 1903; a local government official stated that bananas were the "principal source of wealth."[41] In 1905, exports from Honduras totaled 4.4 million bunches, a figure that continued to rise in subsequent years.[42] By 1912 (the year that United Fruit acquired its first concessions in Honduras), the governor of Cortés estimated that bananas occupied more than 24,000 hectares of land in that province alone. Although the governor's estimate was probably inflated, export banana production expanded significantly between 1899 and 1911.[43]

The magnitude of human activity on the North Coast at the turn of the century should not be overstated. The combined population of the departments of Cortés and Colón was around 30,000 persons plus "a considerable floating population."[44] The National Railroad, which ran some sixty miles inland from Puerto Cortés to the town of Potrerillos (south of San Pedro Sula), was the only significant railway in the region. Banana growers relied primarily upon fluvial transportation networks to carry their fruit to points of embarkation along the coast. Roads were poorly maintained and often impassable during the rainy season. Consequently, production zones were concentrated near ports, navigable inland waterways, and the National Railroad. These early banana zones emerged primarily on account of the efforts of small- and medium-scale growers with limited capital resources. In Honduras, the pre–United Fruit Company era is often depicted as a "golden age" during which *bananeros* walked around with their upturned hats overflowing with money. This perspective is problematic in part because it is overly teleological and implicitly contrasts the late nineteenth century to what at the time was an unknown twentieth-century future. Furthermore, although expanding markets and competition among shippers in the nineteenth century helped to drive up prices paid to growers for their bananas, tensions between cultivators and shippers emerged virtually from the trade's inception. Alongside railroads and docks, fruit buyers and sellers struggled to gain the upper hand in a trade made risky by the banana's intrinsic perishability. The dynamics of these "in-between" spaces in the commodity chain would play a crucial role in shaping landscapes and livelihoods in export banana zones.

IN-BETWEEN FARM AND MARKET

On the night of April 24, 1891, Eugenio Muenier was boarding a ship bound for New Orleans when, fearing that he was being pursued by assailants, he drew a revolver and fired a shot into the darkness. The bullet struck and killed a soldier named Juan Escobar. Following the incident, Muenier, a French citizen who worked as an agent for the Laffite Fruit Company in La Ceiba, fled Honduras before officials could apprehend him. The following August, a group of prominent businessmen, bankers, and shippers asked Honduran President Luis Bográn to pardon Muenier so that he could return to work in Honduras. Describing the shooting as a "tragic accident," the written appeal noted that the Laffite Fruit Company had "suffered enormous losses" due to the absence of their agent, prompting the company to suspend its operations in La Ceiba. Muenier's defenders were confident that if Bográn issued a pardon, the company would "immediately restore" shipping routes to La Ceiba.[45] Two months later, President Bográn granted the pardon, citing Muenier's law-abiding conduct prior to the shooting incident, his solid reputation in La Ceiba, and the "important services" that he had provided for the fruit trade— services that he would continue to provide in the future.[46] Muenier's pardon resulted from his social and business ties to an international network of men who held important positions in commerce and local politics. He was neither the first nor the last shipping agent on the North Coast to find himself at the center of a controversy; conflicts between growers and shippers often erupted over fruit prices, grades, and rejections.

The process of transporting bananas to markets began when a shipper issued an *aviso,* or notice, to fruit growers. For example, an *aviso* distributed on June 13, 1881, announced (in English and Spanish) that a train picking up fruit for the schooner *Etta E. Sylvester* would depart San Pedro Sula four days later.[47] The notice instructed growers to put their fruit along the railway by midday on Thursday. Payments for the fruit would be made once it had been received by a shipping agent in Puerto Cortés. Shipping agents were typically responsible for counting and grading fruit. The location of banana sales often was the site of power struggles that routinely took place between growers and shippers. Not surprisingly, growers often objected when buyers rejected fruit judged to be bruised, overripe, or sunburned.[48] Determining fruit quality was a highly subjective practice linked to fluctuations in market demand; fruit accepted in a period of high demand might be rejected during a seasonal lull in U.S. markets. Shippers often held the upper hand when negotiating fruit purchases because growers possessed a narrow time frame in which they could sell their fruit before it became too ripe.

In an 1889 letter published in *La Gaceta,* Jesús Quirós remarked that the banana trade, which "should have produced immense advantages" for the residents of Tela, was suffering due to the deceitful ways of steamer captains who often took advantage of grower vulnerability.[49] Municipal acts from Tela indicate that inconsistent steamship service hindered the local banana trade in the early 1890s.[50] In 1893 dozens of residents of Tela appealed to Honduran president General Leiva "to lend not only moral but material support" to resolve the "terrible crisis" affecting the port.[51] Specific requests included assistance with normalizing steamship schedules and ensuring the sale of fruit in order to eliminate "the abuses to which we are subject by the current steamship lines." The *teleños* urged the government to exercise direct accounting of fruit sales.

In October of that same year, banana growers saw many of their requests transformed into law. In the first piece of national legislation passed regulating the banana industry, Decree 30 established a system of fruit inspection and taxation.[52] The law restricted fruit sales to designated points on the shoreline; any person caught selling fruit at nondesignated spots would face stiff fines. The decree also called for government fruit inspectors charged with recording each fruit sale. Fruit inspector salaries were to

be funded by the taxes and fines that they themselves collected. A portion
of the tax revenues was earmarked for subsidizing shipping in the hope of
normalizing steamship schedules. Somewhat ironically, the law's imple-
mentation generated discord in Tela, where many fruit growers refused to
pay the export tax, claiming that the inspectors' stem counts did not correspond with the number for which they had been paid.[53] The municipal
council dismissed the allegations and ordered growers to comply with the
law by paying the amount corresponding to the inspectors' lists. Decree
30 did not immediately succeed in attracting more fruit traders to Tela.
In August 1894, the port continued to find itself in a "precarious situation" due to a lack of steamer traffic.[54] The dire economic consequences
were spelled out in clear terms by Tela's municipal government: without
an outlet for bananas, there was no circulation of currency with which to
import goods and foodstuffs.

Banana growers also complained about noncompliance with Decree
30. In 1896, the municipality of San Pedro Sula strongly urged the Minister of Development to punish those who delivered their fruit on board
steam ships.[55] Five years later, the same ministry received a lengthy letter
penned by Omoa Mayor José Ruiz complaining that "higher authorities"
had periodically suspended enforcement of the 1893 decree.[56] According
to Ruiz, some fruit merchants enjoyed "an authorized license" to have
their fruit inspected on board ship. He questioned rhetorically whether
the law was still in effect, stressing the urgent need to enforce the regula-
tion mandating that fruit inspection be done onshore. The mayor's letter
reflected the extent to which Honduran nationalism in banana-growing
regions was redefining itself in opposition to the increasingly dominant
role played by U.S. shipping companies: "The banana farmers (*fruteros*)
of this region are resolved to lose their fruit if the failure to enforce the law
obliges them to deliver their fruit on board, since the American employees, while in the shadow of their flag, believe themselves to be above the
law."[57] In a context of growing U.S. military and economic domination
in the Caribbean and Central America, struggles for national sovereignty
could come down to the distance between a beach and a ship's deck.

However, the relationship between national identity, class, and power
was complex and cannot be reduced to arrogant North Americans and
indignant Honduran growers. In his memoir, *En las selvas hondureñas,*
Francisco Cruz Cáceres describes a Sunday afternoon spent in a bar in
Nueva Armenia, a booming banana town in the early twentieth century.
The joint was filled with *finqueros* who, having just received payment for
their fruit, were "shouting, singing, arguing and tossing money around

with abandon." The revelry was interrupted by the arrival of a man called the "colonel":

> He was an *indio*, of small stature and dark complexion with a few locks of hair hanging out from under his Stetson hat. He wore a pistol and a belt of cartridges over his raincoat . . . [he had] a cigar butt in one hand and a brand new unlit Havana clenched between his teeth.[58]

The man ordered all of the field hands to leave before he turned to address the dozen *finqueros* who remained. He told the group about a recent trip to La Ceiba where he had been approached by several shippers who had become aware that his contract with the Oteri steamship line had expired:

> . . . "Cemori" [Zemurray] don Vicente and Carmelo D'Antoni [Standard Fruit], General Pizzati [Oteri], Dr. Reinolds [United Fruit], that little Cuban fellow who talks like a machine and Peralta were all there. Everyone tried to talk to me privately in order to offer me a contract with their companies except Reynolds . . . they ordered for me glasses of champagne, the finest cognacs, rum, Spanish wines and drink after drink of fine liquors, but they didn't know that I had already promised Reynolds that I would sign with the Trust [United Fruit]. And how could I deny that gringo of everything that he asked me, when he cured *mi negra* of typhoid fever and myself of an *andada de ciempiés?*[59]

The colonel added that he had made arrangements for four other local growers to sell to Zemurray and D'Antoni under new contracts that established higher prices for the fruit. The companies were even buying the inferior fruit of the "poor *poquiteros.*" All of the shippers, the colonel noted with satisfaction, paid well when growers delivered them unbruised, eight-handed bunches (at the time, bananas were not sold by weight; a "hand" consisted of clusters of individual bananas, or "fingers," attached to the fruit stem).

As portrayed in this vignette, the relationship between the shippers and growers was not entirely one-sided, nor was it a purely commercial one. The colonel—who indicated himself to be the largest grower in Nueva Armenia—signed with United Fruit not for lack of other options but because of the nature of his personal relationship with that company's representative. In addition, the colonel's amicable relationships with the other elite shippers prompted him to promise his neighbors' fruit to United's competition—a magnanimous act that underscored the favorable bargaining position in which he perceived himself. Cruz Cáceres's portrait of the colonel's heady optimism and barroom bravado is laced with subtle irony. The Canadian Club whiskey, Spanish wines, Cuban cigars, and U.S. dollars were symbols of the colonel's prominent social position—not just any old *poquitero* could sidle up to the bar with Dr. Reynolds. Yet, the objects so conspicuously consumed were a reminder that the privileged positions enjoyed by local elites were connected to larger economic transformations over which they had little control. Even the colonel's optimistic assessment of the banana trade hints at the market structures—expressed in terms of fruit quality—that could destabilize grower livelihoods, particularly those of smallholders.

Not all small-scale growers were able or willing to place their fates in the hands of a patron like Cruz Cáceres's colonel. In 1894 eighty-five people established the San Pedro Sula–based Sociedad Bananera with the broad objective of "promoting the development of the banana industry by finding the means to overcome the obstacles presently impeding the progress of the industry on this coast."[60] In order to join the society an individual needed to have one *manzana* (.69 hectares) of bananas in a "good state of production," a modest requirement that suggests that the association sought to include small-scale producers. Record linkage with the 1899 survey confirms that a significant proportion of the society's founding members (50 percent) cultivated seven or fewer hectares of bananas.[61] According to one turn-of-the-century report, the Sociedad Bananera tried to support the "small cultivator" (*pequeño agricultor*) who had in the past been victimized by the "evil doings" of "certain large-scale producers." One means by which the society attempted to improve its members' bargaining position was by prohibiting members from buying or selling fruit produced by other growers. The society survived five years before dissolving in 1899 while trying to negotiate a purchase contract. A local government official attributed the society's demise to certain "foreign export houses" committed to undermining the association, but did not provide specific details.[62] However, a memoir written by a San Pedro Sula planter named Catarino Rivas Chácon recalled that during times of high prices, banana growers and shippers alike engaged in speculation and often broke contracts. This potentially explains the demise of the San Pedro Sula Sociedad Bananera during a period of market expansion.[63] Of course, market structures were not the only factors that affected banana growers. A government report from 1900 expressed concern over the situation of the "small scale" producer who, in a majority of cases, relied on loans with "very high interest rates." Revenues from harvests "barely" covered interest payments and the "bare essentials."[64] The report's anonymous author urged the establishment of an agrarian bank to provide loans to cultivators.[65]

In 1895, more than 150 persons, including at least 17 women, created the Sociedad Bananera Gremio Agrario de Omoa in order to "protect the interests of fruit growers."[66] The statutes of the five-year charter laid out administrative structures and membership requirements similar to that of the San Pedro Sula association.[67] The Omoa growers' association outlived its initial charter. A circular from January 1, 1901, announced that the association had yet to sign a purchase contract for the year and urged potential buyers to send a representative to discuss terms.[68] The notice provided monthly production figures for 1900 and added that the association was anticipating a larger harvest as a result of expanded plantings.[69] The circular also exalted the quality of the Omoa banana: "The fruit that has garnered the best prices on the foreign markets and that will earn a superior grade this year at the Buffalo Exposition in New York State, U.S.A., is high quality fruit meticulously cared for, unblemished and not over-exposed to the sun. Qualities guaranteed in our fruit."[70] The contents of the society's promotional material reveals the firm connection between production and marketing: quantity was important, but so too was quality, the standards of which were determined not only on wharves along the Honduran coastline, but also in the exhibition halls of the United States. The mere fact of having been written in 1901 makes the Omoa association's circular significant. Designed to attract "interested parties," the notice calls for potential buyers to send a representative to negotiate a purchase contract. Such contracts were usually entered into prior to the beginning of a calendar year and established fruit prices for a period of one or more years. The Omoa circular suggests that growers in Honduras continued to benefit from the presence of multiple shipping firms following the formation of United Fruit in 1899. In 1902 the Development Council of Atlántida called for an end to shipping subsidies on the grounds that they were no longer necessary in light of the active trade. Other sources indicate that several steamship lines served key ports as late as 1906, a year in which Honduran growers succeeded in negotiating higher purchase prices for their fruit.[71]

But important changes were taking place on the North Coast that would have far-reaching effects on banana production. In 1902, U.S. citizen William Streich received a concession to build and operate a railroad in the municipality of Omoa. The terms of the concession also granted

Streich the right to lease property alongside the railroad in order to establish banana farms. In 1905, the concession passed to one Samuel Zemurray, who, with financial backing from United Fruit Company, purchased Streich's Cuyamel Company. One year prior to Zemurray's arrival in Honduras, the New Orleans–based Vaccaro Brothers and Company received a concession to build a railroad in the newly created province of Atlántida.[72] Like Streich, the Vacarros built their line for the expressed purpose of hauling bananas. The Vaccaros received additional concessions in 1906 and 1910 to extend their railroad and to build a pier capable of handling large steamships.[73] These railroad projects initiated a trend that would eventually leave just two companies in control of the production, transportation, and distribution of export bananas.

However, the process of vertical integration did not take place overnight; as late as 1910, the Honduran government asserted that the country remained the only place where U.S. shipping companies had failed to establish monopolies:

> The growers long ago stopped enforcing the law [Decree 30 of 1893] under pressure from the fruit buyers who, by discrediting Honduran fruit in the United States, have reduced the possibility of attracting the new traders needed to increase competition. In the American ports, the fruit from Honduras is divided on the basis of quality. High quality fruit is sent to markets bearing the name of bananas from Limón [Costa Rica], Jamaica, or Bocas del Toro [Panamá]; the remaining fruit — bruised and rotten — is sold as Honduran fruit. The cause of this hostility is that Honduras is the only free market for bananas, the only one not found under the iron control of the American dealers.[74]

Whether Honduran banana sales suffered from a marketplace conspiracy is unclear, but the government report reflected a heightened awareness of the importance of quality standards set by shippers, distributors, and retailers in distant markets. As the banana passed from being an exotic novelty to join apples, table grapes, and citrus as standard fare in U.S. fruit baskets, defining quality became increasingly important.

THE CONSUMERS

Well before bananas became commonplace in U.S. diets, they entered popular culture as an icon of tropical nature and people. The early-nineteenth-century travels of Alexander Von Humboldt and Aimé Bonpland generated some of the first descriptions of bananas and plantains to circulate widely in the United States. Both men were particularly impressed by the productivity of plantains, estimating that an acre of plantains produced nearly twenty times as much food as an equal area of wheat. The travelers drew a sharp contrast between the "vast spaces" covered with grains in Europe and agricultural landscapes in the "torrid zone" where "a small spot of cultivated land suffices for the wants of several families." Humboldt believed that the different agrarian landscapes produced distinct societies: "These considerations on the agriculture of the torrid zone involuntarily remind us of the intimate connection existing between the extent of land cleared, and the progress of society. The richness of the [tropical] soil, and the vigor of organic life, by multiplying the means of subsistence, retard the progress of nations in the paths of civilization."[75] In other words, the perceived fecundity of tropical soils enabled residents to subsist on small plots of land, a mixed blessing that fostered social isolation and cultural stagnation.

The writings of Humboldt and Bonpland distinguished the plantain from the banana, but popular sources tended to blur the distinction while emphasizing the linkage of bananas and barbarism. For example, an 1832 article in *The Penny Magazine* entitled "The Banana, or Plantain" reproduced both Humboldt's estimate of the productivity of plantains and its sociological consequences: "the facility with which the banana can be cultivated has doubtless contributed to arrest the progress of improvement in tropical regions."[76] An accompanying drawing of a dark-skinned human figure standing near a thatched dwelling in a small clearing shaded by banana plants and coconut trees served to reinforce an image of "the poor Indian" who, content with "gathering the fruit of his little patch of bananas," was barely elevated above the "inferior animal."[77]

The interweaving of ideas about race, nation, and civilization can also be seen in nineteenth-century North American humor. In 1875, Alfred Sedgwick published a musical comedy skit, "The Big Banana," in which Hans, a German immigrant in New York City, considers going to Cuba to strike a "bonanza" mining for gold. However, Hans's limited command of English results in a malaprop as he sings: "I'm off to the Big Banana! / I'm bound for the Big Banana! / I'll sail for the Big Banana! / I'll work like any nigger, / And when my pile gets bigger / I'll cut another figure, / And make *ein schurne schien*." Anna, the woman that Hans is courting, corrects his word usage before responding angrily to his desire to travel in search of fortune: "Better go and eat a big banana, / That's much more in your line."[78] She flatly rejects the idea of going to Havana ("the place where they slaughter free Americans without judge or jury"), preferring to stay put and "work for my living." The story ends predictably enough, with Hans making the decision to stay with Anna; life for poor immigrants in the United States was tough, but surely it was better than the lawless places of tropical Latin America. Sedgwick's wordplay with "Havana" and "banana" conjured images of tropical Cuba, one of the first places from which shippers exported bananas to the United States. His vision of the island as a place where "Americans" get slaughtered and work like "niggers" linked bananas to inferior Latin American and black cultures. The genre is also significant; Sedgwick's skit was an early example of what would become a long line of comedies revolving around bananas.

North American associations of bananas with lazy, backward people were not restricted to popular sources. Describing the results of a research trip to Honduras undertaken in 1897, Harvard University archaeologist George Byron Gordon made little effort to hide his contempt of the "Carib, Xicaque, and Spanish" people who inhabited the banks of the Ulúa River:

> From La Pimienta to the mouth of the river there are 20 or 30 of these villages ranging in size from half a dozen to 50 or 60 huts often completely hidden among the trees and rarely attended with any clearing or cultivated fields. The inhabitants follow the usual occupation of doing nothing. There is an abundance of fish in the river and the forest is full of game, but they seldom take the trouble of procuring either, preferring to subsist on green plantains alone.[79]

Gordon, whose narrative proceeded to contradict itself by providing a lengthy description of the "Indian method" of fishing with a poison extracted from a local plant, misread the landscape because he conflated "clearings" and "cultivated fields."[80] The work of maintaining an agroecosystem based on perennial herbs such as plantains and permanent tree crops (i.e., fruits) did not constitute a legitimate livelihood in the eyes of the North American archaeologist.

Yankees were not the only ones to associate the banana with cultural inferiority. In Jamaica, white planters dismissed bananas as a "nigger crop" prior to the expansion of the export trade.[81] Liberal elites in Central America also tended to view the productivity of bananas and plantains with ambivalence. Juan Narváez, who traveled through Mosquitia the same year that Gordon visited the Sula valley, informed the Honduran Minister of Development that "having visited the villages, the truly backward state—we could say savageness—in which the [Miskito Indians] live has been made clear to me. If the honorable minister were to visit, he would be convinced that the nineteenth century had not shined its light on the jungles in which these men live, jungles that tomorrow could be made useful for their country and family."[82] He added that the people were "little inclined" to work, sustaining themselves during the dry season with fish, game, and a beverage (*atol de guineo*) made from a banana "that practically grows wild" in the flatlands of the region's rivers. One hundred years after Humboldt's journey, literate visitors to the tropics continued to associate bananas and plantains with sloth and backwardness. This view of bananas and their cultural landscapes would be appropriated by both Honduran liberals and U.S. entrepreneurs anxious to demonstrate the need for Yankee ingenuity (and capital) to tap the potential of the tropics. Ironically, the ambivalence expressed by nineteenth-century writers was rooted in the very aspect of banana cultivation—high returns on low labor inputs—that would make it a viable export crop for small-scale growers possessing little or no capital.

If the symbolic meanings of the banana changed little over the course of the nineteenth century, the same cannot be said for its economic importance. The first recorded bunch of bananas to reach New York City arrived in 1804 aboard a schooner from Cuba.[83] During the first half of the nineteenth century, very small shipments of bananas, primarily a variety known as Cuban Reds, reached port cities on the eastern seaboard during the spring months.[84] As late as the 1840s, a single Cuban Red banana sold for twenty-five cents—an indication that the fruit remained an exotic luxury. By 1850, a small number of importers were regularly bringing bananas and other tropical fruits from Cuba to North Atlantic ports. When Irish Catholic bishop James Donnelly traveled in the United States between 1850 and 1853, he tasted a banana, an experience noteworthy enough to make it into his journal.[85] The fruit remained sufficiently exotic—and well known—to draw crowds at the Philadelphia Centennial exhibition in 1876. Popular descriptions of the banana continued to refer to the tall plant as a "tree" and seldom distinguished between dessert bananas and plantains.[86] In 1880, the chef of Delmonico's restaurant in New York City prepared a banana mousse as one of several desserts featured at a posh dinner for General Winfield Scott Hancock, an indication that the fruit retained something of its exotic status. Four years later, the U.S. government lifted duties on banana imports and customs officials began listing "bananas" as a statistical category for the first time. In 1892, more than 12 million bunches of bananas passed through U.S. ports (principally New Orleans and New York City). Two years later, one contemporary observer declared that the banana had joined the apple as a "staple article" in U.S. diets.[87]

The rise in U.S. consumption of bananas and other fresh fruits coincided with the diffusion of steamships and locomotives that were capable of transporting bulky and perishable commodities great distances at previously unattainable speeds. The diffusion of railroads and climate-controlled boxcars enabled fruits to reach distant marketplaces in saleable condition. One 1893 source noted that the "well organized" rail service between New Orleans and Chicago enabled bananas to sell frequently at lower prices in the Windy City than in New York.[88] In a very real sense, then, the transformation of the banana from a novelty to commodity was a product of the fossil fuel era. But innovations in transportation technologies alone cannot explain the tremendous rise in U.S. banana imports.

When bananas first began to appear in Atlantic ports, patterns of North American fruit eating were decidedly seasonal. Apples, peaches, strawberries, and melons enjoyed widespread popularity, but fresh fruits were generally scarce in the winter and early spring months. U.S. banana consumption also tended to vary by season: demand peaked between March and July and declined in the fall and early winter months. This pattern reflected both the seasonality of domestic U.S. fruits—banana consumption slacked when fresh peaches, melons, and apples were available—and the fact that many small fruit dealers who lacked insulated storage facilities stopped carrying bananas during the winter. However, the fact that bananas were harvested throughout the calendar year enabled them to become the first seasonless fresh fruit available for mass consumption in the United States.

Bananas were also affordable. By the 1890s, expanding production in the tropics, combined with the replacement of schooners by steamships, enabled traders to lower wholesale and retail prices. A source from 1893 indicated that "Italians and other foreigners" in mining regions depended heavily on bananas, which were "cheaper than bread."[89] Alfred Sedgwick's 1875 comedy skit also suggests that bananas were not unknown to working-class immigrants. Ironically, the perishable nature of bananas helped to bring them within the economic reach of the working classes by giving rise to a discount market for fruit that reached U.S. ports in an overripe condition. Known as "ship ripes" or "dock fruit," overripe and/or otherwise low-quality fruit would be sold immediately at dockside to local retailers at a fraction of the price of first-class fruit.

Bananas also entered the diets of the expanding middle classes during an era when authors of cookbooks and home economics manuals promoted fresh fruit consumption. For example, Maria Parola advised her readers in 1882 that fresh fruits were "very necessary to perfect health" and recommended apples, figs, dates, and bananas.[90] Hester M. Poole's 1890 housekeepers' manual, *Fruits and How to Use Them,* praised fruits in an age when society was threatened by "too great concentration—whether it be found in social life, in wealth, or in food."[91] Citing scientific data related to "food values," Poole noted that a diet of fruits and grains was superior to one based on animal proteins and fats. She also criticized the "smothering" of fruit with sugar and cream as unhealthful and instead urged an appreciation for the "natural flavors skillfully compounded by the Great Chemist in nature's own laboratory."

Fruits and How to Use Them considered bananas to be "among the most important of all fruits." Poole praised the banana plant's productivity and the fruit's reasonable retail price, its ease of preparation, and year-round availability before providing about a dozen recipes featuring bananas. The majority of the recipes featured the banana as a breakfast item or a sugary dessert such as banana fritters, baked bananas, banana pudding, or banana pie. The author's concern about "heavy foods" notwithstanding, most of the recipes also called for fat-laden dairy products such as cream and butter. Other recipes published around this same time period combined bananas with sugar, eggs, and/or dairy products.[92] Mary J. Lincoln, principal of the Boston Cooking School, published recipes for banana ice cream, banana fruit salad, Banana Charlotte, and "Tropical Snow," a dessert consisting of oranges, coconut, sherry, lemon juice, powdered sugar, and red bananas.

But the most popular way to eat bananas—as a fresh fruit—seldom appeared in cookbooks. In fact, some late-nineteenth-century publications warned against eating raw bananas: "In countries where the banana is indigenous, only the most delicate varieties are eaten uncooked; the bananas that are brought to our markets cannot be eaten safely until they have been cooked."[93] Many nutritionists and health care professionals expressed particular concern about feeding bananas to children. One source urged that children be fed bananas that had been cut or mashed in order to facilitate digestion; another recommended cooking bananas for children unless the fruit was very ripe with black skins. Entering the twentieth century, concerns about the banana's digestibility remained sufficiently widespread to prompt the United Fruit Company to produce booklets with instructions on how to determine the ripeness of bananas. Although nutritionists often compared the banana to the potato in terms of nutrient content, the notion of cooking and eating green bananas and/or plantains as a starchy food did not take hold in the United States. In contrast to its place in many Caribbean cuisines, the banana entered into U.S. diets as a mildly sweet "fruit."[94]

The rise in per capita banana consumption in the United States coincided with a decline in the types of bananas imported. At least four varieties reached New York and Philadelphia markets in the 1880s. An 1885 cooking magazine explained to its readers that many of the best varieties of bananas did not reach New York because the "lazy and ignorant people who live where bananas grow do not take any trouble to cultivate the best kinds to make their shipment anything of a business."[95] An 1889 Arbuckles coffee advertisement stated that "there are two kinds [of bananas], the yellow and the red. The latter is considered the best, and the season for them is from March to September; the season for the yellow ones continues to the middle of October."[96] The Boston Cookbook's "Tropical Snow" dessert called for using red bananas, an indication that they were both available for purchase and highly regarded by epicures. As late as 1905, a Portland, Maine–based wholesaler regularly carried red bananas and sold them at double the price of yellow bananas.[97]

However, by the 1890s, the vast majority of the bananas reaching U.S. ports were "of the yellow variety," that is to say, Gros Michel fruit.[98] Banana-eaters enjoyed the variety's flavor, aroma, and peel color, but references to other varieties found in cookbooks and magazines suggest that aesthetic values alone did not account for the Gros Michel's popularity in export markets. The interests and desires of shippers and fruit dealers played a major role in determining the Gros Michel's prominence. Shippers praised the Gros Michel's relatively thick, bruise-resisting skin and its symmetrical, tight bunches that facilitated packing in ships' holds (prior to the late 1950s, nearly all of the bananas exported to the United States traveled on the full stem with minimal padding). Gros Michel fruit also possessed a sufficiently long ripening period to increase the chances that fruit shipments would reach their destination in a marketable condition (i.e., not overripe). Shippers also valued large bunches of bananas: The greater the number of "hands" on a bunch, the higher its grade and, therefore, its market price. As late as the 1880s, a bunch with seven or more hands could be a "first"; bunches with six or fewer hands were second- or third-class fruit. By the 1890s, important shipping firms, including the Boston Fruit Company, were raising the standard "bunch count" to eight and nine hands, a move that favored varieties such as Gros Michel that tended to produce high bunch counts.

Correspondence sent from Boston Fruit Company executive Andrew Preston to his buying agents in Jamaica during the 1890s reveals a heightened interest in defining and standardizing fruit quality. In an 1891 letter the Boston-based Preston hammered away at the theme of fruit quality: "The time is past when importers can make a profit on thin and ordinary fruit . . . and I trust our Jamaica people will keep it in mind at all times."[99] One year later, Preston acknowledged that his emphasis on quality was causing tension within the company, but he refused to lower his standards:

> I presume your people [in Jamaica] think we are disposed to criticize your selections but we are driven to it by the power of competition — naturally our best customers want the best fruit and I assure you we find it difficult to hold them with fruit of poorer quality than our competitors offer them. It is very plain to my mind that the successful company of the future is the one that controls the growing of its own fruit.[100]

By integrating production, shipping, and marketing, Preston believed that a company could better control both the quantity and quality of the fruit reaching U.S. markets and thereby lower the financial risks associated with trading a highly perishable agricultural commodity. In 1899, Preston played a central role in turning his vision into reality by helping to form the United Fruit Company. For the next sixty years, the fortunes of United Fruit would be entwined with Gros Michel — the variety around which late-nineteenth-century consumer markets formed their notions about just what constituted a "banana."

Chapter 2

Space Invaders

But the day arrived when, due to soil exhaustion or some other reason, a disease invaded the farms that has almost totally destroyed them, bringing ruin to the small producers and turning many communities into ghost towns whose inhabitants little by little are leaving.

GOVERNOR OF ATLÁNTIDA, 1929

Yes, we have no Bananas!
We have no bananas today
We've string beans and honions, cabbahges and scallions
And all kinds of fruit and say,
We have an old fashioned tomahto, Long Island potahto
But yes we have no Bananas
We have no bananas today

FRANK SILVER AND IRVING COHN, 1923

On a cold December night in New Orleans in 1910, deposed Honduran President Manuel Bonilla slipped aboard Sam "Banana Man" Zemurray's private yacht moored on Lake Pontchartrain. The yacht carried the ex-president across the lake and into the Mississippi Sound, where it rendezvoused with a second boat that Bonilla had purchased with money borrowed from Zemurray. Accompanied by a group of armed mercenaries that included General Lee Christmas and Guy "Machine Gun" Maloney, Bonilla set course for the North Coast of Honduras. A couple of weeks later, Bonilla's small forces landed on the island of Roatán. From there they launched an attack on Trujillo, taking control of the port after facing minimal resistance. Shortly thereafter, Bonilla's supporters occupied the port of La Ceiba. The invasion took place during a period of political instability in Honduras: just three years earlier, Nicaraguan forces had invaded Tegucigalpa and ousted Bonilla from power. Miguel Dávila assumed the presidency in the aftermath only to lose most of his political support when his government signed a treaty with the United States giving the latter the right to oversee Honduran customs receipts.[1] Sam Zemurray was among those who opposed the treaty for fear that it would bring an end to the generous duty exemptions held by his fruit company. The Dávila administration further irritated Zemurray by leasing the National Railroad—a key transportation artery for banana exporters—to a rival U.S. investor. In contrast, Bonilla had previously granted important land and railroad concessions to Zemurray. Little wonder, then, that Zemurray was willing to provide financial backing for Bonilla's "invasion."[2]

With the rebels occupying La Ceiba, Roatán, and Trujillo, President Dávila appealed to the United States for support. A U.S. warship entered Honduran waters and impeded the advance of Bonilla's force while simultaneously keeping government troops at bay. Dávila then offered to step down from power provided that the United States agree to arbitrate a settlement between the competing political factions. The negotiations, which took place aboard the U.S.S. *Tacoma,* culminated with the naming of Francisco Bertrand as interim president. Bertrand's appointment was a victory for Dávila's opponents and set the stage for Bonilla's triumph in presidential elections held in November 1911.[3]

That same year, United Fruit sold its interests in Cuyamel Fruit, and Zemurray subsequently incorporated his company with an initial capitalization of five million dollars. These legal maneuvers in Honduras and the United States set the stage for a veritable bonanza of concessions approved by Bonilla during his first year in office. Zemurray secured two concessions in March that included a lease on 10,000 hectares of land plus the rights to develop port facilities in Omoa. In April 1912, Bonilla approved a railroad concession in the name of Cuyamel Fruit Company executive Hillyer V. Rolston. Two months later, Rolston transferred the concession to Zemurray, who in 1913 passed the concession to the Tela Railroad Company, a subsidiary of the United Fruit Company. The transfer was a payback of sorts for the financial backing that United Fruit had provided for Zemurray when he first entered Honduras. United Fruit acquired a second major railroad concession in 1913 via J. B. Camors, who one year earlier had assumed control over the concession originally granted to the Fairbanks Syndicate, an investor group led by a brother of former U.S. Vice-President Charles W. Fairbanks. After failing for more than a decade to establish a foothold in Honduras, United Fruit secured two key concessions thanks largely to the political maneuverings of Manuel Bonilla and Samuel Zemurray.[4]

The railroad concessions provided the legal means by which the U.S. fruit companies established control over vast quantities of resources. Although not identical, most of the concessions granted by early-twentieth-century Honduran governments followed a similar formula: in return for constructing and operating piers, railroads, and telegraph lines, the concessionaires received rights to soil, timber, water, and mineral resources in addition to tax and duty exemptions.[5] For example, the Tela Railroad Company received 6,000 hectares of national lands (including timber rights) for every 12 kilometers of railroad completed.[6] In what would prove to be a futile effort to prevent the company from monopolizing lands, the concession stipulated that land grants be made in alternating lots along the railway such that the national government retained ownership of every other lot. The concession also granted the Tela Railroad Company regional transportation monopolies by prohibiting the construction of competing lines. In addition to generous tax and duty exemptions on imported building materials and equipment, the company enjoyed the right to hire foreign laborers. In return, the concession obligated the company to build and operate a railroad from the port of Tela to El Progreso, Yoro. Government employees and mail were allowed free passage on railways. The length of the contract was indefinite, but the government reserved the right to purchase the infrastructure after sixty years.[7]

If it is true that Bonilla's approval of the 1912 concessions represented a payback to Zemurray and his friends, it also reflected a long-standing practice of Honduran governments rooted in late-nineteenth-century liberal economic policies that created the framework for luring international investors with generous concessions. For many Honduran elites, railroads were the ties that would bind the nation-state both by linking the North Coast to the highlands and by generating revenue for other state-building projects. The Vaccaro Brothers and Company's 1910 concession stipulated that a railroad line be constructed from La Ceiba to the city of Yoro; the 1912 concession acquired by the Truxillo Railroad Company (United Fruit's second major Honduran subsidiary) stipulated that the company build and operate a railway from the port of Trujillo to Juticalpa, Olancho. From there, the government hoped to extend the line to Tegucigalpa. Explaining its support for an amendment to the 1912 concession, the Honduran National Congress declared that "the more railroads that exist, the more we will cultivate and export, giving rise to healthy competition . . ."[8]

Not everyone was thrilled with the railroad concessions; conflicts over property claims surfaced between the state, the fruit companies, land speculators, and small-scale cultivators, many of whom lacked legal title to their farms. In February 1905, William Streich, head of Cuyamel Fruit, complained to government officials in Tegucigalpa that he was having "great trouble" selecting and surveying lands in accordance with the terms of his concession. He added, "I can no longer wait for the adjustment of private claims of title but must begin planting and railroad construction at once to meet the impatience of my associates."[9] If and how the competing parties resolved their claims is unclear. Similar conflicts arose as a result of the 1912 concession acquired by the Tela Railroad Company. Less than three weeks after the text of the contract appeared in the public record, the Honduran Minister of Agriculture sent a telegram to Héctor Medina, an official in La Ceiba, requesting that he suspend the processing of fourteen pending requests for property titles. Eight of the titles were for lands in the municipality of Tela that apparently were also claimed by the Tela Railroad Company. Medina's response expressed his concern over the government's failure to adequately survey and title land claims made in the region.[10] He was particularly worried that "poor campesinos" would be thrown off their lands and urged that a government-supplied surveyor be dispatched to measure and issue proper titles to those who could not afford to hire a private surveyor. Acknowledging the need to locate the lands claimed by the railroad builders, Medina tactfully reminded his superior that the properties in question had been ceded sometime beforehand. He therefore urged that the titling process continue.

Medina's doubts about the ability of poor farmers to title their lands were reiterated by Ulises Meza Calix in 1918. In a telegram sent to the Ministro de Fomento, Calix explained that he was frequently approached by small-scale cultivators who were anxious to title their long-held lands but prevented from doing so due to the expenses involved (titling procedures had to be done in far-off Tegucigalpa).[11] Calix recommended that the central government allow regional offices to title properties not exceeding 25 hectares. A telegram sent to the Ministro de Fomento that same year confirmed Calix's concerns. Writing from San Francisco, Atlántida, Jesús A. Ballestrosa explained that he represented some seventy families that for eight years had been occupying national lands. The families cultivated more than 400 hectares of bananas and other crops, including corn, beans, and rice. However, the Vaccaros (Standard Fruit) were seeking to evict them from these lands, an action Ballestrosa considered "counterproductive and unjust since the land is not included in its titles and besides, we have been paying rent during the time that we have occupied these lands."[12] The telegram is not explicit about the legal status of the land, but the author's choice of words (*ocupantes* and *ocupación*) strongly suggests that the families did not possess written leases or titles.

Conflicts and confusion over land titles persisted well into the twentieth century. In 1923, the National Congress passed a temporary measure prohibiting the transfer of national lands to third parties. According to U.S. consul Robert L. Keiser, the act was passed in response to popular protest over the transfer of lands to "foreign interests." He added that the immediate effect of the legislation would be to end "much undesirable activity on the part of various persons of influence in the controlling political party in obtaining concessions and immediately disposing of them to foreign interests at exorbitant profits."[13] Two years later, legislation setting aside national lands for family parcels (*lotes de familia*) sparked numerous claims by squatters. On September 10, 1925, an official from the Ministry of Government based in La Ceiba, Melecio Zelaya, complained that the "foreign companies'" efforts to keep "Honduran workers" off of their properties had resulted in numerous complaints back and forth since "... everyone claims to have rights to land."[14] He called for the creation of a government-appointed commission headed by a "trustworthy engineer" to carry out land surveys in order to know "once and for all" which lands belonged to the nation and "above all" which ones were legally owned by "the foreign companies." That same month, Zelaya received complaints from the Tela Railroad Company that "many individuals" were occupying its lands near Tela.[15] In Yoro, an agent of the Cuyamel Fruit Company allegedly prohibited residents from establishing their *milpas* (cornfields) in a place known as Laguneta.[16] El Negrito mayor Vicente Nolasco explained that the farmers of Laguneta had held the land for more than twenty years and requested that the national government help recover "our rights." In this case, verifying property lines was complicated by the fact that local records had been lost in a fire.[17]

Following six months of traveling through the North Coast in 1930, Rafael Barahona concluded that the need to survey national lands in the region was a matter of "transcendental importance."[18] He suggested that "all of the banana companies" be required to place stable boundary markers visible from a distance of 100 meters, to indicate the extensions of their properties. Then an "honorable and competent commission" should be established to verify the companies' markers. The measure, Barahona added, would benefit the national treasury in addition to small-scale cultivators since it would provide a clear basis for determining property taxes and rental fees.

The railroad concessions, then, provoked a considerable number of conflicts between small-scale cultivators and the fruit companies. The inability and/or unwillingness of the national government to conduct land surveys only served to exacerbate tensions and left local and regional officials in the awkward position of suspending titling procedures on lots claimed by the fruit companies via the terms of their concessions. Of course, the fact that the companies employed lawyers in Tegucigalpa to represent their interests ensured that they would hold the upper hand in most land disputes with North Coast farmers. That said, land disputes resulted partly because the railroads added value to the places through which they passed by connecting potential banana-producing areas to mass markets. Between the generous terms of government concessions and profit-seeking land speculators, there was probably little need for the fruit companies to resort to strong-arm tactics to secure the soil resources necessary to expand production.

Within a year of acquiring its railroad concession, the Tela Railroad Company assembled five hundred workers and imported construction materials to the port of Tela.[19] By 1915, the company's workforce had laid more than 75 kilometers of main and branch lines and planted 725 hectares of land in bananas.[20] That year, felling crews cleared some 20 kilometers' worth of forest. As workers extended the main line in a southwesterly direction toward the Ulúa River, they encountered a mosaic of forests (including hardwoods, manaca palms, and bamboo), wetlands, and non-company banana farms.[21] A branch line ran east from Tela to the Leán River valley, where workers created farms on properties that company surveyors described as "heavy" forest, "virgin woodlands," and "large trees and bamboo."[22]

The transformation from forest to banana farm began when survey teams selected and mapped out an area for planting. Contract workers cut the underbrush and small saplings with machetes while other laborers dug drainage ditches. Well-drained soils were considered essential for export banana production, particularly in the heavy, clay soils common to the North Coast. By the late 1920s, the United Fruit Company used steam-powered drag lines to excavate major canal ways, but the irrigation and drainage ditches that ran through the farms were hand-dug by *paleros,* or ditchdiggers. The field was then staked and planted with three- to four-pound "bits," or pieces of root stock selected from vigorous Gros Michel plants growing on other farms. Bits would be spaced anywhere from 18 to 24 feet apart. Following planting, teams of ax- and saw-wielding workers

FIGURE 2.1. *Land-clearing activities in Caribbean Costa Rica (1920s). United Fruit Company Photograph Collection. Baker Library, Harvard Business School.*

began the hazardous work of felling the large trees that up to that point were left standing. Perched on a *barbichú*, an elevated platform erected at the base of a tree, workers hewed through trunks at a point above the wide, buttressed base common among tropical hardwoods. Felling crews hacked at the tree until it began to give way, at which point they jumped off of the platform to avoid the falling trunk.[23] As the tree fell to the ground, it yanked on the ubiquitous vines (*lianas* or *bejucos*) woven throughout the forest canopy. These vines often pulled down additional branches and even entire trees that could strike an unsuspecting worker. The logs usually remained in the midst of the farm, where they deteriorated rapidly in the humid, warm environment. On occasion, the fruit companies extracted valuable timber such as mahogany for shipment to the United States; the trunks of guanacaste trees were prized by locals for canoe making.[24]

The extension of the Tela Railroad Company's railroads coincided with increased banana production in the area: between 1915 and 1920, exports from Tela nearly quadrupled from 1.2 million bunches to 4.6 million.[25] By 1921, the company operated fifty farms (about 18,600 hectares of bananas) linked by more than 300 kilometers of railroad. That year, a U.S. consular agent called the port of Tela "the largest banana exporting point in Honduras, and one of the largest in the world."[26] By the end of the decade, the Tela Railroad Company's main line extended 64 kilometers along the eastern bank of the Ulúa.[27] Near El Progreso, land covered with "heavy timber and wild cane" gave way to thousands of hectares of banana farms and pasture.[28] In addition, some 27,000 meters of drainage canals had been dug and more than 13,000 meters of dikes erected to protect the farms from seasonal flooding. In 1928, the El Progreso district alone produced 8.5 million bunches of bananas.[29]

When U.S. botanist Paul Standley visited the Tela region between November 1927 and March 1928, he described a landscape that had been radically reworked by banana production.

> Practically all of the land within this area that is fit for the purpose is covered with banana plants, which, however beautiful when standing alone or in moderate quantities, become exceedingly monotonous when massed in plantations many miles in extent.[30]

He also observed several large pastures where cattle, horses, and mules grazed on Guinea grass, and many *guamiles,* abandoned farmlands giving way to young forest species: "Nearly everywhere along the whole line of the Tela Railroad, except when passing by marshes or very swampy woods, one sees nothing else but second growth and banana plantations."[31] Standley contrasted the rich biological diversity found on the sloping lands of Lancetilla, United Fruit's experimental garden, with the radical reduction in plant diversity in banana farms: "where bananas are grown there is no other vegetation of interest to the botanist."

In the botanist's eyes, the most interesting plant communities were found precisely where export bananas were not growing:

> Between banana plantations however are large areas unsuited for their cultivation. These consist, near the coast, of wide marshes and of densely wooded swamps which cannot, or at least have not, been drained. The most spectacular of these unused areas is the great Toloa Swamp that is crossed by the railroad as it approaches the Ulúa River from Tela. It is like many other swamps or marshes in Central America, a shallow lake with an abundance of aquatic plants, and such a profusion of water birds as one sees only in the tropics.[32]

FIGURE 2.2. *A young Gros Michel farm in the Sula valley (1920s). United Fruit Company Photograph Collection. Baker Library, Harvard Business School.*

Standley's observations, if not entirely surprising coming from a field biologist with a demonstrated fascination with tropical plants, represented a view of the tropics that diverged sharply from those offered by popular writers, public health officials, and the banana companies, which stressed the inherent unhealthiness of lowland tropical environments. From Standley's perspective, marshlands were rich repositories of diverse life forms, not "pestilential swamps" in need of draining.

When University of Chicago ornithologist James Peters visited the same area a few months later, Tela Railroad Company workers had already started excavating a canal in order to drain a large portion of the Toloa Swamp that had captivated Standley.[33] Peters described the short-term ecological change that he observed in the area:

> [M]uch of the vegetation has died off and floods have deposited
> large amounts of sediment, resulting in a wide expanse of mud flats
> interspersed with pools of stagnant water. In such situations waterfowl
> of all sorts abound. Never in my experience have I seen such numbers
> of Herons or Wood Ibises as have flocked there to feed. But it can only
> last for a short time, as eventually these flats and marshy areas will be
> completely drained and planted to bananas.[34]

Ironically, the drainage operations provided a fleeting home for water-fowl, but the end product of the transformation — a banana plantation — afforded little habitat for most forms of avian life.[35] The ornithologist also visited Toloa Lagoon, where he saw Everglade Kites inhabiting a land-scape of alternating marsh grasses and open areas of water. In time, much of this area would also be drained following the construction of another canal.[36] The expansion of export banana farms, then, altered both plant communities (e.g., forests) and local hydrological systems.

The environmental changes that took place in the Ulúa valley were by no means unique. In 1915, United Fruit initiated a second major railroad-building operation in the department of Colón. In contrast to other parts of the Caribbean lowlands, Colón had not been a center of nineteenth-century export banana production. Agricultural activity prior to the 1910s consisted of small-scale production of coconuts, rubber, plantains, yuca, tubers, and grains. A handful of prosperous landowners near Trujillo maintained several hundred hectares of cattle pasture. Although mahogany cutters had operated in the region for more than a century before the arrival of United Fruit, logging was generally restricted to the banks of the Aguán River. A 1911 government survey of the river valley described "great forests" filled with "precious woods and medicinal plants."[37] Another government source described forests of "great fertility" crossed by rivers and streams whose "crystal clear waters" were suitable for drinking.[38] The first assessments made by United Fruit's surveyors predicted that the region's extensive tracts of "virgin soil" would potentially yield 20 million bunches of bananas annually.[39]

By 1920 workers had finished 86 kilometers of main line that stretched from Puerto Castilla (near Trujillo) to a small work camp situated in the lower Aguán valley.[40] Company banana farms covered more than 2,000 hectares. Eight years later, Gros Michel monocultures sprawled over nearly 13,000 hectares; pasture covered an additional 3,500 hectares.[41] A journalist described the view from the company train in 1927 as "one immense plantation."[42] Irrigation systems supplied about one-third of the farms with water from the Aguán, Bonito, Cuaca, Mamé, and San Pedro rivers.[43] Between 1922 and 1928, exports rose from 1.1 to 7.6 million bunches. During this expansionary phase, the Truxillo Railroad Company (United Fruit's second Honduran subsidiary) razed a quantity of timber sufficient enough to cause some of its employees to speculate that the extensive deforestation of the Aguán valley was the cause of a series of severe droughts that hit the region.[44] The company also expanded into the Black River valley where some 10,000 hectares of "virgin land" were slated for cultivation in 1927.[45] By the early 1930s, the company had twenty-three farms along the Black River in addition to forty properties that stretched along the southeast bank of the Aguán River for dozens of kilometers.[46] All told, the Truxillo Railroad Company controlled nearly 70,000 hectares of land in Colón.[47]

The activities of United Fruit's two principal competitors in Honduras wrought similar environmental transformations. The landscape through which the Cuyamel Fruit Company's railroad passed was similar to that found around Tela. Departing from the port of Omoa, the railroad passed through many wetlands and mangroves where the herbaceous *gamolita,* wild sugar cane, bamboo, and plantains mixed with several varieties of swamp plants.[48] In better-drained alluvial soils, numerous "large trees" grew in addition to "many dense bamboo forests."[49] In 1913, the company had 27 kilometers of railroad built and another 23 under construction.[50] By 1920, there were some 6,900 hectares of bananas in Omoa; a Honduran official reported that both the fruit company and non-company growers had cleared "large areas" of forest in order to establish farms.[51]

Around this same time, Sam Zemurray secured a highly controversial concession to administer the National Railroad that ran from Puerto Cortés to a point south of San Pedro Sula.[52] Shortly thereafter, he directed the construction of branch rail lines that serviced several export banana zones in the Sula valley.[53] Between 1920 and 1925, banana exports from Puerto Cortés increased steadily from 2.3 million to 5.1 million bunches.[54] One observer attributed the trend to both the "clearing and planting of virgin acres" and the conversion of preexisting cropland to banana farms.[55] In 1927 Cuyamel Fruit obtained the right to construct irrigation systems provided that they did not disrupt river transportation and that waterways were returned to their "natural courses." Surface water use was taxed at the annual rate of one dollar per hectare; groundwater could be tapped tax-free. By 1930, the company and its subsidiaries had nearly 6,300 hectares of land under irrigation. Zemurray's companies also constructed spillways and canals in order "to encourage flood overflows" into wetlands in order to build up layers of silt that over time would form arable soils.[56]

In the department of Atlántida, the Vaccaro Brothers (Standard Fruit) oversaw the construction of 155 kilometers of railroad between 1910 and 1915.[57] The company's main line proceeded west from La Ceiba, across the narrow coastal plain, and into the Leán River valley. One observer described the landscape through which the railroad passed as "luxuriant forests well suited for the cultivation of bananas and other crops."[58] The expansion of the railroad led to a concomitant rise in exports, from 2.7

million bunches in 1913 to 5.5 million in 1919.[59] By the late 1920s, Standard Fruit's subsidiaries controlled some 23,000 hectares of land in Atlántida.[60] In addition to bananas, the company cultivated forage, citrus fruits, coconuts, and sugarcane.

By the end of the 1920s export banana production dominated the major river valleys of the Costa Norte. In 1929 a record 29 million bunches left Honduran shores, a volume that exceeded the combined exports of Colombia, Costa Rica, Guatemala, and Panama.[61] Some 1,500 kilometers of railroad, stretching from the Guatemalan border to the Black River, linked banana farms to the region's major ports, including Puerto Cortés, Tela, La Ceiba, and Puerto Castilla. United Fruit's subsidiaries possessed more than 160,000 hectares of land, including some 30,000 hectares of bananas and 6,000 hectares of pastures. The Cuyamel Fruit Company held 55,000 hectares of land that included 22,000 hectares in bananas, sugar, and coconuts. Standard Fruit's Honduran subsidiaries owned or leased 23,000 hectares in the department of Atlántida, in addition to several thousand hectares in Colón.[62] Non-company banana farms occupied an additional 10–12,000 hectares of land.

The rapid expansion of export banana production between 1912 and 1930 transformed the North Coast's landscape. Vast expanses of forested lowlands gave way to railroads, banana plantations, pasturelands, and human settlements (between 1910 and 1935, the region's human population tripled, rising from 65,048 to 198,836 persons).[63] Extensive systems of irrigation ditches, drains, spillways, dikes, and canals reshaped the region's hydrology. The export banana industry's invasion of space unquestionably reduced biological diversity. Still, the image of a "sea of bananas" should not be pushed too far. Many ecological zones, including swamps, mangroves, hillsides, and mountains were not conducive to export banana production. Significant areas of land were taken up with coconut groves, pasture, sugarcane, corn, beans, and other crops cultivated for subsistence and local markets. Entering the 1930s, then, the North Coast's major alluvial valleys consisted of thousands of hectares of Gros Michel monocultures interspersed with more biologically diverse landscape patches.

People were not the only organisms drawn to the North Coast during this period of rapid change. Sometime between 1910 and 1915, banana growers began to notice yellow and withered leaves on some of their Gros Michel plants. Upon cutting the plants' pseudostems with a machete, cultivators found purple-brown vascular tissues that gave off a strong odor. Most significantly, the diseased plants generally produced very low quality fruit, if they produced any at all.[64] In 1916, United Fruit Company soil

FIGURE 2.3. *United Fruit Company pastures near Tela (1920s). United Fruit Company Photograph Collection. Baker Library, Harvard Business School.*

surveyors detected the disease on at least two farms in its Tela Division.[65] Three years later, a U.S. official in La Ceiba reported on the "appearance of a plant disease in the nature of a blight which has attacked some of the best plantations."[66] In 1922, employees of the Truxillo Railroad Company detected the disease in Colón.[67] By that point, word must have been spreading quickly along the Costa Norte: *la mata muerta,* or Panama disease, was invading export banana farms.

The disease took its name from the place where it was first widely observed: banana growers on the Atlantic coast of Panama reported wilt-like symptoms as early as the 1890s.[68] Within a decade, the disease was causing serious problems on the Atlantic Coast of Costa Rica.[69] By the time growers first noticed Panama disease in Honduras, major outbreaks had already occurred in Surinam (1906), Cuba (1908), Trinidad (1909), Puerto Rico (1910), and Jamaica (1911).[70] In 1910, U.S. researcher Erwin F. Smith isolated a fungus on diseased banana tissues from Cuba that he named *Fusarium cubense.*[71] However, that same year, a U.S. Department of Agriculture scientist in Panama suggested that the pathogen was a bacteria.[72] Scientists continued to disagree about the identity of the pathogen until 1919 when E. W. Brandes demonstrated that *Fusarium oxysporum* f. *cubense* could produce all of the characteristic symptoms of the disease under controlled conditions. Two years later, United Fruit investigators in Panama successfully replicated Brandes's experiment using Gros Michel banana plants.[73]

The geographical origin of *F. oxysporum* is uncertain, but there is no doubt that human activity has played a major role in spreading the pathogen.[74] The fungus was probably introduced to Caribbean and Central American soils well before the export banana boom. Observers in British Guyana, Cuba, and Surinam reported that the apple and silk banana varieties—introduced to the West Indies prior to 1750—displayed Panama disease–like symptoms prior to the expansion of Gros Michel monocultures.[75] The disease also affected non-export banana varieties that cultivators in Panama had historically grown as food and shade crops.[76] In addition to bananas, some native plants, including *Heliconia,* may have served as a host for *F. oxysporum* in forest environments.[77] However, prior to the rise of the export banana trade, epidemics were rare because "plantations were small and scattered."[78] The landscape mosaics of small farms and banana-free blocks of land inhibited the movement of the soil-borne pathogen, and consequently, infected populations remained isolated.[79] Also, for cultivators who planted bananas primarily as a shade crop and/or for home consumption, a couple of wilting plants would not generate much concern because the farmers' livelihoods were not tied to maximizing production of a single banana variety. But when thousands of people cleared forests and planted Gros Michel banana plants for export, the significance of plant and pathogen changed in reciprocal fashion.

The expansion of export banana farms transformed ecosystems characterized by a high diversity of plants and low population densities of individual species into an agroecosystem comprised of monocultures of extremely limited diversity. Within individual banana farms, dense plantings of Gros Michel clones favored the plant-to-plant dispersal of Panama disease.[80] On a regional level, the removal of vast tracts of lowland forests; the installation of drainage and irrigation canals; and the building of railroads that carried field workers, tools, animals, and planting materials all but guaranteed the pathogen's spread between farms. Finally, increased steamer traffic between Caribbean banana ports facilitated the pathogen's movement across geopolitical boundaries. In sum, if Panama disease can be thought of as an invader, it was a secondary one that followed in the wide ecological swath cut by expanding Gros Michel production.

Growers and government officials initially responded to the epidemic by establishing quarantines and destroying diseased plants.[81] In Honduras, United Fruit's subsidiaries ordered their field workers to apply a disinfectant to their shoes and tools.[82] Ironically, one of the biggest problems faced by growers was how to eliminate infected banana plants efficiently. The labor-intensive process included digging out rhizomes and roots, chopping the plants into small pieces, and burning them with large quantities of fuel.[83] In spite of these measures, the companies had a difficult time ensuring that their workers did not unknowingly introduce infected planting materials to new farms. Little could be done during the rainy season to prevent flood waters from spreading the pathogen far and wide.

In 1916, United Fruit hired Samuel Prescott, a researcher at the Massachusetts Institute of Technology, to direct a soil survey of company farms in Colombia, Costa Rica, Guatemala, Honduras, and Jamaica in order to determine the relationship between disease incidence and soil conditions. Two years later, Prescott reported that his research did not identify any "strikingly marked correlations" between the chemical properties of soils and the spread of the pathogen.[84] Prescott and other United Fruit employees tested a slew of chemical compounds and soil treatments (including mulching and fertilizing) for their ability to "disinfect" soils, but these efforts were in vain.[85] In 1923, United Fruit scientist John Johnston noted that some twenty years of study and treatment "by all the customary methods used in the practice of disease control" had failed to yield a solution to the problem of Panama disease.[86] Stymied in their initial efforts to eradicate and/or prevent the spread of the pathogen, both the United Fruit Company and the British colonial government created formal research programs with the intent of overcoming Panama disease.

As early as 1910—well before the scientific community agreed that *F. oxysporum* was the pathogen—a U.S. Department of Agriculture researcher argued that the long-term solution to Panama disease lay in cultivating a disease-resistant variety such as the "Chinese banana" (i.e., a Cavendish cultivar), that was traded in Asia, Hawaii, and the Canary Islands.[87] In 1910 United Fruit provided the Dutch government in Surinam with a banana variety known as "Congo" (a Cavendish cultivar). However, only modest amounts of Congo fruit reached U.S. markets before United Fruit informed Dutch officials that the variety was not marketable due to its comparatively short shelf life and its tendency to ripen unevenly.[88] Both United Fruit and British researchers initiated breeding programs during the 1920s with the shared goal of developing disease-resistant varieties.[89] United Fruit researchers initially tried to breed healthy-looking Gros Michel plants found in diseased soils, but even apparent survivors of the epidemic eventually succumbed to the pathogen. The company next sought to create a hybrid variety with disease resistance. The first generation of professional banana breeders undertook their experiments possessing very limited knowledge about the cytology, genetics, and taxonomy of the genus *Musa*.[90] However, they were aware of one critical trait shared by the Gros Michel and most other banana cultivars: the plants were parthenocarpic, meaning that they did not have to be fertilized by pollen in order to produce fruit. As a result, their fruit tended to be seedless, a characteristic for which human cultivators selected over the course of centuries if not millennia.

Parthenocarpy posed a major challenge for plant breeders who struggled to obtain seeds and pollen from the highly infertile Gros Michel. In fact, crosses with Gros Michel were possible only because the plants could be induced to set seeds in small numbers when pollinated by "wild" (seeded) bananas. But fertility rates were extremely low. In one breeding experiment conducted by British researchers in Trinidad during the 1920s, pollination trials were carried out with six varieties of bananas, including Gros Michel. About 20,000 pollinated flowers yielded fewer than two hundred seeds, fifty of which were empty. The remaining seeds came from just two varieties, Gros Michel and Silk; all had been pollinated by one of the seeded varieties. Only seventeen seeds germinated, and a mere five survived to the fruit-bearing stage. The sheer size of banana plants helped to make breeding trials a costly endeavor—20,000 banana rhizomes planted at conventional densities would take up some 25–30 hectares of land.[91] Furthermore, the inroads of Panama disease made it difficult to find healthy Gros Michel plants for breeding. The work of early banana breeding, therefore, was tedious, full of uncertainty, and posed a number of logistical problems.

Sensing that successful breeding would require a wide range of germ plasm (i.e., genetic diversity), United Fruit's research director, Dr. Otto A. Reinking, assembled a collection of some 150 *Musa* accessions from Asia, Cuba, and Central America.[92] Between 1925 and 1928, United Fruit scientists in Changuinola, Panama, crossed varieties with distinct chromosome counts on the assumption that some of the offspring would possess the same number of chromosomes as commercial cultivars. The trials yielded fourteen sterile hybrids with edible, seedless fruit pulp, but United Fruit's J. H. Permar noted that they had little economic value since "in no case is their quality equal to the fruits that are generally recognized by the public as 'bananas.'"[93]

In 1930 United Fruit terminated its banana breeding experiments in Panama. Workers transferred some 130-odd varieties to Lancetilla, the company's experimental garden on the outskirts of Tela, where they would

FIGURE 2.4. *"Chinese Banana" (i.e., Cavendish cultivar) on a United Fruit experimental plot (1920s). United Fruit Company Photograph Collection. Baker Library, Harvard Business School.*

be all but forgotten for the next 25 years.[94] The initial failure to develop a commercial hybrid cannot be attributed entirely to the banana's biology. In order to be a commercial success, hybrids had to possess both resistance to *F. oxysporum* and a strong resemblance to Gros Michel fruit—the variety around which U.S. mass markets had formed.

MASS MARKETS, CONSUMER CULTURES, AND THE TOP BANANA

At the same time that Gros Michel monocultures were expanding in the Caribbean and Central America, bananas were slipping into everyday life in the United States. By the 1920s, the symbolic consumption of the banana had achieved a mass scale. As had been the case since the mid-nineteenth century, bananas generally were icons of zany—and increasingly sexual — humor. In 1923, a pair of young musicians in New York City convinced the Skidmore Music Company to publish their pop tune "Yes, We Have No Bananas!" The song title and lyrics were reportedly inspired by an immigrant fruit peddler with a limited command of English — a curious continuity from Sedgwick's 1875 comedy skit involving bananas. The song became an overnight sensation. Copies of the sheet music sold by the tens of thousands, and dance-hall bands played the tune throughout the U.S. and Europe. One of the song's composers, Frank Silver, organized a ten-piece "banana band" that toured the U.S. with a set that included bunches of bananas and a backdrop with an image of a banana plantation.[95] Around the same time, George Gershwin's hit tunes "Let's Call the Whole Thing Off" and "But Not for Me" evoked smiles by playing with the phonetic qualities of the word "banana." Other entertainers, including folk-blues musicians the Happiness Boys and Bo Carter, appropriated the banana as a phallic symbol in their respective compositions, "I've Never Seen a Straight Banana" (1926) and "Banana in Your Fruit Basket" (1931). Silent films and some early talking pictures included banana-peel induced pratfalls. Urban sanitation crusaders incorporated banana peels into children's songs conveying anti-litter messages. Finally, the word "banana" entered into popular lexicon via slang terms including "top banana," "banana boat," "banana oil," "to go bananas," and of course, the enduring "banana republic."[96]

Not all North Americans held a carefree attitude toward banana consumption. While touring western Massachusetts with Henry James in 1904, Edith Wharton found herself unexpectedly spending the night in a summer resort in Petersham on account of car troubles. In a letter to a friend, Wharton offered a scathing critique of bourgeois life in the United States: "I have been spending my first night in an American 'Summer hotel' and I despair of the Republic! Such dreariness, such whining sallow women, such utter absence of the amenities, such crass food, crass manners, crass landscape!! And, mind you, it is a new and fashionable hotel. What a horror it is for a whole nation to be developing without the sense of beauty and eating bananas for breakfast."[97] Wharton's self-described "horror" over banana consumption stemmed from the fact that the act of eating a banana was accompanied by none of the aristocratic (European) traditions associated with the consumption of other tropical commodities such as tea, coffee, and chocolate.[98] Instead, the banana was linked to the "crass" popular culture of the United States shaped by both mass consumerism and democratic ideals. Indeed, what seems to have bothered Whar-

ton—who once referred to herself and James as "wretched exotics produced in a European glass-house"—was the idea that an article of popular
consumption could find its way into the playgrounds of the wealthy.

More than twenty years after Wharton penned her letter, poet Wallace
Stevens affirmed that the less-than-noble banana was unfit for elite Anglo-
American society. In "Floral Decoration for Bananas" (1927), Stevens jux-
taposed the severe elegance of plums served in an exquisite dish with the
rawness of (export) bananas "piled on planks":

> You should have had plums tonight,
> In an eighteenth-century dish,
> And petifogging buds,
> For the women of primrose and purl,
> Each one in her decent curl.
> Good God! What a precious light!
>
> But bananas hacked and hunched.
> The table was set by an ogre
> His eye on an outdoor gloom
> And a stiff and noxious place.
> Pile the bananas on planks.
> The women will be all shanks
> And bangles and slatted eyes.
>
> And deck the bananas in leaves
> Plucked from the Carib trees,
> Fibrous and dangling down,
> Oozing cantankerous gum,
> Out of their purple maws,
> Darting out of their purple craws,
> Their musky and tingling tongues.[99]

Stevens refracted bananas through a primitivist lens in order to create sensual images that both echoed nineteenth-century discourses about
tropical barbarism and anticipated later associations of bananas with
"hot" tropical women, including Carmen Miranda and Miss Chiquita.
The poem may have been further inspired by African-American jazz
dancer Josephine Baker, whose early performances in Paris played to
European fascination with the "primal" sexual energy of dark-skinned

FIGURE 2.5. *Roadside food stand in Alabama with bananas (1930s).*
Library of Congress.

tropical people. In 1925, the nineteen-year-old Baker performed in La Re-
vue Negre whose repertoire included the "Danse Sauvage," a number set in
an African jungle. The following year, during a performance at the Folies
Bergére, she danced the Charleston wearing a G-string adorned with bananas, a costume with which Baker would be identified long after she
struggled to transcend the roles that white producers generally assigned
to black women performers in Europe and the United States.[100]

Other early-twentieth-century writers used bananas as symbols of
societal transformations taking place in the United States. In 1929 William
Faulkner published *As I Lay Dying*, a novel centered around the Bundren
family's sorrowful journey from their rural southern home to Faulkner's
mythical Southern city of Jefferson, where the deceased Mrs. Bundren is to
be buried. The novel's closing scene depicts the Bundren children eating
bananas while they wait for their father in the family's mule-drawn wagon.
When Vardaman, the youngest member of the family, tries to lead his older
sister past a storefront featuring an electric model train, she responds,
"Wouldn't you rather have a banana?"[101] Faulkner's unexpected insertion
of bananas into the novel's closing scene reflects both the fruit's ubiquity

in the 1920s and the author's ambivalence toward the social and economic changes taking place in the New South. The visit to the city exposed the Bundren children to the wonders of mass consumer society: electric toy trains, graphophones — and bananas. If the boy Vardaman could only fantasize about owning an electric train, he could on occasion savor a taste of the tropics that was rapidly becoming as "American" as apple or peach pie. Faulkner's symbolic use of bananas, then, was rooted less in his concern about the erosion of elite culture than in his unease about mass consumption as a remedy for the pain and displacements associated with profound individual, familial, and societal transitions.[102]

Poets, novelists, and musicians were not the only people experimenting with the banana's symbolic value; the fruit companies themselves constructed images of bananas and the tropics through mass marketing campaigns. Lavishly illustrated booklets, often geared toward children, offered a view of production and distribution processes that stressed the benefits that the banana trade brought to both North American consumers and Latin American producers.[103] In addition, writers with close ties to the United Fruit Company published a number of articles and books during the early twentieth century in which modernity arrived to "jungle" landscapes via United Fruit's Great White Fleet. A 1932 article in *Economic Geography* described nineteenth-century Caribbean landscapes as "dark, tangled forests of the swampy lowlands," inhabited by "poison snakes, ferocious animals, myriads of insects, and dreaded diseases." Then, the author noted dramatically, a change took place:

> On the eve of the birth of the present century there was launched in Boston what has become one of the most significant enterprises the world has known — the modern banana industry. Now staunch New Englanders are putting their money into the proved business of banana production and distribution. American engineers are invading the jungles with steam shovels. Swamps are being drained and axes are heard ringing in the woodland. Fruitful banana plantations are appearing as if by magic.[104]

The author, a son of United Fruit attorney Bradley Palmer, stressed the transformative role played by U.S. investors and engineers, while largely ignoring both the past efforts of smallholders and the contemporary contributions of laborers in performing feats of "magic." Palmer was by no means unique; popular and scholarly writers during this time consistently stressed the need to "tame" tropical landscapes and enlighten their human

inhabitants. In these tales of modernization, the export banana symbolized the transformation of tropical Nature into productive agricultural
spaces via the guiding hand of U.S. capital and technology.[105]

People in the United States inscribed the banana with a wide range
of meanings, but both popular and highbrow appropriations often reproduced ethnocentric views of tropical places and their inhabitants. The con-
temptuous view of banana eating expressed by writers such as Wharton
and Stevens, as well as popular associations of bananas with humor and
sexuality, shared historical roots in earlier visions of the tropics as dark,
dangerously fecund, and profoundly different from Anglo America. At the
same time, some writers also linked the export banana trade to progress
by creating images of healthy, hardworking tropical inhabitants enjoying
the civilizing benefits of international trade and applied scientific knowledge. These "developmentalist" discourses, combined with a burgeoning
consumer culture and enduring ideas about the tropics as unhealthy left
little room for public discussions about environmental degradation beyond the isolated voices of naturalists such as Paul Standley and James
Peters who expressed considerable ambivalence about the changes that
they witnessed on the North Coast.

The fruit companies did not make money trading in metaphors, nor
were most consumers drawn to bananas primarily for their symbolic
value. Bananas were first and foremost a food that by the early twentieth century had ceased to be a novelty for most U.S. consumers. In 1910
over 40 million bunches of bananas entered the nation's ports; four years
later, imports neared the 50-million-bunch mark and per capita consumption was around 22 pounds.[106] United Fruit loaned most of its shipping
fleet to the U.S. government and its allies during World War I, leading
to a downturn in banana imports between 1914 and 1918. Consumption
rates rebounded in the 1920s when unprecedented quantities of Honduran
bananas entered the United States.[107] Although the dollar value of U.S.
banana imports paled in comparison to that of coffee, the fruit had unquestionably become one of the most important agricultural commodities in the Americas, constituting 3.3 percent of total U.S. imports and
more than 50 percent of U.S. imports from Central America in 1929.[108]
That same year, a marketing survey conducted for United Fruit found that
more than one-half of the 8,500 households surveyed purchased bananas
"frequently," and the percentage was even higher for households with children. Only 9 percent of those interviewed stated that they "never" bought
bananas.[109]

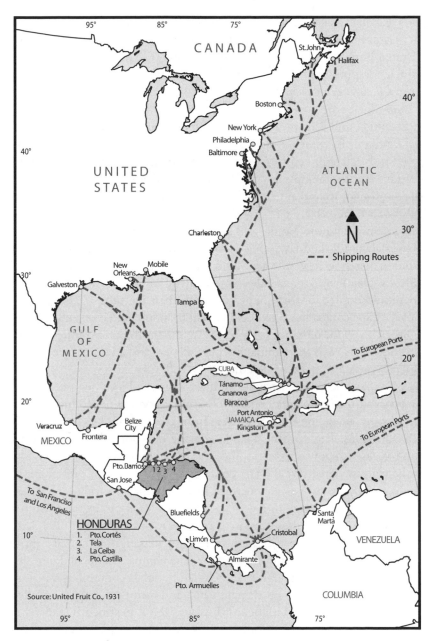

MAP 2.1. *Banana shipping routes, c. 1930*

Bananas reached early-twentieth-century consumers via a commodity chain that included shippers, brokers, jobbers, and retailers. In 1900, United Fruit executives established the Fruit Dispatch Company, a subsidiary responsible for the distribution of bananas in the United States and Canada. Fruit Dispatch established offices in key ports and railroad centers including Boston, Chicago, Kansas City, New Orleans, New York, Pittsburgh, and Richmond. By 1925, the company had representatives in more than fifty North American cities. Fruit Dispatch employees traveled with rail shipments of bananas both to ensure proper storage conditions and to line up sales of "rollers," or railcars of fruit that had not been presold, to brokers and wholesalers along the route. The company also issued numerous pamphlets directed at retailers that provided instructions on how to handle and display bananas. By the late 1920s, Fruit Dispatch handled nearly 53 percent of the total U.S. banana trade, far more than its leading competitors, Standard Fruit (15 percent) and Cuyamel Fruit's subsidiary Banana Sales (13 percent). Combined, these three companies accounted for some 81 percent of the banana trade. At the regional level, single companies often held virtual monopolies. For example, Fruit Dispatch was the only importer servicing the Boston area (United Fruit's headquarters) and the company reportedly controlled 80 percent of the lucrative eastern market (including New York City).[110]

In 1925, the Fruit Dispatch Company convened a conference in Chicago that brought together employees from all phases of production and marketing, including some managers from United Fruit's Central American divisions. High on the agenda was the question of how to market an increased supply of bananas that was catching up with rising demand following the Great War.[111] The conference included both presentations by company executives and reports from regional fruit jobbers assessing the level of competition and the market's ability to expand. United Fruit executives used the occasion to announce the creation of a "Publicity Department" that would be responsible for making the banana "more popular than it has been in the past."[112] The company launched a multimedia advertising campaign that included booklets containing information about the banana's nutritional value and recipes, a magazine called *Unifruitco,* and national billboard displays. The department's leadership pledged to find new outlets for the fruit by working with retailers in order to "feature" bananas prominently in store displays.

The conference's emphasis on finding new outlets for bananas reflected the disjuncture between agroecological processes in the tropics and mass-market dynamics: the local/regional effects of Panama disease were hard to discern in the marketplace due to the continued geographical expansion of production. When United Fruit vice-president George Chittenden addressed the problem of declining production on the Caribbean coast of Panama, he made no reference to Panama disease, but the two options he presented — abandon the area or "plant something else which is still a banana" — clearly indicated that he was talking about the disease. Hoping to salvage some of the company's six-million-dollar investment in the region, the executive delivered a sales pitch of his own:

> We all know about the Cavendish banana (grown in the Canary Islands and Hawaii). It is not very much of a success. . . . There is however, a banana called the Lacatan which can fool most people . . . we can put Lacatan bananas in with a cargo of Gros Michel and the chances are about four out of five that you won't know it.
>
> The [Lacatan] bunches are not very large. The nine [-handed stem] is more occasional than otherwise. The intermediate stage between green and dead ripe is not attractive to look at. Instead of a handsome green it is a rather dull gray green. I don't care how much of a banana expert you are or how well your taste is developed, you cannot tell one from the other when you eat them. We can raise more Lacatan per unit area than we can of the present banana of commerce. If we can raise a third as many more bananas per acre, we give you a margin on which you might very easily be able to move the Lacatan banana. We hope you will think that over.[113]

Chittenden's words reveal the extent to which aesthetic sensibilities held by distributors and wholesalers influenced the fruit company's efforts to find a disease-resistant replacement for the Gros Michel. How the conference audience responded to Chittenden's proposition is unknown, but few jobbers were fooled when United Fruit attempted to export Lacatan bananas three years later.

In September 1928, the Fruit Dispatch Company's Southern Division (based in New Orleans) reported that they had received their largest shipment of Lacatans to date: 15,000 bunches (the division routinely handled 250,000 bunches of Gros Michel per week). Shortly thereafter, the division manager questioned the merits of even this modest shipment of Lacatan fruit:

> Even those firms who are thoroughly familiar with the handling and ripening of Lacatans do not favor this variety. The consuming public,

in the final analysis, are the ones who have the say as to what fruit they desire, and inasmuch as the meat of the Lacatan, even though the skin may be yellow, is not really mellow and not as digestible as the Gros Michel, unless the skin of the former has practically turned black; and in this condition the fruit is uninviting to the eye and hard to sell. There is a question of whether or not we are serving the business properly in trying to force them on the market. This week we are going to have about 2,960 stems of Lacatans and it is my intention to hold the unsold cars here, and have Mr. Rowe's men visit the jobbers who made f.o.b [free on board] purchases, for the purpose of educating them in handling and ripening of the fruit and assisting in every manner possible.[114]

The Weekly Market Report's description of Lacatan fruit contradicts much of Chittenden's rather enthusiastic description of the variety. Lacatan's flavor and ripening behavior were noticeably different from those of Gros Michel. The statement about "forcing" the variety on the market indicates that buyers were rather reluctant to purchase Lacatan bananas when decent Gros Michel fruit was available for a comparable price.

Cuyamel Fruit and Standard Fruit also tried to market Lacatan bananas on a trial basis during the 1920s. Buyers complained that the fruit did not ripen in a satisfactory manner. In addition, the variety was susceptible to a fungal rot that weakened the stem from which jobbers and retailers usually suspended bananas for ripening and display purposes. Although experiments indicated that Lacatan's ripening qualities improved upon exposing the fruit to ethylene gas, jobbers resisted buying a variety that required significant alterations to their routine ripening procedures. Both companies reported that Lacatan sales dropped when Gros Michel fruit was available.[115]

The findings of a 1929 marketing survey commissioned by United Fruit shed additional light on how market structures and aesthetic sensibilities worked to impede the introduction of new varieties. The survey targeted women on the assumption that "the housewife is the authority on the buying and serving habits of the family."[116] The women interviewed were usually at a loss to explain what "impulse" led them to buy bananas: roughly one-third stated that it was a "matter of habit"; about one-sixth credited an "attractive display." Questions directed toward consumers about fruit quality were limited to size and ripening stage; no queries were made in regard to flavor, texture, or preferred way to eat the fruit. More than half of the interviewees preferred to buy "yellow ripe" bananas; about

40 percent favored "fully ripe"; and only 6 percent selected bananas with "green tips." A significant majority (75 percent) favored "large" bananas over "medium" and "small" fruit, but this preference varied by region and income. The study found that six out of ten consumers were not conscious of any season for bananas and purchased them throughout the year. Finally, 75 percent of the people interviewed "never" had difficulty finding fruit of acceptable quality, leading the authors to conclude that the consumer was "not so harsh of judgment as those who *know* banana quality," i.e., fruit jobbers and retailers.[117]

Indeed, virtually all of the jobbers interviewed spoke at length about fruit quality. Premium bananas were large, scar-free, and ripened evenly. For example, a Worcester, Massachusetts–based dealer known as Nick "the Banana Man" explained that "retail sales are better if the fruit is really 'fancy,' clean fruit in nice, fat bunches," an opinion from which few jobbers dissented.[118] They used terms such as "scarred," and "string beans" to describe poor fruit. As was the case with consumers, jobbers apparently did not place much value on flavor, sweetness, or texture when describing fruit quality. Instead, they frequently identified bananas on the basis of the visual appearance of the fruit and, to a certain extent, its port of origin.

Reflecting a trend started in the late nineteenth century, nine-handed fruit bunches garnered the highest prices in the 1920s. For example, the Tsones Brothers—competitors of Nick in Worcester—stated that they only traded nine-handed bunches. They also had started to buy "selected fruit bagged in the tropics" which they admitted cost more but was "good, clean fruit" that arrived in better condition than unwrapped bananas.[119] A jobber with a number of chain store clients in Lawrence, Massachusetts, also sought out nine-handed bunches because the customers liked "large fruit."[120] In contrast, dealers servicing stores with a working-class clientele preferred smaller bunches. For example, in Lowell, Massachusetts, long-time banana dealer Joseph Fielding said that "everyone" in the struggling mill town bought "sevens" because Fielding could not get "a penny more" for larger bunches.[121] Another Lawrence-based banana dealer, George Lampros, concurred with Fielding that stores retailing bananas by the pound sold seven- and eight-handed bunches at the same price, but he bought mostly eights since they "showed up better" and because "people don't buy sevens." In Atlanta, Georgia—"a dumping ground for bananas," in the words of one wholesaler—retailers sought inexpensive, small fruit that they could sell by the dozen. Consequently, the fruit companies usually sent small bunches (fives, sixes, and sevens) and/or eights and nines with thin fruit to Atlanta. Thus, although nine-handed fruit bunches with "fat" fingers set the standard for quality in U.S. markets, demand varied across lines of class and region.[122]

The marketing survey revealed that jobbers perceived themselves to be in a highly competitive business. Virtually all of the jobbers interviewed in 1929 complained about being undersold by small-time and/or seasonal dealers who purchased "decks" (i.e., overripe fruit) and other low-grade fruit for quick sales to retailers during periods of high demand. Such dealers rarely invested in year-round storage facilities and tended to drop out of the trade when demand slackened. Banana Man Nick, who claimed that he bought "mostly nines" from United Fruit, expressed frustration with the "little fellows" who sometimes bought up the "lower quality" fruit and undersold him. The Tsones Brothers noted that United Fruit's practice of selling deck ripes at lower prices allowed jobbers to undercut each other—and they pointed to Nick as an example: "He gets decks, Jamaicas, and some sevens. He never buys first quality fruit."[123] Just who the "little fellows" were seemed to depend upon who was doing the underselling.

The comments of the Worcester-area jobbers notwithstanding, the 1929 marketing survey suggests that small-time fruit vendors such as the peddler immortalized in the pop song "Yes! We Have No Bananas Today" were not the primary threat to wholesaler livelihoods. Instead, the proliferation of cash-and-carry chain stores such as A&P and Krogers reflected the growing consolidation of retail food markets that potentially weakened the position of fruit jobbers. Both retail chain grocers and large-scale agribusinesses staked their financial success on high-volume sales and low profit margins, a shared business strategy that was mutually reinforcing. In the late 1920s, the Midwest-based Krogers chain began purchasing bananas directly from the importing companies. The A&P reported that their stores often used bananas as a "leader" item, sold at cost, in order to lure customers from competitors. However, the dominance of chain stores was by no means complete in 1929: About 40 percent of the consumers surveyed "usually" purchased bananas from chains, but more than 50 percent of the consumers bought bananas from independent retailers, including street vendors, who continued to play an important role in poor and immigrant neighborhoods.[124] Wholesalers and jobbers would remain a crucial link in the banana commodity chain during the first half of the twentieth century.

If it is true that most retail banana sales were transacted through the hands of "housewives," fruit quality standards were set primarily by

FIGURE 2.6. *Fruit jobbers working in a banana ripening room (c. 1930).*
United Fruit Company, "About Bananas" (Boston: 1931).

fruit jobbers (mostly men), who occupied the space between production
and consumption. Both quality standards and processing techniques (i.e.,
storage and handling) evolved around Gros Michel fruit. The failure of
the 1929 marketing survey to generate any conversation about other varieties strongly suggests that the many kinds of bananas cultivated in the
tropics did not exist — at least not as commodifiable things — in the minds
of most consumers. Efforts to introduce a "new" variety such as Lacatan
therefore faced an uphill battle because most wholesalers would have little
interest in a banana that seldom produced nine-handed bunches, required
modified storage facilities in order to ripen, and had a tendency to come
crashing down to the shop floor. Even if the fruit companies were to offer
Lacatan fruit at a reduced price on wholesale markets, it would have faced
competition from discounted Gros Michel bananas.

Of course, the fact that just three companies controlled some 75 percent of the national market left jobbers with few options when buying bananas in the first place. Presumably, the fruit companies could have compelled wholesalers to accept the Lacatan (or some other disease-resistant
variety) had they been compelled to do so. However, the handsome profits
enjoyed by the fruit companies during the 1920s must have satisfied most
investors. The United Fruit Company's cash reserves increased from $11.2
million in 1899 to more than $50 million in 1918. Net profits soared to
more than $33 million in 1920, a sixfold increase over earnings in 1913.[125]

Between 1926 and 1928, United Fruit averaged a remarkable 10 percent annual rate of return on its investment. At the same time, an intense rivalry developed between United Fruit and Cuyamel Fruit during the 1920s. The former held a dominant market share, but many jobbers interviewed in 1929 believed that the latter produced the highest-quality bananas. That same year, Fruit Dispatch officials expressed concerns about being undersold by Cuyamel Fruit, which was reportedly dumping large quantities of nine-handed bunches on the New Orleans market.[126] Under such market conditions, there must have been little incentive to introduce a new banana on U.S. markets. Instead, the fruit companies relied on their economic and political power to ensure continued access to the subsidized soil and water resources necessary to produce nine-handed Gros Michel fruit—the U.S. market's "Top Banana."

SHIFTING PLANTATION AGRICULTURE

Unable to find a marketable, disease-resistant banana, the companies adopted a strategy of shifting plantation agriculture: They abandoned heavily diseased farms, rerouted railroads, and carved new plantations out of forests and wetlands. This practice enabled the companies to maintain and even increase their production levels, but as a contemporary observer in La Ceiba noted, it did nothing to arrest the Panama disease epidemic: "The disease still continues particularly in the older plantations, and only by the planting of new areas can the banana production in this district be maintained or increased."[127] Of course, shifting plantation agriculture depended upon the fruit companies' continued access to soil and water resources. In order to secure such access, the companies renegotiated and/or violated the terms of their original railroad concessions.

For example, during the 1910s, Standard Fruit's railroad building had proceeded in a southwesterly direction from La Ceiba toward the Leán River valley as stipulated in the company's 1910 concession. In 1919, Standard Fruit renegotiated the terms of the concession in order to receive permission to build a railroad east from La Ceiba toward the department of Colón.[128] By the late 1920s, the company had 6,500 hectares of plantations and pasture in the municipality of Jutiapa in addition to two dozen farms in Sonaguera, Colón. Banana exports from La Ceiba reflected the shift to new soils: after falling from 4.3 million to 1.9 million bunches between 1922 and 1926, Standard Fruit's exports rebounded to 6.5 million bunches in 1931.[129]

By that point, the company had almost completely abandoned its farms west of La Ceiba.[130] During the three-month period of peak demand in 1932, only 13% of Standard's exports (1.5 million bunches) came from farms situated in Atlántida.[131] Three years later, the department's governor reported that Standard had not undertaken any new projects in his jurisdiction due to the "impossibility" of combating Panama disease.[132] Around this same time, Standard Fruit agreed to turn over some 25,000 hectares of abandoned land in Atlántida to the national government.[133]

A similar process unfolded elsewhere along the North Coast. By 1930, at least fourteen farms belonging to the Tela Railroad Company had been or were soon to be abandoned. Two years later, the company ceased production in the León valley.[134] In Colón, the Truxillo Railroad Company abandoned nearly 10,000 hectares during the 1920s.[135] In 1928, a Honduran official reported that Panama disease was damaging "the majority of farms, but principally those located along the Mosquitia line."[136] In 1937, only ten years after production began in the Black River valley, the Honduran National Congress, noting "the intense development of some diseases that have caused the complete ruin of the company's bananas," approved a decree giving the company the right to abandon the region.[137] As part of the agreement, the company returned at least 17,000 hectares of land to the state. By 1940, the Truxillo Railroad Company's activities in Colón had all but ceased; observers noted that sun-tolerant plant species quickly inhabited the spaces once occupied by banana plants.[138] Finally, in Puerto Cortés, a U.S. consular report from 1927 stated that the "banana disease" continued to attack new plantings of Gros Michel, reducing the output from Cuyamel Fruit Company farms to "an almost negligible quantity."[139] Following his 1931 inspection of the Omoa-Cuyamel region, Honduran official Alonzo Valenzuela contrasted his memories of banana-covered valleys to the *guamil*-dominated landscape that he observed where banana plants were "seldom found."[140] By 1930, Zemurray's subsidiaries had abandoned more than 10,000 hectares.[141] As the export boom came to a close, Gros Michel "graveyards" littered the North Coast from the Guatemalan border to Mosquitia.

The geographical instability of export banana production cannot be attributed exclusively to the spread of Panama disease. Contemporary observers tended to attribute abandonments to multiple causes, including declining soil fertility. Following his 1927 tour of Central American export banana zones, British researcher Claude Wardlaw criticized the cultivation practices he observed there as little more than "the exploitation of the native fertility of virgin soil with the minimum amount of detailed treatment."[142] He argued that inadequate soil surveys resulted in the establishment of banana farms in poor soils that were swiftly abandoned, leading to the felling of "giant forests." Even on the alluvial plains often considered ideal for banana growing, Wardlaw noted, soils were by no means of a uniform texture or fertility: "Forests will often thrive on soils which, judged from an agricultural standpoint, have a very low standard of efficiency, particularly from the physical and chemical standpoints."[143] Poor soil conditions tended to slow banana plant growth, which in turn provided an opportunity for fast-growing plant species such as grasses to establish themselves and compete with banana plants for nutrients. The resulting increase in labor inputs (primarily weeding) drove up production costs which, combined with poor yields and slow growth rates, lowered profit margins and prompted the abandonment of the land.[144]

Wardlaw further argued that the decision to abandon an export banana farm was not a measure of "complete infertility" but rather of a "non-remunerative standard of productiveness." That is, production could cease despite the ability of a plantation to yield "quite a considerable number of bunches per acre."[145] Evidence from Standard Fruit operations in Honduras confirm that decisions about abandoning farms were not straightforward. For example, during a weekly staff meeting in 1924, a Standard Fruit employee recommended abandoning approximately 1,000 hectares of "unproductive lands" because they no longer annually yielded "60 payables" (export-quality bunches) per manzana (.69 hectares) and therefore would not recover the costs of weeding.[146] However, a comment penned in the margin of the meeting's minutes urged that more "details" be obtained; in the meantime the farms were not to be abandoned because company managers believed that "we may need this fruit." This fragment suggests that the calculus of abandonment involved more than applying cost-benefit formulas on a farm-by-farm basis; other variables, including the anticipated market demand for fruit and the collective ability of the company farms to meet that demand, also affected the decision-making process.

The fruit companies' practice of shifting plantation agriculture, then, resulted from a production-consumption dynamic driven by the banana's peculiar biology, the expansion of interconnected monovarietal agroecosystems, and mass-market structures which, having evolved around Gros Michel bananas, resisted the introduction of Panama disease–resistant varieties. Of course, had the fruit companies been unable to continue to secure concessions from Central American governments ceding them access to the soils, forests, and waters upon which they depended, the strategy of shifting production would have lost its viability.

In May 1928, port officials in New Orleans confiscated $50,000 worth of arms as they were being loaded aboard a Cuyamel Fruit Steamship bound for Honduras. Nearly twenty years after he provided logistical support for Manuel Bonilla's rebellion, Sam Zemurray was once again in the middle of a political scandal. The bungled arms shipment took place during an election year in Honduras. Although unable to prove Cuyamel Fruit's complicity in arms trading, U.S. government officials in Honduras suspected that the company helped funnel weapons to Liberal party supporters in anticipation of a post-election uprising. Zemurray feared that his ability to lobby the national government would be curtailed if the United Fruit–backed National Party candidate Tiburcio Carías Andino were to win the election. He was particularly concerned about maintaining access to the production zone along the disputed border shared by Honduras and Guatemala.

The struggle to dominate this region started in 1915 when Cuyamel Fruit — in accordance with a concession awarded by Honduras — extended its railroad toward the Motagua River where United Fruit had recently established farms on the Guatemalan side of the river. Fearing that the Cuyamel railroad would break its transportation monopoly in the region, United Fruit successfully lobbied the Guatemalan government to protest Cuyamel's activities in the disputed territory. In 1918, the United States government stepped in to mediate the dispute and both countries accepted the creation of a "neutral zone" pending the completion of a boundary conference. The fruit companies apparently struck a deal among themselves, and for six years Zemurray halted operations in the disputed territory. However, by the mid-1920s, the combination of Panama disease and declining soil fertility compelled Zemurray to secure access to additional land. In 1927, the Chacón government in Guatemala amended United Fruit's concession, giving the company the legal authority to operate in the disputed territory. Zemurray responded by reinitiating work on the unfinished railroad, sparking renewed tensions between the two countries.[147]

With troops assembling on both sides of the contested border, U.S. diplomats intervened once again. At this point, Zemurray began to support Liberal Party presidential candidate Vicente Colindres Mejía. The Liberals won the 1928 presidential election but the opposition National Party remained in control of the Honduran congress. Faced with few alternatives and under U.S State Department pressure to strike a truce with his rival, Zemurray traveled to Boston in 1929 in order to negotiate a settlement. United Fruit eventually agreed to purchase the assets of the Cuyamel Fruit Company from Zemurray for 300,000 shares of United Fruit stock. United Fruit acquired nearly 22,000 hectares of land planted in bananas, sugar cane, and coconuts; 23,000 hectares of forest and wetlands; 13 steamships; and control over an additional 13 percent of the U.S. market.[148] Zemurray, now holding United Fruit stock worth $32 million, retired to his family estate near New Orleans.[149]

Both the boundary dispute between Honduras and Guatemala and the rivalry between United Fruit and Cuyamel Fruit predated the appearance of Panama disease in Honduras. However, the fruit companies' response to the epidemic—shifting plantation agriculture—led to repeating cycles of invading people, plants, and pathogens that heightened the importance of soil and water resources on the North Coast. Indeed, the fruit companies faced repeated challenges to their grip on the region's resources from squatters, workers, and local government officials who struggled to maintain (and reinvent) livelihoods in altered landscapes.

Chapter 3

Altered Landscapes and Transformed Livelihoods

The last train on the Truxillo ran on April 5, 1942, and the last purchase of fruit was in March. There will henceforth be no outlet for the small farmers in that section.

ROBERT WHEDBEE, APRIL 18, 1942

"I believe, Honorable Minister, that the true sons of Honduras should not be impeded when we want to work our own lands," wrote a frustrated Víctor Medina Romero on October 8, 1932, in a letter addressed to the Honduran minister of development.[1] Born and raised in the Honduran highlands, Medina first migrated to the North Coast in the 1920s. There he found work as a day laborer (*jornaliando*) for the fruit companies. He later left the North Coast only to return in 1932 with the hope of establishing a farm near the village of Corralitos, Atlántida. Medina's letter explained that because there were no forested lands (*montañas vírgenes*) in the area, he had sought permission to cultivate a *guamil* that belonged to Standard Fruit. When a company official informed him that the land would be made available via lease in the upcoming year, a disappointed Medina turned to the national government for help with gaining access to land that "I need so badly in order to make my own living. The companies only want slaves; the worker remains with nothing after buying his necessities." He concluded his letter by reminding the minister about the difficulties of squatting: "if these companies do not give their consent to work an abandoned farm, they won't want to buy the fruit that one harvests!"

Víctor Medina's brief yet evocative letter sheds light on the dynamic intersection between landscape and livelihood negotiated by those who ventured to the North Coast in the early twentieth century with the hope of tapping into the region's "green gold." However, his self-described identity as a "true son" of Honduras potentially obscures the fact that women also migrated to export banana zones. For example, sometime around 1927, Ángela Coto-Moreno's mother decided to leave her home in southern Honduras and head for the North Coast in the hope of finding some of her children. Accompanied by only seven-year-old Ángela, she made the difficult journey through the mountainous central region of Honduras before reaching the Sula valley, where she found both her children and a job as a labor camp cook. Ángela eventually married and left the banana camps to establish a small farm with her husband.[2]

The experiences of Víctor and Ángela were not unique: thousands of men and women migrated to the North Coast in the first half of the twentieth century. They came from all over Honduras in addition to El Salvador, Jamaica, Guatemala, Nicaragua, Belize, and Mexico. Immigrant life in export banana zones was highly dynamic: people moved from farm to farm and from job to job, blurring the boundaries between campesino/a and obrero/a. Hundreds of small-scale growers produced Gros Michel bananas for export and/or grew a variety of grains, fruits, and vegetables for local markets. Although farming afforded freedoms unavailable to plantation workers, it also held many risks linked to weather, volatile markets, and the fruit companies' monopoly power over railroads and shipping. Panama disease added another destabilizing element to everyday life: the fruit companies' practice of shifting production left residents of abandoned communities to confront the vexing task of forging new livelihoods in altered environments. For squatters, an already tenuous situation was compounded by the threat of eviction, or, as Medina's closing remark suggested, an inability to market one's produce.

In struggles for control over resources, working people frequently employed rhetorics of place that appropriated elite discourses about nation building for their own needs. Working-class visions of the North Coast tended to be as contradictory as the process by which the Honduran state attempted to incorporate the region into an imagined mestizo nation. Spanish-speaking migrants such as Víctor Medina and Ángela Coto-Moreno forged collective identities in opposition to both the hegemony of the U.S. fruit companies and the presence of "black" and "foreign" laborers. The North Coast was a contested contact zone that gave rise to both anti-immigrant campaigns and utopian land colonization projects in places that lay beyond the shadows of the banana plantations.

IN THE SHADOWS OF THE PLANTATION

Contrary to what has commonly been assumed, the expansion and vertical integration of U.S. fruit companies in Honduras did not precipitate a rapid decline in the number of small-scale banana growers. Many late-nineteenth-century centers of small- and medium-scale production, including those in the Sula valley and along the coastal plain in Atlántida, persisted into the 1930s. If the data supplied to U.S. consular officials by company officials can be trusted, the Tela Railroad Company annually purchased between 24 and 41 percent of the fruit that it exported from Honduras between 1921 and 1935.[3] Company purchases climbed from 2.1 million bunches in 1922 to 4.9 million bunches in 1928. Between 1929 and 1933, fruit purchases fell by 30 percent, from 4.3 million bunches to 3.0 million.[4] However, this decline came on the heels of a sharp increase in non-company exports during the late 1920s such that the Tela Railroad Company actually purchased more bananas during the early 1930s than they had during the early 1920s. Also, non-company fruit sales subsequently rebounded to 3.7 million bunches in 1935. Data for United Fruit's other Honduran subsidiary, the Truxillo Railroad Company, are much less complete but suggest that small-scale grower contributions to total exports were significantly less than they were in the Sula valley.[5] Standard Fruit Company documents reveal that the Aguan Valley Company purchased a majority of the fruit that it exported during the first half of the 1920s, including an impressive 76 percent (3.4 million bunches) in 1920. The proportion of the company's exports supplied by non-company growers declined steadily during the second half of the decade, bottoming out at a mere 13 percent (0.5 million bunches) in 1930.[6] Non-company bananas represented less than 5 percent of Standard Fruit's shipments from La Ceiba during the months (March–May) of peak demand in 1932.[7] However, the company's purchases increased significantly in the early 1930s even as its own production dropped sharply; in 1934, non-company growers supplied 33 percent of Standard Fruit's exports.[8]

A Honduran government report documented 955 banana farms operating on the North Coast in 1914. Approximately 61 percent of these farms consisted of less than 14 hectares of bananas; 10 percent of the farms had 70 or more hectares of bananas.[9] In the department of Cortés, *poquiteros* represented a large majority of export banana growers as late as 1926.[10] Out of 179 cultivators recorded on an incomplete 1926 survey, just over half possessed 5 or fewer hectares of bananas and more than 75 percent grew 10 or less hectares of fruit. Growers in San Pedro Sula somewhat bucked

TABLE 3.1. Source of Tela Railroad Company Banana Exports, 1921–1935

	Total Fruit Exported	Fruit Purchased	
Year	In millions of bunches	In millions of bunches	Percentage of total exports
1921	6.7	2.4	35
1922	8.1	2.1	25
1923	7.0	2.2	32
1924	8.5	2.2	26
1925	10.4	2.7	26
1926	8.2	2.7	33
1927	13.3	3.6	27
1928	15.5	4.9	31
1929	17.1	4.3	25
1930	15.9	4.3	27
1931	16.1	3.9	24
1932	13.2	3.3	25
1933	12.3	3.0	24
1934	12.9	3.6	28
1935	9.0	3.7	41

Source: Robert E. Whedbee, "A Brief, Basic Banana Industry Report," 1941, U.S. Diplomatic Post Records 1930–1945 Honduras, roll 28.

this trend: a majority grew more than 20 hectares and several individuals planted more than 50 hectares of bananas. Two San Pedro Sula planters, Domingo Galván (350 hectares) and Henry F. Panting (180 hectares), cultivated large fruit farms.

Many of the cultivators recorded by the 1926 survey grew bananas exclusively, but a larger number raised one or more additional crops, including forage grasses, plantains, sugarcane, maize, and coconuts. *Poquiteros* farming one to three hectares tended to cultivate bananas exclusively. Farmers with a bit more land tended to diversify. For example, Cecilio Machado grew bananas, maize, rice, and sugarcane on 7 hectares in Puerto Cortés; his neighbor Petronilo Aguirre grew bananas, corn, and "other" crops on 7 hectares. Inés García of Omoa grew bananas, plantains, and *zacate* (pasture) on a 5-hectare plot. Most of the wealthy *finqueros independientes* in San Pedro Sula cultivated extensive areas of *zacate* and sugarcane in addition to bananas. In the three municipalities with the

TABLE 3.2. Source of Aguan Valley Company Banana Exports, 1920–1934

| | Total Fruit Exported | Fruit Purchased | |
Year	In millions of bunches	In millions of bunches	Percentage of total exports
1920	4.5	3.4	76
1921	4.3	3.1	72
1922	4.3	2.9	67
1923	3.2	2.0	63
1924	2.7	1.5	56
1925	2.7	1.2	44
1926	1.9	0.7	37
1927	1.9	0.5	26
1928	3.3	0.6	18
1929	3.4	0.5	15
1930	4.0	0.5	13
1931	6.5	0.8	12
1932	5.2	1.0	19
1933	3.8	0.9	24
1934	3.3	1.1	33

Source: Aguan Valley Company, "Detail of Fruit Shipments for Years 1920 to 1930 Inclusive," 5 Mar. 1941, Standard Fruit and Steamship Company Papers, Box 8, Folder 12.

highest concentrations of banana growers—Puerto Cortés, Omoa, and El Paraíso—98 of the 150 growers recorded grew one or more crops in addition to bananas. Consequently, the term "banana grower" must be applied with some qualifications, since many farmers produced multiple crops. The tendency to grow at least two or three market crops in addition to bananas also prevailed in the department of Colón.[11]

On the one hand, the evidence presented here reflects the extent to which the organization of production on the North Coast had changed: small-scale growers, who prior to 1910 accounted for a majority of bananas exported from Honduran ports, supplied no more than 30 percent of the fruit exported during the 1930s. On the other hand, the fact that hundreds of non-company growers sold some 4.7 million bunches as late as 1934 suggests a need to revise historical narratives that emphasize the rupture between the pre– and post–United Fruit eras in Honduras.[12] Geographical centers of late-nineteenth-century export production in the departments of Cortés and Atlántida remained important sites of non-company banana farms well into the twentieth century: in 1914, the two departments accounted for 90 percent of the 955 banana farms operating on the North Coast. Also, the noteworthy difference in the percentage of purchased fruit between United Fruit's two Honduran subsidiaries is consistent with the distinct nineteenth-century histories of the Sula and Aguán valleys in which the companies operated and serves as a reminder that regional contexts mattered in shaping the fruit companies' production practices.

But if small-scale banana producers persisted on the North Coast in the twentieth century, so too did tensions between farmers and shippers. The fruit companies' control over both railroads and steamships placed growers in a precarious position that was further undermined following United Fruit's purchase of Cuyamel Fruit in 1929, a merger that squelched whatever competition existed in the Sula valley, where most of the non-company growers were found. In February 1931, an article in a North Coast newspaper accused Tela Railroad Company fruit inspectors of rejecting "almost all" of the fruit cut by "national growers."[13] One year later, an editorial in a different regional newspaper detailed how rejected fruit reduced the earnings of Luis Caballero, a Sula valley grower who cultivated approximately 35 hectáres of bananas.[14] Caballero apparently did not suffer many rejections during the years 1925 and 1929, when he sold fruit worth US$4,667 and US$4,978, respectively. However, over a nine month period in 1930, Caballero had 807 bunches rejected; that same year, the company lowered the prices that it paid growers for all bunch sizes.[15] In just eight months of 1931, the company refused to buy 2,285 bunches. The rising number of rejections coincided with a dramatic decrease in the number of six-handed bunches that Caballero sold to the company. In 1925, the Tela Railroad Company bought nearly 2,400 sixes (more than 18 percent of the bunches purchased from Caballero). In 1929, the company purchased only 379 sixes; two years later, it all but stopped purchasing six-handed bunches. The case of Luís Caballero illustrates the connection between market demand and shifting quality standards: fruit inspectors tended to be less discriminating about banana quality in "boom" years such as 1925 than they were during the "bust" years of the early 1930s.

Fruit rejections were at the center of a conflict between a large number of Sula valley banana growers and the Tela Railroad Company over the terms of the 1931 purchase contract.[16] The first three clauses of the contract defined quality standards in terms of variety, peel condition, and bunch size. Harvested fruit had to be "fresh, clean, unblemished" Gros

Michel bananas. The company would not accept "bruised, damaged, dirty, or sun-burned" fruit, nor would it buy bunches that were not at the stage of ripeness requested, or that had short bananas (*dedos cortos*). Finally, the company would be obligated to accept only bunches with seven or more hands. The contract also stipulated that the fruit company could issue *avisos* on any day "without exception." Contract growers would be guaranteed a period of at least 12 hours to cut and deliver their fruit to the designated loading spots.[17] Individuals who signed the contract consented to weed and prune their farms with care (*bien limpias y deshijadas*), and to treat plant diseases according to the procedures adopted on company farms. They also agreed to sell their fruit exclusively to the Tela Railroad Company. In return, the company agreed to purchase Gros Michel fruit from contract growers at least once a week, at the rate of 50 U.S. cents for nine-hand stems, 37.5 cents for eight-hand stems, and 25 cents for seven-hand stems.[18] Upon making delivery, the contractor would be given a check or receipt that could be redeemed for cash in the company offices. The contract outlined a grievance procedure that consisted of an arbitration panel whose members were to be named by both the company and the contract grower, but disagreements related to the "variety, classification, maturity, and quality of the fruit" would be resolved by the company "without appeal."

Many fruit growers found the terms of the contract unacceptable; one outspoken critic of the contract predicted that it would lead to far more fruit rejections than in the past.[19] One week after a North Coast newspaper published the contract, the Ministro de Fomento met with a group of banana growers in San Pedro Sula. During the meeting, growers elected a committee to draft a counterproposal.[20] However, as the year came to a close, some 800 growers still refused to sign the contract.[21] In an open letter defending his fellow banana cultivators, Francisco Bográn, President of the Unión Frutera de Cortés, stated that his organization would exhaust all "peaceful and civilized means" to resolve their differences with the company. Shortly thereafter, another grower explained that he had rejected the contract because "individual sovereignty of one's lands and fruit inspectors (*juez de fruta*) are the umbilical cord of the independent farmers."[22] At least some growers believed that having some control over quality standards was absolutely crucial.

In early January 1932, the company lowered its purchase price for nine-handed stems to 30 cents. Many growers responded by refusing to cut their fruit.[23] The combative tone of Eduardo Da Costa Gómez, a spokesperson for the Unión Frutera de Cortés, underscored the heightened tensions between the company and contract growers: "Last night, sympathizers (*manos piadosas*) destroyed fruit that the company had ready [to transport]. We're starting to get New Year's presents (*aguinaldos*)."[24] At virtually the same time, Tela Railroad Company dock and railroad workers went on strike in protest over layoffs and deep wage cuts. The government of Mejía Colindres moved to end the strike by declaring martial law and sending troops to force the strikers back to work. The strike ended with in one week when the company agreed to provide food and housing for dismissed workers.[25] The wage cuts were not rescinded. Contract growers — many of whom were influential members of President Mejía Colindres's Liberal party — fared somewhat better. In mid-January, *El Pueblo* reported that Bográn and Da Costa Gómez met with the head of the Tela Railroad Company in La Lima.[26] The growers requested a reinstatement of the old prices for a period of sixty days, but the company argued that this was impossible due to a downturn in the market. Instead, company officials agreed to increase the price "immediately" when the economic situation improved and to install fruit inspectors who "would give fair receipts." Unsatisfied with these promises, the growers' representatives traveled to Tegucigalpa to meet with government officials. Shortly thereafter, the government consented to lower freight rates on the national railroad provided that the Tela Railroad Company (which under the terms of the contract was responsible for shipping costs) would raise the price paid for non-company fruit a proportionate amount.

Shortly after Sula valley banana growers reached the compromise with the national government and United Fruit, Da Costa Gómez reported that his association had entered into negotiations with Russell English of Mobile, Alabama.[27] Under the proposed terms, growers would sell all of their high-quality (*de primera calidad*) Gros Michel bananas to English.[28] Proposed purchase prices (nine-hand stem: US$.35; eight-hand stem: US$.25; and seven-hand stem: US$.15) were considerably lower than those proposed in the 1931 Tela Railroad Company contract, but higher than the US$.30 offered by that company in 1932.[29] The growers' counterproposal called on English's company to increase prices by 50 percent if and when the market price for fruit reached $2.50 per 100 pounds and/or when average fruit weights exceeded 60, 50, and 30 pounds for nine, eight, and seven-hand stems respectively.[30] In order to verify market prices, growers asked for the right to send a representative to the United States at the company's expense. The counterproposal also stipulated that *avisos* be posted every eight days and remain in effect for 36 hours. For their part, the growers and the government agreed to deliver harvested fruit to Puerto

Cortés and not to raise the shipping rates on the National Railway for the duration of the contract.

Negotiations between English and the growers continued through April.[31] In early May, a letter published in *El Pueblo* pointed out that the contract proposed by English offered growers "great advantages" and a $25,000 guarantee.[32] However, some growers insisted on a $100,000 deposit, and apparently the parties failed to strike a deal. Nevertheless, the negotiations between English and the growers' association revealed the concerns held by many banana farmers. These included ensuring that purchase prices reflected the banana's U.S. market value and creating a mechanism to verify changes in prices. The proposed pricing system also reflected growers' desires to be rewarded for producing heavy fruit bunches and to have more time between harvesting notices and delivery deadlines. The subject of fruit inspectors is absent from the counterproposal, a perplexing omission given the historic importance of this issue. Finally, the proposed contract's stipulation restricting exports to Gros Michel bananas is a reminder that the prospect of a new shipping line did not necessarily create an opportunity to export banana varieties other than Gros Michel.

Around the same time that Sula valley growers were searching for a means to loosen United Fruit's stranglehold on shipping, they became embroiled in a controversy over irrigation water. In February 1932, a member of the Honduran congress proposed reducing the tax on irrigation water applied to banana farms from ten dollars per hectare to three dollars per hectare. As Congress debated the measure, independent growers expressed their opposition to the reform. An anonymous grower wrote, "if they give the water concession they will ruin us; we, Hondurans, do not want irrigation."[33] Da Costa Gómez claimed that the tax concession would result in national growers being "permanently" displaced:

> We will never be able to offer fruit equal to that produced by the company and they'll be justified in not accepting it. The company's production will be sufficient to ruin us and buy up our lands that we would no longer be able to farm due to the high labor costs.[34]

A Puerto Cortés grower added that the reform measure would "harm national growers who will not be able to compete with irrigated fruit; therefore a greater quantity will be rejected."[35]

The concern of the self-identified "national" growers over the irrigation tax was rooted in their belief that the tax rebate would enable the fruit companies to increase their use of irrigation water and thereby produce greater quantities of heavy fruit.[36] Non-company producers, already concerned about fruit rejections, feared that cheap irrigation waters would lead to still greater rates of rejection. However, evidence suggests that the growers' most dire predictions did not immediately come true. The portion of total banana exports consisting of purchased fruit appears to have increased during the three years following the tax reduction. Furthermore, the congressional debate over the amendment revealed that the law establishing a $10 per hectare irrigation tax had not been enforced despite the fact that the companies had undertaken irrigation projects since 1923. Da Costa Gómez reported that the company had pumps operating on at least five company farms, and *El Pueblo* published photos of a pumping station located on the Ulúa.[37] In fact, confidential U.S. State Department correspondence reported that the Tela Railroad Company had more than 10,000 hectares under irrigation at the time of the controversy![38] In other words, the evidence strongly suggests that non-company growers had already been competing against irrigated fruit for nearly a decade, during which time taxes on irrigation water may not have been collected.[39] Nevertheless, contract growers' concerns about their inability to adopt capital-intensive (and resource-consuming) production methods were hardly irrational since the company stipulated that producers operate their farms in conformity with its cultivation practices. As fruit company managers in the tropics adopted novel methods to increase yields of high-quality fruit and U.S. per capita consumption of bananas leveled off, small-scale growers found themselves increasingly challenged to meet evolving production standards.

Fruit rejections and variable prices aside, the U.S. banana companies purchased tens of millions of banana bunches from contract growers during the first third of the twentieth century. For a small number of planters, the banana trade contributed to the accumulation of large amounts of capital. Fruit growers with medium-sized holdings such as Luís Caballero annually sold thousands of U.S. dollars' worth of fruit. For *poquiteros* without a purchase contract, earnings were probably scant.[40] The conflict over the 1931 contract revealed how United Fruit's transportation monopoly, along with its ability to set quality standards, enabled the company to exert considerable control over both *poquiteros* and the so-called *finqueros independientes*. The widespread protests staged by banana growers in 1931–1932 succeeded in securing a temporary government subsidy, but did little to strengthen contract growers' position vis-à-vis the U.S. fruit companies.

THE CROSS-CUTTING EFFECTS OF SHIFTING
PLANTATION AGRICULTURE

Paradoxically, non-company growers felt the limits of their autonomy most acutely when the fruit companies abandoned them. In May 1931, amid rumors that the United Fruit Company was going to suspend its operations in Omoa, Mayor Samuel García dispatched a telegram to the company in order to find out the truth. The mayor received a terse reply from a high-level company official: "I am notifying you that I have received orders to suspend indefinitely the purchase and production of fruit." García also received a telegram sent by United Fruit's William Turnbull explaining that "present business conditions do not allow us to continue absorbing the enormous losses that we have endured for several years in Cuyamel, a situation that we feel has not been appreciated." Mayor Garcia responded to the grim news by convening an open meeting during which some 90 residents from Omoa and surrounding communities signed a petition addressed to Honduran President Colindres Mejía, expressing their outrage over the company's decision:

> There are more than 500 laborers who are losing their daily work and along with it their ability to provide for their families. Many years of struggling, patient labor, perseverance and cooperation with the company are going for naught simply due to an order, as if the labor of an entire community were not worth even the tiniest consideration.[41]

They appealed to the president to intervene in order to prevent the "death of the only activity that provides a livelihood for the people." García pointed out that a suspension of banana-growing activities would likely put an end to local railroad traffic, leaving the community in isolation. The petitioners admitted that the region no longer produced "what it had in the past," but they defended their bananas as being as good as those cultivated elsewhere in the department of Cortés.[42]

One year later, Mayor Garcia's fears became reality when the company began removing branch lines situated between Cuyamel and Omoa.[43] Banana growers made public appeals for help with finding a way to transport their produce.[44] In a 1932 letter to the Ministro de Fomento, Orellano Rodríguez explained that he, along with 25 other growers, stood to lose the investments that they had made in new banana farms located along Cuyamel's railroad line.[45] The minister's response offered little consolation: he informed Rodríguez that the company "has the right to abandon that sec-

tion of railroad; the government has negotiated with company representatives for the line to be maintained but it does not have the right to force
them."[46] The same concessions that gave the fruit companies access to the
region's resources also gave them the liberty to remove their infrastructure—including railroad branches—when the transformed resources no
longer met their needs.

Following his inspection of the Omoa-Cuyamel region in 1933, Honduran official Alonso Valenzuela described the stark contrast between the
boom years of the past and the present economic collapse: "It's a pity to see
the comparison between 1916 and today: then, banana farms covered all of
the valleys and the level of commerce was astonishing; today, everything
is desolate, dead. The valleys are all *guamiles* and it is hard to find a banana
plant."[47] In Cuyamel, Valenzuela noted that the "greater part" of the inhabitants remained in the area. Some residents engaged in the bittersweet
work of dismantling fruit company railroads and buildings. Others cultivated grains and/or raised animals including pigs, chickens, and cattle.
Along a section of railroad that ran close to the sea, small numbers of
cultivators continued to grow export bananas that they transported to
steamers via small boats and canoes. However, by the mid-1930s, banana
exports from the Cuyamel-Omoa region had all but ceased.

By the time that Valenzuela and fellow inspector Pascual Torres arrived in Omoa, the fruit company railroad had already started to deterio-
rate from disuse. Valenzuela and Torres reported that repairing the railroad would require a significant investment on the part of the national
government. Even more problematic, according to the inspectors, was
the lack of potential traffic capable of generating the amount of revenue
needed to meet the railroad's operating expenses. Local people reported
that they generally used canoes and mules as their primary means of transportation because they were more convenient and less expensive than the
fruit trains (whose frequency had been diminishing for several years). In
fact, some residents declared that they had never viewed the fruit company
bridges and railroads as a necessity "to the extent that is being suggested
today."[48] Torres reported that the removal of an iron bridge over the Cuyamel River would not disrupt local livelihoods since the bridge had served
rail cars exclusively. He stated that the people in Cuyamel would be "content" to have a government-provided truck capable of crossing the river
during the dry season and a wooden bridge to facilitate crossing during
the rainy season. The two inspectors may have downplayed the importance of the railroad in order to help build a case for why the government
should forego a costly overhaul of the line in favor of less expensive alter-

natives.[49] On the other hand, their reports may have reflected the extent to which the Cuyamel Fruit railroad primarily served the interests of export banana growers.

If the residents of Omoa-Cuyamel were ambivalent about the fate of the railroad, they were anything but when it came to the fruit company's abandoned land and housing infrastructure. In some cases, local people were already established on former banana farms when the company announced its imminent departure. On a property known as "Cuyamel," several families cultivated annual crops in addition to fruit trees, plantains, pineapple, and sugarcane. They began leasing the land from the Cuyamel Fruit Company at some point in the 1920s and continued to rent from United Fruit following its acquisition of the property in 1929.[50] The renters also occupied company-built houses.[51] When word circulated in 1933 that the national government intended to reclaim the properties, the Junta de Fomento de Cuyamel (Cuyamel Development Committee) petitioned Honduran President Tiburcio Carías to recognize the presence of the renters who had occupied the land "for years."[52] One year later the national government approved the statutes of the Junta de Fomento, investing the body with the power to administer the property.[53]

However, the Junta soon became a target of official criticism. In 1937, Cortés Governor Castañeda listed examples of what he characterized as the committee's inefficiency and corruption: "The former Cuyamel Fruit Company buildings, with minor exceptions, are deteriorating; there are no tires on the truck; the promised investments in the property have not been made; and the land and houses have become the spoils of the Junta."[54] He also accused the committee of tax evasion and fraud. In addition, local police officials reported that a group of "non-Hondurans" living in Cuyamel were dismantling former fruit company houses and selling off the lumber and furniture.[55] In the eyes of Governor Castañeda, the failure of the Junta de Fomento to prevent illegal actions was further proof of its inability to administer the Cuyamel property, and he urged his superiors to dissolve the committee.

In the case of the Omoa-Cuyamel region, then, the fruit company's departure placed severe constraints on local livelihoods by leaving hundreds of laborers unemployed and dozens of non-company banana growers without access to export markets. Railroads and export banana production on the North Coast had developed hand-in-hand during the twentieth century; the loss of one tended to spell the end of the other. But if United Fruit could remove railroad tracks and bridges, it could not haul away the land. In some instances, former workers gained access to abandoned farms and housing that enabled them to cultivate crops for local and regional markets. However, the substitute crops seldom generated the income that export bananas had produced during the boom years, leading many people to migrate to active banana zones. Finally, for some residents, the end of the export banana trade indirectly created opportunities for short-term profiteering and patronage via administrative structures ostensibly created to facilitate local control over abandoned resources and infrastructure.

Although Omoa cannot be held up as a "typical" case of abandonment, similar patterns unfolded in many North Coast communities following the cessation of export banana production. In August 1931, residents of Mezapa (Santa Rosa del Norte), a small village in the municipality of Tela, began "creating difficulties" for workers attempting to remove a branch line operated by the Tela Railroad Company.[56] Shortly thereafter, both the alcalde of Tela, Coronel Modesto Orellano, and Atlántida Governor Adolfo Miralda traveled to the village where they met with nearly 80 residents in order to resolve the matter. Governor Miralda read an official statement from the Ministro de Gobernación, reaffirming both the Tela Railroad Company's right to remove its branch lines and the government's resolve "to protect the rights of the company."[57] He then acknowledged the railroad's importance to the community but explained that he could not compel the company to leave the line intact.

The villagers did not dispute the right of the company to remove the track. Instead, they requested that the bridges over the Naranjo River and several creeks be left in place in order to facilitate the movement of people and animals during the rainy season. They also called for the rebuilding of a bridge over the Naranjo River that had been damaged by flood torrents. Mezapa residents claimed that prior to the arrival of the company, the Naranjo River generally "was dry" and "crossed with great ease." However, the Tela Railroad Company had rechanneled the river and created a network of drainage ditches that combined the flows of several other creeks into the Naranjo. As a result, locals described the river in 1931 as "very deep and dangerous," particularly during the rainy season when the swollen waterway carried trees and other debris down stream. Finally, noting that the fruit company piped potable water from the Mezapa River through the village to its nearby labor camps, the residents requested that, as "an act of justice," four water spigots be installed for the community's use. The following day, Mayor Orellano reported that the matter had been resolved to the satisfaction of all parties.[58] The residents of Mezapa agreed to permit the removal of the railroad in return for the Governor's promise that the bridges would remain intact. The Governor and the Mayor also promised to take up the issues of the water spigots and the Naranjo River bridge with Tela Railroad Company officials.

However, less than one week after the meeting, the assistant mayor of Mezapa, Ciriaco Torres, informed Governor Miralda that he had ordered the workers to stop taking up the rails because the Tela Railroad Company had failed to complete "the construction of the bridge spanning the Naranjo River." The governor's reply to Torres was firm: the village could not insist that the company build a new bridge because one was already in place.[59] But the content and tone of his letter to the Ministro de Gobernación were very different. Miralda explained that many of Mezapa's 400 inhabitants made a living by selling food and other products to plantation workers in the nearby municipality of El Progreso. Between Mezapa and these markets lay the Naranjo River and numerous other creeks that during the rainy season could only be crossed via bridges. Miralda urged his Tegucigalpa-based superior to pressure the company to rebuild the bridge in light of both the environmental changes precipitated by the company's operations and the potential for further resistance on the part of Mezapans:

> I repeat that the villagers have justice on their side because the problem
> has resulted from the channeling work [of waterways] that the
> company has done in that jurisdiction. And I am of the opinion that it
> is the company that has the most to gain by complying with the just
> desires of the inhabitants of Mezapa. The actions that the government
> could take to pacify the villagers would not prevent them from taking
> revenge upon the company.[60]

Unfortunately, the historical record does not indicate whether the bridge was rebuilt, or if the villagers sought "revenge." Nevertheless, the events at Mezapa reveal the historical connections between altered landscapes and transformed livelihoods. The Tela Railroad Company's arrival in the region created new ways to earn a living while altering the landscape. When Panama Disease reached the Mezapa area and reduced the profitability of growing bananas, the company pulled out, removing the infrastructure that it had placed there. However, the Naranjo River and the area's drainage basin remained altered, prompting the villagers to impede the removal of the railroad in order to ensure that the company maintained a series of local bridges essential to the (twice-transformed) local economy.

The bridge over the Naranjo River, then, can be seen as a symbol of the tangible benefits that United Fruit's engineering wizardry brought to the residents of Mezapa. But the company's production practices also changed the region's water and soil resources in two distinct, but historically linked ways: seasonal flooding of the Naranjo River and a decline in banana production due to Panama Disease. These new dynamics in turn triggered another series of linked social processes that included the fruit company's abandonment of the area, Mezapa residents' efforts to maintain their livelihoods, and subsequently new historical meanings for company-built infrastructure. Viewed in this context, the bridge — trembling as it gets pounded by tree trunks — represents the instability of complex agroecosystems shaped by dynamic processes operating at local and international levels.

Two years after the Mezapa protest, the residents of San Francisco, a small village west of La Ceiba, protested Standard Fruit's removal of a branch line. Echoing the concerns raised by his counterpart in Mezapa, San Francisco Mayor Sebastián Figueroa declared that the removal of the track would be a "mortal blow" to his community because it was the only means of transport possible through the swampy terrain in which the village was located. He added that the branch line in question crossed no fewer than 26 bridges. The Ministro de Fomento and the Ministro de Gobernación both contacted Standard Fruit in order to request a suspension of work until the matter could be discussed. Standard Fruit's general manager, A. J. Chute, responded by explaining that the track in question had serviced farms taken out of production due to Panama disease prior to 1929, and that company trains had already ceased to service the branch. However, he believed that with only minor repairs the rail bed could be converted to a roadway suitable for pedestrians and horses. Chute added that at the request of some "local employees and residents of San Francisco," the company had decided to leave two bridges in place.[61]

Chute's reply indicated that San Francisco had already endured an extended period of relative isolation prior to the removal of the branch line. In addition, a government report written four years prior to the incident described San Francisco and its neighboring villages as former "emporiums of wealth that today are barely surviving."[62] This suggests that the removal of the branch line signaled less the beginning of an abrupt transition for the residents of San Francisco than the culmination of an ongoing decline in local economic activity. Whether Mayor Figueroa remained satisfied with Standard Fruit's promise to leave two bridges in place is unclear, but his interest in impeding the removal of useable elements of the fruit companies' transportation infrastructure was consistent with community-based responses to abandonments elsewhere on the North Coast.

Local and regional government officials were not the only ones who initiated negotiations with the fruit companies over resources: many former plantation workers took direct action by squatting on company properties in an effort to create new livelihoods. In 1927, more than a hundred people occupying abandoned (*enguamilado*) Standard Fruit farms near La Masica petitioned Honduran President Miguel Paz Barahona for the right to work 7-hectare plots of land "independently." When Standard Fruit objected to the squatters' presence, Jacobo P. Munguía defended their actions by explaining that the squatters sought permission to plant modest amounts of Lacatan bananas: "Rather than leaving these lands uncultivated, they want to plant them in that disease-resistant variety and should the company find a market for the variety, they will happily sell their fruit to the company."[63] He admitted that the lands belonged to Standard Fruit, but stressed that the company would find the squatters to be reasonable collaborators, not adversaries. Unfortunately for the would-be banana growers, export markets for Lacatan fruit did not materialize during the 1920s. The onset of Panama disease exposed the limited freedom possessed by non-company producers, large and small. Even those willing to gamble on the Lacatan were ultimately forced to abandon the trade, shut off from both transportation and marketing networks.[64]

That same year, members of the Unión Ferrocarrilera de Honduras (Honduran Railroad Workers Union) and a group of campesinos began working "lands around an abandoned camp" of the Standard Fruit Company situated to the west of Sonaguera.[65] Labor leader Zoroastro Montes de Oca requested that the government help to ensure that fruit companies did not seek to evict the workers from the land as apparently had happened elsewhere in the area. He offered the activities of a railroad worker named Luis García as an example of the squatters' industriousness: on some seven hectares of land, García planted maize along with smaller amounts of sugarcane, plantains, bananas (for animal feed), root vegetables (*malanga*), and coffee. According to Montes de Oca, García had unknowingly found "the key to complete freedom" that would enable him to quit his job on the company railroad in favor of farming. He further promised that, if supported by the government, the worker-campesinos would soon form a "great property or cooperative" on the land.

In 1931, a La Ceiba–based workers' organization asked the national government to grant them the free use of "lands abandoned by the banana companies on the North Coast in sufficient quantities to provide for the unemployed."[66] Some 200 signatures were appended to the petition that claimed that at least 5,000 workers were unemployed and that available land was scarce due to the "different railroad and banana companies established on the lands most accessible to centers of consumption." The following year, the Governor of Atlántida, noting the "constant" stream of cultivators who appeared to request protection of their rights to either *ejido* lands (controlled by municipal governments) or those abandoned by the banana companies, authorized municipal chiefs of police to assist cultivators without property titles to establish property boundaries.[67] Efforts to resolve land disputes often proceeded slowly in part due to the inability of municipal governments to cover the expenses associated with a titling process that one local official described as "protracted and costly."[68]

Frustrated with the difficulty of obtaining land in export banana zones, some Honduran worker organizations turned their gaze toward Mosquitia—a large region lying between the department of Colón and the border with Nicaragua that was inhabited primarily by indigenous populations long viewed as primitive by Spanish-speaking highland elites. Honduran labor leaders first proposed colonizing Mosquitia in 1911.[69] During the 1920s, North Coast worker organizations showed renewed interest in the region. In July 1926, the Sociedad Lucha Obrera wrote to the Minister of Development declaring its intention to acquire a land concession in the Mosquitia region, "a place coveted by foreign elements and the only one that remains available to us on the North Coast."[70] A couple of months later, a letter from a La Ceiba–based artisans' guild urged the national government to approve a concession for 50,000 hectares of land "suitable for agriculture" near the Patuca River in Mosquitia.[71] Throughout 1927, guild members donated their labor on Sundays to build a sailing vessel for the purposes of making a preliminary expedition into Mosquitia. The organization also sponsored cultural events, including plays and holiday pageants, in order to raise funds for the project.[72]

In a 1927 address delivered in La Ceiba, Zoroastro Montes de Oca, secretary of the Honduran Railroad Workers Union, wove the language of both class and nationalism in exhorting his comrades to support the Mosquitia project: "How many families can we take to Mosquitia without the help of the state? Every worker's organization in the Republic that holds to the ideal of controlling all of Mosquitia's land for the common good and health of the Republic ought to ask itself that question. As we, the workers, understand it, those lands belong to the nation."[73] In the view of Montes de Oca, workers' claims to the resources of Mosquitia were grounded in ideas about both social justice and the rights and responsibilities of liberal citizenship. If workers loyal to the Honduran nation-state did not act, Mosquitia could easily fall under the control of a foreign interest, be it neighboring Nicaragua or a U.S. corporation.

In August 1928, a group of sixteen workers sailed their vessel eastward from La Ceiba to the mouth of the Patuca River. They proceeded upstream in dugout canoes with the intention of establishing a logging camp. However, by early November, more than half of the workers reportedly had left due to inadequate provisions and swarms of mosquitoes that made sleeping unbearable. The remaining expedition members abandoned the camp in December and returned downstream disgruntled and with little mahogany to show for their efforts.[74] Three months later, the Federación de Obreros Hondureños (FOH) reached an agreement with the Ministro de Fomento that ceded the FOH the right to colonize 40,000 hectares of land along the Patuca River.[75] At least one Olancho newspaper expressed its enthusiasm for the project in an editorial entitled "The colonization of Mosquitia by, and for Hondurans is an unfulfilled need." Describing the region as "majestic plains of great fertility and luxuriant and inaccessible forests yet untrammeled by humans," the newspaper's editors declared that "cultivation is urgently called for whenever there are poor natives, lacking in resources and livelihoods, in a countryside in which benevolent Nature has spilled its cornucopia of abundant gifts."[76]

But not everyone was so optimistic. In January 1929, J. Amado Flores, a logger and self-described supporter of worker causes, wrote a lengthy letter to the FOH in which he praised the organization's efforts to "liberate the fatherland from voracious foreigners" but warned against "blindly pursuing Utopias."[77] Amado suggested that the colonization project was based on a poor understanding of the region's resources. Mahogany trees, he explained, grew in very small, widely dispersed clusters, meaning that logging operations would be labor intensive. As far as cultivation was concerned, the lower portion of the Patuca River was flanked by thin, waterlogged soils. High wages and distant markets would restrict agriculture to high-value cash crops.[78] He estimated that the local population along the Patuca River did not exceed sixty people due to mosquitoes and a harsh climate. This gloomy portrait notwithstanding, Amado stressed that a "Honduran presence" in Mosquitia was vital in light of Nicaraguan "incursions" into the region. He urged the FOH to proceed with the project on a drastically scaled-down basis and offered his personal assistance:

"Being a proud Honduran, I would seek . . . to put these extensive regions in the hands of those who could make them healthy, populate them and make them productive."

Worker organizations appear to have abandoned the Mosquitia colonization project in favor of settling on lands abandoned by the fruit companies. Nevertheless, the failed settlement represented an ambitious and coordinated attempt by artisan/worker organizations to create livelihoods independent of the banana industry. The project also sheds light on the meanings that at least some labor leaders inscribed on the North Coast's resources. The message espoused by Montes de Oca was clear: powerful foreign companies already controlled the best lands along the North Coast; loyal workers needed to ensure that Mosquitia remained under Honduran sovereignty. He and other labor leaders claimed a stake in a territory that they had never seen on the basis of their status as *hijos de la patria* — sons of the fatherland. In order to do so, they appropriated elite visions of a mestizo nation descended exclusively from Indian and Hispanic peoples in an effort to erase the cultural heterogeneity found within the nation's borders and particularly on the North Coast where hispano-Honduran men and women mingled with Garifunas, Jamaicans, Palestinians, and gringos from the United States.[79] Mosquitia became a wilderness without a peopled past — a place to create a mestizo society comprised of male-headed agrarian households free of the social inequities and cultural diversity found on the North Coast.

The utopian vision underlying the Mosquitia project was probably more the exception than the rule among worker-cultivators, most of whom forged livelihoods by migrating in and around export banana zones. As the fruit companies redirected their railroads toward disease-free lands, they left many communities facing economic crises while simultaneously stimulating economic activity elsewhere by injecting capital and providing transportation linkages to regional and international markets. The history of Sonaguera, Colón, illustrates the cross-cutting effects of shifting plantation agriculture. Separated from the Caribbean Sea by the Nombre de Diós mountains, Sonaguera did not participate in the late-nineteenth-century banana boom that took place in and around Caribbean port towns. The municipality remained largely disconnected from the banana trade during the first two decades of the twentieth century, a situation reflected in community leaders' enthusiastic response to a U.S. investor's 1907 proposal to build a railroad from Trujillo to Sonaguera: "[The railroad] is our only salvation since it would both repopulate the

FIGURE 3.1. *Mahogany logs on Standard Fruit train in La Ceiba.*
Author's private collection.

extensive, uncultivated *vegas* of the Aguán River, and put an end to the
constant emigration of our sons to the Costa Norte."[80]

The principal livelihood in Sonaguera in the early twentieth century
was small scale ranching. In 1918, 66 residents reported owning between
1 and 40 head of cattle.[81] In 1920, local officials approved a timber conces
sion for Luís Masnada, a businessman from La Ceiba with ties to Standard
Fruit. The five-year contract agreed to sell Masnada "5,000 mahogany and
cedar trees" averaging 8 feet in diameter.[82] Revenue from the timber sale
was to finance various public works projects, including a new town hall
and schools. The deal strongly suggested that at least part of the municipality contained extensive forests and that existing ranching and agriculture operations did not generate much revenue. One year later, the Mayor
of Sonaguera convened a special meeting to discuss the "near exhaustion"
of forests in the ejidos due to the actions of "certain residents" who were
felling trees in order to plant pasture. Local officials, expressing concern
that such practices would threaten the ability of "poor residents" to establish small farms, agreed to divide the ejido into two zones, one for livestock (*zona ganadera*) and the other for agriculture (*zona mixta*).[83] This
initial effort to limit the expansion of ranching was a portent of the future,
but the shift toward an agricultural base was only beginning; as late as
1923, cattle, horses, and other animals continued to range freely through-

out municipal lands, and the financial burden of erecting fences to protect crops rested squarely on farmers' shoulders.[84]

Life in Sonaguera began to change rapidly when not one but two fruit-company railroads approached the municipality from opposite directions. In 1924, one hundred residents led by Inés Lanza presented a petition to the municipal council calling for Sonaguera's ejidos to be rezoned for agriculture in anticipation of the "foreign companies'" arrival.[85] The petitioners complained that the presence of "all kinds" of roaming livestock was impeding agricultural development. The Sonagueran council, perhaps hoping to avoid rendering a decision on a contentious topic, unanimously agreed to seek advice from higher authorities. The following year, Mayor Martínez reported he had received multiple complaints from the Standard Fruit Company about cattle-related damages on its new plantations.[86] This time the municipal council took action, establishing an agricultural zone on "land pertaining to this jurisdiction" that surrounded the municipal ejido.[87] Ranchers were given three months to corral any livestock and relocate them to ejido lands where free grazing continued to be permitted.

This measure apparently did little to resolve the conflicts between ranchers and cultivators. In March 1926, Nicolas Robles, Adolfo Sarres, Rosalio Escobar, Enrique B. Ocampo, and forty other Sonagueran ranchers petitioned the municipality for permission to erect, at their own expense, a barbed-wire fence in order to avoid damaging the plantations of the "foreign companies" that encircled the ejido.[88] Local officials approved the request, yet the power of the ranchers—who would now bear the burden of preventing damage to agricultural fields—was diminishing. Less than one year later, Robles, Petrona Ocampo, Tomasa Ramos, and some twenty other Sonagueran residents sent a letter to the Ministro de Fomento, complaining about the "severe fines" that they received on account of their cattle entering the banana farms of the Truxillo Railroad and Standard Fruit companies.[89] Describing themselves as "small cultivators and ranchers," the authors claimed that they lacked the financial resources to enclose their pastures and called on the national government to oblige the companies to fence their plantations. The Minister's somewhat ambiguous reply probably brought them little satisfaction: he urged the petitioners to respect the existing regulations that obliged "every owner of cattle and agricultural fields" to enclose their fields, but he made no specific reference to the fruit companies.[90]

By the end of the 1920s, export banana production in Sonaguera had increased dramatically. A majority of the output came from the farms of Standard Fruit and United Fruit subsidiaries, but small-scale cultivators contributed as well. Beginning in 1925, a growing number of people solicited land for agricultural activities. Among the many who sought parcels in 1928 were Porfirio Guerrero and Eladio Zelaya, who each requested 35 hectares in order to plant export bananas. That same year, Alberto Ortíz, Esteban Bardales, Octavio Robles, Juan Bardales Ortíz, and Eugenio Orellano each solicited 7 "forested" hectares on which they intended to grow bananas.[91] In February 1930, a number of residents asked that the ejidos be rezoned for agricultural use.[92] They acknowledged the importance of ranching in the past but noted that the number of cattle had fallen considerably in recent years as residents turned increasingly to banana cultivation on the ejido's "fertile soils." The municipal council agreed to redesignate the ejido as agricultural land, and ordered that fences be erected around existing pastures within a period of six weeks. One month later, the Governor of Colón approved the measure.

Invoking a contrasting view of the local landscape, some eighty Sonagueran ranchers rose to defend their livelihoods before the council: "It is common knowledge in this town that the majority of ejido lands . . . are not adequate for agriculture."[93] They criticized the proliferation of banana farms, a livelihood that from the ranchers' viewpoint "offered no future" since after the second harvest the soils would be "completely exhausted" and yields would fail to cover production costs. Livestock raising, on the other hand, had sustained the region since "time immemorial." The petitioners pleaded with the municipality not to "drown a proven source of wealth for an unknown one." But the ranchers' argument—by no means unreasonable in light of the ongoing abandonment of banana farms elsewhere—was unlikely to convince local officials; by 1930, Sonaguera was Standard Fruit's most important center of banana production and unprecedented amounts of revenue were flowing into municipal coffers.[94] Unsurprisingly, the municipal council dismissed the ranchers' appeal and instructed them to comply with the new ordinance.

Less than ten years after reaffirming the rights of ranchers to graze their animals on ejido land, Sonaguera's municipal council reversed its land-use policy, a reflection of both the changing local economy and the rising political power of banana growers. Small-scale farmers had enjoyed little success in challenging the privileges of ranchers until wayward cattle began finding their way onto the newly established plantations of the U.S. fruit companies. The arrival of the companies, then, provided small-scale growers with both economic opportunities and the political leverage necessary to vie for greater control over local resources. What in retrospect appears to be a straightforward example of U.S. corporate domination may have seemed much more ambiguous to the people who lived the experience.

Sonaguera's participation in the export banana trade was shaped by the unusual condition of having, for a short period of time, two major banana companies operating within its boundaries. In at least one instance, a group of *poquiteros* was able to take advantage of the companies' overlapping zones of influence. In July 1929, forty-five individuals wrote to Honduran Ministro de Fomento Salvador Corleto requesting titles to the farms that they worked in an area lying just east of Sonaguera's ejidos identified as "Lot 19."[95] The cultivators asserted that they had been farming the land in question for ten years and that they had recently signed a five-year contract to sell bananas to the Standard Fruit Company. However, the Truxillo Railroad Company ordered them to stop their activities in the area, alleging that it had bought the property several years earlier from a local landowner. Citing Standard Fruit maps of Lot 19 as evidence, the *poquiteros* claimed that they were occupying national lands and requested that the government deed its members *lotes de familia* as stipulated by the 1925 agrarian law. Two weeks later, the group's representative, Colonel Jesús J. Zelaya, wrote a second letter to Minister Corleto, "on behalf of the village La Paz," in which he indicated that the *poquiteros* had rejected a buyout offer made by the Truxillo Railroad Company because "we want to expand our farms, not sell them."[96]

In November 1929, Minister Corleto's office informed Romualdo López, a farmer in the disputed zone, that Lot 19 belonged to the Truxillo Railroad Company.[97] However, this "fact" did not put an end to the matter. In January 1930, an executive order ceded the growers 2,500 hectares of Lot 19 on which to establish *lotes de familia*.[98] When Truxillo Railroad Company General Manager E. E. Thomas received an order to suspend all company activities in the disputed area, he dispatched a lengthy letter of protest to the Governor of Colón in which he asserted that prior to 1928, no one lived in the forested region where the "imaginary" village of La Paz claimed to be established.[99] According to Thomas, La Paz had its genesis when a group of laid-off Standard Fruit Company workers, assuming that the forested lands in Lot 19 were national, began to clear timber and plant crops.[100] Soon thereafter, Truxillo Railroad Company forest rangers arrived on the scene and prohibited the workers from further clearing.

Sometime later, Thomas's letter explained, Jesús Zelaya, a "rich property owner from Balfate" convinced the workers to renew their clearing activities over the fruit company's protests. Zelaya himself established a "small plantation" in the area before traveling to Tegucigalpa — with funds supplied by the ex-workers — where he published notice of the formation of La Paz village and arranged for the government to parcel out *lotes de familia*.[101] According to Thomas, Zelaya had even seen the company's property title and "accepted" the "undeniable rights" of the company to the disputed land. The fruit company's general manager concluded by requesting that the President's office overturn the decision to cede the land to the *poquiteros*, lift the order halting the company's operations in the area, and protect the property from further acts of trespass.[102]

The respectful yet firm letter, accompanied by several enclosures in support of the company's position, may have convinced the national government, but it did not deter the residents of La Paz. In 1931, the Mayor of Sonaguera reported to the municipal council that La Paz was a "progressive village whose residents cultivate bananas on a large scale."[103] He urged the municipality to support the creation of a school in La Paz, a proposal that elicited a formal protest from the Truxillo Railroad Company. The residents of La Paz maintained a tenuous hold on the land for three more years. In fact, the village appears to have grown despite both the ongoing legal dispute and depressed prices for bananas on international markets. In 1934, La Paz consisted of 172 houses, 431 families, and a school that enrolled 53 students. Residents cultivated approximately 1,200 hectares of bananas, in addition to smaller amounts of *plátano macho*, pasture, maize, and beans.[104] One year earlier, approximately 150 villagers had attended a council meeting in Sonaguera in order to garner official support for their efforts to convince Standard Fruit to build a branch rail line toward La Paz.[105] The municipality agreed to make an official request to the company concerning the line. During the same session, the municipality also authorized a cemetery for the village. Its origins may have been mythical, but La Paz was quickly becoming a tangible reality.

In March 1934, a government commission consisting of Colón Governor Romero, General Sanabria, and a Truxillo Railroad Company official went to La Paz to discuss the conditions by which "an honorable transaction of the fruit" could take place.[106] A declaration submitted by the company to the Governor of Colón reiterated many of the points made in Thomas's 1930 letter, but also contained some important changes in the company's position.[107] Truxillo Railroad Company officials expressed little sympathy toward the *poquiteros*, whom they described as individuals "of diverse backgrounds who violently and without heed to private property" established themselves and planted bananas in a place called "La Isleta." The company's 1934 version of events replaced the complex and morally ambiguous version found in Thomas's 1930 letter with one in which the cultivators' activities were premeditated criminal acts. Also, the letter referred to the disputed area as "La Isleta," and did not acknowledge the formation of La Paz.

However, after declaring its inalienable rights to the property, the company official offered to cut a deal: "The company is willing to consent to the trespassers' (*intrusos*) presence, provided that they remain circumscribed in the area where they are currently established and on the strict condition that they sell their bananas to the company under the same terms as do other independent growers who farm their own lands."[108] The Truxillo offered to facilitate the transport of fruit grown in La Paz by building a branch line that would bring the fruit to the bank of the Aguán River, at which point the fruit would be carried across the river via an aerial tram to the company's main railroad. The company emphasized that any grower who did not accept these terms would be bought out.

But the *poquiteros* were not ready to relinquish their fields. On April 2, 1934, they submitted a document to the municipal council signed by around 100 individuals requesting that the legal status of their settlement be changed from *caserío* (hamlet) to *aldea* (village).[109] In considering the request, the municipal council acknowledged the Truxillo Railroad Company's claim to the land, but pointed to the existence of a school with 53 students as evidence of the community's legitimacy (conveniently forgetting that the council itself had authorized the school's creation). Council members unanimously agreed to designate La Paz as a village with an area of one square kilometer. The language of the act was unwavering in its support: "Should at any time the Truxillo Railroad Co. or any other entity seek to assert a legal claim, the municipality will, regardless of the title presented, ask for the expropriation of the land in the name of the public good in accordance with Article 27 of the Agrarian Law." Ten days later, Sonaguera Mayor Montiel telegraphed the Ministro de Gobernación, appealing for help in preventing the eviction of the 129 *poquiteros*, plus some 500 field hands from Lot 19: "If this comes to pass, what will more than one thousand Honduran workers do without employment or housing?"[110]

On April 23, Governor Romero returned to the disputed property for another meeting with the *poquiteros* that resulted in the signing of an act laying out two options for the future of La Paz: either the settlers would sell their farms to the fruit company at a "fairly assessed rate," or the company would sell the land to the settlers for the same price that it had originally paid.[111] On May 3, government surveyor Camilo Gómez reported that La Paz village was located on lands that were owned by the Truxillo Railroad Company.[112] He added that the company was still extending its offer to purchase the growers' bananas and install the infrastructure needed to transport the fruit to its railroad. However, according to Gómez, the *poquiteros* refused under any condition to sell their fruit to the company, preferring to either sell or purchase the land.

The inhabitants of La Paz continued to present evidence in support of their right to occupy the land during meetings with both government and company representatives in early May.[113] Then on June 1, 1934, following what Governor Romero described as "intense deliberations," the parties struck an agreement whereby the growers would sell their farms to the company.[114] The accord granted the *poquiteros* a period of four months to relocate and permission to continue selling their bananas to Standard Fruit until the Truxillo Railroad Company was able to erect a transportation system. How and where the residents of La Paz village relocated is unclear, but by November 1935, observers referred to the zone as the "La Paz farms of the Truxillo Railroad Company," suggesting that the company had assumed control over the land as agreed upon.[115]

The story of the drawn-out struggle to control the soil resources of Lot 19 does not readily conform to images of omnipotent fruit companies usurping the lands of hapless smallholders. The *poquiteros'* stubborn squatting and shrewd alliance making succeeded in keeping the Truxillo Railroad Company at bay for at least five years. The La Paz growers gained the support of local and regional authorities in spite of evidence indicating that the property had been transferred to the fruit company. The strong statement of support issued by the Sonaguera municipal council in 1934 suggests that if some local elites' initial backing of the *poquiteros* was motivated by little more than opportunism, support for La Paz evolved into an expression of Honduran nationalism. Local officials did not question the sanctity of private property, but they believed in the right of "Hondurans" to access the resources necessary to create dignified livelihoods. Significantly, the La Paz residents sustained local political support through the initial years of President Carías Andino's sixteen-year rule, a period in Honduran political history noted for both its authoritarianism and the far-reaching influence of United Fruit.

Of course, the La Paz villagers' "silent partner" throughout the dispute was the Standard Fruit Company, whose willingness to purchase the *poquiteros'* fruit provided the latter with access to export markets. The fact that Standard Fruit refrained from building a branch line to service La Paz may have reflected the company's reluctance to openly antagonize its powerful competitor. On the other hand, by doing business with

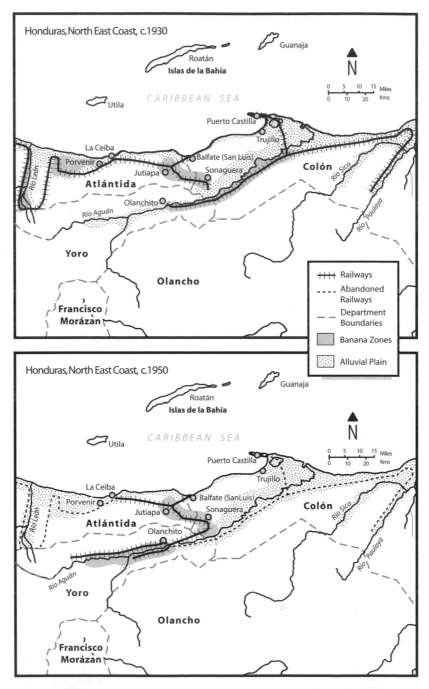

MAP 3.1. *Shifting geographies of production, Standard Fruit and Truxillo Railroad Company between 1930 and 1950*

the *poquiteros* they undermined the Truxillo Railroad Company's efforts to evict the cultivators. Although the company eventually reclaimed the land, its effort to cast the *poquiteros* as criminals largely failed. The persistence of La Paz, then, can be attributed in large part to its geographical location: in contrast to the abandoned farms occupied by squatters along the coast of Atlántida, the La Paz settlement straddled the active production zones of two fruit companies. However, this condition was far from permanent. The rapid spread of Panama disease compelled the Truxillo Railroad Company to abandon dozens of farms in the lower Aguán valley. In 1942 the company made its final purchase of fruit before shutting down its rail service for good.

The fragmentary portraits of North Coast people and communities offered in this chapter reveal the cross-cutting effects of the fruit companies' shifting plantation agriculture. Local economies all but collapsed due to massive layoffs, outmigrations, the drying up of government tax revenues, and a slowdown in commercial activity. The companies often added insult to injury by removing branch railroads. In places like Mezapa and San Francisco, residents challenged fruit company power through collective, direct protests over the removal of transportation infrastructure. But not everyone lost in the cycle of shifting production. As towns along the Caribbean littoral entered a period of acute economic crisis and outmigration, inland communities situated in the region's major river valleys experienced an expansion of agricultural production and immigration. The fruit companies' response to Panama Disease contributed to a process of "uneven development" along the North Coast that did not bring about the extinction of non-company banana farmers, but it exposed the limits of their autonomy. The power that the fruit companies wielded over non-company growers would become all the more apparent when a second fungal pathogen appeared without warning on the North Coast.

Chapter 4

Sigatoka, Science, and Control

The scientific methods used to combat the Sigatoka epidemic require the intervention of experts in plant pathology, experts who carry out their work with great care and thoroughness.

DIARIO COMERCIAL, SAN PEDRO SULA, 1938

As more scientific methods of banana cultivation, including protection against disease, have come into general vogue, the small producer has been placed at an increasing disadvantage. The adoption of irrigation, dusting, and other modern methods of banana cultivation by the independent grower is out of the question because of his lack of large financial resources.

ANTONIO CERTOSIMO, TEGUCIGALPA, 1941

The spray. The effect that it had on a person at that time scared me. I didn't like it. It was the hardest job.

FELICIANO NÚÑEZ, EL PROGRESO, 1995

In late October 1935, a powerful storm struck the Sula valley. After three consecutive days of heavy winds and torrential rains, the Ulúa and Chamelecón rivers overflowed their banks, destroying crops, drowning livestock, and washing out villages, labor camps, and bridges. Water and electricity were temporarily cut off in urban areas such as San Pedro Sula and El Progreso. An eyewitness from one of the Tela Railroad Company's farms reported that floodwaters had carried off the workers' barracks like "match boxes," leaving more than 150 families without basic necessities. As part of the relief efforts, the company evacuated workers from flooded camps, set up relief kitchens, and provided potable water for people left homeless by the storm. For one longtime resident of El Progreso, the storm was a memorable event that brought more than flooding and displacement: "After the great flood of 1935, the banana farms became diseased. Sigatoka came."[1] That the storm and Sigatoka were, and continue to be, linked in the minds of the region's residents is not surprising. The effects of Sigatoka, like those of the hurricane, were dramatic and far reaching.[2]

Tela Railroad Company employees first observed isolated cases of Sigatoka, or leaf spot disease, a couple of months prior to the October flooding.[3] However, it was only in the storm's aftermath that the disease broke out in epidemic proportions. By early December more than 4,400 hectares of company plantations had "some degree of infection." Six months later, the figure had doubled to 8,900 hectares, and fruit yields were in decline on some 1,340 hectares.[4] The epidemic intensified during the second half of 1936 when company officials reported that more than 2,800 hectares were out of production. Between 1936 and 1937, the Tela Railroad Company's banana output fell from 5.8 to 3.7 million bunches.[5] Describing his visit to the North Coast in May 1937, a U.S. diplomat wrote: "the ravages of [Sigatoka] in the farms of the United Fruit Company have created a state of near-panic in the personnel of that organization and the disease and efforts being made by the company to combat it were practically the sole topics discussed in conversations held with officials of the Fruit Company."[6]

Sigatoka did not spare non-company growers in the region. In October 1936, Roberto Fasquelle, a prominent San Pedro Sula *finquero independiente*, alerted Cortés Governor J. Antonio Milla that if government authorities failed to reach an agreement on a means to control the disease, non-company banana growers would "disappear."[7] He provided a sobering assessment of conditions in banana-growing communities situated along the National Railway. In Potrerillos, weekly production had dropped from some forty rail cars to barely four cars. Exports had fallen by two-thirds in the neighboring municipality of La Pimienta. Conditions were even worse in the Chamelecón district, where "not one" of the more than 1,000 hectares of bananas was Sigatoka free and production was "condemned to disappear."[8] Fasquelle described the municipalities of Choloma and San Pedro Sula as less affected than the others, but the pathogen was present on several farms, including his own. Finally, farms situated along the section of the railroad just south of Puerto Cortés were free from Sigatoka, but "seriously infected" with Panama disease. Tela Railroad Company officials confirmed Fasquelle's assessment, reporting that they were rejecting almost all of the fruit offered for sale by non-company growers.[9] By the end of the year, only four of eleven municipalities in the department of Cortés continued to export bananas.[10] Between 1935 and 1937, non-company exports from the Sula valley fell from 3.6 to 1.7 million bunches.

A few months after receiving Fasquelle's letter, a concerned Governor Milla warned officials in Tegucigalpa that "without the banana, there won't be money on the North Coast to import goods, the customs houses will lose revenues, as will the municipalities that depend so much on banana taxes."[11] He added that the National Railroad stood to lose its primary source of shipping revenues. Finally, the Governor noted that Sigatoka threatened production of plantains, "the bread of the poor." In early 1937, the U.S. consul at Puerto Cortés reported that shrinking company and non-company payrolls were leading to the "curtailment of money in circulation."[12] The impact of the epidemic on both banana production and the North Coast economy, then, was severe and swift. However, political leaders in Tegucigalpa were slow to react to the crisis, prompting the fruit companies, non-company growers, and regional government officials to initiate control efforts.

When Sigatoka struck the Sula valley, the Tela Railroad Company's research department had been cut back to three scientists following Samuel Zemurray's takeover of company operations.[13] Zemurray apparently thought little of professional scientists, an opinion that some company scientists attributed to his belief that Panama disease gave United Fruit an advantage over its smaller competitors so long as the company could continue to relocate production.[14] But the speed with which Sigatoka lowered production levels prevented the banana companies from "running" from the problem and compelled a threadbare research staff under the leadership of Dr. Vining Dunlap to explore ways to control the epidemic. Fortunately for Dunlap and his colleagues, Sigatoka had been described in scientific papers prior to 1935. The first documented incidence of the disease occurred on Java in 1902. Ten years later, a widespread outbreak occurred in the Sigatoka district on the island of Vitu Levu, Fiji—an event that gave rise to the disease's popular name. Later epidemics caused major damage to banana farms in Australia (1924) and Ceylon (1928). The first reports of Sigatoka in the Americas came from Surinam and Trinidad in 1933. Between 1934 and 1938, Sigatoka caught the attention of observers in Colombia, Costa Rica, Cuba, Guadeloupe, Guatemala, Jamaica, Mexico, Panamá, and the Windward Islands.[15]

At least two theories have been proposed to explain the intercontinental spread of Sigatoka. In 1962, Robert Stover speculated that air currents

were capable of transporting spores of the fungus associated with Sigatoka disease great distances. A second and more likely means by which
Sigatoka traversed the globe was via the movement of *Musa* propagat-
ing material and banana leaves (often used as packing material). Banana
breeding programs initiated in the 1920s by the British government and
the United Fruit Company received plants from Asia and the Pacific. One
can also assume that other *Musa* specimens reached the Americas via non-
institutional efforts. In addition to banana boats, the growing amount of
merchant marine traffic through the Panama Canal probably increased
the number of intentional and unintentional plant introductions.[16]

The pathogen associated with Sigatoka, *Mycosphaerella musicola*
Leach, was an airborne fungus that infected the young leaves of banana
plants.[17] Infected leaf tissue developed yellow streaks that subsequently
turned into blackish spots. Severely infected leaves eventually ceased functioning and drooped. The loss of leaf area affected the development of
the fruit: diseased plants produced low-weight bunches.[18] Moderately infected plants tended to produce fruit bunches that at first glance were
indistinguishable from bunches on healthy plants. However, upon being
harvested, the bananas quickly turned soft and yellow, rendering them
unfit for export. Such fruit was known as "ship ripes," "leaf spot ripes," or
"Cercospora fruit."

Plant pathologists considered *M. musicola* Leach to be a mild pathogen, greatly affected by environmental conditions, including temperature
and humidity levels. In Honduras, some observers initially hoped that a
seasonal change in temperature and/or atmospheric pressure would check
the pathogen's spread.[19] Unconvinced that weather changes alone would
bring Sigatoka under control on the company's sprawling monocultures,
Vining Dunlap began testing fungicides within weeks of the epidemic's
outbreak. As early as 1914, researchers in Fiji had recommended applying Bordeaux mixtures (copper sulfate and lime) to control *M. musicola*
on banana plantations.[20] During the 1920s, Norman Simmonds tested a
variety of control techniques, including copper-lime dust, on diseased
banana farms in Australia.[21] The general ability of copper-lime and sulfur-
lime compounds to control the fungus was therefore known in 1935,
but their efficacy under the environmental conditions found on Central
American banana plantations remained uncertain. By the end of 1936,
Dunlap reported that Bordeaux mixture (copper sulfate, lime, and water)
applied on seven- or fourteen-day cycles provided adequate control, particularly during the rainy months when many other fungicidal compounds
failed.[22]

He next turned to developing a cost-effective means for applying the fungicide on a large scale. Dunlap experimented with a variety of technologies, including knapsack sprayers, overhead irrigation equipment, and airplanes before settling on a stationary, ground spray system modeled after systems used in U.S. orchards. The system consisted of a central mixing/pumping station where copper sulfate, lime, and water were mixed in 2,000-gallon tanks. Diesel-driven pumps distributed the solution through a network of pipes laid across the farms. Operating in pairs, workers attached hoses to valves found at intervals along the pipes. The workers moved from plant to plant, coating the banana plants with a fine mist of Bordeaux spray applied with a high-pressure nozzle. Upon finishing two rows of banana plants, the hose would be attached to a valve further down the line and the process repeated. Although the ground-spray system was both expensive to install (more than double that of airplane dusting) and labor intensive, Dunlap believed that its superior ability to control Sigatoka compensated for its high cost.[23]

After two years and one million dollars' worth of intensive testing, United Fruit managers decided to invest in ground spraying on a large scale. During 1937 the area serviced by spray systems rose from less than 500 hectares to 8,900 hectares.[24] Two years later, the company had installed equipment on 14,500 hectares in Honduras, and Bordeaux spraying was considered to be a part of "ordinary farm routine."[25] The company introduced the spray system throughout its Central American operations, including its new divisions on the Pacific Coast of Costa Rica.[26] In order to implement the system on a large scale, the company imported pipes, high-pressure pumps, storage tanks, chemicals, and other equipment from Germany and the United States. The company's consumption of copper sulfate (thousands of tons per year) quickly outstripped the available supply on international markets, prompting United Fruit's management to send mining engineers to Honduras in the hope of finding a local source of raw materials.[27] Additional material and labor costs resulted from the need to remove heavy residues from the fruit bunches after spraying. The cleaning process involved dunking harvested bananas into an acid solution several times followed by a water rinse. All told, Sigatoka control procedures increased the cost of production by an estimated 40 percent.[28]

Less than five years after the epidemic hit the Sula valley, Bordeaux spraying enabled banana exports from Honduras to return to their pre-1935 levels. British researcher Claude Wardlaw—who in the past had been highly critical of Central American banana culture—considered the development and rapid deployment of Dunlap's control system to be one of the greatest achievements in the history of plant pathology.[29] But this feat meant little for small-scale growers such as Ángela Coto-Moreno's brother. Unable to afford the "imported medicines" needed to control Sigatoka, he replaced his bananas with food crops for local markets.[30] How many small-scale growers underwent similar transitions is difficult to determine with precision, but the number likely ran into the hundreds because the costs associated with spraying were well beyond the financial means of most non-company growers in the region. Following a tour of banana farms along the Ulúa River in 1937, U.S. diplomat John Erwin reported that "it was very noticeable at some places along the line, where independent banana producers had not used either of the methods of control against the blight, that the plantations were practically destroyed for a considerable distance."[31] Export figures confirm the devastating effect of the pathogen on non-company growers: between 1937 and 1939 their exports plummeted from 1.7 million bunches to a mere 122,000 bunches.[32]

Tela Railroad Company officials apparently advised planters to await the outcome of their fungicide trials in order to avoid investing financial resources in unproven control techniques. Some planters, including Roberto Fasquelle, considered this to be a pragmatic strategy. However, not everyone was willing to assume a passive role while their banana farms succumbed to Sigatoka.[33] Lacking the financial resources to import chemical control equipment, growers in Choloma pruned infected leaves and carefully placed them upside down on the ground in order to prevent the spores from drifting to other plants. This "provisional" measure reportedly slowed the movement of the fungus and permitted a greater percentage of fruit to be harvested.[34] In 1937, William T. Coleman, a wealthy Choloma planter with a 900-hectare farm, rigged a truck-drawn fungicide applicator that functioned effectively regardless of weather conditions.[35] The degree of disinfection was "complete" according to Governor Milla, who reported that the treatment killed "all classes of insects, and other animal pests such as squirrels."[36] However, even for growers like Coleman who could afford manufactured inputs, there was no guarantee that they would be able to control Sigatoka on their farms because spores from untreated banana patches could re-infect plants up to a distance of one kilometer or more.[37] In other words, an individual cultivator had to contend not only with infected plants on his/her property, but also those on neighboring farms since the pathogen paid little heed to property lines.

As early as 1936, Cortés Governor Milla urged the government of Tiburcio Carías to assist "national producers" by purchasing an airplane and the materials needed to make Bordeaux spray, pointing out that the

Tela Railroad Company benefited from exemptions on import duties.[38] Initially, the Carías administration did not consider the threat posed by Sigatoka sufficiently severe to warrant government intervention. Milla's gubernatorial successor, Gustavo A. Castañeda, continued to press Tegucigalpa for assistance in 1938. Writing on behalf of several prominent growers, Castañeda asked that duties be waived on imports of copper sulfate, lime, pumps, and other materials needed to control Sigatoka.[39] However, his request was denied by the Carías administration, which, if increasingly aware of Sigatoka's severity, had little political interest in aiding North Coast *finqueros,* many of whom were prominent members of the opposition (and increasingly marginalized) Liberal party.[40]

In April 1938, the Tela Railroad Company published the outlines of a plan to aid non-company growers in *El Comercio,* a company-owned newspaper. The two-part article began by describing the "collapse" of the banana industry due to Sigatoka, pointing to the "completely unproductive" banana farms along the National Railroad as an illustration of the decline.[41] The company then outlined its proposal to install Bordeaux ground spray systems at a cost of $870 per hectare. In addition, loans of $145 per hectare would be provided to growers with "good lands." The company promised to pay participating growers 25 cents for a nine-handed bunch. According to the article, planters who agreed to participate stood to benefit financially while having the opportunity "to learn modern methods of cultivation and obtain practical knowledge that if applied with care would increase production." Company officials insisted that they were acting in good faith, noting that it would be less expensive to control Sigatoka on their farms in Honduras and elsewhere than to revive non-company production. They emphasized the boost that the plan would bring to the moribund North Coast economy by creating jobs and increasing revenues for the National Railroad and customs houses. In sum, the company promised to return the banana trade to "the conditions that prevailed prior to the appearance of Sigatoka."[42]

But the article's enthusiastic and confident tone concealed the fact that its authors provided few details about the terms of the loan and just who would be eligible. U.S. consul Oury-Jackson reported that the lack of specificity was intentional: "This office has been informed that the plan as outlined . . . is not exact and that the information is given in an ambiguous manner to secure the interest of small banana producers and cause them to make advances and comments directed towards placing a modified plan in effect."[43] After speaking with a high-level company official, Oury-Jackson outlined the company's intentions: "The plan calls for the cultivation of the land by the owner, while irrigation and spraying for the disease will be carried out by the Fruit Company. The latter will lay all pipe lines, install all other necessary equipment for irrigation, as well as spraying, and will actually carry out these operations, all equipment remaining their property under the contract."[44] As described by Oury-Jackson, the proposal hardly represented a return to pre-Sigatoka conditions. The decision to offer the contract only to planters with "good lands" presumably excluded a large number of cultivators. For those who signed onto the plan, the payment received for their fruit — 25 cents per bunch less an additional 5 cents per bunch to cover loan payments — represented a steep drop from the 45 cents previously paid for a nine-hand bunch (and was significantly lower than prices paid during the Depression).[45] Finally, the company's ownership and operation of the Sigatoka control and irrigation equipment threatened to render non-company growers independent in name only.

Presented with few options, several Sula valley farmers accepted some version of agreement described above. Installation of Sigatoka control equipment on non-company farms began in 1939. That year, the company purchased a mere 122,000 bunches;[46] three years later, company purchases exceeded one million bunches, and non-company farms covered 1,900 hectares in the Sula valley.[47] However, a U.S. consular official noted the changed conditions of production:

> During these years the domestic growers became increasingly dependent upon the American companies, both for market outlet and for the increasingly special supplies needed, to such a degree that at present the Tela Railroad Company installs all irrigation and spray systems in the independent farms and supervises their labor and production methods, etc. Nowadays the so-called "independent" grower, in effect, simply collects the rent for his land at the rate of 25 cents per stem of bananas produced thereon.[48]

The Tela Railroad Company's Sigatoka assistance program primarily served to ensure that the company would continue to have access to the region's best banana soils without actually owning or leasing additional lands. By controlling access to markets, key production processes, and financing, the company dominated banana farming in the Sula valley to an unprecedented degree. Increasingly, small- and large-scale cultivators whose soils did not produce the yields needed to turn a profit in the Sigatoka era shifted to other crops and ranching.

The Standard Fruit Company also initiated Bordeaux spraying operations during the mid-1930s. Company employees based in La Ceiba made
frequent visits to the Sula Valley in order to observe the control procedures adopted by the Tela Railroad Company. Standard Fruit, which
did not have a formal research department at the time, installed Bordeaux ground spray equipment similar to that developed by its larger
competitor. When the Sigatoka epidemic reached its farms, the company
was in the process of shifting its operations to the Upper Aguán valley
in the department of Yoro. The region received less rainfall than typically fell on the coastal plain in Atlántida. The comparatively arid climate
helped to limit the severity of Sigatoka outbreaks, but it also compelled
the company to irrigate heavily, an input that required significant investments of labor and capital.[49] The average area sprayed by Standard Fruit
workers increased steadily between 1938 and 1942, rising from 730 hectares
to more than 3,100 hectares. During this period, the company's annual
consumption of copper sulfate nearly quadrupled, from 525 tons to nearly
1,900 tons.[50]

In a process very similar to what had taken place in the Sula valley,
Standard Fruit's adoption of capital- and labor-intensive Sigatoka control
measures marginalized small-scale banana producers without necessarily
dispossessing them of their land. As one La Ceiba-based U.S. consul noted
in 1942, "the company has been able to move, to irrigate, to spray and
to prop (to reduce wind damage), but the small farmers have not. They
stick to the railroad line along the rainy coast, solving only the problem of
transportation, and their yield per acre is small."[51] The report estimated
that 1,000 *poquiteros* scattered along the company's railroad annually sold
around 500,000 bunches of fruit to the company. Both the low per-capita
production levels and the dwindling fraction of total exports that non-
company bananas represented (17 percent of Standard Fruit's total exports
in 1942) reflected the marginalized role played by *poquiteros* in the Sigatoka era.

According to U.S. consul Wymberley Der Coerr, "certain [Standard
Fruit] officials" held the opinion that they should cease buying non-
company fruit because it was often rejected prior to shipping but after
the company had paid for them.[52] Not surprisingly, company officials frequently described *poquitero* fruit as "inferior" in quality to that grown
on Standard's plantations. However, some Standard Fruit managers advo-
cated buying all independent fruit production "for the sake of local welfare and long-time political considerations." For forty years, the company had purchased bananas from small-scale farmers; no doubt some

veteran employees were reluctant to sever long-established relationships. In addition, World War II shipping restrictions led to serious economic losses for non-company growers.[53] Coming at a time when the U.S. government was promoting its "Good Neighbor Policy" in Latin America, fruit company officials perhaps sensed a need to avoid adopting policies that would generate controversy. But Der Coerr's report confirms that, political concerns aside, *poquitero* production was declining in importance because export banana production required costly inputs in order to adapt to dynamic agroecosystems and evolving quality standards. These inputs included knowledge generated by a cadre of professional scientists who would play an increasingly important role in defining and controlling plant pathogens.

THE SCIENCE OF SIGATOKA CONTROL

Although Sigatoka was under control by 1940, United Fruit scientists in Honduras found "no indications" that the pathogen could be eradicated.[54] Consequently, they turned their attention to increasing the economic efficiency of fungicide applications. Their efforts initially showed signs of success: between 1937 and 1939, the cost of spray operations dropped from sixty-three dollars per acre to around forty dollars per acre. This sharp decline in costs resulted from a reduction in the frequency of application.[55] But the downward trend in Sigatoka control costs was short-lived partly because of the variability of climatic conditions. Throughout the 1940s, seasonal increases in disease activity linked to above-average rainfall and cool temperatures prompted the company to shorten spray cycles. Between 1941 and 1951, the average cost of spraying increased from $2.51 to $3.58 per acre.[56] By the early 1950s, United Fruit farms annually received about 15–17 Bordeaux treatments. The high-volume spraying consumed 265 gallons/acre of fungicide solution per application.

United Fruit's near-exclusive focus on chemical controls for Sigatoka contrasted with Caribbean-based research programs. Although growers in parts of Jamaica used Bordeaux sprays, Dunlap's system was not well suited for Caribbean banana zones where predominantly small-scale cultivators often farmed hilly terrain with limited access to irrigation. In addition, non-company farmers in the Caribbean faced a similar set of financial and labor constraints as their Central American counterparts. The distinct agroecological conditions found in the Caribbean compelled researchers to study less capital- and labor-intensive control measures, including the use of shade crops and/or disease-resistant varieties. In 1937, Gerold Stahel, a researcher at the Surinam Agricultural Experiment Station, observed that when he placed banana plants inoculated with Sigatoka spores under a glass roof they did not show symptoms even when plants just outside the roof were covered with spots.[57] Stahel surmised that the fungus would grow only if the plant tissue was covered with a film of water (i.e., dew), a hypothesis confirmed by later researchers.[58] His finding suggested that Sigatoka could possibly be controlled through the use of shade crops.

Three years later, Jamaica-based plant pathologist R. Leach argued that shading could prevent excessive heating of plant foliage and retard the rate of cooling, thereby reducing dew formation. "There is no doubt," he added, "that shade produces . . . a natural control of leaf spot in many districts in Jamaica."[59] Leach considered shading to be a viable Sigatoka control under certain environmental conditions: "Although there may be a prejudice against the use of shade for bananas, it is not improbable that the use of a properly controlled, light shade may ultimately prove the most economic means of control, without the use of sprays, in those areas where dew formation is not excessive during most of the year."[60] Around the same time that Leach published his findings, plant pathologist C. A. Thorold reported that when Sigatoka hit Trinidad, Gros Michel plants grown in monocultures were affected much more than those planted with cacao and/or *Erythrina* trees.[61] The Trinidad Agricultural Department subsequently set up experiments to determine if intercropping Gros Michel plants with cacao or *Erythrina* could reduce the incidence of Sigatoka. Thorold stated that the results "left no doubt that shade effectively checks the Leaf Spot disease so that a normal healthy bunch can be matured."[62] He did not deny the efficacy of Bordeaux spraying, but he doubted whether it would be viable in Trinidad where banana farms were "small and scattered."

Thorold warned that the frequency of scratches and blemishes on banana peels would increase as a result of intercropping because both cacao and *Erythrina* trees provided habitats for tree-dwelling mammals and thrips (*Frankiniella* spp.) that could blemish banana peels. This caveat alluded to the market structures that continued both to shape scientific research and to impede small-scale growers from competing with the high-input, large-scale production processes of the U.S. fruit companies. Shading might have been capable of controlling Sigatoka on small farms at a fraction of the cost of Bordeaux spraying, but scarred fruit would have fared poorly on U.S. mass markets where a premium was placed on visual aesthetic qualities. Scattered studies—including one by United Fruit's Vining Dunlap—produced during the 1950s confirmed the ability of shade to inhibit the rate of Sigatoka infection, but there is no evidence to suggest that United Fruit experimented with shade plants.[63]

Caribbean-based scientists also tried to breed Sigatoka-resistant banana plants. In 1937, Imperial College of Tropical Agriculture (ICTA) researchers reported that several commercial varieties, including the Gros Michel, Congo, Dwarf Cavendish and Governor bananas, all proved to be highly susceptible to Sigatoka "under plantation conditions." A survey of ICTA's collection indicated that eight varieties were relatively resistant to the pathogen, but five of these were cooking bananas (i.e., plantains) and two others were sterile and offered little hope for raising seedlings of commercial importance.[64] Drawing on their experiences breeding for Panama disease resistance, the authors commented that "the numerous other qualities required of a commercial banana remain the same whether it is to be bred resistant to wilt or to a leaf spot, and evidence has accumulated that combining those qualities in a single plant is the real problem of banana breeding, rather than disease resistance alone."[65] Standard Fruit's trials with the IC 2, an ICTA hybrid, reconfirmed the difficulties of introducing a new variety on U.S. mass markets. The company began commercial shipments of IC 2 in 1944. The variety showed a high level of resistance to Sigatoka, shipped well, and ripened like Gros Michel fruit. In 1950, IC 2 exports reached 400,000 bunches, but the success was short-lived; Standard Fruit discontinued IC 2 shipments in 1954 due to the prevalence of "short-fingered winter fruit" that had become "unacceptable" on mass markets.[66]

Neither biological nor cultural controls for Sigatoka were widely adopted by export banana producers in Central America. Nevertheless, a comparison of United Fruit scientists' approaches to Sigatoka and those of Caribbean-based researchers illustrates the relationship between the production of knowledge about Sigatoka and the contexts in which scientists worked. United Fruit's initial turn toward fast-acting chemical fungicides to control Sigatoka was no doubt linked to the sense of urgency created by the swift-moving pathogen, but the system also reflected the company's deep financial resources, the flat, well-watered conditions found in the Sula valley (recall the fruit companies' irrigation concessions), and large-scale production units. In addition, the historical significance of Sigatoka, like that of Panama disease, resulted from mass production/mass consumption dynamics. Although the fruit companies' responses to the two pathogens were quite different, they were similarly circumscribed by both mass-market structures that impeded the adoption of disease-resistant varieties, and the agroecological structures associated with monocultures.

By the early 1940s, both the processes and the organization of export banana production had changed dramatically since the early twentieth century. The small- and medium-scale cultivators who had formed the backbone of the banana trade all but disappeared. The decline of non-company growers in Honduras resulted from a historical conjuncture of processes occurring on local and international scales. The spread of Sigatoka created a crisis for non-company growers whose economic wellbeing was already weakened by both the severe international economic crisis of the early 1930s and the 1935 flood. For the reduced number of *finqueros independientes* who persisted on the North Coast, the demands of disease control greatly eroded their already limited autonomy. But the direction in which modern disease control proceeded was by no means a purely "technical" process informed by neutral scientific evidence. Dunlap's Sigatoka-control systems favored large-scale producers with capital reserves and high-yielding soils. The system's logic was a self-reinforcing one that only made sense in a specific context shaped by regional agroecologies, mass markets, and the fruit companies' large labor forces.

THE WORK OF SIGATOKA CONTROL

In December 1937, U.S. diplomat John D. Erwin observed Sigatoka control operations while touring the Tela Railroad Company's farms:

Near Progreso, [Tela Railroad Company manager] Mr. Cloward stopped the [rail] car and had us go into the edge of one of the banana farms to watch the spraying process in operation. The chemical solution which is used necessitates pipe lines laid in the fields at two-hundred foot intervals and the native employees, with a hose, spray the plants from four sides to make certain all the fungi are destroyed. Then the "stem" of bananas, which is cut off the plant, is carried to a tank alongside the electric railway, where it is dipped in another chemical solution to nullify the effects of the first solution; and, then as a last treatment, it is dipped into a tank of water to remove all of the chemicals from the first before shipment. It was obvious that this is a rather costly operation, because each stem or stalk of bananas has to be dipped eight times in the chemical tank and four times into the water tank to bring it to a state where it is ready to be shipped.[67]

FIGURE 4.1. *A pair of* veneneros *applying Bordeaux spray (1940s). United Fruit Company Photograph Collection. Baker Library, Harvard Business School.*

Erwin's image of residue-laden banana bunches being dipped repeatedly in vats of acid and water suggests that Sigatoka control required more than imported technologies: the ground spray system required "native employees" to carry out tedious, messy, and physically demanding tasks. The Tela Railroad Company used an average of 10–12 spray gangs on a daily basis per farm. During the 1930s and 1940s, each two-person "gang" typically sprayed around 2 hectares (5 acres) per day. On any given day, at least 1,000 people worked to control Sigatoka on company farms in Honduras.[68] Each farm also had a "spray master" and one or two spray foremen

FIGURE 4.2. *Working the "mono": A pair of United Fruit Company workers remove Bordeaux spray residue from bananas prior to loading onto a rail car (1946). United Fruit Company Photograph Collection. Baker Library, Harvard Business School.*

who monitored both disease incidence and workers' spraying techniques in the field.

As might be expected, United Fruit's scientific staff tended to describe the organization of Bordeaux spraying exclusively in terms of control and efficiency. For example, a research bulletin authored by Vining Dunlap in 1950 explained that the two members who comprised a spray team received the same pay and status because the company found having a sprayer aided by a lower-paid assistant to be "impractical," since the latter would "almost invariably shirk and hold up the nozzle man making him pull his own hose part of the time."[69] Dunlap provided three reasons why spray gang members should swap tasks at short intervals: "(1) Each one willingly pulls hose, for the other man will help him in turn. (2) Variety of work rests each man and increases efficiency. (3) It is good insurance to have both men capable of handling the nozzle at any one time."[70] A subsequent section of the bulletin describes the work of the spray team in precise, methodical terms.

Not surprisingly, fruit company managers and scientists were concerned first and foremost with controlling the pathogen and disciplining the human spray applicators to work efficiently. In an effort to lower labor costs and increase control over fungicide applications, company researchers began experimenting with an overhead spray system during the 1940s. The overhead system's purported advantages included "the elimination of the human element to a large degree, in the application of spray." Other potential benefits included lower costs due to more efficient use of fungicides and a reduction in the number of laborers needed.[71] Company researchers continued to run trials with overhead sprayers as late as 1951. Echoing earlier reports, the technicians noted that the experimental system lowered the per-acre cost of controlling Sigatoka in addition to providing "indirect savings in housing, schooling, and hospital facilities" by eliminating workers.[72] One year later, the research department reported that field crews using overhead spray applicators worked with nearly three times the efficiency of those using the ground spray system. However, the new system required more thorough supervision than did hose spraying: "the quality of supervision of spray operations should be stressed by the selection of conscientious foremen and spray masters. Supervisory personnel must pay close attention to all details such as pressure, wet leaves, wind, timing of application, etc."[73] To judge by its internal reports then, United Fruit's research department saw fieldworkers as little more than pieces of a puzzle that needed to be carefully interlocked with other inputs in order to establish control over persistent pathogens.

The distanced, analytical descriptions of Sigatoka control produced by fruit company scientists during the 1950s stand in sharp contrast to the images of spray work found in Ramón Amaya Amador's 1950 novel, *Prisión verde*. For Amaya Amador, head of the Honduran Communist Party and an outspoken critic of U.S. imperialism, Bordeaux spraying was not only disagreeable and hazardous—it epitomized the injustice of the plantation regime. The contested meanings of Sigatoka control work are best captured by the terms used to describe the workers themselves: fruit company documents referred to Bordeaux applicators as "spray gangs," but Amaya Amador—and the workers themselves—preferred the term *veneneros* (poison applicators).

Early in *Prisión verde*, readers meet Martín Samayoa, a former *poquitero* who, having sold his land to the company, finds himself broke and without a livelihood. When a sympathetic worker offers to secure him a position as a Bordeaux spray applicator, Martín hesitates:

He remembered all that he had heard said of the *regadores de veneno;* that the spray entered into the lungs and the brain; that everyone ended up with tuberculosis; that in the hospital, the doctors had opened up several *veneneros* and had found even their intestines to be blue-green. Even the strongest of men wasted away in a matter of months.[74]

Putting his fears aside, Martín decides to give it a try. On his first day, he is assigned to work with Don Braulio, "a tall, thin man, with pale skin and the face of one suffering from tuberculosis."[75] As the two unrolled their hose, Don Braulio gives Martín some pointers: "When the *veneno* starts, we can't waste any because if the foreman sees us he'll fire us on the spot." He added, "the work is not as hard as ditching or weeding, you'll just go along dragging the hose. I'll help guide you. The nozzle man is the one who has to trouble himself more. You have to spray one plant at a time until all the leaves are well coated."[76] After explaining to Martín the difference between Sigatoka and Panama disease, Don Braulio observed ironically, "we're all sick here, some with Sigatoka, others with *mata muerta,* malaria and tuberculosis. Some will get better if they get away in time; but some of us are practically dead and buried! You see me? I'm no longer a man. I'm a shadow, nothing more."

Amaya Amador's fictional account of Bordeaux spraying suggests that exposure to the fungicide produced both acute and chronic affects on the workers:

> Taking the nozzle, don Braulio . . . began to spray the plants with the blue liquid. The spray arced above the tallest leaves before falling upon them like rain, covering the leaves with a blue ashen dew. Martín sensed a caustic odor that provoked sneezing and a nauseous feeling.
>
> "When one begins," the nozzle man explained with a cough, "you lose your appetite; you get a nasty cough. . . . But humans are strange creatures, they adjust to everything. Some exceptionally strong workers endure years in this work, but others leave after just a couple of weeks, spitting blood."[77]

He then advises Martín to place a handkerchief around his mouth but for Don Braulio such protective measures are futile. Later in the novel, on a particularly cold and rainy day, Don Braulio dies in the field. The heavy-handed symbolism of the fallen *venenero* is reinforced by the words of a fellow worker: "The plantation ate him up! He died with the spray nozzle in hand, serving foreign masters."[78] *Prisión verde* was both a literary and political project written to expose what its author viewed as unjust social conditions on banana plantations. The "Green Prison" was a metaphor for a system of export agriculture that subjugated working people and undermined Honduran sovereignty. Therefore, the image of a fieldhand dying, spray gun in hand, should not be interpreted literally. At the same time, Amaya Amador's depiction of spray work bears a strong resemblance to the procedures outlined in Dunlap's research bulletin. This is not surprising considering that the author worked briefly on Standard Fruit's banana plantations where he experienced Bordeaux spraying first hand. Equally significant is the fact that both *Prisión verde* — part novel, part primer on labor organizing — and Dunlap's bulletin on Sigatoka control were largely prescriptive narratives: both texts sought to present the meaning of spray work in unambiguous terms.

The memories of former Bordeaux spray applicators simultaneously resonate with, and complicate, scientific and literary depictions of Sigatoka control work. Cantalisio Andino worked for the Standard Fruit Company during the 1940s in the Aguán valley — not far from the birthplace of Amaya Amador. First hired by the engineering department to assist with land surveying, Cantalisio later switched to Bordeaux spray work in order to earn higher wages.[79] He recalled earning 3 lempiras ($1.50) per eight-hour day, significantly more than the 2 lempiras he had been making as a land surveyor. Each spray team was assigned to a farm section (*calle*) consisting of five valves. Workers proceeded from valve to valve, making designated entries (*entradas*) into side paths designed to ensure that plants were thoroughly sprayed. Cantalisio noted that close cooperation was required between the *escopetero* (sprayer) and the *manguerero* (hose-hauler): a skilled hose-handler could anticipate where to place the hose so that spraying would be more or less continuous. He also stressed that foremen closely supervised spray teams in order to ensure that proper techniques were employed. For example, *escopeteros* had to spray with an arc-like motion (*media luna*) above the plants so that the spray fell as a rain onto the leaves: "If they saw you spraying the leaf directly, the foreman or spray master reprimanded you." Foremen also watched to ensure that *manguereros* pulled the heavy hose fully into the *entrada* in order to ensure thorough spraying.[80] If a foreman was unhappy with the effort, he might get off of his mule and give the worker a lecture. According to Cantalisio, supervisors were less inclined to assist *escopeteros:* "The thing that the *capitán* hated to do was help one with the nozzle. Because it splattered and stained; it left one's body splattered with blue." Cantalisio learned how to turn this unpleasant aspect of the job to his advantage: "If the foreman was hanging around being a pest, you just started to spray over where he was standing. At first I didn't know how to do it, but my god-father taught me how to work."

Cantalisio maintained that a skilled *escopetero* could avoid getting splattered by the spray, but the details of his story contradicted this claim. For instance, he wore a handkerchief over his mouth and two shirts. He also put a sack over himself to absorb the spray: "I had confidence that this would protect me and I didn't believe that my body was exposed." However, he changed his mind after his wife discovered something unusual:

> I used to sleep in a bed made of leather. One day my wife says to me, "I was cleaning and I noticed that the underside of your bed is blue." I told her, "Damn, I'm not going back to work with that stuff." My body—and there was nothing on top of the bed. It was the under-side that was blue. When I realized this, I told myself, "This means you're poisoned." I never went back . . . it scared me to see my bed so blue. I remember that I worked with a shirt and then the sack on top, and still the poison penetrated my skin.[81]

Cantalisio worked "about two or three years" in Sigatoka control. He did not complain about any acute or chronic health problems resulting from his work, but he recalled an "unconscientious" coworker who did not take any protections and suffered from chronic health problems. For Canalisio, the perception that spray work could be dangerous was not linked to the onset of personal health problems, but rather to the realization that the Bordeaux solution could penetrate his body in spite of his improvised protective gear.

The memories of other former workers contain similar themes and images. For example, Neche Martínez remembered starting the day off in white clothes and ending in blue-green ones. After a few weeks on the job he recalled, the blue penetrated his skin.[82] In fact, every former spray worker with whom I spoke recalled the blue-green stain that penetrated their clothing and skin: "when you sweated, it was blue," one assured me.[83] Bricio Fajardo, an ex-Standard Fruit employee who worked as both a *manguerero* and *escopetero*, explained "we always used to call it 'poison'—it turned people blue-green." But Fajardo believed that the spray did more than stain clothing and penetrate the pores of human skin: "It [Bordeaux spray] also killed people; it killed many people."[84] Although his memories of workers dying on the job resonated with the fate Don Braulio in

Prisión verde, Fajardo's memory pointed toward a complex set of factors that contributed to worker illness:

> Look, people, maybe already sick with the flu or something . . . if one didn't report to work they'd fire you. People had to go to work out of necessity. Before, there weren't any infirmaries or anything of the sort. Many single people died because there was no one to care for them.[85]

Here, the image is less one of spray workers succumbing to exposure to a toxic chemical than to a more general condition of deprivation characterized by inadequate medical care, job insecurity, and weakened kinship ties.

Bricio was not the only ex-worker to identify Bordeaux spray as an occupational health hazard. Former Tela Railroad Company field hand José Almendares Ortiz offered an analysis of the health risks associated with spray work that interwove biomedical and social explanations:

> Weak persons were harmed by the *veneno.* The spray contaminated them and ruined their lungs. Yes, and the brain too; they operated on one fellow and found that his brain was blue. He suffered from headaches and [subsequently] died. . . . Many people worked too much and wore themselves out. The human body is a machine. If the machine is overworked, it shuts down.[86]

In this case, a former worker drew a link between exposure to Bordeaux spray and specific symptoms, including headaches and pulmonary disorders. Almendares worked just one year on a spray gang before changing jobs out of concern for his health. However, he commented that many people "worked all the time" and ruined their health. According to Almendares, sick workers often returned to their birthplaces in the highland interiors of Honduras. Feliciano Núñez also linked Sigatoka control work to respiratory illness: "This spray was the reason why there were so many cases of tuberculosis. They did not have any protection. Nothing."[87] Several other retired Tela Railroad Company workers drew connections between Sigatoka control work and the prevalence of tuberculosis. However, only one of the ex-sprayers interviewed recalled suffering from acute and/or chronic maladies linked to Bordeaux spray.[88]

Not all ex-workers considered Bordeaux spraying to be hazardous. Víctor Reyes, who worked on a spray gang for five years, recalled the work with fondness (*"era bonita"*) and indicated that claims about its dangers had been greatly exaggerated. He associated spray work with relatively high wages and short days. Reyes rejected the idea that exposure to Bordeaux spray was a health hazard, but his story confirmed the image of spray applicators covered with blue-green stains and smelling of copper sulfate. His memories of spray work also drew an indirect link between the job and respiratory disease. Reyes believed that sickness among spray workers was due to the personal hygiene habits of workers who bathed immediately after working, while still sweaty and hot (*agitados*): "I had a younger cousin who was in the habit of bathing as soon as he finished work. I'd say 'Look, cousin, don't bathe while you are hot and sweaty. Wait until later.' But no, he was always going to visit his girlfriend and did not want to be seen with spray stains."[89] According to Reyes, this habit was unhealthy, a belief shared by at least one other former worker.[90]

Camilo Rivera Girón, who worked seven years as a spray master for the Tela Railroad Company prior to becoming a political and business leader in San Pedro Sula, recalled trying in vain to discourage workers from referring to themselves as *veneneros*. However, he vacillated on the hazards posed by spray work: "Even though they got sick, there were not any laws; no one was thinking—but no, it's not true that they got sick, because I would have become sick too. I was there."[91] Rivera Girón declared that "never even once did my lungs bother me," but his job as spray master did not require him to apply, or even directly supervise, fungicide treatments on a regular basis. Furthermore, his position as a spray master meant that he was an *empleado de confianza* who received better housing and medical care than the vast majority of field workers. Significantly, Rivera Girón's conflicted memory of spray work both denied the possibility that the fruit company was responsible for creating a hazardous working environment and implicitly linked Bordeaux spray to respiratory ailments.

Written sources related to the health effects of Bordeaux spraying in Honduras are few. However, a 1950 report prepared by a Honduran congressional committee that spent a week investigating labor conditions on the North Coast stated that "the work of those who spray *veneno* deserves special mention. Although some are of the opinion that the spray is innocuous, a greater number believe that it produces damaging effects."[92] In Costa Rica, where spray workers called themselves *pericos*, or parakeets, on account of the indelible blue-green left on their clothes and skin, documentary evidence confirms that Bordeaux spray work was closely associated with respiratory maladies.[93]

Headaches, coughing, and a loss of appetite were among the acute re-

actions that workers associated with Bordeaux spraying. Long-term exposure produced respiratory problems, weight loss, and in some cases, death.
Many observers believed that spray work brought on tuberculosis. Certainly the chronic symptoms linked to spraying—coughing, fatigue, and
weight loss—are not unlike those associated with tuberculosis. During
the 1920s, tuberculosis, along with bronchitis, pneumonia and other pulmonary illnesses was not uncommon among the United Fruit Company's
workforce. The numerous references made by former banana workers to
respiratory disease is not surprising given the congested living spaces in
which they rested, ate, and slept. The frequent movement of workers from
camp to camp further facilitated the spread of human illness. Lourdes
Mejía, a former administrator in the Tela Railroad Company's labor relations department, helped to process workers diagnosed with tuberculosis during the late 1940s.[94] The company provided sick employees with
100 lempiras in compensation, after which many "returned to their home
towns to die." Although she did not share Amaya Amador's political
views, Lourdes considered his portrayal of spray work in *Prisión verde* to
be accurate.

The pervasiveness of respiratory diseases among plantation workers
in general fails to explain the perception that *veneneros*—more so than
other workers—fell prey to debilitating, tuberculosis-like symptoms.
However, from an epidemiological perspective, the likelihood of a direct link between copper sulfate exposure and tuberculosis incidence is
remote.[95] Although little information exists on the effects of long-term,
occupational exposure to copper sulfate, a small number of studies from
grape-growing regions in Portugal and Spain have linked copper sulfate
exposure to respiratory ailments in field workers.[96] A study published
in 1969 reported two cases of what the researchers termed "Vineyard
sprayer's lung."[97] Both cases involved Portuguese men in their mid-thirties
who had worked as Bordeaux sprayers in vineyards. One individual developed shortness of breath on moderate exertion. The other suffered from
weight loss, general weakness, and a cough. The two workers had previously been treated with antibiotics for tuberculosis even though neither
one tested positive for the bacteria. When their conditions failed to clear
up entirely, doctors made chest incisions that revealed "the intensely blue
aspect of the visceral pluera [outer lining of the lung] which could not be
explained by known pathological conditions."[98] Microscopic lesions detected on the lungs had silicosis-like nodules that contained a "substance
rich in copper."[99] The Portuguese researchers did not attempt to determine disease incidence among vineyard sprayers, but they believed that

only a "limited number" of workers developed scarring on their lungs because the disease seemed to be influenced by a "patient (host) factor," in addition to the "chemical factor." The study, which noted that the lesions could partially clear if the affected subject was removed from contact with the spray, concluded by calling for the adoption of protective measures for vineyard spray workers.

A follow-up study examined the clinical records of 14 men and 1 woman who had been diagnosed with vineyard sprayer's disease over a five-year period in Portugal.[100] All of the persons had a history of exposure through inhalation to Bordeaux for varying periods of time. Their symptoms generally consisted of weakness, loss of appetite, and marked weight loss, followed by breathlessness often accompanied by a cough. Biopsies of three acutely affected patients revealed blue-green patches on the surface of their lungs and microscopic lesions that tested positive for copper. The study stressed that "routine laboratory work" and immunological data contributed little to the diagnosis of vineyard sprayer's disease, which was "easily confused" with pneumonia, lung abscess, and tuberculosis.[101] In six cases, the disease remained dormant until an additional factor, such as a bacterial or viral infection, triggered its progression at a later date. In other subjects, the disease progressed chronically, forming "tumor-like, massive opacities" in the upper region of the lungs. Five of the patients examined died due to various forms of respiratory failure. On the brighter side, improvement was seen in some patients when their exposure to Bordeaux ceased.

Although data on vineyard sprayer's lung is limited, the juxtaposition of the Portuguese studies from the 1970s with the oral testimonies of ex-*veneneros* offers new ways to interpret the historical meanings of Sigatoka control work.[102] The similarities between the symptoms of vineyard sprayer's lung and those described by banana workers—lethargy, loss of appetite, weight loss and coughing—are noteworthy. The symptoms also correspond to tuberculosis and pneumonia, diseases that were commonplace among fieldworkers living in banana camps. The difficulty of distinguishing vineyard sprayer's lung from tuberculosis through clinical diagnosis raises the possibility that respiratory problems linked to the accumulation of copper in banana workers' lungs were sometimes "misdiagnosed" as tuberculosis. Of course, "vineyard sprayer's lung" had yet to enter medical discourse, nor did antibiotics (e.g., streptomycin) exist to treat tuberculosis prior to the 1950s. Consequently, the findings from Portugal serve less as evidence of negligence on the part of the fruit companies' medical staffs, than to provide a plausible epidemiological explanation for the popular perception that *veneneros* suffered disproportionately from respiratory problems.[103]

Evidence from both Costa Rica and Honduras indicates that spray workers did not use masks or respirators on a regular basis. Instead, spray gang members tried to protect themselves by layering clothing, placing handkerchiefs over their mouths, and teaming up with an experienced applicator who knew how to minimize exposure. Such efforts were largely in vain. During the course of a day's work, laborers were routinely exposed to what must have been a considerable amount of Bordeaux mixture. They absorbed the liquid through their skin, they inhaled it, and at times they probably ingested it.[104] The most effective way to avoid exposure was to seek a different job; in Honduras field workers frequently quit their comparatively well paying positions on spray gangs after one or two years. In Costa Rica, spray work was similarly disliked by field hands and tended to be carried out by young migrant workers seeking short-term cash income.[105]

The work of Sigatoka control marked the onset of an era in which the export banana industry relied upon chemical inputs in order to overcome problems associated with plant diseases, pests, and declining soil fertility. Nearly ten years before DDT became widely available for use in agriculture, thousands of field workers on export banana farms began applying high volumes of copper sulfate. Bordeaux applicators, often wearing improvised and largely ineffective layers of clothing, inhaled and absorbed unknown quantities of copper for up to eight hours a day. Although memories of blue-green brains, beds, and sweat cannot always be taken literally, the recollections of former spray workers in Honduras and Costa Rica, combined with limited medical evidence related to copper toxicity among Mediterranean vineyard sprayers, strongly suggest that exposure to Bordeaux spray could lead to the accumulation of copper in the lung tissue and the onset of respiratory illnesses. Significantly, both medical and folk understandings of the risks associated with exposure to copper sulfate emphasized the role played by the environmental and social-cultural contexts in which spray work took place. In other words, copper sulfate exposure per se was not considered to be responsible for worker illness and death, but it contributed to the hazardous environments in which field workers lived and labored—Amaya Amador's "green prison."

Chapter 5

Revisiting the Green Prison

All day the draining work of the field hands continued until dusk, when, with their legs trembling with exhaustion, they left the green prison of the plantation for the stark prison of the empty barracks.

RAMÓN AMAYA AMADOR, *PRISIÓN VERDE* (1950)

The way in which workers could cheat the company was by slacking off on the job. The company asked them to do a good job but they did it however they felt like. If the foreman signed off on the job, it was a done deal. A crew might do a full day's work in half a day—but poorly done.

JOSÉ MARÍA LARA, INTERVIEW (1995)

Juan Sotano awoke and rolled out of his hammock when the first rays of dawn were more imaginary than real. Bending over to pull on a pair of muddied shoes, he felt a dull throbbing in his forehead—a reminder of the previous night's *guaro* drinking. Sheathing the machete that lay at his side, Juan stepped outside of his mud-and-grass-walled *champa*. He cast a glance of pity toward a group of young Olanchanos who had arrived the previous week and were forced to sleep outside for want of shelter. The contractor, Señor Martínez, had promised to build more *champas,* but the pressing schedule of the company afforded little time for activities beyond clearing the land. Juan sat down at a large table with several co-workers. His wife Elena brought him breakfast: a large flour tortilla, beans, cheese, a portion of oatmeal, and sweetened coffee. She gave him a quick smile before hurrying off to fix another plate. Elena had been up for some time, building a fire, making tortillas, and fetching water from a nearby stream. The contractor's wife, a distant cousin of Elena, had offered her a job as a cook. The hours were long, but at times she made more money than her husband, especially on paydays, when workers eagerly bought her tamales and enchiladas. After eating, Juan headed off with his felling crew to continue clearing trees and brush. On the way to the work site, he thought about moving to an established farm where he could work as a harvester or ditch digger. The other day he had narrowly avoided being struck by a felled tree. Mosquitoes were a constant annoyance around the makeshift camp. And then there were the snakes; he hadn't seen a *barba amarilla* in a while, but one never knew—the foreman's shout jarred Juan from his thoughts. Drawing his machete, Juan sighed and began hacking at the underbrush of the receding forest.

This imagined scene never happened, but similar ones took place nearly every day in banana camps along the North Coast during the first half of the twentieth century.[1] The transformation of the North Coast's landscape resulted from the labor of thousands of people (mostly men) who cleared forests, dug drainage ditches, planted and tended the fields, and harvested mature fruit. Thousands of other people (mostly women) worked in and around the camps, preparing meals, washing clothes, fetching water and firewood, and raising children. This multitude of migrant, poor, and largely illiterate farmworkers inspired Ramón Amaya Amador to write *Prisión verde,* a novel that revolved around the lives of a group of *campeños,* or plantation workers. Amaya Amador was born and raised in Olanchito, Yoro, in 1916. In an adulthood spent working as a teacher, banana plantation worker, and political organizer, he witnessed firsthand the social and ecological transformations wrought by export banana production following the arrival of first the Truxillo Railroad Company and later the Standard Fruit Company to his hometown. He also experienced the political repression of the Carías regime (1933–1948), fleeing the North Coast in 1947 for Guatemala, where he wrote novels about working-class lives in Honduras and helped to create a clandestine communist party.[2] By depicting banana plantations as sites of exploitation and misery, he challenged fruit company and government discourses that portrayed the North Coast as a beacon of modernity in an otherwise backward country. Amaya Amador's narrative problematized images of *campeños* as drunks and gamblers prone to violence by constructing a world in which profit-driven U.S. corporations and their Honduran cronies trapped workers in a cycle of grinding poverty from which few escaped. The prison metaphor conveyed the physical and psychological degradation of workers wrought by a production system rooted in social and economic inequities.

The life histories of twenty-four individuals who worked on the fruit companies' plantations between roughly 1930 and 1950 resonate forcefully with Amaya Amador's portrait of demanding work regimes, insalubrious living conditions, and material impoverishment. However, they also reveal the limitations of the author's bipolar vision that unambiguously located characters either inside or outside of the prison. The memories of former laborers offer a much more dynamic and morally complex view of life on banana plantations than the one portrayed in *Prisión verde*. They temper Amaya Amador's rigid structuralism by revealing some of the strategies devised by *campeños* to endure the hardships and uncertainties associated with living in a world where civil liberties were few, job security minimal, and daily life was shaped by distant marketplace structures and regional agroecologies. Sketches of individual life histories also help to bring women into view as important actors in plantation economies. During the first half of the twentieth century, women seldom, if ever, worked on the banana farms of the U.S. fruit companies. Instead, they forged livelihoods on the plantation peripheries that were both vital to daily life and an important source of cash income for themselves and their families. Far removed from the main stage of national politics, working-class men and women used the intimate spaces of the fields and barracks to negotiate—with varying degrees of success—the terms under which they worked and lived.

FIGURE 5.1. *United Fruit worker housing after a flood in the Aguán valley (1924). United Fruit Company Photograph Collection. Baker Library, Harvard Business School.*

FIGURE 5.2. *A "standard" six-room labor camp in the Sula Valley (1924). Note the abundance of ornamental plants. United Fruit Company Photograph Collection. Baker Library, Harvard Business School.*

LANDING (AND LOSING) A PLANTATION JOB

Between March and September 1928, the Truxillo Railroad Company ran a notice in *El Olanchano,* a Juticalpa, Olancho–based newspaper, seeking 500 workers for "railroad building, forest clearing, ditching, planting" and other jobs in the Black River district of Colón.[3] Another company advertisement in the same paper promoted jobs for up to 1,000 workers in the Sico River valley. Potential workers were enticed by offers of free medical service and rail transportation from Olanchito. In 1929, the editors of *El Olanchano* referred to the constant movement of people between the North Coast and Olancho as a "local fever."[4] The paper lamented that workers often returned to the highlands with little more than a case of malaria to show for their efforts. After recuperating for a spell, many people, "bored and without occupation," returned to the North Coast and "its vices." Although the editorial's image of the "unhappy and futile" lives led by banana workers was incomplete, it effectively captured the "push-pull" factors that drove the migrations: temporary jobs created by the fruit companies' expanding operations attracted unemployed and underemployed people from near and far. The remark about the "vices" found on the North Coast reflected—albeit critically—the fact that the region's image as the land of "green gold" (*oro verde*) did not stem merely from the large number of available jobs. Export banana zones were dotted with the symbols of modernity. Fruit company commissaries and other merchants sold an array of foodstuffs, clothing, and manufactured goods from the United States and elsewhere. Paved streets lined with electric lamps, hospitals, ice plants, and breweries were just some of the amenities to be found in company towns such as La Ceiba, Tela, and Puerto Cortés. Novel consumer technologies such as Victrolas and imported recorded music found their way to the work camps, where they filled the air with sounds from Argentina, Mexico, and the United States.

But if visions of modernity's material comforts lured people to the North Coast, the ability to find work is what kept them there for extended periods. Most ex-workers remembered the 1930s and 1940s as a time when one could land a fruit company job with relative ease. Payroll statistics confirm an overall upward trend in hiring. During the 1920s, the export banana industry provided jobs for 15–20,000 people (about 10 percent of the North Coast's total population at the time).[5] Twenty years later, the combined payrolls of the Tela Railroad Company (24,000) and Standard Fruit (6,000) approached 30,000. In the early 1950s, the two companies' combined payrolls fluctuated between 32–36,000 workers.[6] The increasingly high-input practices of the fruit companies along with the opening up of new lands and the reclamation of old ones in the Sula and Aguán valleys created many jobs during this period.[7] In addition to the multiple tasks associated with Sigatoka control, new jobs emerged in conjunction with expanding use of irrigation, fertilizers, and wooden stakes to prevent wind-related losses. Not all of the job growth during this period took place on the plantations. In 1949, the Tela Railroad Company's 11,000 farm hands represented only about half of its employees. The company's engineering and construction, mechanical, buildings and grounds, merchandise, and medical departments all had large payrolls.

In twentieth-century Honduras men almost always outnumbered women in and around banana camps, a situation that prevailed throughout Central American banana growing regions.[8] The men employed by the fruit companies possessed diverse ethnic, national, and racial identities. For example, in 1929, the Truxillo Railroad Company's employees consisted of "Hondurans" (59%), "West Indians" (11%), "Central Americans" (10%), "Honduran Caribs" [Garífuna] (9%), "North Americans" (3.9%), and "Bay Islanders" (3.2%). The remaining four percent included "Europeans," "South Americans," "Mexicans," and "Asians."[9] There can be little doubt that the North Coast was far and away the most cosmopolitan region in Honduras. However, the anti-black and anti-immigrant campaigns waged by worker organizations during the 1920s and early 1930s, along with the passage of legislation restricting the immigration of non-whites, appear to have succeeded in slowing West Indian migration to the region.[10] Another factor that led to a decline in the number of black workers was the termination of the Truxillo Railroad Company's activities in Colón where the proportion of immigrant black workers appears to have been greater than in the Sula valley where Salvadorans formed the largest immigrant group. West Indians and Garífuna men continued to work for the fruit companies as stevedores, railroad workers, and machinists through the 1930s, but their presence on the farms diminished drastically. In 1938, the Tela Railroad Company reported that Hondurans (8,300) and Salvadorans (3,665) formed the bulk of its workforce; West Indians and British Hondurans comprised less than three percent of the company's payroll.[11]

Many individuals began laboring for the fruit companies as youths. For example, Pastor Martínez left his birthplace in Olancho for Standard Fruit's plantations at the tender age of thirteen.[12] Bricio Fajardo also started working as a thirteen-year-old following the death of his father. El Salvador native Manuel Canales began grinding corn for a labor contractor at the age of fifteen. Sixteen-year-old Francisco Portillo worked as a "yard-boy" (yardero) for an overseer.[13] Female kitchen workers also commonly began working as pre-adolescents often, but not always, alongside their mothers.[14] Census data confirm that the North Coast's population during the first half of the twentieth century was a youthful one. In 1935, 38 percent of the inhabitants of Cortés were under fifteen; people under 40 comprised 84 percent (63,026 of 75,000) of the department's population. In the neighboring department of Atlántida, youths under 15 constituted 39 percent of the population, and people under 40 years of age comprised 82 percent (35,850 of 43,862) of the population in 1940.[15]

Regardless of age, individuals seeking employment on a fruit company plantation generally had to approach a labor contractor. Both Standard Fruit and United Fruit relied heavily upon contractors to supply field workers during the first half of the twentieth century.[16] The fruit companies began hiring farm workers directly in the mid-1940s, but the process remained highly decentralized: farm foremen hired and fired workers according to their discretion. As late as 1950, the Tela Railroad Company did not maintain centralized personnel files and continued to recruit laborers on a "semi-contractual basis."[17] Contratistas enlisted workers for periods of time ranging from days to weeks depending upon the task. In the early 1930s, wages ranged from US$1.50–$2.00 per day.[18] Some contractors enticed newcomers to join their crews by offering clothes, shoes, and machetes.[19] They also hired cooks to prepare meals for workers who paid about 1 lempira (US$.50) per day for food. Providing meals fulfilled a practical need since banana farms were often far from stores and markets, but the practice may have contained an element of coercion: many ex-workers recalled that contractors compelled them to eat exclusively in their kitchens by threatening to fire those who ate elsewhere. However, some women who worked in camp kitchens did not remember this practice. Labor contractors probably varied in this regard, but there is little doubt that they played, for better or worse, a crucial role in the lives of field workers.

New arrivals to export banana zones also relied on family connections, friends, and word-of-mouth in order to find work. For example, following the sudden death of his father in 1942, Bricio Fajardo began working on a Standard Fruit farm after family friends convinced "the bosses" to give him a job on a propping crew.[20] In 1946, Víctor Reyes set out from Santa Cruz de Yojoa for El Progreso where he found a job with the Tela Railroad Company "through a friend." According to Reyes, getting a farm job at the time involved few formal procedures:

> If I arrived in a camp in the middle of the day and you knew me and that I had come from another camp because I was not making much or did not have enough work, then you'd say, "go over to such and such section of the farm [to work.]"[21]

The experiences of Juan Gavilán, an Olancho native, confirm that personal contacts were important, but not essential, for finding work. Gavilán landed his first job—weeding on a Tela Railroad Company farm—by approaching a contractor who he did not know. Sometime later, Juan relocated to the Aguán valley where he weeded for Standard Fruit. However, he considered the job to be "too much work" for the pay. Fortunately, a brother-in-law found him a position in the company's irrigation department. In Gavilán's case then, a family contact helped him to leave a job that he disliked for a more favorable one.[22]

Single women seeking work in camp kitchens often relied upon a network of friends and extended family to land a job in much the same manner as their male counterparts. For example, Gladys Nieves was raised on a banana farm where she worked in the kitchen of her mother who single-handedly "looked after" some men workers in addition to her daughter.[23]

When she was still a child, Gladys left the camp and resettled in the department of Comayagua only to return to the North Coast at the age of eighteen. A girlfriend helped her find work with a *patrona* (spouse of contractor) cooking and washing clothes for about 20 men. Gladys continued to cook for workers after she married a fieldhand. Ángela Coto-Moreno's introduction to the camp kitchen also came at an early age. Her single mother brought her to a Tela Railroad Company camp near El Progreso when she was only seven. By the age of ten, she was "working hard" grinding corn and fetching water for her mother who cared for some thirty or forty men. Ángela left the camp kitchens after marrying a man with whom she operated a small farm on the periphery of the plantations.[24] Women who married labor contractors often set up kitchens to provide meals for their husband's work crew. In some instances, contractors maintained "houses" that provided meals for 20–30 workers. Isabel Mangandí de Duarte considered cooking for her husband's workers to be less of an obligation than a necessity since the work site lay a considerable distance from area villages. Serving a satisfying meal was a source of great pride for Isabel who recalled that she and her husband did not profit much from providing meals due to the costs of serving "extras" such as bread, oatmeal, fish and eggs.[25] José María Lara confirmed that the quality of the food served was a consideration when male workers assessed the merits of individual labor contractors.

If finding a plantation job was not particularly difficult, holding onto one was nearly impossible because most farm work was done on a short-term contractual basis. As Charles Kepner wrote in 1936, "Much employment in banana districts is intermittent. Fruit is not cut every day, longshoremen are needed only when ships are in port, task workers are busy as long as their tasks last."[26] The observations of a US diplomat recorded fourteen years later reveal that short-term stints of employment remained the norm through mid-century: "Each of the fifty farms in the [United Fruit] company's Honduran division has frequently hired and fired laborers as needed. This frequently has meant that workmen discharged at one farm, for whatever reason, moved on to other farms where they were hired if needed."[27] This instability resulted largely from seasonal variations in annual production and consumption cycles. For example, employment levels tended to be highest during the first half of the calendar year when exports and U.S. market demand both peaked. By contracting out most farm tasks, the fruit companies benefited from flexible payroll obligations. As one former Standard Fruit Company worker recalled, when a particular task was completed, "three-quarters of the employees" were laid off.[28] These structural layoffs often lasted for weeks. Another ex-worker recalled that field hands could be fired at the discretion of their supervisors: "If they [the bosses] saw you slacking off a little, they'd say, "don't bother coming tomorrow" and the next day you did not go because they would not give you work."[29]

In the absence of any legal recourse, dismissed workers were forced to solicit work on another farm. Migrating between farms also provided the means to escape conflict with bosses. For example, when a *mandador* ignored Juan Gavilán's complaints about the difficulty of applying Bordeaux spray with a heavy hose, Juan and his spray partner protested with their feet and headed to another farm. In another instance, after he was fired for drinking on the job, Gavilán was able to find work on a different farm.[30] At times, workers took advantage of the fruit companies' decentralized hiring systems by quitting jobs and/or changing farms as an assertion of personal autonomy. As Cantalisio Andino explained, "If you were unhappy with your job, you could find something else through another *mandador* or captain. . . . There were no identification numbers or anything like that, so one went from farm to farm without any problem."[31] Although Cantalisio may have exaggerated the ease of finding a desirable position on a new farm, his experiences, along with those of other former *campeños,* confirm that field workers moved frequently. Over a span of twenty years, Manuel Canales worked as a weeder (*chapeador*), pruner (*deshijero*), harvester (*juntero* or *cortero*), and Bordeaux spray applicator (*venenero*) for the Tela Railroad Company. He usually spent at least one month (workers were paid monthly) at a given position at which point if he wasn't satisfied he moved on to another farm. Upon re-locating, Manuel sometimes had to fill temporary positions, but he added that, "as time went on, and the foremen got to know you, they gave you regular work."[32]

Pastor Martínez also remembered the ease with which one could change jobs: "I was a harvester, *apoyador* (plant staker), hose-man, nozzle-man [Bordeaux sprayer], and I worked in irrigation too—I've worked in 99 percent of the jobs." He added that it was "unusual" to find a person who had worked one job exclusively. The flexibility provided Martínez with an escape from the tedium of manual labor: "Suppose that I worked six months hauling fruit. Then, the situation might change and I'd decide that I no longer want to keep that job. So I went to work in irrigation. Then something else—say, weeding. Later, when I got tired of that, maybe I'd look for pruning work."[33]

José María Lara's work history reveals a similar pattern of transition and instability. Born in the department of Ocotepeque, Lara first worked as a teenager for United Fruit in Guatemala. After contracting malaria, he returned to Ocotepeque to recover. Between 1937 and 1940 he harvested bananas and installed irrigation systems on the plantations of the Tela Railroad Company. He then worked briefly as a Bordeaux applicator before shifting to ditch digging. Lara excavated ditches (*zanjos*) on three different farms. In the early 1940s, the company eliminated contractors for drainage projects and began directly contracting individual *paleros* or ditch-diggers. Around 1944, Lara went to Guatemala where he joined a small guerrilla group comprised of Hondurans who sought to depose the Carías government. Following this self-described "adventure," he returned to the Sula valley in 1950, two years after Carías stepped down from power. Lara found work on a company farm through a Sigatoka foreman who was married to his niece. Later, he returned to ditch digging.[34]

Few workers duplicated the trajectories of individuals like José Maria Lara. Nevertheless, they frequently left banana plantations to pursue some other livelihood. For example, Cantalisio Andino grew up in a small farming and ranching village outside of Olanchito. He started working for Standard Fruit during the 1940s when the company was extending its plantings into the Upper Aguán valley. Cantalisio began in the engineering department, assisting with land surveys before switching to Bordeaux spraying. He quit and/or was fired more than once. On such occasions, Cantalisio returned to his village "where there was always work," albeit poorly paid (less than half of the prevailing wages on banana farms). In the early 1950s, he left the company and re-settled in his village where he tended cattle, raised hogs and cultivated a milpa.[35] For Cantalisio then, plantation work meant an opportunity to earn higher wages without severing ties with the village of his birth. Crossing the eco-social boundaries that separated banana plantations and neighboring villages was not unusual in the Aguán valley where many of Standard Fruit's workers lived in communities situated on the arid slopes that lay above the fertile *vega* lands where the company established its banana farms. Village life did not offer many opportunities for capital accumulation, but it could provide an escape from the rigors and tedium of plantation life.

In addition to facing cyclical layoffs linked to the production calendar, workers also lost their jobs en masse due to international economic downturns, wartime shipping restrictions, and the spread of plant pathogens. During the 1930s, the conjuncture of international market depressions and the spread of Panama and Sigatoka diseases created an employment crisis in Colón. In 1934, the region's governor reported that no fewer than 600 unemployed workers were sitting idle in Puerto Castilla with more arriving by the day.[36] The United Fruit Company's decision to pull out of Colón and dissolve the Truxillo Railroad Company precipitated a wave of out-migration in the late 1930s. Among those who left were Feliciano Núñez and Margarita Gonzales. Feliciano Núñez had first migrated to the North Coast in the late 1920s when he worked briefly as a banana harvester for an independent grower in the Ulúa valley before returning to his birthplace in a mountainous region south of Tegucigalpa.[37] Around 1931, Feliciano returned to the North Coast (a ten-day journey on foot) where he had brief stints with both Standard Fruit and the Truxillo Railroad Company. He subsequently turned to farming a small tract of land. This venture ended in failure and Feliciano found himself once again harvesting and hauling bananas, this time for *poquiteros* in the Aguán valley. In December 1938, the imminent closure of the Truxillo Railroad Company's farms and concomitant decline in rail service prompted Feliciano, Margarita, and their two children to leave the area. Traveling aboard fruit company trains and steamers, the family joined hundreds of unemployed people in search of new livelihoods.

In Puerto Cortés, Feliciano and Margarita tried to find work through a godmother whose North American husband was a *mandador* for the Tela Railroad Company. However, jobs were scarce and the godmother could only arrange for Feliciano to work one day per week in the U.S. consulate. On Christmas Eve, the family boarded a company train bound for El Progreso. Feliciano recalled the grim situation on the farms: "There was nothing by way of work. Nothing. Everyone there was just hanging out in the camps. One group was playing cards, another group playing *maule*, another group played *trompo;* others played domino. They used beer and soda bottle caps for chips."[38] The couple's luck began to turn when they came upon some friends who offered Margarita a position as a cook on yet another farm. The job enabled Margarita to feed her two daughters, but Feliciano was forced to get by on charity. He worked irregularly until the early 1940s when he landed a position as a *subcomandante* (a security guard on the payroll of the Tela Railroad Company) responsible for keeping the peace on the company's farms. He continued to work for the company until 1954. Over a period spanning twenty-five years, Feliciano migrated frequently and engaged in a variety of livelihoods. He weathered a period of prolonged unemployment and dislocation by drawing on the support of extended family, friends and his spouse.[39]

The fruit companies laid off thousands of workers during World War II when shipping restrictions led to a sharp decline in U.S. banana imports. For example, between April and June 1942 — historically a period of high market demand — Standard Fruit cut its payroll from some 7,000 to 4,400 employees.[40] Many idled workers "drifted back" to family fincas; those without land were reportedly "loafing" around the company's camps. Standard Fruit officials allowed some of the jobless to remain in company housing, but the commissaries refused to extend credit.[41] Individuals who were lucky enough to retain their jobs endured severe pay cuts.[42] In 1943, "large numbers" of workers migrated to southern Honduras to work on the Pan American highway. Still others found jobs on local public works projects or growing produce for area markets.[43]

The temporal and spatial fluctuations that characterized export banana production during the first half of the twentieth century, then, forced farm workers to endure frequent periods of unemployment. They often responded by migrating both within and beyond export banana zones. "Farm-hopping" enabled field hands to avoid cyclical layoffs, harsh bosses, or boredom, but this strategy was less viable during periods of sustained, widespread slowdowns in production. Of course, geographical mobility should not be conflated with social mobility; the lack of stable employment, along with stagnant or even declining real wages rendered the accumulation of capital difficult. Assessing the status of the "average worker" on the North Coast during the 1930s and early 1940s, a U.S. official based in La Ceiba painted a mixed picture: "Generally he [the average worker] may be said to be about as well off now [1944] as at most any time in the last ten years but at best his condition is not an enviable one."[44] Of course, wages alone reveal little about the historical experiences of workers on export banana farms. Daily life in the fields involved carrying out tasks that required manual dexterity, stamina, and knowledge about banana cultivation. It also meant living and working in environments that posed both short- and long-term health hazards.

WORKING ENVIRONMENTS

The "work day" began during the middle of the night in banana camps. As one retired worker recalled, "around three in the morning they would begin shouting at the cook to get up and make breakfast." Aside from disrupting their sleep, cooks' predawn start exposed them to one of the most insidious threats to human health found in export banana zones: the malaria-transmitting anopheles mosquito. Ángela Coto-Moreno recalled contracting malaria when she was a child helping her mother prepare food in an open-air kitchen: "The camps were breeding grounds for

FIGURE 5.3. A "typical kitchen" in Caribbean Guatemala (1920s). United Fruit
Company Photograph Collection. Baker Library, Harvard Business School.

mosquitoes (*zancudales*). There was no metal screening in the kitchens.
Ay, the malaria! One day when I was a child, I caught a fever. Then chills set
in—what shivering! Then, the high temperatures came back—a burning
fever. There were people who died from malaria."[45]

During the 1920s, the fruit companies' hospitals treated thousands
of cases of malaria on an annual basis. In 1926, the admission rate to
United Fruit Company hospitals of employees with malaria was 254/1,000;
in other words, one in four employees who sought medical treatment did
so for malaria.[46] In 1926, United Fruit implemented a multifaceted malaria
control program that combined reducing mosquito breeding grounds
via insecticide applications, mandatory treatment of sick employees, and
chemotherapy (quinine and Plasmochin). United Fruit medical reports
indicate that both mortality and morbidity rates for malaria fell significantly through 1931, the last year for which published reports exist.[47] However, malaria remained the "predominant disease" among Tela Railroad
Company workers during the 1930s.[48] In 1935, the number of treated cases
among Standard Fruit's employees exceeded seven thousand.[49] One year

later, the Truxillo Railroad Company's medical department attended to some 4,600 cases of malaria. The company's medical department implemented a malaria prevention program that included weekly applications of crude oil and insecticides "in all of the camps" and along the banks of rivers, streams and swampy areas.[50] In addition, the company distributed tens of thousands of quinine tablets and Plasmochin.

The annual reports issued by United Fruit's Medical Department indicate that the type of work most often associated with malaria during the 1920s was land-clearing, a pattern that had less to do with the "pestilential" nature of the woodlands than with the provisional nature of worker housing.[51] In an article published in 1926, William Deeks, a physician employed by the United Fruit Company, concluded that his research in Honduras demonstrated that "the house is a factor of primary importance in the acquisition and spread of malaria."[52] This awareness did little for the workers contracted to clear land, who were forced to sleep in hastily built structures with manaca (palm-thatched) roofs. Feliciano Núñez recalled swarms of mosquitoes hovering above his hammock when he worked for a contractor clearing forests in the Aguán valley in the early 1930s. Not surprisingly, he came down with malaria. Through the 1940s, land-clearing crews continued to be housed in crowded structures that afforded little protection from mosquitoes.[53] Even as the fruit companies waged multi-pronged campaigns to bring malaria under control, their practice of relocating production locations in response to Panama disease placed workers in high-risk environments. Shifting plantation agriculture then, depended not only upon the availability of land but also upon men and women who were willing to work in places that heightened their chances of contracting malaria.

Beyond mosquitoes, perhaps no other non-human inhabitant of banana plantations inspired as much dread among field workers as the *barba amarilla* (*Bothrops atrox*), a venomous snake with a bright yellow chin and a reputation among *campeños* as an unusually aggressive serpent. The bite of a *barba amarilla* could produce temporary blindness, bleeding, paralysis and, if untreated, death. In the mid-1920s, concern over snakebites prompted United Fruit to support studies of the *barba amarilla* in collaboration with the Antivenin Institute of America and Harvard University's Museum of Comparative Zoology.[54] The company helped to establish a serpentarium near Tela where snakes could be studied and bred for purposes of extracting the venom needed to produce antiserum. The prevalence of snakebites among plantation workers is unclear; United Fruit's Medical Department reported a handful of life-threatening cases each year, but company physicians noted that many workers sought out treatment for snakebites from local healers.

In 1928, the serpentarium's curator, Douglas March, reported that the *barba amarilla*'s aggressiveness was "somewhat exaggerated."[55] Both March and Raymond Ditmars, a curator of the New York Zoological Park, attributed the frequent encounters between farm workers and the *barba amarilla* to ecological changes associated with export banana production: banana farms created habitats in which the serpent's prey—including rats and opossums—thrived. Consequently, in areas of expanding banana production, the large *barba amarilla* tended to abandon woodlands in favor of plantations. The fact that the snake was a nocturnal hunter probably lowered the frequency of snakebites since most plantation work was carried out during daylight hours. However, field workers seldom took chances and quickly struck down any snake within reach of their machetes—much to the consternation of the herpetologists who encouraged field hands to capture—not kill—snakes encountered in the course of their work. To judge by the data published in the Antivenin Institute's journal, the reported number of snakebites was small and certainly paled in comparison to the number of people who contracted malaria. On the other hand, United Fruit's investment in the serpentarium, along with the prominence of the *barba amarilla* in popular stories about life on banana plantations suggests that encounters with poisonous snakes were commonplace.

Venomous snakes and malaria-carrying mosquitoes instilled widespread fear among *campeños,* but other, mundane elements of export banana agroecosystems—including wind, rain, soils, weeds, mules, and the banana plants themselves—also conditioned workers' daily experiences and earnings. One of the gloomiest moments in the novel *Prisión verde* is a particularly harsh rainy season that left "hundreds of workers with their arms folded." Idled workers "watched the hours and days pass with heavy eyes, cursing the storm and enduring long and horrible nights . . . in their rooms with no more heat than that produced by their own bodies."[56] Former workers recalled that on exceptionally rainy days they "did not earn hardly anything" because many jobs, including ditch digging and Bordeaux spraying, were halted.[57] Local wind storms, or "blow downs" also prompted the fruit companies to lay off workers. For example, between March and June 1949, Standard Fruit's payrolls dipped from 13,600 to 10,800 due "mainly" to lower production stemming from inadequate rainfall and a major "blow down."[58] Frequent references to blow downs in annual reports produced by United Fruit's Department of Tropical Re-

FIGURE 5.4. *Idled workers in the Sula valley on United Fruit farm shortly after a "blow down" (1925). United Fruit Company Photograph Collection. Baker Library, Harvard Business School.*

search during the first half of the twentieth century provide indirect evidence that the susceptibility of tall Gros Michel plants to high winds had a significant impact on workers' livelihoods.

Variations in soil conditions also affected the earnings of contract workers. By the late 1920s, the fruit companies used steam-powered drag lines to excavate primary drainage canals but lateral ditches, or *zanjos,* were excavated by hand. Ditch digging was remunerated on a piece-wage system.[59] Soil conditions significantly affected earnings: loose, sandy soils could be excavated with much less exertion (and therefore potentially faster) than compact clay soils. *Paleros* received extra pay for removing tree trunks and other surface obstacles, but wage rates did not vary on account of soil conditions. According to José Almendares, individuals who complained about having to dig clay soils were told to "take a hike" (*andáte*).[60] José María Lara recalled that a skilled *palero* could earn up to

6 lempiras ($US3) per day, considerably more than at jobs such as weeding and pruning.[61] But the arduous work was not for everyone: one young North American supervisor who tried it reported that "my back muscles were not sufficiently developed to swing a spadeful of wet dirt the required distance out and away from the ditch."[62] Little surprise, then, that some *paleros* devised strategies to work less for their pay. For example, when not under the vigilance of a foreman, workers used their machetes to hack off small lengths of the stakes placed by company engineers to indicate the desired depth. This sleight of hand gave the appearance that the ditch had been dug to the proper depth when in reality it was shallower than ordered. Another labor-saving technique used by some workers when building dikes and retaining walls alongside irrigation ditches was to cut stalks from old banana plants and place them in a line along the canal border. Dirt was then shoveled on top of the stalks. This trick enabled *paleros* to move less earth, but the banana-stalk berms tended to spring leaks and collapse when water entered the ditch.[63]

If farm supervisors could not measure the depth of every ditch, neither could they monitor how low weeding crews (*chapiadores*) swung their machetes. Weeding was a notoriously low-paying, tedious task: as late as 1954, *chapiadores* on Tela Railroad Company farms earned two lempiras (one U.S. dollar) per acre, an area that could be, but was not always, completed in a day.[64] The length of time needed to clean an acre reflected both the density of the weeds and the care with which the work was done. One ex-employee explained that by thoroughly weeding (*bien bajito*) sections near well-traveled routes, areas less frequently traversed by foremen could be weeded superficially. Of course, workers were not the only ones capable of manipulating the piece-wage system to their advantage: former United Fruit employee Jay Soothill wrote that company overseers could reduce labor costs by lengthening the time between weeding cycles. In so doing, they compelled *chapiadores* to either move to another farm or agree to work for less pay.[65]

In contrast to the isolation and tedium associated with weeding and ditching, the work of harvesting fruit bunches — "the most important day in the life of a banana farm" — was fast-paced and team-oriented.[66] When farm managers issued notice of a *corte,* they unleashed a frenzy of activity — rain or shine — that lasted between 24 and 48 hours. Harvesting teams generally consisted of nine members including mule-drivers (*muleros*), cutters (*corteros*) and backers (*junteros*). According to one longtime farm supervisor, a *cortero* was "the skilled man of most farm operations" who made crucial decisions about selecting which fruit to harvest

FIGURE 5.5. Cortero y juntero *harvesting bananas in Caribbean Guatemala (1925). Note height of Gros Michel plants. United Fruit Company Photograph Collection. Baker Library, Harvard Business School.*

on any given *corte*.[67] Through the 1940s, grading was done largely by eye: supervisors displayed representative bunches to the *corteros* in order to give them an idea about what their teams should harvest. This was no trivial matter since fruit that was either too thin or too far along in the ripening process would be rejected by fruit inspectors. *Corteros* also provided farm managers with crucial information about the volume of fruit that would be available for future *cortes*.

Harvesting the large fruit bunches produced by tall Gros Michel plants required coordination among workers. Using a blade attached to the end of a lightweight, eight-foot pole, a *cortero* made a small gash in the plant's stalk so that the weight of the fruit bunch (between 40 and 80 pounds) would cause the plant to double over until the bananas came to rest on the padded shoulder of a waiting *juntero*. The padding notwithstanding, heavy bunches often broke when they made contact with a *juntero*'s shoulder suggesting that workers' backs absorbed considerable pounding in the course of harvesting hundreds of bunches. The *juntero* then carried the fruit to another worker who loaded it onto the backs of mules that would subsequently carry the fruit to a *bacadía,* or railroad siding.[68]

Prior to the introduction of tractors in the mid-1950s, mules played a critical role in transporting fruit. The Tela Railroad Company maintained more than 6,300 pack mules that required "extensive pastures" and imported feed. Mule drivers did not take their animals for granted; uncooperative mules could throw off or even eat their cargo. New mules often gave workers fits and were broken in by placing heavy sandbags on their backs.[69] On harvest days, *muleros* headed to the corral in the early hours of the morning to find their teams using only the light of a lantern or flashlight. The mule driver who arrived late to the corral ran the risk that a fellow worker would "swap" a rebellious mule for a reliable one. In order to avoid bruising during the ride, canvas padding was layered between the mule and the fruit. However, as one ex-Standard Fruit worker noted, the combination of heavy rains and unpaved roads all but ensured that the fruit would be bumped and jostled during its ride to the *bacadía:* "Everything was mud. The fruit suffered as much as the worker. It got rather battered."[70] According to Bricio Fajardo, mule drivers commonly hauled 200–300 bunches during a day that extended for twelve or more hours: "We got up at two in the morning to prepare the mules and perhaps at six or seven at night we'd return them to the corral . . . it was terrible, we would be plastered with mud."[71] Slogging through rain and mud "up to one's knees" was a memory shared by many former Tela Railroad Company workers as well.[72]

Not surprisingly, harvesting crews tried to devise ways to increase their earnings under the piece-wage system. Some contractors eliminated the *juntero* position. Feliciano Núñez recalled that his six-person crew, "working like crazy," could harvest and transport more than 1,000 bunches in an eighteen-hour period. In order to ensure that workers did not sacrifice quality for quantity, foremen closely supervised harvesting crews, taking them to task for improperly padding the fruit and/or overloading the mules. Of course, the same set of environmental factors that could make life miserable for harvesters must have rendered close supervision difficult and unpleasant.[73] Bananas had to be cut and transported

FIGURE 5.6. *Workers—under watchful eye of overseer—hauling bananas with mules (c. 1925). United Fruit Company Photograph Collection. Baker Library, Harvard Business School.*

with speed and care, but rain, mud, and darkness combined with workers' own initiatives to increase their earnings lowered the odds that the two goals could be consistently met.

The work of ditch digging, weeding, and harvesting shared in common a piece-wage system that attempted to accelerate the pace at which *campeños* labored while simultaneously placing the burden of dealing with subtle but significant agroecological variations upon workers. In much the same way that ditch diggers encountered a range of soil conditions, harvesters confronted fickle mules, inclement weather, and variable hauling distances.[74] Workers also tended to bear the burden of ensuring that the fruit they harvested conformed to the grade and quality standards of export markets. Squeezing extra earnings out of the piece-wage system took considerable creativity and guile. Some individuals tried to earn more by cutting corners; others tried to work less through deception. Whatever their ploy, workers had to take care not to upset their *capataz,* or foreman, upon whom they depended for keeping their jobs. Foremen occupied a middle ground in the plantation hierarchy, responsible for translating— often quite literally—the orders of central managers to labor contractors and their crews. As a result, they played a crucial role in determining the quotidian experiences of *campeños.*

CAMPEÑOS AND CAPATACES

Arguably the most despicable character in *Prisión verde* is a Honduran *capataz* known as "capitán Benítez." Throughout the novel, he is repeatedly depicted as deceiving Honduran workers in order to serve the interests of Standard Fruit. In the banana fields, he spies on workers "to listen to their conversations in case they were talking about him or the *gringo* managers."[75] Later, during a strike, he and other *capataces* distribute rum to workers in order to elicit the names of the strike organizers. Finally, at the novel's end, readers learn that Benítez was an accomplice in the murder of a popular worker. Amaya Amador further symbolizes Benítez's betrayal of his Honduran roots by having the character speak in a broken "Span-glish." As one of the characters in *Prisión verde* explains, "before rubbing elbows with the *gringos* he [Benítez] spoke Spanish; but he has gringo-ized himself so much that now he speaks neither Spanish nor English."[76] The indignity of enforcing the company's will, Amaya Amador seems to suggest, stripped foremen of their very identity. However, the portrait of Benítez is weakened by its excessive functionalism. His unambiguously vile actions lend the impression that the line separating (oppressed) workers from (repressive) bosses was firmly and irrevocably drawn. In the end, Benítez is reduced to a pawn all but lacking agency. As a result, the irony of his "gringoization" is largely lost.

Amaya Amador's decision to use the character of a Honduran *capataz* to personify the injustice of the "green prison" is not surprising given the crucial position that foremen occupied in the plantation hierarchy. The fruit companies administered their sprawling operations in a highly decentralized fashion. Each of the Tela Railroad Company's farms was managed by an overseer (*mandador*) assisted by a timekeeper (responsible for managing the payroll), a spray-master (in charge of Sigatoka control) and several foremen, or *capataces.* Foremen's responsibilities included hiring and firing laborers in addition to supervising work crews. They also submitted personnel rosters and tally sheets used to determine monthly payrolls. As one former farm superintendent recalled the *capataces* "really ran the business."[77]

During the 1910s and 1920s, West Indians often served as field bosses along with Mexicans, Nicaraguans, Hondurans and some North Americans. By the mid-1930s, the majority of farm foremen were native Spanish-speakers.[78] Some ex-field hands recalled the presence of Honduran *capataces* with a bitterness similar to that of Amaya Amador, but they also indicated that foremen who knew the ins-and-outs of banana cultivation earned their respect. On the other hand, supervisors who lacked hands-on experience were ridiculed in stories that circulated among workers. One popular anecdote described a North American manager's first day on a banana farm: Upon witnessing a worker cut down the stalk of an already-harvested banana plant, the new supervisor angrily accused the worker of destroying company property. The supervisor did not calm down until someone gently explained to him that banana "trees" only bore fruit once. Although such tales usually poked fun at the ignorance of *gringo* managers, *campeños* expressed a similar contempt toward Honduran bosses whose knowledge of banana cultivation came primarily through reading books, not handling a machete.[79]

For a small number of ex-*campeños,* the opportunity to be promoted to foreman represented a rare opportunity for social mobility.[80] In *Prisión verde,* when a new worker asks an experienced one how to become a *capataz,* the latter explains that there are various pathways but that the fastest route was to have a well-connected *padrino,* or godfather. This may have been the case with Ramón Vallecillo, who arrived in the Aguán valley with a letter of recommendation that he presented to Standard Fruit's superintendent of irrigation. Following brief training in both Bordeaux spraying and irrigation, the twenty-two-year-old Olancho native was made a Bordeaux spray captain. He worked only a few months in that position before the company transferred him to another farm to fill an opening in irrigation. Vallecillo spent four years as a *capataz* in Standard Fruit's irrigation department working twelve-hour, rotating shifts. Every other week, he pulled a double shift and worked a twenty-four-hour day. Traveling on mule-back, he made sure that crews properly managed the overhead irrigation system. On the night shift, he and his crews worked by lantern light. Vallecillo did not recall having any difficulties managing his crew but he admitted that he lacked confidence in them: "I always had to supervise them."[81] The long hours notwithstanding, Ramón considered himself very lucky: "They always gave me a letter so that I would be placed in charge of a crew. I worked very little. Most of the time I just shouted at people." He attributed his good fortune to the fact that he came recommended.[82]

José María Lara's chance to climb up a rung on the plantation social ladder came through a combination of luck and talent. His first opportunity to supervise came on a day in 1952 when a drunken *capataz* failed to dispatch his crew to a job site. Lara was placed in charge of twenty men who were replanting a field. Later, a *mandador* named Luís Fasquelle asked Lara to repair a badly damaged irrigation pipe. A few days after successfully completing that assignment, Lara was promoted to *capataz*. His starting salary was 60 dollars per month (the company deducted two percent for medical care). The company also provided him with a small house. Lara did not consider the starting pay to be a major incentive ("the only thing that changed was the work") but the combination of prestige, better housing, and liberation from taxing physical labor must have been hard to turn down.[83] Interestingly, Lara's promotion came after his lengthy hiatus as a guerrilla in Guatemala — presumably not the sort of sabbatical experience favored by United Fruit's North American managers.

As Ramón Vallecillo's reminiscences suggest, foremen bore the responsibility of reprimanding laborers who loafed on the job and/or failed to follow company procedures. Many ex-workers recalled being taken to task for a variety of infractions, such as over-loading pack mules, failing to properly protect fruit, or applying Bordeaux spray haphazardly. José María Lara recalled that confronting slackers could be a dicey proposition:

> I used to check all of the stakes [for a drainage ditch] and if I found that they had been tampered with, I'd call the worker over and ask "why did you raise this stake?" It was humorous, but at times risky too, because many workers would become angry and want to fight. But things always worked themselves out.[84]

The mixture of humor and fear described by Lara reflected the beneath-the-surface tension that marked the daily relations between field workers and their immediate bosses. These tensions resulted not only from the awkward social position of *capataces* like Lara who at times found themselves exercising authority over former coworkers, but also from the organization of plantation space. Maintaining control over a work crew was a tenuous proposition on large plantations where help was not always around the corner.[85] Firearms were carried openly by North American managers, *capataces*, contractors, and many workers. Small daggers could be purchased in company stores, along with the ubiquitous machete. Although there is no evidence that worker assaults on foremen were common, the potential for violence likely prompted bosses to act with considerably more tact than that displayed by Amaya Amador's Benítez. Supervisors who humiliated workers could find themselves in trouble.[86]

Conflict was only one possible outcome of the daily contact between foremen and workers. Although former field hands complained of being verbally harassed by foremen and/or fired, they also recalled amicable relations with *capataces* who provided favors such as issuing medical passes, or granting time to run off-farm errands. According to one retired employee, "many" *capataces* colluded with workers to extort money from the companies.[87] Foremen, who were responsible for submitting daily work sheets to timekeepers, could manipulate the number of hours worked and/or add assignments that had not been completed. Another simple yet hard to detect swindle was signing off on hastily completed work. For example, a *capataz* could accept a ditch that had not been dug to the required depth in return for a small cash payment from the *palero* responsible for completing the task. This form of agreement enabled foremen to pad their salaries while shortening the workday for field hands. Of course, the fact that a foreman could fire an individual who refused to embezzle the company meant that there was a fine line between collusion and extortion.

The frequency with which farm supervisors and workers swindled their employers is difficult to determine. Describing a conversation held with the Tela Railroad Company's La Lima–based general manager William Turnbull in 1950, a U.S. diplomat concluded that central management's power over its farm personnel had limits:

> However forward looking and progressive the policy of the United
> Fruit Company laid down by Boston and headquarters in La Lima may
> be, overseers and time-keepers and other petty officials in the remoter
> areas are admittedly arbitrary and inconsiderate of some of their
> workmen.[88]

By attributing the unjust treatment of workers to the "arbitrary acts" of "petty officials," the consular official—and presumably Turnbull—attempted to divert attention away from the production processes and wage structures created by the company's central management. In this sense, Turnbull's statement can be interpreted as lending support to Amaya Amador's depiction of Honduran bosses performing the dirty work for the U.S. fruit companies. However, viewed from a different perspective, the remark points toward the difficulties confronted by fruit company executives when trying to monitor the actions of widely dispersed farm managers.

If the autonomy vested in overseers and foremen enabled chief executives to deflect criticisms of company policies, it also provided farm managers with opportunities to subvert the rule of central managers who largely isolated themselves from fieldworkers. During the 1950s, the Tela Railroad Company rotated its farm managers every year or two in order to discourage patronage.[89] The authority vested in foremen, the fact that they seldom performed physical labor, and the fringe benefits that they enjoyed unquestionably set them apart from field hands, but they did not uniformly reconstruct themselves as "company men." Many foremen had started in the fruit companies as field hands and shared common backgrounds and language with the people that they supervised. The memories of ex-*campeños* suggest that the plantation environment provided workers and foremen with room for confrontation, collusion, and an uneasy co-existence.

LIVING ENVIRONMENTS

The physical distance that separated the places inhabited by fruit company executives such as William Turnbull, and *capataces* and *campeños* did not exist by accident. High-level U.S. employees and their families resided in *zonas americanas* that were physically demarcated from other neighborhoods by fences and gated entry points. The architecture and landscaping—including golf courses and swimming pools—reflected the aesthetic sensibilities and cultural practices of its predominantly white U.S. residents. Foremen and fieldhands inhabited a world apart, eating, resting, and sleeping in company-owned camps that usually lay in very close proximity to the farms.

During the first half of the twentieth century, United Fruit's Honduran subsidiaries housed workers in six-unit wooden barracks; separate kitchens lay behind the sleeping quarters. The structures lacked indoor plumbing and electricity. In 1925, a public official in Trujillo reported that he had met with Truxillo Railroad Company management to discuss worker housing that did not "meet the necessary standards of hygiene . . . the majority of the workers are victims of a terrible plague of mosquitoes."[90] That same year, Dr. William Deeks, a United Fruit Company physician, published a pamphlet on malaria that stressed the need for "mosquito-proof" housing in order to prevent the disease. But, United Fruit's Medical Department reported that screening was impossible be-

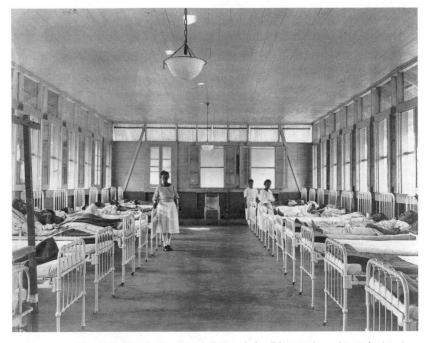

FIGURE 5.7. *The United Fruit Company's "second class" hospital ward in Tela (1923). United Fruit Company Photograph Collection. Baker Library, Harvard Business School.*

cause workers failed to use it properly. One former worker agreed that screening cut down, but did not eliminate, exposure to mosquitoes: "Since there were so many workers in a single room, a good portion of whom were drunk, the door at times got left open and mosquitoes came in."[91] As Charles Kepner pointed out in his 1936 study, even if screens were properly installed and maintained, mosquitoes could easily enter worker housing due to the absence of ceilings and openings between the walls and the floorboards.

The crowded, poorly ventilated barracks found in banana camps along with the constant farm-to-farm migrations, contributed to high rates of respiratory illnesses among workers. In fact, between 1914 and 1931, far more United Fruit employees in Central America died from respiratory illnesses than from malaria. In Honduras, pneumonia accounted for many more deaths (602) than malaria (234) between 1923 and 1926. Tuberculosis was also responsible for many deaths.[92] In contrast to their aggressive campaign against malaria, the fruit companies did little to address the housing conditions contributing to high rates of respiratory illness. According to one U.S. embassy official, Tela Railroad Company workers who contracted tuberculosis around 1950 were "normally given 100 lempiras . . . and a ticket to travel overland to their homes."[93] A former employee of the company's labor relations department confirmed that many field workers diagnosed with tuberculosis were given a small compensation before returning to their home towns "to die."[94] Standard Fruit also tried to get "native employees" suffering from tuberculosis "off the farms and back, as quickly as possible, to the place from where they originally came."[95] As was the case elsewhere in Central American export banana zones, the fruit companies showed much less interest in healing individual workers suffering from respiratory diseases than in preventing the spread of illnesses to other workers. More significantly, the companies seldom acknowledged the degree to which production processes and the organization of plantation spaces contributed to the spread of human — as well as plant — pathogens.

The cramped living spaces inhabited by field workers afforded little privacy. One worker recalled that contractors slept in small private rooms in the barracks; laborers slung hammocks in a long corridor.[96] Francisco Portillo did not have fond memories of life in the barracks:

> We lived in the rooms packed like hens. The people returning from the farm did not even bother to wash their feet before lying down in their hammocks with their feet practically under their neighbor's nose! Many workers were in the habit of chewing tobacco, too. They'd spit on the walls and all over the place. You lived like an animal.[97]

Other workers confirmed the lack of hygiene that characterized many work camps. José Maria Lara recalled camps without toilets or showers. People went to the fields to relieve themselves. Bathing was sometimes possible in one of the many canals and ditches that coursed through the farms, but after 1936 these were often contaminated with Bordeaux spray. More often, workers bathed in nearby rivers and lagoons. Many camps had wells that supplied bathing and cooking water, but the wells were often shallow and the water not always potable. Sanitary conditions did not differ significantly in the camps of Standard Fruit. Bricio Fajardo remembered that pit toilets often over-flowed during heavy rains; unfortunate souls who did not pay attention when walking near the latrines left with their shoes — as Bricio politely explained — "plastered in poop."[98]

Following World War II, the United Fruit Company began to re-design plantation living spaces. In 1945 company engineers developed a prototype living space that improved sanitary conditions while preserving a strict social segregation.[99] At one end of the camp lay the overseer's residence, a large bungalow-style house surrounded by a yard that included a servant's quarters, chicken coop, and garden area. One former worker recalled that overseers' residences were surrounded by picket fences that represented less of a physical barrier than a social one: "If you needed to speak with the overseer, you could approach only as far as the fence gate; from there you explained to him what you wanted."[100] Adjacent to the overseer's residence were houses for the timekeeper and the spray-master. The interior living spaces, yards and gardens were smaller than those allotted to the overseer and they shared a chicken coop and servant's quarters. A riding stable was situated nearby. Separating the three managers' houses from the workers' camp was an orchard area and a large garden plot shared by the foremen and medicine dispenser.[101]

Foremen lived in modest, single-family houses with small yards that literally occupied the middle ground between management and labor: only about fifty feet separated them from the nearest row of worker housing. Living units for workers with families consisted of a 12′ × 24′ space divided into two 12′ square unfurnished apartments usually elevated about eight feet off of the ground. Concrete patios below the raised structures provided additional living space. Separate, enclosed kitchens were located behind each house. Camps also had multiple "bachelor barracks" (72′ × 18′) divided into six rooms. Worker housing lacked interior plumbing and electricity; camp residents shared drinking water faucets, toilets, and showers. Housing was laid out in straight rows around a soccer field, a reflection that banana camps remained largely masculine spaces. The plan did not allot garden space for workers because, according to a U.S. official, it "would entail excessive use of valuable lands."[102] A commissary, medical dispensary, and a recreation hall lay in close proximity to worker housing units.

Few social spaces played a role as central—and controversial—to camp life as the commissaries, or company stores where workers could purchase a range of products, including dry and canned foods, men's work clothes, and farm tools such as machetes and axes. Commissaries also retailed grains, beans, and other produce grown by local farmers. In addition to maintaining stores, the Tela Railroad Company brought freshly butchered meats and milk by rail from their Puerto Arturo pastures (near Tela) to company farms in the Sula valley. Víctor Reyes recalled that peddlers sold items such as meats and shoes, but that the company stores offered "everything" at lower prices, a perception generally shared by several other former *campeños*.[103] A 1947 U.S. consular report supported this

FIGURE 5.8. *Women filling water buckets in United Fruit Company labor camp (1946). United Fruit Company Photograph Collection. Baker Library, Harvard Business School.*

view, noting that the Tela Railroad Company sold "essential foods" at or below cost to workers. Losses were made up on "non-essentials."[104] Company officials reported that for the fiscal year 1946–1947, commissaries sold nearly $US 3 million worth of goods, and maintained a net loss of $10,000. However, Thomas McCann, a Boston-based United Fruit Company executive who started with the company as an office boy in 1952, asserted that company accountants shifted operating costs in order to conceal the sizeable profits turned by the commissaries in the early 1950s.[105] Regardless of profit levels, the commissaries enabled the fruit companies to recapture a significant portion of the cash wages that they paid out to agricultural workers. One former Standard Fruit employee recalled that company officials collected cash receipts from commissaries in order to meet monthly payrolls.[106]

The company commissaries enjoyed some critical advantages over other North Coast merchants. Loosely interpreted clauses in the companies' railroad concessions enabled them to import many consumer items duty-free. In addition, the commissaries were located in or very close to labor camps. Workers could reach them by foot, in contrast to many of the merchant houses located in towns that lay many miles away from the farms. Although railroads linked farms and towns, the fruit-company-controlled train schedules did not always accommodate shopping trips. For example, in order to travel the relatively short distance from Standard Fruit camps near Coyoles to Olanchito, a person had to board the train for La Ceiba that did not return to Coyoles until the following day. This meant that workers would have to find a place to spend the night in Olanchito and potentially lose a day's wages. Nevertheless, camp residents occasionally traveled by rail and by foot to outlying commercial centers including El Progreso, La Lima, and Olanchito in order to purchase items (such as women's clothing) not sold in company stores.

The living spaces inhabited by workers, then, were largely defined by the control that the fruit companies exercised over the movement of people, money, and consumer goods. Within the camps, the organization of space served to reinforce prevailing inequalities. By separating the private residences of farm managers from workers' dwellings with fences, orchards, and foremen's living quarters, the camp design created a distance that was at once physical and social between managers and farm workers. Soccer fields and recreation halls served to channel worker leisure time into activities deemed acceptable by company management. What the architectural plan left unsaid—that the company owned the entire complex and therefore could evict a dismissed worker—spoke volumes about the ways that work and living spaces overlapped. Of course, the blueprint for prototype camps represented an idealized ordering of space; in practice, camp residents periodically appropriated social spaces for their own ends. At no time was this more evident than on paydays (*pagos generales*) when work camps converted into boisterous (and often violent) *ferias* where consumption and revelry were the orders of the day (and night).

The *pago general* usually took place on the last Saturday of each month.[107] An armored rail car traveled from farm to farm disbursing payments to workers and contractors. Workers lined up to cash in their time-checks—a process that often extended well into the evening. Drawn by the infusion of cash, peddlers, prostitutes, and even tax collectors descended on the camps. Peddlers hawked wares ranging from practical items such as locally made work shoes (*zapatos burros*) to indulgent imports that included Cuban cigars, white silk shirts, and English cashmere. *Guaro*-fueled workers picked guitars and belted out folk songs, while phonographs spun Mexican rancheros and Argentine tangos. Prostitutes visited barracks and set up temporary palm huts where they performed sexual acts for one lempira. If paydays provided men with opportunities to re-lax and consume, they gave many women a chance to supplement their earnings from kitchen work by preparing and vending a variety of special foods, including tamales, enchiladas, breads, and sandwiches, along with a variety of drinks—including some illicit ones.

By virtually all accounts, drinking among men was commonplace in banana camps, particularly on paydays and holidays. Commissaries offered beer (in bottles and kegs) and whiskey, but they did not sell what was perhaps the most popular drink—*guaro*—whose sale was officially prohibited. As early as 1930, Honduran President Colindres Mejía tried to ban the sale of liquor in banana camps on paydays. When the Truxillo Railroad Company came under criticism for continuing to sell alcoholic beverages wholesale, company officials maintained that they had tried to prohibit liquor and beer sales, but that drinking continued unabated due to "numerous persons who operate the contraband trade with im-punity."[108] Ángela Coto-Moreno recalled how her mother secretly distrib-uted *guaro:* "She had a short, little barrel that she would fill with *pachos* (about half of a liter) of *guaro.* Then she'd sit on the barrel and all of the men would know that she was selling." Periodic visits by the authorities required deft diplomacy: "The head of the police would pass by and say to my mom—who was dark-skinned, '*Negra,* they say that you sell *guaro.*' She would reply, 'No, I don't sell any of that. I've got my little supply here, but it's just so I can add a drop to flavor the punch that I sell. Won't you try some?' Then she would give the police a glass of punch—my mom knew how to take care of herself.[109]

Guaro and other alcoholic beverages were also available in many out-lying villages that lay within walking distance of the plantations. This was particularly true in the Aguán valley, where many of the farms that Stan-dard Fruit established in the late 1930s and 1940s borrowed their names from adjacent communities. Several ex-workers remembered paydays as times when "everyone went to the villages," some to "look for girls (*mucha-chas*), drink beer and rum," and others to gamble or visit brothels.[110] How-ever, for some workers, villages were not merely a place for weekend so-cializing, they were home. For example, Neche Martínez, was born and raised in a small village on the outskirts of Standard Fruit's Aguán val-ley farms. He continued to live there throughout his years of employment with the company, once turning down a promotion offer because it would have required moving his wife and children to a company camp. Martínez did not consider camp life to be a healthy setting in which to raise a family: "Life in the work camp was not the same as village life . . . there was a lot of fighting . . . and quite a bit of freedom . . . for girls and all that. I did not want that for my family."[111] In all likelihood, Neche's circumstances and his decision to turn down a promotion were unusual, yet his case demonstrates the diversity of worker experiences, perceptions, and values that guided individual pathways.

In addition to visiting local villages, some workers spent their free time fishing in nearby rivers and hunting in the forest fragments that bordered banana farms. Juan Gavilán hunted deer (*venado*) that once abundantly populated the forested lands found "very close" to Standard Fruit's Coyoles operations. He attributed the decline of the local deer population to the proliferation of firearms among workers, suggesting that hunting was a popular activity. In the Sula valley, Víctor Reyes hunted deer, *tepescuintle* (Querétaro pocket gopher), and feral hogs (*chancho del monte*) in a forested area near El Progreso. Other camp residents preferred fishing. Bricio Fajardo spent free afternoons fishing for catfish, *dormilón* and *tepemechín* in the Aguán River. Cantalisio Andino also recalled catching "large" *dormilón* in the Aguán when its waters ran low during the dry season. In the Sula valley, José María Lara used to canoe the Ulúa River and cast nets to catch catfish, bass and other river-dwelling species. For at least some individuals then, the non-human world was not entirely encountered through labor processes.

Hoping to raise the consciousness of the Honduran working class, Ramón Amaya Amador stressed the ways in which a capitalist production system and U.S. imperialism erected oppressive social structures that imprisoned plantation residents in a bleak world from which there was little hope of escape. However, the narratives of former workers reveal that they were constrained — but not immobilized — by the weight of being on the bottom of the plantation hierarchy. Most workers found the means — through the help of friends, spouses, sympathetic bosses and their own ingenuity — to endure the hardships and uncertainties that characterized plantation life. In some instances, individuals "escaped" the confines of company plantations by pursuing livelihoods not directly linked to banana production. Others labored decades for the company, shifting jobs frequently, and occasionally getting promoted to low-level management positions.

If field workers found ways to endure and at times even enjoy life in the banana zones, exceedingly few were able to accumulate much capital. About 25–50 percent of an average wage (2–3 dollars per day between roughly 1930 and 1950) went to pay for prepared meals. Work clothes (shirts, pants, and shoes) cost the equivalent of several days' wages. Some workers found ways to boost earnings by working faster under a piece-rate system, but any savings that individuals were able to accrue could quickly disappear during periodic layoffs. Finally, most workers were no more inclined to asceticism than their North American managers: young men and women indulged in any number of "vices," including food, drink, sex, and stylish footwear.

The Second World War and its aftermath would bring a number of economic, political, social, and technological changes to Honduras and the United States that would affect North Coast landscapes and liveli-hoods. Fruit company employees would play a major role in fomenting change by organizing a massive strike in 1954 that precipitated a wave of social reforms in Honduras — reforms that would be monitored closely by both banana company executives worried about dwindling profits and U.S. State Department officials preoccupied with containing communist "threats" in Latin America. Meanwhile, in the United States, World War II introduced the consuming masses to yet another seductive image of tropi-cal exoticism.

Chapter 6

The Lives and Time of Miss Chiquita

"[T]he banana industry is no longer a gypsy industry that can move on to new land as PD [Panama disease] or other pests invade the old plantations. We must now hold the front and in order to do so are having to make tremendous investments in flood fallowing, Sigatoka control and insect control to bring back this land and maintain it in maximum production."

L. G. COX, VICE-PRESIDENT FOR RESEARCH, UNITED FRUIT 1954

I'm Chiquita Banana and I've come to say
Bananas have to ripen in a certain way.
When they are fleck'd with brown and have a golden hue,
Bananas taste the best, and are the best for you.
. . .
But bananas like the climate of the very, very tropical equator.
So you should never put bananas in the refrigerator.

THE CHIQUITA BANANA SONG, 1944

Miss Chiquita was born on the airwaves in 1944. That year, the United Fruit Company launched a nationwide radio campaign that featured the voice of Patty Clayton singing the "Chiquita Banana Song." The tune, set to a calypso beat, achieved hit status and found its way onto the play lists of radio disc jockeys, juke boxes, and the repertoire of the Boston Pops.[1] Both the lyrics and the medium reflected changes taking place in U.S. consumer culture. Written by a New York City advertising agency, the jingle's often-quoted couplet, "But bananas like the climate of the very, very tropical equator / So you should never put bananas in the refrigerator," conjured images of middle-class homes equipped with electric appliances such as refrigerators and radios. This vision of domestic life stood in sharp contrast to the scene of an urban street peddler hawking produce depicted in the 1923 pop hit "Yes, We Have No Bananas!" The post–World War II era witnessed important changes in consumption patterns in the United States, but the "poor man's luxury" remained a fixture in the appliance-filled kitchens of the increasingly suburbanized middle classes.

World War II shipping restrictions sharply reduced banana imports and lowered per capita banana consumption to 8.2 pounds in 1943, but consumption rates rebounded quickly following the end of the war, peaking in 1948 at an estimated 22 pounds per person. Over the next ten years, per capita consumption rates fell to 17–19 pounds.[2] This trend was consistent with a general decline in fresh fruit consumption that coincided with the proliferation of processed foods. Bananas remained among the most popular fresh fruits, but with the exception of a small demand for banana puree for baby food, no major markets emerged for processed banana products as was the case with apples and oranges. The Chiquita Banana Song's lyrics, then, reflected both the banana's enduring popularity and changes in U.S. foodways that would limit the ability of the banana market to expand.

The medium through which Miss Chiquita reached her audience— the radio—further reflected changes taking places in advertising and mass media. Prior to the 1940s, United Fruit's advertising consisted primarily of informational pamphlets, billboard displays, and the company's *Unifruitco* magazine. In the 1930s, United Fruit's promotional materials began replacing text-heavy pamphlets with ephemera that featured elaborate artwork and photographic layouts. Recipe books from the period featured a cartoon banana figure with masculine features who instructed consumers on how to evaluate fruit ripeness. Following the airing of the Chiquita Banana Song, the cartoon figure appearing in the company's print advertisements shifted from the man-banana to Miss Chiquita. She cut a striking figure with her smooth, blemish-free skin, long, flowing skirt, high heels, and an oversized hat adorned with tropical fruits. United Fruit's decision to "transgender" their icon is not surprising given the immense popularity enjoyed by another woman often associated with bananas during the 1940s: Carmen Miranda.

Dubbed the "Brazilian Bombshell" by the U.S. media, the Portuguese-born Miranda took both Broadway and Hollywood by storm during World War II.[3] The bananas that often dominated the sets of her musical numbers provided a visual association between her "hot" rhythms and a sensual—yet never quite locatable—tropical region. Nothing conveyed this more explicitly than Busby Berkeley's 1943 Hollywood musical *The Gang's*

*A new easy way
to cook bananas*

BAKED BANANAS
IN THE PEEL

4 firm bananas*
1½ tablespoons melted butter
    or margarine
Salt

Use all-yellow or slightly green-tipped bananas

Cut off the tips of both ends of each banana.
Remove a lengthwise section of the peel, about
1 inch wide, extending from end to end. Brush
exposed portion of the pulp with butter or
margarine and sprinkle lightly with salt. Place
into baking dish. Bake in a moderate oven
(375°F.) 15 to 20 minutes, or until peels are
dark and bananas are tender . . . easily pierced
with a fork. Serve hot as a vegetable.
Four servings.

*IMPORTANT: When browning is desired, place
the baked bananas under broiler heat about 1 to
2 minutes.*

HAM BANANA ROLLS

With Cheese Sauce

4 thin slices boiled ham
Prepared mustard
4 firm bananas*
1½ tablespoons melted butter or
    margarine
Cheese Sauce

Use all-yellow or slightly green-tipped bananas

Spread each slice of ham lightly with mustard.
Peel bananas. Wrap a slice of the prepared ham
around each banana. Brush tips of bananas with
butter or margarine. Place Ham Banana Rolls
into a greased shallow baking dish, and
pour Cheese Sauce over them. Bake in a
moderate oven (350°F.) 30 minutes, or until
bananas are tender . . . easily pierced with a
fork. Serve hot with the Cheese Sauce from the
baking dish. Four servings.

Cheese Sauce

1½ tablespoons butter or margarine
1½ tablespoons flour
¾ cup milk
1½ cups grated sharp American cheese

Melt butter or margarine in saucepan; add flour
and stir until smooth. Stir in milk slowly. Add
cheese and cook, stirring constantly until sauce
is smooth and thickened.
Makes about 1 cup sauce.

3

FIGURE 6.1. Chiquita Banana's Recipe Book. *New York: United Fruit Company, 1956.*

All Here, in which Carmen Miranda sang "The Lady in the Tutti-Frutti Hat" while a chorus of women straddled oversized strawberries and bananas. Miranda infused her performances with a humor that undercut the sexual tension created by her performances and ensured that neither she nor the banana would threaten the moral standards of the era. The light-skinned Miranda brought a nonthreatening form of tropical exoticism to the North American stage and screen through her costumes (including her signature headwear based loosely on styles worn by Bahian market women), her music (samba rhythms performed by Brazilian musicians), and her often amusing (and calculated) mix of Portuguese and English. Both Carmen Miranda and the banana became popular culture icons of the sexy and the comic, a combination that does much to explain their broad popularity.

The commercial success enjoyed by Carmen Miranda was also linked to changes in U.S. policy toward Latin America. Seeking both to neutralize German influence in the region and to ensure access to strategic raw materials, President Franklin Delano Roosevelt promoted a "Good Neighbor" policy toward Latin America. The United States pledged to end military interventions and to strengthen economic and cultural ties in the hemisphere. As part of its World War II propaganda campaign, the U.S. government enlisted prominent Hollywood motion picture studios to produce movies that depicted the people of the Americas united in the struggle against Nazi Germany.[4] Carmen Miranda's films, including *The Gang's All Here, Down Argentine Way, Weekend in Havana,* and *That Night in Rio,* became the vehicles through which Fox Studios imagined the hemisphere's harmonious relations. In the opening scene of *The Gang's All Here,* Miranda appears alongside a ship, the S.S. *Brazil,* performing the "Uncle Sam-ba" while stevedores unload Latin America's quintessential agroexport products: coffee, fruit, and sugar.[5] How audiences in the United States received such less-than-subtle messages is hard to say, but Miranda's extremely popular movies (the opening of *Weekend in Havana* outsold *Citizen Kane*) attempted to present a Latin America that was both sensuous and a "good neighbor."[6]

These were the cultural and geopolitical contexts in which United Fruit registered "Chiquita Banana" as a trademark in 1947. Shortly thereafter, some U.S. wholesalers sought to capitalize on the logo's high profile by placing colored bands with the name "Chiquita" around consumer-sized units of bananas in retail outlets.[7] United Fruit officials noted that banded fruit was well suited for self-service supermarkets, but they were slow to exploit Chiquita's potential marketing value. For the most part, the company's advertising campaigns of the 1950s updated well-worn themes that encouraged consumers to eat more bananas, or borrowed from in-vogue modernization discourses to call attention to United Fruit's role in bringing greater prosperity to the Americas. United Fruit's marketing strategy would undergo a transition in the early 1960s as part of a larger company makeover in response to a set of political, economic, and agro-ecological changes that left the company with historically low profits at the end of the 1950s. Not surprisingly, in the scramble to reinvent the company's image, United Fruit executives would turn to Miss Chiquita for help.

At the same time that the Chiquita banana song was filling the air-waves across the United States, Panama disease continued its silent in-vasion of export banana farms in Honduras. Between 1939 and 1948, the Tela Railroad Company lost more than 6,700 hectares of banana farms. The rate of abandonment accelerated over the next five years (1949–53) when the company removed more than 9,600 hectares from production.[8] Compounding the problem of rising rates of Panama disease incidence was the diminishing amount of prime banana soils on the North Coast. In 1946, nine farms occupying some 3,200 hectares of "freshly-cleared jungle land not previously cultivated" were in "various stages of development."[9] Although appreciable, the new farms could not make up for land that United Fruit had already abandoned and the prospect of obtaining for-ested lands in the future was dim. Consequently, the company increasingly turned its attention to areas considered marginal for export banana cul-tivation, including extensive wetlands lying between the lower portions of the Ulúa and Chamelecón rivers. The "land reclamation" projects used an extensive series of dykes and spillways to divert the rivers' flood waters to swamps where the silt-laden water slowed, and solid particles settled, eventually forming a layer of soil in which Gros Michel bananas could be planted.[10]

One of the largest silting projects undertaken by the company in the mid-1940s was a 4,500-hectare site appropriately named El Pantano ("The Swamp"). Workers erected levees—the longest of which extended almost five miles—that were capable of holding water to a depth of twelve feet. In 1947, workers drained the land with the aid of turbine-driven pumps that both removed standing water and ensured that groundwater did not rise to unacceptable levels (not an easy task in a lowland area situated be-tween two rivers and subject to heavy rains during the wet season).[11] The El Pantano project and others like it demonstrated United Fruit's engi-neering prowess but also the rising inputs—and concomitant increase in

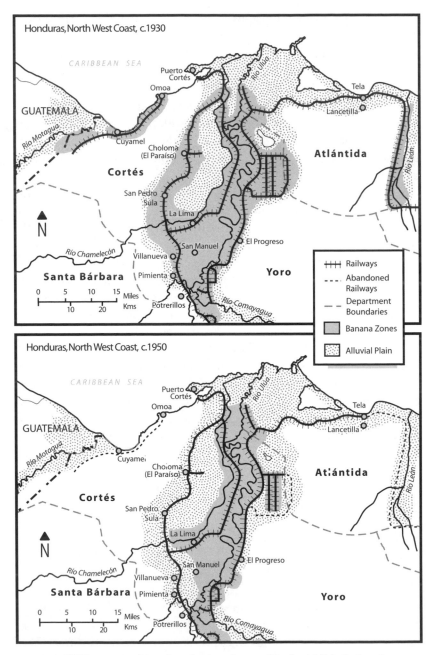

MAP 6.1. *Shifting geographies of production, Cuyamel Fruit and Tela Railroad Company between 1930 and 1950*

FIGURE 6.2. *Aerial view of Sula valley showing drainage canals built by United Fruit (1949). United Fruit Company Photograph Collection. Baker Library, Harvard Business School.*

costs — associated with growing bananas in the Sula valley at mid-century. Of course, such projects could only be carried out by businesses with hefty amounts of capital at their disposal; in 1949, "more and more" non-company banana farms were being abandoned and/or converted to other crops on account of plant diseases.[12]

The soil-building projects yielded an unexpected benefit: scientists observed that soils infected with Panama disease produced "first class" fruit for a number of years after having accumulated several rainy seasons' worth of silt. This observation inspired United Fruit's Dr. Vining Dunlap to begin a series of experiments in 1939 aimed at reclaiming Panama disease-infected soils.[13] Dunlap and his assistants temporarily transformed diseased banana farms into shallow lake beds that were filled

FIGURE 6.3. *Aerial view of United Fruit plantation under flood fallow (1949). United Fruit Company Photograph Collection. Baker Library, Harvard Business School.*

with water. After a period ranging from three to eighteen months, workers drained and replanted the land with disease-free rhizome materials. In 1942, Dunlap reported that his "flood-fallowing" technique was showing "some success."[14] Five years later, the company had more than 4,000 hectares in various stages of flood fallowing. The early success of the experiments, combined with the accelerated spread of Panama disease entering the 1950s, made "all the more urgent" the need for "extensive flood fallowing operations."[15] By 1953, company workers had flood-fallowed and replanted some 5,700 hectares of land in the Sula valley.

Standard Fruit Company executives also faced the dilemma of dwindling soil resources in Honduras. In 1941, the company possessed some 25,000 hectares of abandoned banana and coconut lands.[16] By that point, Standard Fruit was in the process of shifting its production to the upper Aguán valley where it established offices, workshops, and worker housing in Coyoles, a short distance from Olanchito. Mulling over future planting projects in a 1941 memorandum, general manager A. J. Chute wrote, "There is not enough good land at Olanchito for us to be justified in passing any of it up."[17] The company began buying small and large properties in order to create contiguous blocks of land with soils suitable for banana cultivation. Between 1935 and 1945, company workers planted nearly 4,900 hectares of new banana farms in the area, while abandoning nearly 1,300 hectares following the spread of Panama disease.[18] During the mid-1940s, long-time company employee John Miceli engaged in protracted negotiations with local landowners in order to acquire "everything plantable south of the Aguán River."[19] In late October 1945, Miceli wrote triumphantly that he had succeeded in his mission: "I told you I would get the lands on the south side of Aguán River and I got them. I could have gotten through much quicker if I would have paid the price they asked and [was] authorized to pay but I wouldn't. As it is, in spite of the price they asked at first, I do not believe that all this land has cost the company more than 25 dollars per acre [$61.75 per hectare]."[20] Miceli managed to piece together a 2,200-hectare block of land on the south bank of the Aguán that he anticipated would take care of the company's land needs for five years.

Local climatic conditions complicated Standard's efforts to expand rapidly. Because the upper Aguán lies in a rain-shadow created by the Nombre de Diós mountains that lie to the north, the region has a pronounced dry season. Export banana farms therefore required heavy irrigation that both taxed the valley's water resources and elevated production costs.[21] For example, in 1946, a Standard Fruit official reported that an 800 hectare block of land could not be planted due to "insufficient water"; existing farms were already taking all of the available water from the Aguán River.[22] Company records from that year indicate that installing and operating an overhead irrigation system represented more than forty percent of the total costs associated with creating a banana farm in the region.[23]

In addition to diverting the flow of the Aguán River for irrigation needs, Standard Fruit also took advantage of the region's forests. Beginning in the 1940s, the company tried to reduce wind-related losses by supporting the banana plants with *varas,* or wooden stakes. Logging contractors extracted hardwoods, including oak, mahogany, and guaruma, from the mountains that surrounded Standard Fruit's Coyoles farms.[24] Working in teams, fieldhands dug holes into which they placed a *vara* alongside plants bearing heavy bunches. A *vara* typically lasted four or five harvests before being replaced, provided that it was not stolen by workers for firewood. Former Standard Fruit researcher Henry Muery recalled that his company experimented with bamboo props as early as 1951, but continued to harvest *varas* from mountain forests and Tiki wood from marshes on the island of Utila into the 1970s.[25] The company also established Eucalyptus plantations near its Coyoles operations. The Tela Railroad Company used bamboo for propping. The fruit companies' combined use of *varas* easily ran into the tens of thousands per year, a significant, if seldom-considered impact of export banana production on surrounding ecosystems.[26]

New soils, irrigation, and propping could help to boost yields, but they did little to impede the spread of Panama disease in the Aguán valley. Consequently, Standard Fruit experimented with the Tela Railroad Company's flood fallowing technique. In January 1947, Standard Fruit's top executives unanimously agreed to lease about 7,500 hectares of national lands on the north side of the Aguán River.[27] The properties, previously cultivated and abandoned by the Truxillo Railroad Company, were considered to be the only place in the valley with sufficient water to undertake large-scale flood fallowing. Standard's general manager A. J. Chute considered the project's completion, whose estimated cost was 500,000 dollars, to be "imperative."[28] However, when the press in Tegucigalpa published news of the company's planned acquisition, President Carías received a number of telegrams and petitions from residents in the region protesting the proposed deal. Coming in the midst of an election year — in which a formidable opposition was forming for first time in more than a decade — Carías suspended negotiations with the company.

Alarmed Standard Fruit officials sent a representative to meet with the President in the hope that the reason for the delay was "a nonpolitical one" that "with money . . . could be adjusted."[29] The company was prepared to pay as much as one hundred thousand dollars [in bribes] in order to secure the land. During an hour-long meeting with President Carías, Standard Fruit's spokesperson stressed that Panama disease was rapidly infecting the company's farms in Olanchito and that the company was prepared to invest half a million dollars in order to restore the previously abandoned lands. He also noted that the region was filled with "ghost towns" that would be revitalized if banana farms and rail service returned. The lobbying efforts apparently paid off because two years later, a U.S. consular official reported that Standard Fruit was going to spend nearly $5 million over a five-year period preparing dykes in preparation for flooding.[30] Operations were scheduled to get underway in 1950. However, Henry Muery, who joined Standard Fruit's recently established research department in 1951 to work on flood fallowing experiments, recalled that the company halted the project after having constructed only a few lakes due to the high costs incurred.[31] Standard Fruit's foray into flood fallowing illustrated how agroecological change limited its power: the company managed to wrangle land concessions from the national government, but the capital needed to turn Panama-diseased soils into productive export banana farms prevented the company from transforming its political influence into profits.

Political changes in Honduras and elsewhere further complicated matters for the fruit companies. Following the defeat of fascist regimes in World War II, authoritarian governments in Central America came under internal and external pressures to democratize political institutions. In 1948, faced with growing opposition led by university students and radical Liberal party factions, President Carías stepped down from power after ruling Honduras for sixteen years, paving the way for his vice-president and former United Fruit Company lawyer, Juan Manual Gálvez, to assume the presidency.[32] The following year, university students and others openly protested the terms of a concession sought by United Fruit, a clear signal that the fruit companies' influence in Tegucigalpa was waning. In 1950, President Gálvez signed legislation creating a 15-percent income tax on the banana companies' in-country earnings. Five years later, the national government raised the tax rate to 30 percent. At the same time, the Honduran state began promoting cattle, coffee, and cotton exports in order to diversify the national economy and lessen its dependence on banana exports for revenue.[33]

The Gálvez administration also initiated labor reforms at a time when both the U.S. State Department and the American Federation of Labor (AFL) were pressuring Central American governments to promote the formation of anti-communist trade unions. In 1950, Gálvez signed an Organization of American States (OAS) charter pledging to defend workers' right to associate. Two years later, the Honduran congress created the Bureau of Labor and Social Welfare in order to implement reform measures that included shortening the work day, restricting the use of child labor, and creating worker compensation. Ex-fieldhand Francisco Portillo recalled the joy with which workers greeted the eight-hour day: "I was working in irrigation. We usually left the fields really late. Then one day, another crew showed up to relieve us. It was two in the afternoon. We all stood in the field shouting, "Viva Juan Manual Gálvez!"[34] According to historian Darío Euraque, that was precisely the type of reaction that the government hoped to elicit. Gálvez did not envision his reforms as stepping stones leading to the formation of powerful unions, "but rather as part of a state apparatus that would serve to mediate labor disputes."[35]

However, communist organizers (including writer Ramón Amaya Amador), radical Liberal party members, and activist workers had ideas of their own. The Comité Coordinador Obrero (Workers' Coordinating Committee, CCO) formed in 1950 with the intention of organizing Honduran mining, factory, and agricultural workers. The CCO, along with the Partido Democrático Revolucionario Hondureño (PDRH) began publishing underground newspapers that circulated widely on the North Coast.[36] In April 1954, Tela Railroad Company dock workers walked off the job after the company refused to pay them overtime for working on Easter Sunday (as stipulated by Gálvez's reform legislation). Shortly thereafter, nurses and other employees of the company's hospital in Tela presented management with a list of demands that the two sides swiftly resolved. A few days later, dock workers, machinists, and other company employees went on strike in Puerto Cortés. When police authorities detained a pair of strike leaders, a mass protest by workers succeeded in winning their unconditional release. May Day celebrations in El Progreso and La Lima drew several thousand people who turned out to express their support for the striking dock workers. Two days later, the entire work force of the Tela Railroad Company's El Progreso division walked off the job. They were soon joined by thousands of coworkers in La Lima, Puerto Cortés, and Tela. Within a week, some 15,000 Standard Fruit Company laborers also went on strike. For the first time since 1932, a general strike paralyzed export banana production on the North Coast.[37]

The striking United Fruit workers demanded wage increases, improved medical care, paid vacation time, housing for all workers, free schooling for employees' children, and the provision of protective work clothing, among other things. Standard Fruit's employees sought the immediate dismissal of three company administrators, a fifty percent, across-the-board wage hike, paid vacations, and other benefits. A government-appointed mediator succeeded in bringing the Standard Fruit strike to a relatively swift conclusion when the company consented to both make modest wage increases and replace the three administrators named in the strikers' petition. However, some workers rejected the settlement and remained on strike until the government intervened. The Tela Railroad Company strike lasted sixty-nine days before the two sides reached an agreement following the intervention of President Gálvez, the development of deep fissures among the workers' leaders, and the U.S.-supported arrest of strike organizers with ties to communist organizations and the PDRH. Workers won modest increases in wages and benefits. More importantly, the Tela Railroad Company agreed to recognize collective bargaining units. Shortly thereafter, labor leaders created the Tela Railroad Company Workers' Union (SITRATERCO).

Both Gálvez and the U.S. State Department insinuated that the Guatemalan government under the leadership of Jacobo Arbenz helped to foment the strike, but workers received far more support from San Pedro Sula's business leaders than from communist-influenced foreign governments. In fact, the U.S.-orchestrated overthrow of the Arbenz government notwithstanding, the events of 1954 ultimately served to weaken United Fruit's power. In the United States, the Department of Justice's anti-trust division opened an inquiry into the company's marketing practices. In Honduras, the candidate of the resurgent Liberal Party, Ramón Villeda Morales won a plurality—but not a majority—of the votes in the election that followed in the aftermath of the strike. In the absence of clear majority, Julio Lozano Díaz, vice-president under Gálvez, assumed dictatorial powers. Lozano Díaz's government promulgated a Charter of Labor Rights that guaranteed workers the right to collective bargaining, legalized about fifty unions, and recognized the right to strike.[38]

Coming only seven years after the end of the sixteen-year Cariato, the legislation marked both the growing power of pro-labor Liberal party leaders and the reluctant acknowledgement on the part of some National party leaders that in the rapidly shifting geopolitical contexts of the Cold War, the United States frowned upon the repression of anti-communist labor organizations. Villeda Morales at last assumed the presidency in 1957, following the overthrow of Lozano Díaz in 1956 by Colonel Oswaldo López Arellano. The armed forces' motives for the coup were multiple, but by forcing the discredited Lozano Díaz out of office, the coup leaders created an opening for the increasingly popular Liberal party to come to power. During the presidency of Villeda Morales (1957–1963) the previously marginalized voices of workers and small-scale farmers resonated loudly, expanding the boundaries of political discourse in Honduran society and reshaping state-led development projects. In 1959, the Villeda Morales administration created the Institute of Social Security (1959) and promulgated a new national labor code (1959). Three years later, the Honduran government approved agrarian reform legislation.

Unsurprisingly, the U.S. banana companies did not stand still in the wake of the profound changes that took place between the end of World War II and the early 1960s. In Honduras, the companies reacted to the rising power of organized labor by finding ways to reduce the size of their work forces. Under the terms of the strike settlement, the company promised not to take reprisals against strike leaders, but it reserved the right to transfer and/or release workers for "general economic reasons, acts of God, and unforeseeable events."[39] Company executives must have prayed hard because two months after the strike concluded, severe flooding wiped out thousands of hectares of bananas in the Sula valley. The company responded by dismissing some 3,000 workers in November 1954, striking a blow to the fledgling Tela Railroad Company Workers Union.

SITRATERCO officials reported to the press that they had convinced company management to refrain from laying off an additional 7,000 employees, but a company-issued statement only acknowledged that management had agreed to keep the number of firings to the "fewest possible."[40] A U.S. embassy official reported that rank-and-file members were upset over the inability of union leaders to prevent mass layoffs. The Tela Railroad Company made small severance payments to dismissed workers and allowed them to cultivate crops on company lands that lay fallow. In addition, the Honduran government requested relief supplies from the United States and organized an emergency public works program that provided highway-building jobs for laid-off banana workers. However, a U.S. official warned that any long-term solution to the unemployment problem would remain out of reach until the company "settles the basic question of whether operations will be built up again to 'normal' or pre-flood levels, or will be resumed on permanently lower levels."[41]

An answer came two years later when the Tela Railroad Company organized a tour of its rehabilitated operations for representatives of Honduran banks, commercial establishments, industry, and the national press. Company officials explained that the spread of Panama disease, combined with market demand for "high quality" fruit, reduced the viability of recuperating "marginal lands." Consequently, the area under production would never again equal pre-1954 levels, nor would the company "maintain as many employees as in the past."[42] This proved to be an understatement: between 1953 and 1957, the Tela Railroad Company slashed its Honduran payroll nearly in half (from about 26,000 to just over 13,000 workers) while land under active banana cultivation declined from some 16,000 hectares to 11,300 hectares between 1953 and 1959.[43] The number of employees hired by United Fruit fell to a low of 8,800 persons in 1961. Standard Fruit's response to the 1954 strike was equally dramatic: after expanding both its banana plantings and its workforce in the early 1950s, the company cut its payroll from 13,000 to 9,000 between 1954 and 1955. Entering the 1960s, the company employed fewer than 5,800 persons.[44] Standard's payroll continued to diminish through 1967, when it dipped below the 5,000 mark.

The fruit companies pursued two basic strategies for cutting jobs: contracting out labor-intensive production processes and investing in labor-saving technologies. Efforts to shift production to non-company farms actually began prior to the 1954 strike, coincident with the Gálvez administration's labor reforms. In 1952, the Tela Railroad Company established an "associate growers' program" that provided one hundred former company employees with twenty hectares of land each in El Higuerito, an area that lay to the south of the company's La Lima headquarters. The associate growers, who assumed responsibility for managing the labor-intensive tasks of planting, weeding, and harvesting, consented to sell their bananas exclusively to the Tela Railroad Company at prices set by the latter. Under the terms of the contract, the company agreed to install drainage, irrigation, and road infrastructure; operate irrigation and Sigatoka control systems; and coordinate daily cultivation activities through a central office in La Lima. The company promised to transfer the property titles to individual growers upon recovering its investment.[45]

Former Tela Railroad Company District Superintendent Camilo Rivera Girón recalled that the national press generally opposed the El Higuerito project because it provided the company with the means to "alleviate itself of its responsibilities [to the workers]."[46] As part of an effort to sway public opinion, Rivera Girón led newspaper reporters on a tour of El Higuerito in order to demonstrate the project's merits. But, newspaper editorial boards were not the only ones with reservations about the associate grower projects. SITRATERCO officials argued that the program would depress wages. In October 1957, a group of Bordeaux sprayers and other workers from the El Higuerito farms joined SITRATERCO in order to defend themselves against what the union's newspaper termed "wide-spread and capricious firings."[47] Four months later, SITRATERCO representative Pastor Zúniga Ramírez complained that the company was unjustly dismissing workers in El Higuerito. Company management denied the accusation, stating that those fired were employees of associate growers. However, the El Higuerito growers contended that they only hired harvesting and weeding crews. In 1958, SITRATERCO declared that the company "directly contracted" the laborers who worked in irrigation, Sigatoka control, and fertilizer application on the associate grower farms. On paydays, the union asserted, "these workers present pay stubs created in the offices of the company to the associate grower . . . often, this is the only contact that the grower has with the workers."[48]

Union opposition failed to deter the company from expanding its associate grower programs. In May 1958, four former *mandadores* signed leases with the Tela Railroad Company for 120-hectare lots in San Manuel, a municipality that lay to the south of the company's La Lima headquarters.[49] The terms of the leases were very similar to those found in the El Higuerito contracts: the company agreed to install plantation infrastructure in return for exclusive rights to purchase export-quality fruit grown by the lessees. The San Manuel growers assumed responsibility for all aspects of production with the notable exception of Sigatoka control which remained in the hands of the company. In 1960, the Tela Railroad Company initiated two additional associate grower projects involving eight former high-level Honduran employees and more than 800 hectares of land in the Sula valley.[50] That same year, Thomas Sunderland, the newly installed president of United Fruit, told shareholders that their company's "future" lay in associate producer programs.[51] In 1961, the company spent approximately one million dollars on disease control, irrigation, and fertilizer inputs on more than one hundred associate grower farms in Honduras. That year, associate producers sold more than two million bunches of bananas to the company.[52]

Company managers did not publicly state their long-term objectives for the associate growers program in Honduras, but in private conversations held separately with Honduran and U.S. government officials in 1960, they confirmed that they were seeking to get out of banana farming. One U.S. official reported that Honduran President Villeda Morales received the news like a "body blow." At least one member of congress called for the immediate nationalization of company properties and railroads.[53] No expropriations took place, but pressure from organized labor prompted Villeda Morales to order the extension of several clauses in SITRATERCO's contract, including those related to minimum wages, holidays, medical benefits, and housing, to "all farms in the Tela RR Company's zone and to future entities who may acquire lands of the company."[54] This measure notwithstanding, SITRATERCO's leadership continued to criticize both the "poor prices" paid to associate growers for their bananas, and a clause in associate grower contracts that prohibited producers from selling fruit rejected by company inspectors to other buyers. Such measures, the union claimed, tended to drive down the wages paid to fieldworkers.[55]

Camilo Rivera Girón became an associate grower in 1960 after working for many years for the Tela Railroad Company. Rivera Girón recalled being at the company's mercy: "The Tela's fruit inspectors would arrive and say 'this bunch is not good, that one is no good' — but what were we going to do? There wasn't any other buyer." He recalled that the wages paid to workers on associate grower farms were "about half" of those paid by the company. In addition, associate growers did not provide workers with the housing and medical benefits enjoyed by the company's unionized workers.[56] For Rivera Girón, the Tela Railroad Company's use of associate growers was a clear response to the growing power of organized labor: "When they [company management] gave the workers better wages, they had to reduce the personnel so that their profits would remain the same, right? They had to lay off people so that the fixed costs—the costs of administration and labor—would be lower and employee productivity higher."[57]

If in retrospect Rivera Girón viewed the fruit company's cutbacks as a logical business decision, he was less sanguine about the threat of layoffs when he served as Governor of Cortés in the early 1960s. Following the Tela Railroad Company's announcement that it was suspending investments in Honduras in protest over proposed land reform measures, Rivera Girón complained to a U.S. official that the company's action was a crude attempt at blackmail that undermined the spirit of President John Kennedy's Alliance for Progress. Girón was not the only one upset with United Fruit; U.S. consul Robert Ashford received a "barrage of complaints" from "friendly sources," who expressed "amazement" that the U.S. government could not more effectively control the actions of the fruit company.[58] Ultimately, both land reform legislation and the associate grower program (which meshed nicely with Alliance for Progress approaches to poverty reduction) proceeded ahead. Entering the 1970s, United Fruit's associate producers cultivated around 3,100 hectares of bananas in Honduras.[59]

Standard Fruit began laying the groundwork for an "Independent Planter Program" (IPP) in 1965. The move came one year after the San Francisco-based Castle and Cook Corporation acquired a controlling interest in the company.[60] Castle and Cook executives favored freeing up the company's capital by finding Honduran investors to grow bananas. The IPP bore a strong resemblance to United Fruit's associate producers program: Standard Fruit planned to assist growers by securing bank loans, providing technological inputs, and serving as the exclusive market outlet. Company officials predicted that the initiative would double the company's existing acreage and create 6,000 new jobs over a two-year period. Not surprisingly, union officials opposed the IPP on the grounds that the "independent" planters would not be bound by the terms of collective bargaining agreements between the union and the company. Standard Fruit officials countered this criticism by asserting that growers would be able to pay union wages and make a profit. However, U.S. State Department officials doubted this claim, noting that existing non-company growers tended to pay about one-half the minimum wages paid by the fruit companies.[61] In order to weaken union opposition, Standard Fruit included a clause in the 1965 labor contract that established an incentive system for employees based on the total number of bunches shipped from its Honduran division regardless of whether the fruit came from a company-run farm. This apparently swayed many of Standard Fruit's employees — a majority of whom did not work in harvesting operations — who came to view the union's opposition to the IPP as preventing them from earning extra pay.[62] After a modest beginning in 1966, the Independent Planter Program grew swiftly: in 1971, IPP farms occupied approximately 3,800 hectares.[63]

Contracting out banana production enabled the fruit companies to cut labor costs, but it did not resolve the problems posed by Panama disease. Running low on both disease-free soils and facing an uncertain political climate following the 1954 strike, Standard Fruit's management abandoned efforts to undertake capital-intensive flood fallowing in favor of renewing the search for a pathogen-resistant banana to replace Gros Michel. At some point during the early 1940s, Standard imported Bout Rond plants from Puerto Rico and Giant Cavendish from Santos, Brazil, along with the IC 2, a hybrid created by British breeders at the Imperial College of Tropical Agriculture that resisted both Panama and Sigatoka pathogens.[64] In 1944, Standard began small commercial shipments of the IC 2 hybrid variety. Exports peaked in 1950 (less than 0.5 million bunches) but the company discontinued IC 2 production four years later due to the variety's relatively low yields and short-fingered fruit.[65] Standard's first planting of Giant Cavendish (a modest 40 hectares) took place in 1943.[66] Shortly thereafter, the company began intercropping Bout Rond bananas among diseased Gros Michel plants so that as the latter went out of production, the former would serve as a replacement. General Manager Chute described both Bout Rond and Giant Cavendish as "fine, large bananas, resistant to Panama disease."[67] However, the fruit bunches did not ripen in the same manner as Gros Michel fruit. Bout Rond and Giant Cavendish required storage temperatures between 60 and 75 degrees Fahrenheit and exposure to ethylene gas in order to ripen "properly." Chute therefore initially discouraged selling Bout Rond and Giant Cavendish bananas to dealers who would not ripen them "in the proper manner."

By 1953, more than 3,200 hectares of Bout Rond were in bearing.[68] Three years later, Standard Fruit elected to convert all of its production to Giant Cavendish because it out-yielded Bout Rond and possessed greater resistance to wind damage ("Giant Cavendish" was a misnomer; the plant was shorter than either Gros Michel or Bout Rond). The company sold its Cavendish fruit under the trade name "Golden Beauty." As had been the case in the 1920s with Lacatan bananas, the new variety met with considerable resistance from U.S. fruit distributors who complained that the thin-skinned Cavendish was highly susceptible to bruising and scarring while in transit from farm to retail market. As late as 1955, studies of banana jobbers indicated that "the quality and appearance of the fruit" was a "major determinant" of the profitability of their businesses.[69] Gros Michel remained the banana of choice for most fruit dealers, who tended to refer to all other bananas simply as "varieties," a lack of specificity that reflected the extent to which jobbers considered Gros Michel to be without peer.

As the 1950s came to a close, Standard's non–Gros Michel exports suffered a high rate of rejection and discounting.[70] In 1958, the company's public relations department published a statement in a Honduran newspaper claiming that U.S. wholesalers complained about the appearance, shape, and ripening characteristics of Giant Cavendish fruit. The company added, "It's widely known that when there is an abundance of Gros Michel fruit, as was the case in 1957, the price of the Giant Cavendish falls dramatically."[71] Several months later, Standard Fruit published another statement claiming that market prices for Giant Cavendish continued to be low and that the company's Honduran division was losing money.[72] Both statements appeared during a period of labor unrest and probably were intended to convince the Honduran public that the claims of striking workers were unreasonable. But they also reflected the continued resistance of market structures to non-Gros Michel bananas.

In 1957, Standard Fruit erected an experimental banana packing plant in Honduras. Workers de-stemmed, washed, and selected hands of bananas before packing the fruit in cardboard boxes. The idea of the experiment was to cut down on the number of times that the delicate Cavendish fruit had to be handled prior to reaching retail markets. After two years of trial marketing in urban areas in the United States, company officials announced in 1960 that they were on the verge of "the greatest innovation in the history of the banana industry—precooled, plantation boxing."[73] In fact, the idea of packing bananas in boxes was far from revolutionary; Standard Fruit had experimented with exporting boxed bananas in the early 1930s. Driven in part by the growth of self-serve supermarkets, fruit jobbers in the United States began to deliver bananas to retail outlets in boxes before World War II. By the mid-1950s, jobbers cut, packed, and weighed virtually all of the bananas that they handled.[74] Not surprisingly, Standard Fruit officials reported that retailers were "unanimous" in their approval of boxed bananas because they were well suited for self-service supermarkets that by 1960 accounted for about 75 percent of food sales in the United States. That year, Standard Fruit introduced consumers to boxed "Cabana" bananas.[75]

United Fruit continued to grow and export Gros Michel fruit through 1960, but tensions were growing between the company's research staff and top-level management over how to resolve the Panama disease problem. In 1957 United Fruit's top scientists gathered in Palo Alto, California to develop a long-range research agenda. The company's research director, Dr. Jesse E. Hobson, opened the meetings by stating that "a major problem" facing the company was the rising cost of production. He noted that plant diseases were largely responsible for the trend: "Panama disease is costing millions of dollars per year. Sigatoka is costing millions more per year to control."[76] In addition, the company was annually abandoning around 2,000 hectares of land throughout its far-flung tropical operations. Flood fallowing accounted for about 50 percent of the company's Honduran production, an indication of the shrinking amount of disease-free soils in the Sula valley. The staff scientists and consultants assembled in Palo Alto concluded that United Fruit was "running out of land" and that the company would no longer be able "to avoid problems by moving to new land."[77] Two years later, Dr. Robert Stover, writing in the research department's newsletter, called banana breeding "the only hopeful long-term approach to the solution of the banana disease problem."[78] On a short-term basis, some company scientists believed that the Lacatan banana, which the company was already producing in Jamaica for European markets, should be planted on abandoned farms.[79]

However, United Fruit's top executives remained reluctant to replace Gros Michel as late as 1959. Jesse Hobson believed that management's lack of interest in solving the Panama disease problem could be traced to former company president Samuel Zemurray who considered the pathogen to be a "blessing" to the company that helped to limit competition.[80] However, there is little evidence to substantiate this claim and much circumstantial evidence—including the company's long-term investments in research on Panama disease—against it. The complacency of Zemurray and other "banana men" was more likely rooted in their perceptions of U.S. markets. Thomas McCann, who began working for the company in 1953, recalled that "the old-timers swore by all they held sacred that there was just no way to replace it [Gros Michel], that anything else would be thrown out of the markets, that nothing would grow on our plantations except 'Big Mike.'"[81] But the banana trade familiar to the "old timers" had all but ceased to exist by the late 1950s. In 1952, Ecuador passed Hon-

FIGURE 6.4. *Banana farm with Panama disease (1955). Note irregular pattern of highly infected areas. In the foreground is a model United Fruit banana labor camp. United Fruit Company Photograph Collection. Baker Library, Harvard Business School.*

duras as the world's leading banana exporter. By the end of the decade, 40 percent of U.S. banana imports came from Ecuador's Panama disease–free soils.[82] The result was a glut of inexpensively produced bananas at a time when production costs were on the rise in Honduras and both per capita consumption and the average retail price of bananas in the United States were flat.[83] Between 1950 and 1960, United Fruit's earnings fell precipitously from $66 million to $2 million; share prices plummeted from $70 to $15 over the same period.

To make matters worse for United Fruit, the anti-trust investigation initiated by the U.S. Department of Justice in 1954 concluded in 1958 when company officials signed a consent decree in which they agreed to sell off the company's Guatemalan assets.[84] That same year Samuel Zemurray—the quintessential "banana man"—resigned as Chairman of United Fruit's board of directors. Thomas Jefferson Coolidge (a direct descendant of Thomas Jefferson) succeeded Zemurray for one year before being replaced by forty-year-old George Peabody Gardner. With profits and stock values plummeting, Gardner began to "clean house," forcing out long-time executives including CEO Kenneth Redmond and Almyr Bump, vice-president of agricultural operations.[85] In 1958, Gardner hired Thomas Sunderland to be the company's president. Sunderland, who had previously served as vice president and general counsel for Standard Oil of Indiana, was an industry outsider who had made his reputation handling antitrust litigation, not bananas. He quickly moved to reduce United Fruit's operating costs both in the U.S. and the tropics. Noting that the annual cost ($18 million) of replacing Panama disease-infected farms throughout Latin America was more than four times greater than the estimated annual costs ($4 million) of converting to pathogen-resistant varieties, Sunderland gave the go-ahead for a conversion to Cavendish bananas.[86]

In 1959, United Fruit's research division added a "Plant Breeding and Genetics" department.[87] The company enlisted botanists Paul Allen and J. J. Ochse to travel to Southeast Asia in order to expand the genetic resources available for banana breeding.[88] Both the United States Department of Agriculture and the State Department provided logistical support for the expeditions, the first of their kind carried out by the company since Otto Reinking's work in the 1920s. Allen and Ochse sought out both varieties of *Musa* whose fruits resembled Gros Michel (i.e., seedless triploids) and those likely to possess disease resistance (including seeded diploid varieties). In other words, the botanical missions sought to collect a wider range of *Musa* specimens—including uncultivated varieties—than had previously been assembled. United Fruit's new-found interest in diploid plants reflected important changes in approaches to banana breeding. Observing that seed-bearing diploids tended to possess disease resistance but seldom produced fruits whose shape, size, and color resembled export bananas, British breeders in the 1940s began to develop hybrid diploids with "improved" fruit quality. These "elite" diploid lines were then crossed with Gros Michel.[89] This strategy guided banana-breeding programs in the Caribbean and Central America during the second half of the twentieth century.[90]

With the Southeast Asia expeditions still in the field, researchers in Honduras initiated trials of several cultivars maintained at Lancetilla, the company's experimental garden near Tela.[91] In 1962, the research staff reported that three members of the Cavendish group—Giant Cavendish, Valery, and Grand Nain—were giving "extremely high production." United Fruit test-marketed boxed Valery bananas in the U.S. Midwest and received a favorable consumer response. An independent taste panel found both the flavor and aroma of the Valery to be "distinctly superior" to that of the Gros Michel.[92] By the end of 1963, United Fruit workers had planted nearly 4,400 hectares of Valery bananas and built 29 boxing plants in Honduras.[93] Two years later, virtually all of the company's Central American farms were planted with Panama disease-resistant, Cavendish varieties.[94]

Ironically, banana breeders considered both Giant Cavendish and Valery varieties to be closely related to Lacatan—the cultivar that U.S. mass markets had largely rejected in the 1920s. Yet, by the 1960s, new political and agroecological contexts in Honduras, and the expansion of self-serve supermarkets in the United States enabled boxed Cavendish varieties to become a viable solution to a problem that was more than half a century old. The export banana industry's conversion to Cavendish varieties is noteworthy because in contrast to the history of other major food crops, hybridization did not play a significant role in reshaping production processes following World War II. The varieties that replaced Gros Michel bananas were popular cultivars from South and Southeast Asia. For example, United Fruit's Valery plant stock had been collected by Otto Reinking in the 1920s during his excursion through Saigon (Vietnam). After dramatically reducing the biological diversity of lowland tropical landscapes in Central America for seventy-five years, the export banana industry tapped into the pan-tropical diversity of *Musa* cultivars in order to overcome Panama disease.

The Cavendish era also gave a second life to Miss Chiquita. Under the direction of Thomas Sunderland and Executive Vice-President Jonathan Fox (another industry outsider hired by Sunderland) United Fruit launched new marketing initiatives in conjunction with the conversion to boxed bananas:

Boxing has cleared the way for developments in merchandising which have never been possible before in the banana business. We are now ready to consider changing our business from the sale of a commodity item to the sale of a branded, identifiable item, which, if adopted, will enable us to advertise *our* bananas, instead of bananas generally.[95]

By turning an agricultural commodity into a retail product distinguishable by a brand name, United Fruit hoped to create demand for a "premium" export banana for which it could charge higher prices and recuperate some of the added expenses associated with boxing.[96] The company created a new executive position, Director of Quality Control, that was responsible for setting and maintaining quality standards. In 1963, United Fruit launched a multi-million dollar advertising campaign in order to promote its new product. Company officials chose "Chiquita" for the brand name after marketing surveys revealed that consumer recognition of "Miss Chiquita" remained extremely high (surpassed only by Elsie, the Borden cow, according to one trade journal).[97] Workers in packing plants began placing blue and gold stickers on retail units of bananas that featured a Mirandaesque figure wearing a fruit-laden hat and the word "Chiquita." Supermarket displays featured oversized versions of the blue and gold icon accompanied by the phrase "This seal outside means the best inside."[98] Once a mere salesgirl, Miss Chiquita was now United Fruit's top banana.

Meanwhile, popular culture in the United States continued to appropriate the banana as an icon for sex and humor. In 1967, national media outlets reported that "hippies" were smoking dried and shredded banana peel fibers. The smoke, dubbed "mellow yellow," reputedly produced hallucinogenic effects similar to LSD. One U.S. congressperson proposed a banana-labeling act in order to halt what he described, tongue-in-cheek, as "an invasion of the fruit stand by a generation of thrill seekers."[99] In fact, the recipe for smoking banana peels started as a satire in the *Berkeley Barb* and was later picked up by other counter-culture periodicals, including the *Village Voice*.[100] Subsequently, the story gave new meanings to British pop singer Donovan's hit tune "Mellow Yellow." However, the humor was lost on straight-laced United Fruit Company officials who, along with the U.S. Food and Drug Administration, conducted laboratory experiments to discredit the notion that burning fruit peels could produce hallucinogenic effects. Counterculture movements of the 1960s also revived the banana as a phallic symbol, most notably in the Andy Warhol–designed jacket for the rock album classic, *The Velvet Underground and Nico*, released by Verve Records in 1967. The cover featured a yellow banana that peeled off to reveal an orange-pink colored fruit that was highly suggestive of a penis. Significantly, during a period when scholars, university

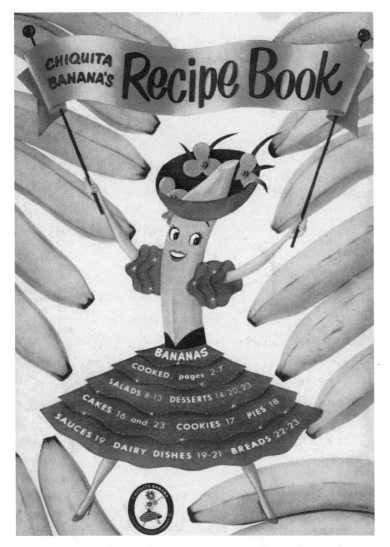

FIGURE 6.5. *United Fruit's "Miss Chiquita" (1956). New York: United Fruit Company, 1956.*

students, and liberal politicians in the United States increasingly criticized their government's foreign policies in Latin America and elsewhere, the banana continued to be appropriated to tease, mock, and arouse in contexts far removed from the places where bananas grew.

United Fruit's advertising campaigns during the 1960s appropriated both turn-of-the-century images of the tropics and elements of contemporary U.S. pop culture, including rock music and bikinis. In 1969, the company sponsored a search in Latin America for two women to be "Señorita Chiquita USA" and "Señorita Chiquita Europe." The winners, Ximena Iragorri of Colombia and Ana María González of Guatemala, were young, petite, and had prior experiences in television and fashion modeling. United Fruit promotional material noted that the two women would "attract lots of attention with their mod banana-looking outfits," that included a "short, flippy little petal dress;" a "floating chiffon dress;" a "banana-kini;" and a "sleek jumpsuit."[101] Company publicity thus portrayed Iragorri and Gonzalez as sexy Latin singles. However, both the cosmopolitan backgrounds of the two women (the trilingual Iragorri had attended a French school in The Hague while Gonzalez learned English in a California high school) and the contest prizes — college scholarships — suggested that both women possessed skills and aspirations that belied the Miss Chiquita image.

Three years later, Miss Chiquita returned to the airwaves in a television commercial featuring Barbara Carrera, a New York–based model and performer who sang a "driving Latin Rock" arrangement of the Chiquita Banana Song:

> I'm Chiquita Banana and I'm back to say
> I am the top banana.
> Chiquita's top banana in the world today.
> There's only one —
> You'll know me when you see me.[102]

The revised lyrics reflected changes in marketing strategies since the 1940s: advice about storing (generic) bananas was replaced by a message that not all bananas were the same: Chiquita fruit was superior to the competition. An article in the company magazine described Carrera as a "vivacious new Miss Chiquita" whose roots were "definitely Latin." Conjuring up the ghost of Carmen Miranda, the company quoted the Nicaraguan-born Carrera as saying "Eef they hadn't chosen me, I would have lost faith in the beezness. I was raised on bananas."[103] As late as the 1970s then, fruit company advertising continued to get mileage out of worn stereotypes of Latin American women. In fact, United Brands' 1972 annual report stated that new advertising campaigns would stress the "nostalgia" of the Chiquita Brand image during an era when anti-Vietnam war protestors, feminists, civil rights activists, and environmentalists appeared to threaten the social order.[104]

But consumer longings for bygone days could not single-handedly sell Chiquita bananas. At the heart of the campaign was an effort to inculcate consumers with the idea that not all bananas were the same. The Chiquita and Cabana brand names tried to re-define what consumers considered to be a quality banana by emphasizing features such as bunch symmetry, the fullness of individual bananas, and blemish-free peels that ripened uniformly. In order to bear the Chiquita label in 1970, a banana had to be a minimum of eight inches long and free of a long list of "defects" primarily related to the visual appearance of the fruit.[105] Standard Fruit also based its quality ratings on the number of "outward defects" and the "fresh appearance" of the peel.[106] Achieving and maintaining these new quality standards required new production techniques and new forms of labor. The most important innovation was the on-farm boxing of fruit.

The *empacadora,* or packing plant, became the key component of the industry's "post-harvest" operations designed to ensure greater quality control. Former Standard Fruit employee Henry Muery noted that the *empacadoras* virtually eliminated "in-farm defects," and enabled the fruit companies to export "essentially blemish-free" fruit.[107] Boxing bananas was a multi-step process. At one end of the plant, workers armed with sharp knives removed the hands of freshly harvested bananas from their stems and placed them in tanks filled with water. The bath served the dual purpose of cleaning the peels and cooling the temperature of the fruit prior to boxing. A gentle current carried the fruit to the other end of the long, rectangular tanks where another group of workers sorted the premium grade fruit (e.g., "Chiquitas") from both the second grade bananas (known as "specials") and the rejects. Export grades were then treated with chemicals to prevent fungal rots before being weighed, stickered, and packed into boxes.

The *empacadoras* provided novel employment opportunities for Central American women. Although women had found employment in the offices, hospitals, and schools of the fruit companies, the work of growing and shipping bananas remained a masculine domain in Central America prior to the creation of packing plants. In Honduras, United Fruit began using women in packing operations no later than 1962. Women entered Standard Fruit's *empacadoras* no later than 1967.[108] Both companies initially hire women for packing plants in small cohorts. These first hires often had family connections that helped them to secure a position. For example, Esperanza Rivera Nájera was offered a packing plant job by her husband's supervisor in 1968. She recalled that "if you weren't related to an employee, you were not able to get a job." Other women secured positions in packing plants through fathers and stepfathers.[109] This was nothing new; male field hands historically landed jobs by exploiting personal contacts. In fact, kin networks may have become even more important by the late 1960s, when the companies were reducing the size of their unionized work forces.

Women worked selecting, weighing, stickering, and packing bananas. The work pace in *empacadoras* followed a rhythm set by harvesting operations: the larger the *cortes,* the longer and more frenetic the shifts for packers. Days could be particularly strenuous for women like Esperanza, who had three children when she began working in the *empacadora* at the age of twenty-three:

> We got up at 4:00 in the morning and ate breakfast on the way to work, because sometimes there wasn't time to eat at work. The day was stressful. We started at 6:30 and we didn't finish working until 6:30 in the evening. Twelve-hour shifts. We had one half-hour break at 11 in the morning and that was it.
>
> When a woman leaves her family to work it's a struggle because one has obligations to her children and also to her job. Sometimes I got up at 3:00 in the morning to wash clothes.[110]

Other women who began working in packing plants in the mid-1960s recalled a similar routine of rising early and working long days (up to 16 hours) with few breaks. Long shifts in the *empacadora* were punctuated by days when the plants operated at less than full capacity or shut down completely in the absence of harvesting activities. For women like Olivia Zaldívar, periodic lulls in packing activity provided an opportunity to catch up on domestic work: "The days that the *empacadora* did not operate were spent washing clothes."[111]

Olivia worked for six months in a Tela Railroad Company packing plant in 1964 during which time she met a man with whom she had a child who died in infancy. Two years later, Olivia had a second child with another man, but when the father refused to provide any financial or emotional support, she returned to the *empacadora,* "motivated" by the need to take care of her child. Olivia's status as a *madre soltera,* or single mother, was a common one for women in the boxing plants. Indeed, some women suggested that single mothers formed a majority of the female employees. According to Olivia, the *empacadoras* not only attracted single mothers, they also helped to create them: "There are women who are married when they start working, but you know that when a woman works she frees herself. When she is not working [outside the home] a woman is dependent on her husband. But if she is working, how can the man say no?" Olivia described herself as a "libertine" in her youth, a characterization that may have been shaped by her conversion later in life to evangelicalism. In retrospect, she viewed the breakup of couples with children as undesirable since the kids "are the ones that suffer the most."[112]

Juana Meléndez was another *madre soltera*—in this case a young widow who worked long days in order to raise her children. Juana never remarried. She described herself as a "Tom-boy" during her childhood, a characterization confirmed by a long-time male friend who recalled that Juana had dressed "like a boy," played with boys, and tended to cattle.[113] Juana's physical and mental strength served her well in the packing plant where she simultaneously annoyed and won the respect of both her fellow workers and supervisors for her fast work pace and quick tongue. She recalled an occasion when she led an impromptu work stoppage in order to protest the supervisors' failure to maintain sufficient water in the washing tanks (a situation that increased the likelihood of bruising to the fruit). She subsequently became a union steward, but she "complained so much" about working conditions that she soon found herself back among the rank-and-file. Juana's strong will may have been exceptional, but her memories resonated with those of other women packers whose stories mingled images of maternal sacrifices and personal autonomy.[114]

Regardless of their marital status, women who worked in the *empacadoras* depended upon other women to assist with child-care. In Olivia Zaldívar's case, she relied upon her mother to watch her son on days that she worked as a fruit packer. Other women, including ones with spouses such as Esperanza, hired *muchachas* (girls or young women) to care for their children and attend to household chores. Having to pay for child care cut into women's net earnings, but the ability to employ domestic help also reflected the benefits of having a steady—and in some cases dual—income. Esperanza relished the opportunity to earn wages so that she could "buy things for her house," and pay for her children's education. Olivia Zaldívar described packing plant work as *muy sacrificado* but added in the same breath that "everyone" wanted to work for the company because it was relatively steady employment. Women entering the packing plants in the 1960s benefited from the existence of unions, labor law reforms, and collective bargaining contracts that were the legacy of the 1954 strike. They earned hourly wages and received medical and retirement benefits. However, "steady employment" did not mean a fixed work schedule since the volume of fruit harvested fluctuated due to the vagaries of weather and mass markets. Furthermore, the number of women who managed to get full-time jobs in the packing plants during the 1960s was small and initially limited to individuals with a spouse or male family member employed by one of the companies.

The opportunity to work in a packing plant exacted both physical and emotional costs. Women uniformly described their days in the *empacadoras* as exhausting. They performed repetitive tasks at a high rate of speed for anywhere from ten to fourteen hours. Breaks were limited to a half-hour lunch break around 11 and a second break in the late afternoon on occasions when packing operations extended into the late evening. The work environment could also be debilitating. Fruit selectors constantly had to dip their hands into the water tanks in the process of grading the bananas. Some women considered this to be the least desirable job in the *empacadora*. Pepe Puerta, a former packing plant supervisor for Standard Fruit, recalled that "they [the women] used to say that the dampness affected them."[115] He also believed that some workers developed tumors as a result of their exposure to the chemicals used in the *empacadoras* to prevent crown rot (a fungus) from developing while the bananas were in transit. From the fruit companies' perspective, severe cases of crown rot rendered the bananas "commercially unacceptable."[116] United Fruit initially used a Dithane dip to prevent crown rot. Around 1965, the companies began adding chlorine to the water tanks in order to control the fungus. Three years later, the industry switched to a systemic fungicide (Thiabendazole) following its approval for use on bananas by the U.S. Food and Drug Administration.[117] Workers applied Thiabendazole with the aid of a sprayer that showered the fruit just prior to boxing.

Throughout the 1960s and 1970s, there is no evidence that either the fruit companies or union officials provided packing plant workers with safety instructions and/or protective apparel such as gloves or masks. Esperanza recalled that she worked ten years in the *empacadora* "without protecting myself, always wet, with my arms exposed to the sprays [fungicides]."[118] Other women confirmed the absence of protective clothing. An illustrated instructional manual for United Fruit's packing plant workers makes no mention of protective clothing and depicts a bare-handed worker dipping fruit into a solution of "disinfectant" (presumably dithane) strongly suggesting that the women and men who labored in packing plants during the 1960s and early 1970s received frequent exposure to more than just dampness.

Although some workers in the packing plants, including the ex-supervisor Pepe Puerta, expressed concerns about chronic exposure to cancer-causing chemicals, long-time packing plant workers suffered from other ailments including arthritis and skin problems. In addition, Esperanza recalled that when she began working in the late 1960s, bathroom facilities were crude and inconveniently located, and the water available for drinking tasted like "pure salt." The 1974 collective bargaining agreement signed by Standard Fruit and the workers union SUTRASFCO included clauses requiring the company to install toilet facilities, drinking water, electric fans, and wall clocks in all of its *empacadoras*. The company also agreed to provide places for workers to eat lunch and a room for women to change their clothes.[119] The extent to which the company complied with these clauses is unknown, but the terms of the contract suggest both that a significant number of packing plants lacked basic amenities as late as 1974, and that union officials and company executives sought to address at least some women employees' concerns.

Because only men filled supervisory roles in the *empacadoras,* women were potentially vulnerable to sexual harassment. However, former workers indicated that cases of blatant abuse were rare. On the other hand, women's memories point toward a more subtle tension created by the tendency for women in the *empacadoras* to be viewed simultaneously as possessing stereotypical feminine qualities (e.g., delicate hands) and potentially threatening levels of autonomy—the *madre soltera*. The limited number of women's testimonies presented here point to the existence of a fine line between "liberated" and "libertine," and "outspoken" and "troublemaker." Finally, if women viewed their packing plant jobs as the best way to ensure a secure future for their families, they also regretted spending entire days away from their young children who would often be fast asleep by the time they returned home.

By the mid-1960s, United Fruit officials declared the Chiquita marketing campaign a success. The company enjoyed record sales' volumes and rising profit margins. Miss Chiquita had helped to save the day for the company's new management who watched profits rise from $1.7 million to $25 million between 1963 and 1966. The successful financial turnaround led to a dramatic takeover attempt by Wall Street trader Eli M. Black that culminated in the merger of United Fruit and Black's AMK corporation in 1969.[120] The following year, the new company changed its name to United Brands. After nearly seventy years, the tight relationship between United Fruit and Gros Michel bananas was irrevocably severed.

The rebirth of Miss Chiquita, therefore, provided an aura of continuity to a period of political, economic, environmental, and social transformations in both Central America and the United States. Banana workers in Honduras helped to bring about some of these changes by forming labor unions and pressing for land reform. But organized labor was not the only force that compelled the fruit companies to alter their production processes; the inexorable spread of Panama disease drove up production costs and rates of soil abandonment at a time when the fruit companies' extensive landholdings in the Caribbean and Latin America were under severe public scrutiny and threats of expropriation. The industry's solution to the problem — boxed Cavendish bananas — created unexpected opportunities for women as wage laborers in packing plants. Ironically, the nostalgic return of Miss Chiquita coincided with changing roles for women in the tropics.

Chapter 7

La Química

The direction of research in the labs follows the philosophy that the banana, the soils, and the various enemies of the banana, are a three-dimensional biological system in which factors affecting any one variable can be expected to affect all other variables.

NORWOOD C. THORTON, 1959

I had to take a friend of mine who had been applying Nemagon to the emergency room, and there were quite a few cases like that. If you happened to be passing through the farm you immediately noticed the smell in the air . . . there were dead fish in the rivers and creeks, a lot of dead fish.

NECHE MARTÍNEZ, 1995

One day in the early 1950s, United Fruit Company research assistant Jorge Romero was supervising a work crew applying an agrochemical through the irrigation system.[1] As the sun climbed in the tropical sky, the smell of the rapidly vaporizing chemical penetrated the protective masks worn by the workers, forcing them to complete their tasks quickly in order to avoid being overwhelmed by the fumes. When a crew member named Benito removed his mask, Jorge pleaded with him to put it back on before approaching the irrigation equipment. But Benito refused, declaring "*soy indio salvadoreño bruto*" ("I'm a tough *indio* from El Salvador"). Just watch." Romero described what happened next: "Benito didn't take more than five steps toward the sprinkler when plop! He fell to the ground with blood running from his nose, ears, and eyes. We pulled him out of there and rushed him to the hospital." Jorge, who spent more than thirty years in the Tela Railroad Company's research department, used the anecdote to illustrate what could happen when a worker adopted a "superman mentality" and failed to play by "the rules of the game." The story also helps to convey how the "game" of growing export bananas was changing in important ways for fieldworkers.

As late as the mid-1940s, the primary chemical input on export banana plantations was copper sulfate used to control Sigatoka. Following World War II, both the spiraling costs of Bordeaux spraying and the increasing availability of petroleum-derived pesticides prompted United Fruit to strengthen its ties with chemical companies. In 1948, Dr. Norwood Thorton left his position with Union Carbide and Carbon Chemicals Corporation to become United Fruit's head plant pathologist. Four years later, United Fruit's Director of Research Hartley Rowe encouraged his staff to establish "close contact and cooperation with those chemical companies working in the field of modern, scientific insecticides and fungicides."[2] That same year, Dr. Thorton presented a paper at the conference of the American Phytopathological Society entitled "The Use of Fungicides in Central and South America." Noting that "the need for fungicides is evident on every hand," he expressed confidence that the future of Central American agriculture lay with chemical controls.[3] In Honduras, company researchers set up dozens of test plots treated with fungicides supplied by major U.S. chemical manufacturers including DuPont, Union Carbide, Esso, and R. T. Vanderbilt. Both DuPont and Vanderbilt sent their top agricultural scientists to Honduras to study the Sigatoka problem.[4]

By the late 1940s, United Fruit was making use of organochlorinated insecticides such as DDT, Methoxyclor, Chlordane, and Toxaphene to control flies, ticks, mosquitoes, and leaf-cutting ants. The research department's annual report for 1949 displayed what at the time was a typical lack of concern about human exposure to insecticides:

> Widespread application of high concentrations of DDT are effective, but usually leaves a heavy residue deposit that may be unsightly in a residence. To overcome this, we have, in the case of a few residences, made applications of Chlordane and DDT at one percent concentrations to the exterior of buildings only. The flooring, sills, uprights and ground areas under the house, the thick bushes, flowering trees and in special cases, even the lawns were sprayed. Application of the spray mixture has always been light and in most cases no unsightly residue was left.[5]

If unaware of the health hazards posed by exposure to DDT, company scientists quickly realized its limitations. As early as 1951, the research department reported that it had "conclusive evidence" that house fly populations acquired resistance to DDT. They urged rotating the use of various insecticides in order to slow the build-up of resistance: "It is likely that a new population of resistant flies will develop, but probably not to bothersome proportions before six months to one year."[6] This curiously shortsighted strategy for dealing with the problem of pesticide resistance would dominate fruit company practices for the remainder of the twentieth century.

By the early 1970s virtually every phase of production — from plant propagation to boxing operations — involved chemical inputs. Daily plantation work increasingly revolved around disease and pest control. Workers sanitized banana rhizomes before planting them, disinfected their pruning tools, walked the fields on the lookout for disease symptoms, and applied fertilizers, fungicides, herbicides, insecticides, and nematicides. The prominent role played by agrochemicals following World War II was captured by both the official and unofficial names given to the research complex opened in La Lima by United Fruit in 1953. Formally christened the "Vining C. Dunlap Laboratories" in honor of the former research director who developed the Bordeaux spray system, the labs were popularly referred to as "La Química."[7] The banana industry's rising use of agrochemicals can be attributed to several factors. Following World War II, there was a dramatic increase in the number of pesticides that chemical companies marketed to agribusinesses and farmers.[8] Also, the conversion to boxed Cavendish bananas ushered in an era of heightened quality standards that could only be met through regular applications of fertilizers, insecticides, and nematicides. Finally, following the 1954 strike, the fruit companies in Honduras went to great lengths to cut payroll costs; new fungicides and herbicides enabled the companies to control Sigatoka and weeds with only a fraction of the labor inputs once required.

The impact of the 1954 strike on the fruit companies is visible in the unpublished annual reports of United Fruit's Department of Tropical Research. During the 1940s and early 1950s, company researchers pursued a wide range of projects, prompted in part by the exigencies of World War II. A "New Crops Program" inaugurated in 1942 focused on cultivating "emergency crops" such as *abacá* (*Musa textilis*), rubber, and oil-bearing plants. In 1950, plantings of African oil palm covered more than 1,300 hectares of former banana lands. Company workers also reforested more than 4,000 hectares of land.[9] All told, by 1951 United Fruit's non-banana crops covered a remarkable 12,150 hectares of land in Honduras.[10] That same year, non-banana subject matter filled one half of the research

FIGURE 7.1. *The Vining C. Dunlap laboratories in La Lima, Honduras (1953). United Fruit Company Photograph Collection. Baker Library, Harvard Business School.*

department's annual report. But the company's interest in new crops diminished rapidly following the 1954 strike. In 1955 the New Crops Program all but ceased to exist following the transfer of its personnel to other projects. The notable exceptions were African oil palm and cattle whose production would continue to expand.[11]

The research department's annual reports for the remainder of the decade focused almost entirely on banana production. In 1958, research director Jesse Hobson declared that his staff was "properly directed at helping to improve the company's earnings through increased production per acre and through reducing costs of production."[12] The statement reflected the pressures on Hobson and his colleagues to generate findings that could help United Fruit overcome production problems that were cutting sharply into company profits. In the face of dwindling earnings and declining stock value, a new generation of executives boosted the research budget from about $1.5 million in 1958 to $2.5 million in 1959. The number of scientists swelled to 94 (including 45 with doctorate degrees) in a range of disciplines including agronomy, entomology, genetics, microbiology, plant pathology, and statistics.[13] The Standard Fruit Company also invested in research during the 1950s, establishing a formal research program for the first time in the company's history. The banana industry was placing its future largely in the hands of university trained research scientists armed with a growing array of chemical weapons with which to combat the "enemies" of the banana.[14]

Following the 1954 strike, United Fruit's research staff played a central role in revamping production processes in order to make them more labor efficient. The most dramatic changes took place in the area of Sigatoka control. By the mid-1950s, United Fruit was annually spending around 20 million dollars (6–7 percent of its total operating costs) to protect its Gros Michel plants from Sigatoka.[15] One company official estimated that workers annually applied enough Bordeaux spray to fill a 2,000-acre lake to a depth of one foot. With both labor and material costs on the rise, the fruit companies sought out alternative chemical fungicides. However, field trials of at least 55 different fungicidal compounds carried out by United Fruit researchers between 1936 and 1952 failed to yield a viable alternative to high-volume applications of copper sulfate.[16] In addition to its high fungicidal activity, Bordeaux spray's "spreading and sticking" qualities protected plant tissues for up to four weeks. The spray also provided protection against various kinds of leaf-eating caterpillars and locusts. Finally, the same blue residue that caused such consternation for workers aided supervisors responsible for monitoring spray operations. The situation began to change in 1955, when French researchers in Guadeloupe made the surprising discovery that low-volume applications of orchard oils effectively held Sigatoka in check.[17] Two years later, United Fruit scientists reported that small-scale testing indicated that various oil compounds provided better Sigatoka control than Bordeaux spray. However, they refrained from endorsing a switch to oil-based sprays prior to the completion of a more thorough study.[18]

In November 1957, SITRATERCO decried the company's efforts to eliminate the Bordeaux spray system: "This time the company is trying to eliminate an enormous amount of its workers (nearly 33 percent) in one fell swoop."[19] The union reminded its members of past failures with aerial applications of fungicides and pointed out the potential health problems associated with inhaling fungicidal dust. A return to aerial spraying, SITRATERCO's leaders warned, would expose workers to toxic chemicals and condemn them to the list of "white plague" victims.[20] In a press release issued one month later, SITRATERCO officials reiterated their concerns about the risks that aerial fungicide applications posed to human health:

"upon being sprayed by planes, the caustic chemical ingredients will be inhaled by workers and damage their lungs."[21]

These published statements indicate that union leaders were envisioning aerial dustings of fungicidal powders—a technique temporarily used in Honduras during the first outbreak of Sigatoka in 1936–1937. Although Dunlap's reports from those years make no mention of adverse health effects associated with aerial dusting, a 1940 study from Australia described dusting as "extremely unpleasant in spite of the use of dust-hoods and respirators, and with few exceptions, growers condemn this method of control."[22] Union references to the "white plague" reflected the widespread belief among workers that exposure to copper sulfate produced tuberculosis-like symptoms in some individuals. In light of these antecedents, the union's assumption that the proposed aerial applications would endanger worker health was hardly surprising. Interestingly, SITRATERCO publications did not mention workers' concerns about the health affects of ground spray work, presumably because the fledgling union was primarily concerned about the prospect that hundreds or even thousands of jobs would be eliminated if the company switched to aerial crop dusting.[23]

In 1958, United Fruit's Boston-based management, anticipating annual savings of $15 million, ordered its banana-growing divisions to adopt oil-based fungicides as rapidly as possible. The following year, aerial applications treated more than 12,100 hectares of bananas. But laboratory studies conducted that same year indicated that the presence of spray oil on banana leaves inhibited photosynthesis and resulted in fewer bunches per hectare and lower fruit weights.[24] Oil sprays also failed to control certain insect pests whose populations had been (incidentally) held in check by Bordeaux spray. In light of these findings, United Fruit's director of tropical research wrote to Dr. Hobson in August 1959, urging a return to Bordeaux spraying. One month later, company officials in Boston hastily ordered that Bordeaux spraying be restored on as many farms as possible.[25] A U.S. embassy official in Tegucigalpa, noting that oil spraying had enabled the fruit companies to offset rising labor costs by reducing their workforces by "more than ten percent," called the news "extremely serious."[26] Hoping to hold down labor costs, the Tela Railroad Company eliminated the *manguerero* position, forcing individual workers to manage the hose and spray nozzle.[27]

This partial reprieve for Bordeaux applicators was short-lived. After screening nearly 100 fungicides in 1960, United Fruit scientists reported that a new product, Dithane M-22 (a dithiocarbamate), provided excellent Sigatoka control and "markedly" increased fruit weights over copper fungicides.[28] That same year, company researchers detected extremely elevated levels of copper in some banana farm soils in Honduras, a finding that raised additional concerns about continued use of Bordeaux spray.[29] In 1961, aerial Dithane applications achieved "unquestionable success" in controlling Sigatoka on more than 11,000 hectares of bananas in Honduras. The new system led to a sharp decrease in Sigatoka control costs ($67 per acre/year in 1951 to $40 per acre/year in 1966).[30] Standard Fruit also phased out Bordeaux spraying in the early 1960s in favor of orchard spray oils applied by workers using knapsack sprayers. In 1968, Standard began using aerial applications of Dithane.[31]

The era of the *veneneros* was over. Under the new system, the fruit companies employed a very small number of men as flaggers (*bandoleros*) who helped to guide the pilots (hired by contract) in their runs over the plantations. Víctor Reyes, who worked five years as a *venenero* for the Tela Railroad Company recalled that "thousands lost their jobs" as a result of the switch to aerial fungicide applications.[32] Between 1957 and 1961, the Tela Railroad Company cut its labor force from 13,000 to 8,800 employees.[33] How many of the 4,200 dismissed workers were *veneneros* is hard to judge based on available evidence. Equally difficult to pin down is the number of laid-off employees who were rehired by the company when its payroll expanded in the early 1960s in conjuncture with the conversion to Cavendish varieties. A considerable number of people must have been exposed to Dithane, including the small number of workers who served as *bandoleros,* and a much larger number of residents living in company housing that lay adjacent to the farms. However, Dithane was not acutely toxic and its potential carcinogenic effects were not common knowledge in the 1960s. Consequently, SITRATERCO's immediate reaction to the company's conversion to aerial applications of Dithane was to protest the loss of jobs, not the creation of new occupational health hazards.

Aerial applications of Dithane-based fungicides proved to be more effective in helping to eliminate human workers than fungal pathogens. In 1973, a heavy outbreak of leaf spotting occurred on some 1,200 hectares of banana farms in the Sula valley that could not be attributed to "typical Sigatoka."[34] The symptoms possessed characteristics of both Sigatoka and black leaf streak, a malady first recorded on the island of Fiji in 1963. Researchers in Honduras dubbed the new disease "Black Sigatoka" on account of the dark spots that appeared on infected leaves, and described the pathogen as a "new, undescribed race" of *Mycosphaerella musicola.*[35] Observers also reported that the new pathogen "mostly replaced Sigatoka" on the farms in which it appeared. This raised the possibility that some environmental factor triggered a mutation in *Mycosphaerella musicola* Leach giving rise to the newly dominant Black Sigatoka strain that proved to be much more virulent than Sigatoka. Researchers subsequently classified Black Sigatoka as *Mycosphaerella musicola fijiensis,* a fungus that United Fruit pathologist Robert Stover detected on preserved plant tissue samples collected in Fiji in the 1920s, indicating that the pathogen did not have its genesis in the Sula valley. Nevertheless, the consistent pattern of Black Sigatoka replacing Sigatoka leaves open the possibility that changing production practices—including the use of Dithane—altered agroecological conditions in such a way as to favor the proliferation of Black Sigatoka.[36]

The company brought the initial outbreak of Black Sigatoka under control through multiple applications of Benlate, a systemic fungicide that company scientists first field-tested in 1967.[37] A second outbreak of Black Sigatoka occurred in 1974 following Hurricane Fifi. When aerial spraying resumed after the storm, about 4,800 hectares of infected farms received Benlate treatments every other week. Benlate proved to be an effective short-term control for Black Sigatoka but the rapidity with which populations of fungi developed resistance to the fungicide limited its potential as a long-term solution. In order to slow the buildup of Benlate-resistant strains of the pathogen, United Brands' scientists ordered that applications of Dithane be made every third cycle. The company achieved a tenuous control over the pathogen through high frequency applications (35–45 times/year) of systemic fungicides. Not surprisingly, the cost of Black Sigatoka control rose sharply following 1974 and within a decade accounted for about 26 percent of all pre-harvest production costs in Honduras.[38] Standard Fruit began alternating cycles of Dithane and Benlate in 1975. Within five years, the buildup of resistant pathogen populations prompted the company to switch to another systemic fungicide called Bravo. In 1982, following a heavy outbreak of Black Sigatoka in the Standard Fruit's Aguán valley farms, the company began to rotate Bravo with applications of a Dithane-oil-Benlate-water "cocktail."[39]

For the remainder of the twentieth century, the export banana industry would be "running to stand still" on a treadmill driven by expensive agrochemical inputs and ever-evolving populations of fungi. The history of Sigatoka and Black Sigatoka control on export banana farms calls into question the widely held notion that post–World War II innovations in chemical pesticides reduced economic losses from pests and pathogens in commercial agriculture.[40] The switch to low volume applications of fungicides helped the fruit companies to reduce labor costs in the early 1960s,

FIGURE 7.2. *United Fruit Company workers pruning young banana plants in Honduras (1946). United Fruit Company Photograph Collection. Baker Library, Harvard Business School.*

but the appearance of Black Sigatoka in the 1970s reversed the trend in control costs. Through the early twenty-first century, Black Sigatoka remained the most costly and complex aspect of export banana production.

Black Sigatoka was not the only new pathogen that shaped banana production in Honduras during the Cavendish era. Bacteria wilt (*P. Solanacearum*) reached Honduras in the late 1950s, probably arriving via infected Gros Michel planting stock imported from Costa Rica.[41] Disease symptoms included the yellowing and wilting of plant foliage, deformed roots, stunted growth, and fruit that ripened prematurely. Bacteria wilt first gained notoriety in late-nineteenth-century Trinidad when it threatened to wipe out a widely cultivated plantain variety called Moko from which the disease acquired its popular name in the Caribbean and Central America.[42] The disease did not draw the attention of United Fruit researchers until the mid-1950s when it appeared on banana farms in Costa Rica.

Prior to that time, growers and scientists assumed that Moko transmission took place primarily via plant roots. However, company studies found that under plantation conditions Moko almost always infected banana plants via the machetes and knives used by weeding and pruning crews. The company responded by devising a control program based on tool disinfection, the prompt removal of infected plants, and re-planting with sterilized rhizomes.

Cases of Moko remained few and scattered in Honduras until 1961 when an outbreak occurred that could not be linked to tool infection.[43] United Fruit scientists discovered that a range of flying insects, including bees (*Trigona* species) wasps (*Polybia* species) and fruit flies (*Drosophilia* species) were transmitting a particularly virulent strain of the bacteria. In just two years, bees and other flying disease vectors transported the pathogen up to 150 kilometers.[44] Once established in the plantation environment, Moko spread via the roots of the densely set Cavendish plants and the tools of unwary workers. Outside of the plantations, the bacteria infected the same plantain variety (known as "Chato" in Honduras) that had been devastated in Trinidad. Concerned that the pathogen would persist in scattered patches of plantains, United Fruit worked to eliminate Chatos in the vicinity of its plantations.[45] Achieving this goal required a certain degree of cooperation from area farmers who had to be convinced to stop growing the popular crop. However, the effects of Moko may have been sufficient to convince farmers to give up on the variety. In 1963, after visiting one of the places where the "original build up" of Moko had occurred, a fruit company scientist predicted that "people will continue to destroy Chatos on their own when they see that they will remain unproductive."[46] He added that many Sula valley growers had already replaced their plantains with corn and other crops. In 1965, the company reported that it was providing the Honduran government and area cultivators with rhizomes of a resistant "Chato-like" plantain for planting.[47]

That same year, Standard Fruit reported to the U.S. embassy that Moko was causing severe problems for thousands of small-scale cultivators who depended on Chatos to feed both their families and animals. Some people traveled for two days to Standard Fruit's Aguán valley farms in order to obtain discarded green bananas as a substitute for plantains.[48] Company officials, emphasizing that they had never seen such levels of hunger in the region, strongly urged the U.S. government to provide emergency assistance. In the meantime, a Standard Fruit employee inspected areas lying on the periphery of the company's farms for signs of Moko infection. Upon detecting patches of diseased Chato, the company inspector paid farmers one or two dollars to cut down their plantains, an offer that Standard Fruit officials claimed most cultivators readily accepted because their plantings had already ceased to be productive.

The fruit companies' reports from this period tend to identify Chato patches as sources of Moko infection that needed to be eliminated. Of course, this view represented the perspective of export banana growers and ignored the likelihood that the fruit companies bore primary responsibility for introducing the pathogen to Honduras. It also failed to acknowledge that disease vectors moved in multiple directions. There was no reason to doubt that certain bee species, capable of carrying the bacteria for miles, traveled back and forth between plantain patches and export banana farms. Moreover, the large areas planted in Moko-susceptible banana varieties enabled bacteria populations to grow much larger than they would have in the absence of dense host populations. In other words, export banana farms probably constituted greater reservoirs of bacterial wilt than plantain farms. The history of Moko then, reveals a noteworthy agroecological interaction between export and non-export agriculture that acutely affected the livelihoods of small-scale cultivators in Honduras and elsewhere in Central America during the 1950s and 1960s.

Moko control also changed the work routines of field hands by both creating new jobs and altering existing ones. The companies trained workers to carry out Moko surveys and record the locations of diseased plants so that other workers could swiftly eradicate them.[49] Ironically, the resiliency of banana plants—easily damaged but hard to eradicate—impeded the fruit companies' efforts to control Moko. The multi-step process involved cutting down the infected plant and its neighbors and spraying the area with herbicides. If the infected plant was bearing fruit, workers also applied an insecticide to kill any potential disease-carrying insects. Moko crews revisited the site in subsequent weeks and reapplied herbicides to any sprouts that emerged from the cut banana stalks.[50]

Since it was impractical to maintain constant supervision of Moko inspectors, the companies relied on indirect forms of monitoring. One ex-Standard Fruit employee recalled that inspectors were always assigned to cover the same area so that if a Moko outbreak occurred, managers would be able to identify which worker had failed to be vigilant.[51] Another former Standard Fruit worker held similar memories:

No one was watching to see if you were doing a thorough inspection. I could have entered my area and laid down to rest and no one would have been the wiser. But, if they found a diseased plant in my section,

I was held responsible. And one time they found a [case of] Moko that
I had missed — they wanted to suspend me but the foremen never did
it — however, it put me on my toes.[52]

United Brand's 1972 *Banana Operations Manual* instructed foremen to
maintain up-to-date lists of their Moko inspectors. All personnel changes
had to be cleared through a district supervisor (a degree of centralization
that did not exist prior to the mid-1950s). The manual also instructed foremen to assign inspectors to the same area so that "if an old Moko case is
found which was obviously missed on the previous cycle, it is then possible to pin point which man was lax in his work. If men know [that] their
work can be checked, they will be more efficient."[53]

Highlighting the need for careful supervision of Moko inspectors,
United Brands' researchers described a "classic example" of what could
happen when all controls were not "strictly enforced":

> When the experiment was initiated, the farm overseer was very
> interested in Moko control. . . . This overseer was transferred and
> another took over [who] initially did not pay attention to Moko and as
> a result there was a general relaxation of control measures, the most
> serious being the surveys. The surveyors are to cover an area based on
> an eight-hour day. In San Juan [farm] surveyors often left the field by
> 10:30 which means they worked 4–5 hours and only superficially
> covered the assigned acreage. In addition, surveyors are sometimes
> used for other work so there might be only five surveyors instead of
> eight. Irregardless [*sic*], they still manage to leave at approximately
> the same early hour.[54]

The hasty survey work resulted in a sharp rise in Moko some two months
after the new overseer took charge. From the scientists' perspective, the
moral of the story was clear: effective Moko control required conscientious workers and vigilant supervisors. But the research department's reports also revealed some of the underlying tensions in the company's
attempts to minimize fruit losses and labor costs simultaneously. For
example, Moko inspectors worked under two-week contracts that paid
them on a per-acre basis — hardly terms of employment likely to promote
thorough inspections. In a 1971 report, company scientists acknowledged
that the only way to reduce the costs of Moko control would be to lower
the frequency of surveys, suggesting that wages could not be realistically
diminished.[55]

The fruit companies also went to great lengths to prevent the spread of Moko via routine cultivation practices. During the 1950s United Fruit required its pruners to work with two machetes and a scabbard filled with a ten percent formaldehyde solution. Company foremen instructed workers to rotate their machetes constantly so that the blades would be immersed for at least ten seconds in the formaldehyde solution in between uses.[56] United Fruit devised various means to ensure that workers complied with this seemingly simple measure. In 1957, the company issued a Spanish-language manual that urged field hands to "[u]se disinfectant to clean your machete regardless of whether the plant is diseased . . . add fresh *formulina* [formaldehyde solution] often."[57] The manual concluded with two cartoons. The first image featured a worker, shiny machete in hand, standing between a drum of *formulina* and a healthy banana plant with a dollar sign hanging from it. The second image depicted an unkempt worker with a dirty machete next to a dead banana plant; neither *formulina* nor the dollar sign were anywhere to be seen. By 1970, the company required pruners to add a violet dye to the otherwise clear formaldehyde solution so that foremen could inspect plants for telltale stains in order to monitor worker compliance with tool disinfection procedures.[58]

Fieldworkers generally disliked working with formulina because their fingers came into frequent contact with the disinfectant due to the constant rotation of pruning knives and machetes. Former Standard Fruit employee Abel Posas believed that constant exposure to formaldehyde caused permanent damage to many workers' fingers. He added that the disinfectant also produced a burning sensation in one's eyes.[59] Ramón Vallecillo, another ex-Standard Fruit employee, recalled having "little drops" of formaldehyde solution fall into his eyes. In addition to causing an intense burning sensation, he believed the chemical left his vision permanently impaired.[60] Posas and Vallecillo were not alone in their dislike of formaldehyde. Standard Fruit researcher Henry Muery's unpublished memoir refers to "constant complaints by laborers" in the early 1970s that forced the company to replace formaldehyde with a disinfectant called Beloran.[61] United Fruit began experimenting with Beloran in 1967. Although research department reports made no reference to worker complaints about formulina, they described Beloran as "effective but odorless and non-irritating" suggesting that the same could not be said about formulina.[62]

This description of routine Moko control work reveals the complicated dynamic between fruit company researchers, field workers, banana plants, and plant pathogens. Cultivation practices were primarily responsible for the spread of Moko within the confines of fruit company farms, but banana plantations were not closed systems and itinerant bees carried the infection back and forth across property lines. Also, the rapid and large-scale movement of planting material in connection with the conversion to Panama-disease resistant varieties greatly increased the probability that workers introduced diseased plants to locations where the disease had not been present. These conditions prompted the fruit companies to adopt a two-pronged control strategy based on plant inspection and tool disinfection. However, the Moko control program did not meet with immediate success due largely to the difficulty of disciplining field workers to perform tasks that were tedious, irritating, and potentially hazardous.

Dynamic pathogens and the companies' desire to increase labor efficiency were not the only forces shaping production processes during the Cavendish era. Revised quality standards led to the increased use of insecticides, nematicides, and fertilizers. United Fruit first experimented with fertilizers in the late 1920s as a means of stimulating the growth of young banana plants in marginal soils. These early studies demonstrated that banana plants treated with nitrogenous fertilizers yielded more bunches per acre (500) and higher average bunch weights (60 pounds) than plants that did not receive fertilizer (357 bunches/acre and 53.5 pounds).[63] Following World War II, the fruit companies began importing millions of pounds of sodium nitrate into Honduras from the United States.[64] The effect of fertilizer use on yields was dramatic. In fact, when export volumes are measured by weight and not bunch counts, the "decline" in Honduran banana exports from 1929 to 1950 is called into question. Although United Fruit's subsidiaries exported 3.5 million fewer bunches in 1950 than in 1929, the weight of the 1950 shipments exceeded those of 1929 by 75,000 tons due to large increases in average bunch weights.[65]

The conversion to Cavendish varieties—planted at much higher densities than Gros Michel—prompted a major increase in fertilizer use. For example, between 1952 and 1962, Standard Fruit's annual fertilizer use increased from 50–80 pounds of urea per acre to 270 pounds per acre. In the 1970s, the company applied around 300 pounds per acre. United Fruit applied urea at the rate of 1,000 pounds/acre on its densely planted Valery farms.[66] Each farm received four applications per year. Under this fertilizer regime, average Valery bunch weights ranged from 80 to 100 pounds.[67] Yields on Standard Fruit farms followed a similar upward trajectory during this period.[68] United Fruit workers applied fertilizer by hand and through overhead irrigation systems. Frequently working without gloves, daily contact with urea left many laborers with burns on their hands and arms.[69]

The fruit companies also incorporated herbicides into their production practices as part of their strategy to boost yields. In the early 1970s, United Brands's weed control included both manual weeding with machetes and herbicides. According to the company's 1972 operations manual, herbicides reduced weeding costs by 30–50 percent, lowered the risk of spreading Moko, and proved more effective in eradicating species of plants that were potential pathogen hosts. Herbicides used on banana plantations during the 1960s and 1970s included Dalapon, Diuron, and Paraquat. Workers applied Dalapon-Diuron mixtures with mistblowers; the manual advised that Diuron-Paraquat mixes be applied with knapsack sprayers in order to minimize damage to banana plants from drifting herbicides. The operations manual further instructed field supervisors to use knapsack sprayers when applying Paraquat because it is "toxic to human lungs," but it added that workers had to wear masks when applying Paraquat with mistblowers suggesting that the latter situation occurred at least on occasion.[70] United Brands also instructed supervisors to provide water for workers to wash their hands and faces before eating, drinking, or smoking.

The intensive use of fertilizers and herbicides was largely a result of the fruit companies' interest in boosting yields, but hefty bunch weights alone did not make a first-rate banana. Following the conversion to boxed Cavendish varieties, research agendas increasingly focused on factors influencing the visual appearance of the peel. For example, in 1966 United Fruit's research department declared that "a major portion" of their disease control agenda focused on fruit spot diseases "in view of the importance of unblemished fruit in the Chiquita quality program."[71] The company's fruit spot control program combined the removal of dry leaves from banana plants, weekly fungicide (Maneb) treatments, and fruit bagging (covering maturing bunches with polyethylene bags). Covering banana bunches with plastic bags provided protection against a number of pests and increased bunch weights, but the bags created very humid microenvironments in which populations of aphids grew rapidly. The aphids themselves were not considered to be a problem, but a fungus (sooty mold) that grew on the honeydew secreted by aphids "detracted" from the fruit's appearance.

As early as 1959, Standard Fruit began adding insecticides to the plastic bags in order to control aphid populations. United Fruit workers dusted bags with Diazinon, an acutely toxic chemical.[72] Using both electric and hand blowers, workers coated the insides of polyethylene bags with a 25 percent Diazinon powder. One pound of the powder treated about 200 bags. In Honduras, the bagging operation required 75 dusters and a "sub-

stantial" labor force. Goggles, masks, and protective clothing were recommended for workers who handled Diazinon. In addition, bag-dusters
were to work only one week followed by three weeks doing other tasks
in order to limit exposure to Diazinon.[73] In 1971, United Brands researchers reported that the concentration of Diazinon could be reduced to 10
percent and remain effective. They also noted the development of a new
method to treat the bags "for greater worker safety."[74]

The reference to worker safety was unusual; research department reports generally were silent on issues related to occupational and environmental health. On the occasions when worker health issues did surface in
the reports, they tended to be framed in terms of labor efficiency. For example, in a section on fruit spot control, the 1969 annual report stated,
"Thylate which continues to perform well in controlled field trials, did
not appear to do as well in the field, perhaps because its irritant action
on the workers' skin influenced the efficiency of application."[75] In general,
company guidelines for handling pesticides were ambiguous and placed
the burden of responsibility for limiting exposures to toxic chemicals on
workers by emphasizing the need for personal hygiene.[76] Furthermore,
United Fruit's standard operating procedures ignored how the organization of work gave rise to social practices, including eating and smoking
on the job, which made strict adherence to safety measures difficult. The
masks, gloves, and rubber boots sometimes provided to workers were ill
suited for use in the hot and humid climate in which banana plants thrive.
Of course, personal experience convinced workers like Neche Martínez
to take precautions: "With these asphyxiating poisons, if you tried to
eat, you immediately turned green and they hauled you off [for medical
treatment]."[77]

To argue that fruit company research staffs paid little attention to
occupational exposures to pesticides is not to suggest that agrochemical
use on banana plantations was indiscriminant. Fruit company scientists
quickly became aware that sustained use of certain classes of pesticides
could alter agroecological processes and give rise to new problems in the
form of pesticide-resistant pest populations, chemical residues, and/or
new pests. The multiple considerations that influenced decisions about
agrochemical use on banana plantations are illustrated by the histories of
two pesticides—Dieldrin and DBCP (Nemagon)—employed to kill parasitic organisms often found in the soils of banana plantations.

The root borer, or banana weevil (*Cosmopolites sordidus*), damages
the roots of banana plants by tunneling in and feeding on rhizome material during the grub stage. Infected plants generally produce smaller

than average fruit bunches and are very susceptible to uprooting during windstorms.[78] In 1950, United Fruit experimented with controlling root borers through an intensive trapping method designed to kill adult weevils.[79] Three years later, a study concluded that trapping was "effective in reducing the populations [of root borers]," but was not as "efficient" as the insecticide Dieldrin which reportedly could control root borer populations for up to two years after application.[80] In 1954, the company began applying Dieldrin spray at a recommended rate of once per year except where root borer populations were "extremely high."[81] United Fruit later applied Dieldrin in the forms of granules and dusts that provided longer-lasting control than spray formulations. As late as 1960, United Fruit's Norwood Thorton declared that "chemicals continue to be the main weapon for root borer control," and cited an example in which a single application of Dieldrin had brought a major infestation of borers under control within two months.[82]

However, not everyone on United Fruit's research staff was enthusiastic about the use of Dieldrin. In the mid-1950s the department's newsletter urged farm managers to control borer populations through cultural practices such as planting insect-free rhizomes. A subsequent newsletter stressed the need to practice farm sanitation in order to make conditions "unfavorable" for pest populations. The letter concluded by exhorting farm managers to "reduce your insect populations without the use of sprays!"[83] In 1956, a Cornell University toxicologist studied residue levels of Dieldrin in soils and concluded that "frequent applications" could result in a potentially dangerous build-up of the insecticide.[84] That same year, United Fruit entomologist Furber S. Roberts gave a paper at the 10th International Congress of Entomology that provided several examples in which Dieldrin applications eliminated "beneficial insects" such as ants and lady bugs, provoking subsequent surges in populations of herbivorous insects with no previous history as "pests." By disrupting patterns of predation and parasitism among insects, Dieldrin and other persistent insecticides helped give rise to new "enemies" of the banana plant. Roberts concluded by stating that biological and cultural methods appeared to be the most satisfactory means to control root-borer populations.[85] One year later, after observing that an application of Dieldrin had destroyed ant populations that played "an important role" in controlling other insects, United Fruit's research department warned farm personnel that "indiscriminate use of insecticides may not be economically sound and could lead to problems greater than those for which control was attempted."[86]

A broad-spectrum killing power was only one of Dieldrin's drawbacks. As early as 1961, United Fruit researchers declared that there was a "great need" to find a substitute for Dieldrin on account of root borer resistance to the insecticide.[87] In 1965, the company stopped using Dieldrin in favor of Kepone (another organochlorinated compound) following the latter's clearance for use on bananas by United States' regulatory agencies. Two years later, United Fruit received an extension on its Kepone clearance because the insecticide was "important in the banana borer control program."[88] However, by 1970, growing concerns about the long-term environmental effects of organochlorinated pesticides prompted the U.S. government to consider a ban on Kepone. United Fruit and Kepone's manufacturer, the Allied Chemical Corporation, subsequently entered into negotiations with the U.S. Food and Drug Administration over use of the insecticide on bananas. That same year, United Fruit scientists began testing the ability of other insecticides, including an organophosphate (Dursban) and a systemic carbamate (Furadan), to control root-borers in banana plantations.[89] Then, in 1973, United Fruit's Golfito division in Costa Rica discontinued all insecticide use in favor of biological controls. Within two years, populations of root borers and other insects fell to acceptable levels. By the late 1970s, all of the company's Central American operations had drastically lowered their use of insecticides to control root borers.[90]

Root borers were not the only organisms capable of weakening banana root systems. In fact, early studies of the effects of root borers on banana production may have overlooked the extent to which parasitic nematodes (*Radopholus similis*) also contributed to lowering yields. As early as 1957, United Fruit scientists reported that populations of *R. similis* were causing "considerable damage" to banana plants in Panama.[91] That same year, the Shell Oil Company began marketing a nematicide called Nemagon (dibromochloropropane or DBCP) that the company claimed would boost yields of "exportable bananas."[92] In 1958, United Fruit researchers noted that early reports on DBCP's effectiveness were favorable, but recommended controlling *R. similis* populations via fallowing and planting nematode-free rhizomes. Two years later, research department experiments confirmed earlier findings that nematicide treatments could increase the amount of "marketable" fruit defined at the time as an "eight-handed, American grade stem" that weighed more than 70 pounds.[93] In 1961, the U.S. Food and Drug Administration approved a temporary clearance for the use of DBCP in banana "seed" beds. United Fruit scientists subsequently recommended using DBCP in company nurseries, but they refrained from endorsing its use on a large scale pending further trials.

Instead, the company relied upon a combination of clean seed material and fallowing to control populations of R. *similis* throughout the 1960s.[94]

Continued problems with plant uprooting and the rising costs of fallowing — a process that involved leaving soils out of production for at least two years and treating them with herbicides — prompted United Brand scientists to reinitiate nematicide trials in the early 1970s. Experiments conducted in Honduras revealed that applications of DBCP increased bunch weights and reduced losses from uprooting. Nevertheless, researchers concluded that the value of the increased output did not offset the costs of the treatment. Instead, they recommended propping as a less expensive alternative to DBCP on farms where uprooting was serious. However, in Costa Rica and Panama, where rates of nematode infestation were much higher than in Honduras, United Brands began applying DBCP in 1973.[95]

Standard Fruit began using DBCP on a commercial scale in 1967, after field tests conducted in Honduras indicated that its use increased yields. Researcher Henry Muery wrote that average bunch weights on Standard Fruit's Coyoles farms increased from 70 pounds to 90 pounds between 1967 and 1971.[96] The positive effect that DBCP had on fruit weights prompted some former Standard Fruit field workers to refer to the nematicide as *abono* (fertilizer).[97] In Honduras, the company first applied DBCP through overhead irrigation systems. Working twelve-hour night shifts, laborers applied the product at the rate of 4–6.7 gallons/acre.[98] Cantalisio Andino, who worked part-time mixing DBCP, said that his skin regularly came into contact with the chemical: "I didn't take many precautions because the man [supervisor] never told me, 'Be careful, this stuff is poison.'"[99] Other laborers remembered being repeatedly exposed to DBCP-laced irrigation waters.[100] In the words of one former applicator, "We didn't take care of ourselves, we didn't use any protective clothing or gloves, nothing."[101] Neche Martínez recalled being issued safety equipment, but maintained that it was not always foolproof: "they gave us gloves and masks but in spite of these measures . . . people always became ill, maybe two or three workers would vomit and have diarrhea."[102]

Irrigation workers were not the only plantation residents potentially exposed to DBCP. When pruning crews entered farms in the early morning, they invariably brushed up against wet banana leaves and walked through puddles filled with the previous night's DBCP-laced irrigation water. DBCP, along with other pesticides and fertilizers, ran into drainage canals where they killed a variety of fauna (including fish, shrimp, opossum, and skunks) whose corpses could be seen floating in the ditches during the early morning hours.[103] DBCP also drifted over company-owned

worker housing units situated alongside the farms. One former camp resident recalled that drifting pesticides sometimes poisoned chickens and
other domestic animals.[104] Worker complaints apparently prodded Standard Fruit to install new sprinklers that reduced the amount of drift.
At some point in the 1970s, the company began applying DBCP in a
granular formulation that workers injected into the base of banana plants.
This method significantly reduced the contamination of plantation living
spaces but left applicators vulnerable to exposure.

Public concern about the effects of DBCP exposure on human health
did not surface until 1977 when a group of male workers in a California
chemical plant learned that they were sexually sterile. That same year, the
U.S. government greatly restricted DBCP use. Standard Fruit continued to
use the product on its Central American banana farms for two more years.
The consequences of the fruit companies' use of DBCP are still being un-
raveled. In Costa Rica some ten thousand people may have suffered serious health effects (including cancers and sterility) from their exposure to
DBCP. In Honduras, the number of individuals affected by the nematicide could be as high as 2,500, but a precise figure will never be known.
Lori Ann Thrupp found that economic considerations largely drove Standard Fruit's decision to use DBCP in Costa Rica, which was less expensive
and equally effective (when applied at high frequencies) as less hazardous
alternatives.[105] This perceived financial incentive, combined with the sup-
pression of toxicological studies by the manufacturers of DBCP and fruit
company research agendas that prioritized keeping banana plants—not
banana workers—healthy, all explain the use of DBCP in Central America
and elsewhere for more than a decade. The broad outline of the DBCP
story is a distressingly familiar one for Latin American farmworkers who
have often lacked the resources and political power to ensure a safe work
environment.[106] But the story of DBCP cannot be fully explained in political and economic terms: changing agroecological conditions gave rise
to the nematode "problem" in the first place.

As is the case with fungal pathogens, parasitic nematodes have a dynamic relationship with their hosts and the surrounding agroecosystem.
In Central America, the emergence of a burrowing nematode problem
coincided with the industry-wide conversion to Cavendish cultivars.[107]
Cavendish-type plants are highly susceptible to nematode infections. Furthermore, the routine pruning and fertilizer applications intended to
boost yields tended to exacerbate the degree of damage caused by nematode infestations. Pruning—an operation dating back to the nineteenth-

century export trade—removed most of the young suckers from banana plants so that nutrients would be concentrated in one or two stems. This technique helped to produce full, long-fingered bananas, but it deprived plants of the structural stability provided by the lateral shoots. Heavy fruit bunches in turn placed great stress upon the stems and roots, leaving fruit-bearing plants vulnerable to uprooting.[108] In other words, the impact of *R. similis* on export bananas was not an entirely "natural" phenomenon; a singular emphasis on high yields helped to create the problem.

Soil conditions and land-use histories also influenced the incidence of nematodes. The comparatively low populations of *R. similis* on United Fruit's Sula valley farms resulted from both the company's clean-seed program and its earlier silting and flood-fallow projects that yielded the unanticipated benefit of lowering nematode populations.[109] Under the soil conditions in the Sula valley, United Fruit scientists determined that the most economical means to reduce the incidence of uprooting was by propping. Standard Fruit researchers, operating in a distinct agroecological setting, concluded otherwise and urged wide-scale use of DBCP to boost yields. This seemingly technical footnote in the history of banana cultivation is vital for understanding how United Fruit's field workers in Honduras largely avoided exposure to DBCP and the health problems that have afflicted tens of thousands of banana workers elsewhere in Central America.

The varying approaches to root borer and nematode control reflected the complex economic calculus involved in defining agricultural "pests" in a world of changing markets and evolving agroecosystems. In both cases, financial considerations—"the bottom line"—played a central role in decision-making about agrochemical use, but forecasting the economic risks and benefits associated with Dieldrin and DBCP was by no means simple. The close relationship between the chemical industry and the fruit companies shaped the direction of research in the tropics, but fruit company scientists were wary of adopting new pesticides prior to extensive field-testing. At the same time, there is little to suggest that agronomists, entomologists, plant pathologists, and other scientists possessed the knowledge and/or motivation to monitor the effects of agrochemicals on field hands. Instead, they focused almost exclusively on how new agrochemicals affected yields. In the case of Dieldrin, secondary pest outbreaks and the rapid buildup of resistant root borer populations led United Fruit researchers to favor biological and cultural controls that the fruit companies eventually adopted. However, the lengthy delay between the initial warnings about long-time use of Dieldrin and the adoption of non-chemical control measures suggests that fruit company executives tended to pay less attention to their scientific staffs and field hands than to their stockholders and U.S. government regulatory agencies. In the case of DBCP, the product boosted yields and had no discernable negative effects on banana plants, prompting the fruit companies to use the nematicide under certain soil conditions. The companies continued to use DBCP in Central America even after governmental regulatory agencies in the United States acted to restrict its use due to occupational health concerns.

There can be little doubt that, as Jorge Romero's anecdote about Benito suggests, individual decisions and behaviors contributed to workers' levels of exposure to pesticides. At the same time, changing production practices created working environments that were permeated with agrochemicals. Bent on maximizing labor efficiency and fruit yields, the fruit companies' researchers tended to raise concerns about chemical inputs only when they showed signs of being toxic to banana plants and/or sufficiently irritating to workers to lower productivity. Consequently, the fruit companies sometimes found ways to reduce exposures to acutely toxic substances but displayed little concern for understanding the long-term effects of agrochemicals on worker health and the surrounding environment.

In the late 1960s, export banana production/consumption dynamics began to be influenced by powerful environmental movements in the United States and Europe that sought to regulate the use of pesticides. Inspired largely by Rachel Carson's widely read book *Silent Spring,* U.S. environmentalists succeeded in restricting and/or banning the use of some persistent organochlorines (e.g., DDT) capable of causing long-term damage to people and wildlife. Regulations restricting pesticide use tended to be based on residue levels — thresholds that provided a degree of consumer safety but did little to protect farmworkers.

In spite of the United Farmworkers' early calls for a ban on DDT and organized consumer boycotts of California table grapes, it was Carson, not Cesar Chavez who became the most prominent symbol of the U.S. environmental movement.[110] In some instances, pesticide reforms actually increased risks to farmworkers by encouraging greater use of chemicals (including organophosphates) that broke down quickly in the environment but that were acutely toxic to humans. The environmental movement in the United States largely failed to alter the banana companies' basic approach to controlling the "enemies" of the banana: trials of fungi-cides, herbicides, and nematicides continued to dominate research agen-das throughout the 1970s. Ultimately, the daily hazards faced by farm-workers in Central America remained a largely unaccounted-for cost of late-twentieth-century U.S. banana consumption.

Chapter 8

Banana Cultures in Comparative Perspective

The worldwide expansion of capitalism and the creation of a global market of commodities has been driven by the profit-seeking effort to control not only cheap labor, technology, or markets, but also nature.

FERNANDO CORONIL, 1997

When Hondurans turned on their radios the morning of April 22, 1975, they learned from the Supreme Council of the Armed Forces that Colonel Juan Melgar Castro was the new Chief of State, replacing General Oswaldo López Arellano, who two weeks earlier had been accused of accepting a bribe from the United Brands Corporation.[1] When López Arellano prevented a special Honduran investigating committee from examining his foreign bank accounts, he was ousted in a bloodless coup. The bribe was discovered during the U.S. Security and Exchange Commission's (SEC's) "routine" investigation into the death of United Brand's former president Eli Black, who had committed suicide by jumping out a window of his office on the forty-fourth floor of the Pan-American building.[2] Following a *Wall Street Journal* report on the investigation, United Brands released a public statement on April 8, revealing that a $1.25 million bribe had been paid to a "high official" of the Honduran government.[3] Eli Black reportedly authorized the bribe in order to obtain a reduction in the banana export tax. The SEC charged United Brands with fraud for failing to inform stockholders of the bribe; after several months of litigation, the company agreed to a federal court injunction that required it to correct its financial reports "with respect to unlawful payments to officials and employees of foreign governments and unlawful foreign political contributions."[4]

From the days of Sam "Banana Man" Zemurray to the late twentieth century, U.S. banana companies employed both legal and extralegal measures to gain access to land, restrict competitors, evade taxes and duties, hold down wages, and expand market shares. Only the most ardent apologists for the fruit companies can relegate such activities to a distant past that has no bearing on the present. However, as this book has demonstrated, the fruit companies' political and economic power conditioned, but did not determine, the historical trajectory of export banana production in Honduras and elsewhere. Export banana farms were simultaneously linked to international commodity chains and a web of agroecological relationships that constrained, resisted, and confounded the power of the fruit companies and their allies.

In tracing the transformation of a tropical plant into an everyday food consumed in the United States, I have tried to uncover how cultural practices and biophysical processes have shaped economic institutions (including corporations and markets) and vice-versa. This framework reveals the limitations of explanatory models in which capital exercises power "globally" and subaltern actors respond "locally." Clearly, vast asymmetries of power existed between U.S. banana companies and the worker-cultivators who lived on the North Coast. Nevertheless, even the United Fruit Company had to exercise its power through people situated in specific localities stretched along a transnational commodity chain.[5] Moreover, people were not the only dynamic element with which the fruit companies had to contend. The plants and pathogens that the companies needed to control in order to generate profits from the production, transport, and distribution of bananas were neither passive nor predictable. Viewed from the ground level, export banana production appeared more like a series of improvisations (both creative and destructive in nature) than a well-scripted global power play.

Acknowledging the role of contingency, the particularity of place, and the entangled agency of people, plants, and pathogens does not preclude efforts to draw comparisons with other regions and commodities in order to formulate new explanatory models capable of informing policy debates and political projects. In this final chapter, I draw upon scholarship on other agricultural commodities in order to place export bananas in a comparative perspective. A comprehensive comparison would require writing another book; my more modest endeavor selectively compares bananas to two other important agricultural commodities in Latin American and Caribbean histories: coffee and sugar. For a twist, I also examine commercial fruit orchards (including oranges and pears) and vineyards in California in order to recast models of "export" agriculture by juxtaposing commodities that travel great distances both within and across national borders.

In keeping with the main themes of this book, my comparison concentrates on the dynamics of mass production and mass consumption, and the connections between social and environmental change. The first half of the chapter compares the emergence and evolution of mass markets for bananas, coffee, sugar, and California fruits in the United States during the nineteenth and twentieth centuries. Simply put, I argue that consumption was uniquely "super-sized" and selective. People in the United States annually consumed billions of bananas, oranges, cups of coffee, and teaspoons of cane sugar. However, mass desire for individual commodities was not insatiable, and as per capita consumption rates leveled off in the twentieth century the increasingly consolidated industries went to great lengths to limit competition, standardize their products, and sell "quality." Advertising campaigns often incorporated images of production spaces that stressed both the fecundity of the land and the contentedness of the people who worked it. Miss Chiquita, Juan Valdez, and the Sun Maid not only distracted consumers from injustices by romanticizing daily life in places of production, but also played a significant role in shaping production/consumption dynamics, less by "creating" demand per se than by shaping the aesthetics of consumption.

The second half of the chapter compares production across commodity sectors. As a number of scholars have demonstrated, export economies in Latin America and the Caribbean gave rise to a remarkable diversity of experiences over time and space. William Roseberry suggested that the explanation for the diversity lay in the different contexts or "fields of power" into which commodity traders and capital moved.[6] Unfortunately, few scholars have analyzed the literal fields from which investors, traders, farmers, and workers struggled to create wealth and livelihoods. In the final section, I focus my comparison on both human and non-human elements of agroecosystems — soils, plants, pathogens, and herbivores — in order to account for both similarities and differences found within and among different commodity sectors. Integrating non-human actors runs the risk of filling history's score card with an incomprehensible number of players. However, my intention is to compare the dynamic relationships among actors, not to expand the lineup of autonomous entities. I conclude by identifying some common features and problems associated with agricultural commodity webs as a first step toward fostering both new research agendas and socially just and ecologically resilient farming systems.

BIG APPETITE: THE EMERGENCE AND
EVOLUTION OF U.S. MASS MARKETS

The rise in U.S. consumption rates of tropical agricultural commodities in the late nineteenth century was unprecedented. Between 1870 and 1920, total sugar consumption grew by seven times while annual per capita consumption more than doubled from 35.3 pounds to 85.5 pounds. During this same time span, U.S. coffee imports rose from 231 million pounds to approximately 1.5 billion pounds. Between 1883 and 1900, per capita coffee consumption jumped from 9 pounds to 13 pounds. As late as the mid-1880s, citrus was a luxury item; by 1914, people in the United States were eating approximately 40 oranges per person each year. During this time period, California emerged as the major source for many kinds of deciduous fruits. For example, between 1882 and 1891, shipments of raisins from Fresno County increased from 80,000 pounds to 45,000,000 pounds![7] In 1909, the entire state produced 31.5 million bushels of fruit, including three-quarters of all citrus consumed in the United States.[8] Of course, food was not the only thing being consumed in greater quantities during this period; a slew of manufactured goods ranging from sewing machines to soap to cigarettes proliferated in both urban and rural areas in the United States.[9]

A number of explanations have been offered to account for this extraordinary increase in consumption. Sidney Mintz and Michael Jiménez have linked rising consumption of sugar and coffee to changes taking place in industrial capitalism, including the formation of a large, urban-dwelling working class. Environmental historian John McNeill includes population growth and technological innovations as the "engines of change" that powered twentieth-century resource consumption. Business historian Alfred Chandler has identified a "managerial revolution" in late-nineteenth-century business, which, along with a series of U.S. Supreme Court decisions, gave rise to corporations possessing sufficient capital (and limited liabilities) to achieve the economies of scale and vertical integration necessary to increase productivity, lower unit costs of production, and enforce quality standards.[10]

There is little doubt that increases in food consumption coincided with a set of interrelated demographic, economic, legal, and technological changes. Between the 1870s and the 1920s, the population of the United States increased from approximately 38.5 million people to more than 100 million. During this period, domestic and international migrations (including more than 23 million arrivals from Europe) swelled the populations of industrial cities, creating large, dense markets. Improved public health measures, ranging from vaccinations to sewage systems, lowered mortality rates. Workers' discretionary incomes also rose, enabling increases in per capita consumption of foodstuffs and other goods. In mining, milling, manufacturing, transportation, and other industries, corporations capable of producing and selling commodities at previously unattainable scales proliferated (United Fruit was hardly unique for its time). In order to "scale up," these corporations frequently invested in processing and transportation technologies that enabled them to accelerate the pace of production, distribution, and sale of commodities while cutting labor costs. Increasingly, fossil fuels (mostly coal) powered the machinery of mass production and mass transportation.

Consideration of the above processes is essential for understanding what made possible mass consumption in general, but they are far less helpful in accounting for the popularity of specific commodities. Explaining mass desire for certain things and not for others requires consideration of cultural contexts. For example, Sidney Mintz has demonstrated the power of sweetness in driving sugar production/consumption dynamics. Sweetness seems to have wide appeal across cultures, but Mintz and others locate the emergence of a preference for sucrose (refined white sugar) over other sweeteners in parts of sixteenth-century Europe.[11] In the nineteenth-century United States, the consumption of both sugar-based confections and sugar-sweetened hot beverages connoted European cosmopolitanism. The increasing availability of once "exotic" and expensive goods produced in the tropics became an everyday sign of rising U.S. hegemony in tropical Asia and Latin America.

The widespread availability of refined sugar (sucrose) contributed to the rising consumption of other commodities. Many U.S. coffee drinkers spooned sugar into their cups in order to sweeten their daily caffeine "fix."[12] At the same time, the psychoactive properties of coffee may have simultaneously increased demand for refined sugar via a kind of nineteenth-century "synergy." Sugar and coca extracts were key ingredients in Coca-Cola, which, along with other sweetened carbonated beverages like Hires Root Beer, would eventually supplant coffee as the most widely consumed beverages in the United States. The popularity of coffee probably contributed to a decline in hot cocoa drinking, but refined sugar helped to give rise to novel forms of cocoa consumption in the form of solid milk chocolate, a shift in taste that Milton Hershey both capitalized upon and promoted via the mass production of five-cent chocolate bars and Hershey's Kiss candies. In order to ensure a steady supply of sweetener, Hershey purchased 65,000 acres of land and financed the building of a large sugar refinery in Cuba.[13]

Bitter-tasting tropical commodities were not the only ones whose consumption in the United States was closely associated with sugar: California canneries used refined sugar as a preservative for peaches, pears, grapes, and other fruits that were packed in a sugary syrup. In addition, citrus growers favored varieties of oranges — one-fifth of which were destined for juice production by the 1930s — with high sugar contents.[14] Finally, bananas entered U.S. diets as a mildly sweet "fresh fruit"; their few popular uses in cookery and baking were confined largely to sweet breads, pies, and ice cream desserts. Starchy cooking bananas, or plantains, did not acquire mass appeal in the twentieth century United States. Sweetness, then, was a common denominator among this otherwise mixed set of food and beverage commodities for which mass markets emerged in the late nineteenth and early twentieth centuries.

A second common denominator was mass advertising and product branding. From a comparative perspective, the U.S. banana companies' decision to brand Cavendish bananas in the late 1950s was rather delayed. As early as 1865, the Arbuckle brothers sold packaged coffee beans throughout the United States under the brand name Ariosa. California fruit packers began shipping their delicate products in crates featuring colorful labels in the 1880s. The California Fruit Growers' Exchange adopted the Sunkist name in 1908 and subsequently began wrapping individual oranges in tissue paper stamped with the Sunkist label. In 1912, the California Associated Raisin Company introduced Sun-Maid raisins. By that time, grocery shoppers could find Domino sugar on the shelves along with products such as Quaker Oats, Nabisco's Uneeda Biscuits, and Kellogg's Toasted Corn Flakes. According to historian Susan Strasser, manufacturers used brand names in order to foster customer loyalty and diminish the ability of wholesalers and retail grocers to steer shoppers toward competitors' products.[15]

Brand names were only one form of advertising. Public exhibitions (including World's Fairs), pamphlets, recipe booklets, billboards, and newspaper and magazine advertisements were other forms of mass media used to promote products in the early twentieth century. Eventually, radio and television would become key media for advertisers. The United Fruit Company and its subsidiaries took advantage of all of these media, printing text-heavy informational pamphlets in the 1910s, shifting to billboards, recipe booklets, and marketing studies in the 1920s, and launching "The Chiquita Banana Song" on the radio during the 1940s. California fruit growers, coffee roasters, and sugar refiners pursued similar market-ing strategies.[16] However, the undeniable rise of mass marketing and ad-vertising budgets in the early twentieth century should not be taken as evidence that the masses were seduced (or duped) into their consuming habits.[17] For the commodities examined here, the steepest climbs in per capita consumption took place in the second half of the nineteenth cen-tury, prior to the creation of national advertising campaigns directed at end-consumers. In fact, national advertising campaigns for bananas, cof-fee, and deciduous fruits from California did not begin in earnest until consumption rates began to plateau during the early 1920s. As U.S. his-torian Steven Stoll has observed for the case of California fruit-grower cooperatives after World War I, marketing campaigns sought to redefine a condition of "over-production" as one of "under-consumption."[18]

If the emergence of professional advertising agencies cannot be cred-ited with creating demand, they were quite adept at identifying—selec-tively and with considerable distortion—the changing social and cultural contexts of consumption. For example, as the twentieth century unfolded, United Fruit's advertisements shifted from rather detailed descriptions of production and distribution processes to a changing set of images that conveyed consumers' desires—for health, for sex, for humor, and of course, for good-tasting food. Advertising, according to U.S. cultural his-torian Jackson Lears, created widely circulated "fables of abundance" in which industrial efficiency—be it in a steel mill or in an orange grove —guaranteed a cornucopia of pleasures. The fetishized images of com-modities created by advertising agencies reflected their creators' highly selective visions: the connections between resources, workers, and mass consumption were seldom discernable. In 1932, the editor of *Printers' Ink,* an important U.S. trade journal for advertisers, proposed replacing the "full dinner pail" (an image strongly associated with factory work) with the "full cereal bowl" as the icon for an emerging generation of "full-fledged consumers." One cannot help but wonder if the editor imagined a sliced banana topping off his symbol for "the future of America."[19]

The editor's optimism—even during the Great Depression—was not entirely unfounded: the mass production of foodstuffs enabled lower- and middle-class people to eat and drink what was once restricted to the tables of the elite. In fact, processed cereal with a banana was a quintessen-tial urban-industrial meal that reflected larger changes in when and how working people prepared and took meals.[20] Daily life in the United States increasingly moved to the synchronized beats of standardized time. Time zones, punch clocks, watches, school bells, and hourly wages reconfigured the activities of daily life. Eating became more harried, as evidenced by both ritualized "snacking" (e.g., coffee breaks) and the rising consumption of highly processed or ready-to-eat foods.

Advertisers also recognized that women bore primary responsibilities for making meals in most households, and they frequently appropriated ideals of domesticity by defining consumers as "mothers" and "housewives." However, to the extent that these marketing tactics worked, they tapped into the anxieties of an expanding number of middle-class women who juggled domestic responsibilities with work outside of the home. As women increasingly carved out new social spaces for themselves, they also had to make time to occupy them (since most men were not inclined to take on domestic meal preparation). Highly processed foods helped to reduce the amount of time needed to prepare meals. In other words, new social roles for women—which in many ways undermined the ideals of domesticity—may have played a large part in shaping the significance of buying and eating easy-to-prepare foods. Here the connection between production and consumption is entangled: industrial food processors often paid female workers to perform what was essentially kitchen work—washing, peeling, cutting, and preparing foods—on a massive scale. The same can of peaches bought by "office girls" in Chicago signified factory jobs and opportunities for new kinds of social relationships (including union membership) for immigrant women in California packing plants.[21]

Food consumption in the twentieth century also became tightly linked to ideas about health and morality. For example, in order to counter the perception that bananas were difficult to digest, some of the United Fruit Company's earliest informational pamphlets stressed both the nutritional value of bananas and the importance of proper ripening. Coffee marketers also worked to win the support of health care professionals in order to dispel concerns about the physiological effects of their product. The Joint Coffee Publicity Committee (a coffee industry lobby) turned to Massachusetts Institute of Technology industrial microbiologist Samuel C. Prescott—the same expert enlisted by United Fruit—to secure "scientific" confirmation of the health benefits to be derived from coffee.[22] But if some people viewed coffee consumption as an unhealthy habit, many employers and social reformers saw it as an alternative to alcohol consumption that they associated with worker absenteeism and immoral behaviors. This was no small consideration in an era when powerful temperance movements campaigned successfully to ban the sale of alcoholic beverages. Prohibition would not last, but the importance of the moral meanings of consumption is clearly reflected in the history of cocaine, whose status shifted from that of a medicinal tonic to a "fiendish" illicit drug by the early 1920s.[23]

Continued economic expansion, population growth, and a mass culture of consumption that helped tie together an otherwise divided nation ensured that the United States would remain the largest single market for coffee, bananas, sugar, and fresh fruits throughout the twentieth century. However, trends in per capita consumption varied considerably by commodity.[24] The lifting of shipping restrictions following the end of the Second World War enabled banana consumption to return to pre-war levels by 1947. Per capita consumption of bananas subsequently declined slightly and remained flat through the 1960s. In the late twentieth century, banana consumption rose steadily, topping 27 pounds per person in 1997. California deciduous fruit trades followed a distinct trajectory: the consumption of fresh citrus, including oranges and grapefruit, declined from a peak of more than 60 pounds per capita during the mid-1940s to less than 28 pounds in the early 1970s. Since that time, consumption of fresh citrus has remained relatively flat. However, between 1970 and 1997, individuals in the United States routinely consumed an additional 90 to 100 pounds of citrus per year in the form of processed juices. Consumption of other fresh fruits widely cultivated in California, including grapes, peaches, and pears, either declined or remained virtually unchanged in the second half of the twentieth century; but as was the case with citrus, consumption of these fruits in processed forms tended to rise.[25] Comparing bananas to other fruits, then, underscores the uniquely narrow niche occupied by bananas in U.S. cuisine: bananas have rarely been consumed in dried, canned, jellied, jammed, or juiced forms.

Coffee consumption increased steadily between 1925 and 1945. Entering the 1960s, coffee was the most popular beverage consumed in the United States. But coffee consumption fell by 26 percent between 1965 and 1987, a trend that continued through the late 1990s, when per capita consumption of both sweetened soft drinks and alcoholic beverages surpassed coffee.[26] The popularity of soft drinks notwithstanding, per capita consumption of sucrose (from sugarcane and sugar beets) declined from more than 100 pounds in 1970 to about 66 pounds in 1997. This counter-intuitive trend is explained by the rising popularity of sucrose substitutes, including high-fructose corn syrup. However, there continue to be marketing "synergies" between coffee and cane sugar: the emergence of a rather large market for "specialty coffees" in the late twentieth century was accompanied by the appearance of semi-refined cane sugars. Marketed under names such as "Sugar in the Raw," the non-white sucrose sweetener is pitched to consumers seeking "natural" or "artisanal" food products.[27]

Unsurprisingly, this comparison of long-term trends in commodity consumption confirms the centrality of various fruits, coffee, and sucrose in twentieth-century U.S. diets. It further indicates that the biggest leaps in per capita consumption occurred in the nineteenth century. Consumption rates fluctuated considerably during the twentieth century, but they generally leveled out in the 1950s. This is not to suggest that markets for these commodities have remained static since midcentury; they all became increasingly integrated as shippers, processors, and distributors sought to increase their market shares and lower costs. As industries consolidated, commodities became increasingly standardized. Fables of abundance gave way to discourses on quality.

SELECTIVE TASTES: THE EVOLUTION OF QUALITY STANDARDS

As late as the 1880s, none of the commodity sectors considered here had undergone significant integration; farmers, shippers, processors, wholesalers, and retailers tended to be distinct entities although by no means independent. However, this changed dramatically over the course of the twentieth century. By the 1910s, just three U.S. banana companies had achieved a very high degree of vertical integration, controlling the production, shipping, and marketing of their product. California fruit growers also integrated production, packing, and marketing operations in the early twentieth century, but they did not control rail transportation. Some sugar companies, including United Fruit, had operations that integrated cultivation, milling, and refining processes. The coffee industry remained fragmented during the first half of the twentieth century. Following World War II, coffee roasting in the United States began to consolidate, but even then, roasters seldom owned coffee farms or processing mills (*beneficios*) in Latin America. Significantly, consolidation generally occurred first in the middle nodes of commodity chains; shippers, processors, and distributors integrated before producers and retailers.

Getting commodities to mass markets required mass transportation: in the late nineteenth century, fossil fuel–powered railroads and steamships (along with mules and canoes) carried unprecedented volumes of cargo at record-breaking speeds. Bananas, coffee, and sugar, along with deciduous fruits from California, all required processing and/or packing prior to transport in order to ensure that the product arrived in saleable condition. The importance of shipping and processing is reflected in the tendency across diverse commodity sectors for capital and power to concentrate precisely in the places that lay in between farms and kitchens. For example, coffee mill owners, merchants, and roasters "directed and profited from the coffee economy far more than did growers."[28] A similar tendency prevailed in the twentieth-century sugar industry, where power and wealth accumulated primarily in the hands of the families and corporations who owned the *centrales,* railroads, and refineries. Legendary "banana men," including Lorenzo Dow Baker, Minor Keith, the Vaccaro brothers, and Samuel Zemurray, began their careers as shippers, railroad builders, and wholesalers, not planters. In California, fruit packers became key mediators between growers and wholesalers.

Throughout the Americas, the expansion of export commodity production went hand in hand with railroad construction. For example, between 1834 and 1837, Cuban sugar planters financed the building of the first railroad in Latin America (and the seventh built in the world).[29] In Costa Rica and Guatemala, coffee interests financed the building of railroads that in turn stimulated export banana production along the Caribbean coasts of those two nations. United Fruit's two Honduran subsidiaries were tellingly named "railroad"—not banana—companies. Finally, the completion of a transcontinental railroad in the United States helped to make possible the rapid overland transport of bulky commodities from California to Midwest and Eastern markets.

For all of the commodities in question, post-harvest processing was crucial for transforming plant materials into marketable products. However, there were some important differences. In the case of coffee, the valuable part of the plant is the seed (i.e., the coffee "bean"). The fruit pulp is removed via washing or drying, processes that have historically taken place in close proximity to coffee farms. Once depulped, "green" coffee can be stored for extended periods prior to roasting; once roasted, vacuum-sealed coffee has a relatively long shelf life. Also, roasters could, and often did, blend coffees from different regions. In the case of sugarcane, railroads served to transport cut cane to large mills where cane juice was extracted as quickly as possible in order to maximize sucrose content. The semi-processed product was then shipped to the United States where it was further refined into white, granular sugar. In sum, both coffee and sugar historically are highly processed in ways that completely change their appearance and flavor.

In contrast to coffee and sugar, bananas and oranges needed only minimal processing prior to shipment. In fact, the less the fruits were handled on their journey from farm to wholesale outlets the better. Transportation therefore had to be fast, smooth, and climate-controlled in order to be able to deliver "fresh" fruit throughout the calendar year in temperate climates. Significantly, the Armour Packing Company, an early innovator in shipping refrigerated meats, was among the first large-scale enterprises to establish fruit packing plants in California in order to fill refrigerated cars on their return journey east. But refrigeration and railroads were insufficient to overcome the intrinsic perishability of fresh fruit. Harris Weinstock, a London-born merchant, and G. Harold Powell, a New York–born horticulturalist, played leading roles in encouraging early-twentieth-century growers in California to standardize their products and form what historian Steven Stoll has called "corporate cooperatives."[30] In a process that anticipated the future of the export banana trade, Powell devised fruit packing techniques based on closely supervised fruit harvesters and packers to ensure quality. In the 1940s, California cooperatives incorporated chemical baths into the packing process in order to prevent the growth of mold on citrus during transit.[31] As was the case with bananas, a desire to lower the chance of spoilage and standardize quality played a key role in prompting a reorganization of the California fruit trade.

In addition to transporting and physically transforming plant materials into desired commodities, shippers and processors also developed discourses about "quality" as part of an effort to standardize production processes. Standardization was central to achieving and maintaining the economies of scale that enabled corporations to turn profits. For example, historian César Ayala argues that the Havemeyer family dominated the "sugar trust" that formed in the United States in 1887 largely because its refinery was able to produce both high-quality "cut loaf" sugar and "low-grade" sugars. The Havemeyers and other sugar refiners ensured acceptable profit margins by working to control the price margins between "raw" and "refined" sugar. They successfully lobbied the U.S. federal government for tariff schedules that favored the importation of unrefined sugars known as muscovadoes.[32]

The tariffs reflected the political power of the U.S. sugar industry and also the power that the United States government exercised over Cuba during the years of the Platt Amendment (1901–1934). They also reflected the premium that U.S. mass markets placed on white sugar, a preference in sweeteners apparently transplanted to North America from Europe. At some point in the eighteenth century, sugar refiners began grading raw sugar based on color and appearance in accordance with a system known as the "Dutch Standard." This grading system remained in use until the late nineteenth century, when refiners began using polariscopes, instruments that measured the refraction of light through sugar crystals, to grade sugars with a previously unattainable level of precision.

The diffusion of both polariscopes and centrifugal machines capable of rapidly separating sucrose from molasses led to changes in quality standards. By the 1890s, trade journals quoted prices for only two grades of raw sugar based on polariscope measurements. Some refiners continued to refer to the lower of the two grades as "muscovadoes" even though the product was rather distinct from sugars bearing that name in the mid-nineteenth century. Historian Alan Dye argues that the ability to determine grades with precision enabled refiners to purchase raw sugars without making direct inspections. Trading centers subsequently shifted from Havana to New York City, where buyers created a futures market for sugar. Dye also notes that the use of centrifugal machines reduced the moisture content of raw sugars, thereby lowering both spoilage rates and shipping costs.[33] However, muscovado sugars, which contain varying amounts of molasses that affect the color, flavor, and texture of the sweetener, have been, and continue to be, widely consumed by people in cane-growing regions of Latin America, where they are known as *rapadura* (Brazil) and *panela* (in much of Spanish-speaking Latin America).[34] The evolution of quality standards for sugar then, reflected technological innovations, the economic interests of shippers and refiners, and deeply rooted cultural beliefs that associated whiteness with "purity."

Coffee importers also pushed for standardization of green coffee— the semi-processed state in which beans were typically exported. In the early 1880s, New York–based coffee merchants founded a coffee exchange. Shortly thereafter, similar entities appeared in major European coffee trading cities. These organizations, which effectively created a futures market for coffee, developed standards to evaluate the size and "roasting potential" of imported beans, information that traveled across continents via telegraph lines. The development of a futures market for coffee meant that buyers no longer inspected specific beans; indeed, they often purchased "beans" that had yet to become a reality. But determining both quality and origins of coffee bean shipments remained problems for buyers and roasters. The passage of the 1907 U.S. Pure Food and Drug Act created federal regulations for a wide range of ingestible commodities. In response to reports that some coffee roasters adulterated their products with heavy metal–laden dyes and fillers, the law included labeling regulations for coffee.

Shortly thereafter, coffee roasters in the United States formed a national organization to self-regulate coffee quality as part of an effort to capture market share from neighborhood grocers who sold green beans and/or roasted coffee to order for retail customers. In fact, the movement for national standards for processed foods and drugs enjoyed the support of many large food manufacturers who found it easier to comply with regulations than their smaller competitors.[35] After several years marked by tensions between New York–based importers and Midwest roasters, in 1928 the two groups established the National Coffee Association (NCA), an organization dedicated primarily to marketing and lobbying activities. NCA members were important players in the negotiations among the U.S. government and the governments of coffee-producing nations in Latin America that led to the signing of the Inter-American Coffee Agreement (1940–1948) and the International Coffee Agreement (1962–1989). Driven in part by the geopolitical preoccupations of the United States during World War II and the Cold War, the agreements sought to stabilize prices and standardize quality through quota systems. By 1962, the NCA was dominated by corporate roasters (including General Foods and Folgers) who controlled a large portion of the U.S. market for ground coffees. The integration of the coffee trade, then, was a complicated process that occurred some three to four decades after the consolidation of the banana and sugar industries.[36]

In California, fruit growers faced a dilemma similar to that of banana growers when dealing with buyers. This is not surprising considering that deciduous fruits, like their tropical counterparts, were fleeting commodities that accrued and lost their market price in a matter of days. In order to gain leverage over distant brokers and wholesalers, California growers formed large cooperatives that, among other things, developed standards and grades for their produce. In 1917, the California Fruit Growers' Exchange successfully lobbied the California state legislature to pass the Fresh Fruit, Nut, and Vegetable Standardization Act. Shortly thereafter, the United States Department of Agriculture established standards for fresh produce in order to resolve disputes between buyers and sellers. As was the case with bananas, size and visual appearance tended to be key characteristics for fresh fruits: Sunkist oranges were washed, dried, waxed, and polished prior to being sorted into categories such as "Extra-fancy," "Fancy," and Choice."[37]

Historians are just beginning to consider the significance of standardization for the history of commodities. Nevertheless, a comparison of bananas, coffee, sugar, and California fruits permits the formulation of some preliminary propositions. Perhaps the most important point to emphasize to readers living in an era when market institutions and discourses reign supreme is that quality, as one scholar of coffee has observed, is a "curious thing."[38] The evidence that I have reviewed for four important food commodities indicates that "quality" is a floating signifier subject to change: there is no universally accepted "best" cup of coffee, banana, grape, or sweetener. This is not to deny that social groups living in particular times and places often possess similar tastes for goods. However, this tendency has less to do with objective, measurable criteria than with the subjective meanings that goods and their consumption acquire.

Moreover, there appears to be a link between quantity and quality: as mass markets became saturated (i.e., as per capita consumption began to level off), notions of quality tended to acquire a new sense of importance. Consequently, historians of agricultural commodities need to give much more attention to how quality standards have shaped contractual agreements (and disputes) between growers, buyers, laborers, and state regulators.[39] Evidence indicates that marketplace intermediaries (roasters, refiners, wholesalers, and shippers) have functioned as key arbiters of taste and quality. Advertising campaigns, directed toward both businesses and individual consumers, may have had their greatest impact in shaping quality discourses related to taste, appearance, and aroma.[40] This is not to imply that the consuming masses did not exercise agency in twentieth-century production/consumption dynamics: popular culture must be taken into consideration in order to understand why, for example, coffee and bananas were more widely consumed than tea and plantains in the twentieth-century United States. Nevertheless, analyses of consumption should avoid idealized notions of market economies in which individual consumer preferences prevail and "superior" quality triumphs over the "inferior." Instead, much closer scrutiny should be given to the practical needs, economic interests, and aesthetic sensibilities of the "middlemen" who worked in the nearly invisible spaces that lay between farms and kitchens.[41]

Finally, it is important not to view export markets as monolithic. The commodities compared here generally entered segmented mass markets. Standardization paradoxically contributed to market segmentation by enabling distant buyers to acquire knowledge about the origins and other features of commodities deemed to be important. For example, many European coffee buyers have historically paid premiums for arabica coffee beans produced at high altitudes. In contrast, mass markets for coffee in the United States became the primary destination for Brazilian arabicas cultivated at comparatively low altitudes. In the 1950s, markets emerged in the United States for instant coffee, a product that often included blends of arabica and robusta coffee beans. Then, in the 1970s, affluent U.S. coffee drinkers turned increasingly to "specialty coffees," high-priced arabicas that until recently were sold primarily by local and regional roaster/retailers.

European and U.S. banana markets have also differed significantly from one another. In the Caribbean and Central America, workers harvested Gros Michel bananas bound for Europe at a slightly younger age than bunches bound for the United States in order to compensate for the longer sea journey to European ports. As a result, Europeans became accustomed to eating bananas that on average were smaller than those available in the United States. Also, European markets imported Cavendish bananas from the Canary Islands long before U.S. markets accepted them. In Jamaica, growers reoriented their production toward Britain in the 1930s after the British Empire Marketing Board began subsidizing bananas produced in colonial territories. In 1947, the British Ministry of Food approved the importation of Lacatan bananas. Jamaican producers responded by replacing Gros Michel with the Panama disease–resistant Lacatan variety more than ten years before Cavendish varieties replaced Gros Michel in the United States.[42] In the late twentieth century, additional market segmentation occurred with the rising demand for "organic" and "fair trade" bananas, coffee, and other tropical commodities in Europe and the United States.

My research also suggests that quality standards can function to segment mass markets by class and region. For example, in the early twentieth century, U.S. fruit jobbers and retailers catering to affluent customers bought and sold top-grade bananas, while those operating in working-class communities carried lesser grades. In addition, at least some jobbers distinguished markets by region (recall the perception of Atlanta as a "dumping ground" for inferior bananas). However, in contrast to coffee markets, banana markets within the United States were not consistently segmented on the basis of variety or place of origin. Instead, grading tended to be based on the size and physical appearance of Gros Michel fruit when it reached U.S. ports. One suspects that a similar form of market segmentation prevailed for fresh and canned fruits from California.

In many ways, the twentieth-century evolution of quality standards for food commodities represented an effort to overcome, or at least control, variable biological processes. The environmental rootedness of agriculture ensured that product uniformity was more of an advertising claim than a reality: even export bananas, harvested from asexual plants with a high degree of genetic uniformity, varied over time and space. Standardizing plant products was achieved through the use of disciplined laborers and technological inputs. Ultimately, mass markets, no matter how large and powerful, were entangled in a dynamic relationship with processes of mass production.

FIELDS OF POWER: PRODUCTION AND ENVIRONMENTAL PROCESS

The most basic connection between mass markets and mass production was a spatial one: an abundance of land in nineteenth-century California, the Caribbean, and Latin America indirectly facilitated mass consumption by enabling farmers to produce massive quantities of agricultural products.[43] This abundance was not a fortuitous gift of nature or what sometimes is referred to as a "commodity lottery." The quantity and quality of land available at the rise of the export boom resulted primarily from historical ruptures and ecological jumblings initiated in 1492 that gave rise to what might be thought of as "modernity's nature." The voyages of Columbus and his companions marked the beginnings of the Columbian Exchange, an intercontinental transfer and mixing of biota (including plants, animals, bacteria, and viruses) whose scope and scale were without historical precedent.[44] The introduction of human pathogens from Europe and Africa resulted in waves of epidemics during the sixteenth and seventeenth centuries that, combined with warfare, enslavement, and political crises, precipitated a demographic collapse throughout the Americas. The effects of the Columbian Exchange were not uniformly distributed, but by the mid-eighteenth century few places in the Americas remained unaltered. One outcome of the precipitous decline in human population was an overall expansion of forest cover.[45] These new, post-Columbian forests provided nineteenth- and twentieth-century cultivators with "forest rents": wealth created by removing forest cover in order to gain access to soils, water, and wood fuel that provided high, short-term yields with minimal investments of labor and capital. As the history of the export banana industry reveals, forest rents generated wealth not only for "backward" campesinos, and "feudal" *fazendeiros,* but also for "modern" U.S. multinational corporations.

The abundance of land should not be understood exclusively in terms of environmental process. As dependency theorists noted many years ago, Latin America's export economies relied on an emerging class of national elites who saw foreign capital and markets as means by which to accumulate wealth and modernize their societies. Government officials and intellectuals frequently referred to regions where export agriculture expanded as "frontiers," "wastelands," or "deserts," terms that tell us much more about the worldviews of the writers than about the actual places where production occurred. Educated elites' views of forests and grasslands were tightly bound to their perceptions of the people who inhabited these landscapes: indigenous groups, escaped slaves, and poor mestizo settlers were considered to be "backwards" at best and "savage" at worst.[46] State legal codes and institutions seldom recognized—and often sought to undermine—the territorial rights of social groups whose ideas about livelihoods, family structures, and ownership were at odds with urban-based elites whose gaze was fixed on London and Paris as models of modernity. Latin Americans' own fables of abundance or "vastness," then, resulted from long-term environmental processes and the exercise of power by states seeking to create "neo-European" societies. Throughout much of the Americas, elite fantasies would outlive the forests.[47]

More research is needed to qualify this rather sweeping statement about the relationship between the Columbian Exchange, expanding forests, and the rise of agroexport economies in the Caribbean and Latin America. In some regions, including many Caribbean islands and parts of Mexico and Peru, colonial-era agriculture, mining, and ranching operations consumed forests and altered preexisting environmental processes long before the nineteenth-century agroexport boom. Elsewhere (e.g., the pampas of Argentina and the Central Valley of California) arid climates limited the formation of forest cover. As many historians of California have noted, large-scale state-subsidized irrigation projects were crucial to transforming the Central Valley into a center of export agriculture. Finally, the forests themselves varied considerably in terms of soil conditions, species composition, and degree of human modification, meaning that not all forest soils were equal in their capacity to generate short-term rents. The expansive forests and grasslands found in the Americas, then, did not guarantee or predispose regions to export agriculture; rather, they provided many farmers with a temporary comparative advantage.

Paradoxically, the universalizing tendencies of both mass markets and liberal state institutions did not result in homogeneous production systems. Scholars of Latin American coffee societies have argued that single commodity production gave rise to "radically distinct experiences" across time and space.[48] Although the coffee industry's very limited degree of integration during the boom years was unique, recent research on other export commodities shows that coffee's diverse production scales and labor systems were not unusual. For example, while it is true that large-scale plantations dominated export banana production in Central America during most of the twentieth century, the leading role played by small- and medium-scale growers during the late nineteenth century when mass markets for bananas first emerged can no longer be denied. Furthermore, small- and medium-scale banana cultivators drove Ecuador's export boom in the 1950s, and they formed the backbone of late-twentieth-century production in the British and French Caribbean.[49] In the case of sugar, the influx of U.S. capital in Cuba and Puerto Rico following 1898 created enormous *centrales* (mills) that in turn stimulated a proliferation of *colonos,* small-scale cane growers who sold their harvests under contract to sugar mills. César Ayala argues that *colonos* were a crucial element in a period of mass production characterized by subcontracting, flexible production, and "just-in-time" delivery.[50] Finally, in pre-Depression California, tens of thousands of small-scale vineyards and orchards existed alongside the state's more familiar "factories in the fields."[51] In sum, the only remarkable aspect of mixed production scales in export agriculture seems to be scholars' continued surprise at (re)discovering their existence![52]

But if farm size varied considerably, the varieties of plants that farmers cultivated for export markets were few. The banana trade's reliance on a single, globetrotting variety was not unusual. The mass production of coffee, citrus, grapes, and cane sugar was derived from an extremely limited number of varieties introduced to the Americas by European colonizers and African slaves over the course of centuries.[53] These crop plants had long histories before they became internationally traded commodities. They comprised a wide range of plant types, including herbaceous plants (bananas and sugar cane) from Southeast Asia, trees and vines (citrus and grapes) from the Mediterranean, and trees (coffee) from Africa. Some of the plants (bananas and sugar cane) originated in hot, humid lowlands while others (citrus and grapes) came from sea-level climates with extended dry seasons. Only one (coffee) thrived in mountainous regions. Regardless of origin, all of these plant types co-evolved with other organisms, including bacteria, fungi, insects, and viruses. The intentional exchange of plant materials often facilitated the accidental movement of other organisms, including pathogens and herbivores, that created problems of varying severity for farmers.

For example, sugar cane cultivation in the Americas, which began in the sixteenth century, was based on a single variety that did not acquire a name other than "sugar cane" until the eighteenth century, when the introduction of higher-yielding varieties from the Pacific known as Bourbon or Otaheiti canes (*S. officinarum*) prompted growers to refer to the older variety as "Creole cane."[54] By the early nineteenth century, the fast-maturing and high-yielding Otaheite canes became the principal variety grown in the Americas. Otaheite canes also provided planters with a woody bagasse that served as a fuel for the mills. As forests in Caribbean cane-growing regions receded and firewood became more difficult to procure, cane bagasse acquired a new importance.[55]

The spread of plant diseases in the second half of the nineteenth century prompted Caribbean cane growers to shift to varieties introduced from Java. As was the case with bananas, the movement of cane varieties inadvertently spread pathogens because disease-tolerant plants seldom displayed symptoms when infected by pathogens, making it difficult to establish effective quarantines. Initial efforts to breed cane varieties were stymied by the failure of popular cane varieties to produce seed under field conditions (a characteristic shared with Gros Michel bananas). However, cane growers began establishing breeding stations in the late nineteenth century following the realization that some varieties could be induced to set seed. One scholar credits the subsequent development of cane hybrids as a factor that enabled Caribbean cane growers to compete with European beet sugar growers in the early twentieth century.[56] However, new varieties sometimes encountered opposition from planters and field workers. In the 1910s, mosaic disease invaded cane fields in Cuba where a majority of planters favored Crystalina (a Javanese cane) and other varieties that were highly susceptible to the pathogen. *Colonos* and owners of *ingenios* balked at the idea of planting disease-resistant hybrids because the sucrose content of the new cane varieties differed from that of Crystalina. In order to overcome this problem, *colonos* and mill owners devised new contracts based on Crystalina's sucrose yields. Subsequently, trained chemists were enlisted to determine the sucrose content of *colono* cane shipments. Opposition to new cane varieties also surfaced among Jamaican and Haitian cane cutters who disliked harvesting the new hybrids because the canes' spiny surfaces shredded their hands. More research is needed to understand the roles played by mill owners, *colonos,* and field workers in influencing decisions about cane varieties in Cuba and elsewhere, but the example illustrates the ways in which agroecological change affected rural people's livelihoods.[57]

Latin American coffee production has been based on varieties of just two species: *Coffea arabica* and *Coffea canephora* (commonly referred to as

"Robusta"). Varieties of *C. arabica* reached the Americas in the early eighteenth century and formed the basis for production in the French colonies of San Domingue (Haiti) and Martinique. The collapse of exports from San Domingue following the Haitian Revolution contributed to an increase in Brazilian coffee exports in the early nineteenth century. Brazil's dominant position in the world market also resulted from outbreaks of coffee leaf rust (*Hemileia vastatrix*) on *arabica* coffee farms in India and Ceylon in the 1860s. Some growers in Asia abandoned coffee production in response to the disease; others converted to rust-resistant Robusta varieties cultivated in various parts of Africa.

However, the New York Coffee and Sugar Exchange banned the importation of Robusta beans as part of its drive to standardize coffee quality. The ban effectively impeded the cultivation of rust-resistant species in Latin America.[58] Consequently, most coffee growers in the Americas planted rust-susceptible varieties of *arabica* through the first half of the twentieth century. For example, just two *arabica* varieties dominated coffee production in Costa Rica from the 1850s to the 1930s.[59] However, for reasons that remain unclear, leaf rust did not raise alarms in Latin America until the 1970s. Even then, outbreaks in Brazil (1970) and Nicaragua (1976) did not create problems on the same scale and intensity as they had elsewhere in the world.[60] Nevertheless, the threat of leaf rust, along with the lifting of the ban on Robusta imports in 1960, prompted coffee growers in many parts of Latin America to adopt new varieties in the late twentieth century.[61] A rising number of agrochemical inputs often accompanied the conversion to new varieties. However, Arabica coffees still constitute 75–80 percent of world production.[62] Coffee growers in Latin America, then, shared a tendency with banana and sugarcane producers to cultivate a limited number of varieties for mass markets. However, disease epidemics do not appear to have played a direct role in altering coffee production/consumption dynamics.

In California, the drive toward standardization also prompted fruit growers to stake their fortunes on a handful of varieties. For example, by the 1920s, 80 to 90 percent of California's pear crop consisted of Bartletts, a favored variety due to its appearance, shipping qualities, and early harvest. Just two varieties of oranges (Washington Navel and Valencia) dominated the orchards of the growers belonging to the California Fruit Growers Exchange.[63] The aridity of the Central Valley reduced the dangers posed by fungal pathogens, but herbivorous insects proved to be another story. Between 1860 and 1920, planters introduced hundreds of trees and vines to California in the hope that they would "acclimatize" to their new

surroundings.[64] An unknown number of herbivorous insects and parasites "hitch-hiked" aboard the introduced plants. By the 1880s, farmers
regularly reported losses due to pests, including *Phylloxera vastatrix,* a
tiny insect that damaged the roots of grape vines. In 1886, a University of
California researcher succeeded in grafting susceptible European vines to
the roots of resistant grape varieties found in the eastern United States.
This technique controlled the economic damages caused by *Phylloxera* but
compelled growers to incur considerable replanting costs. Subsequently,
the state of California assumed an increasingly active role in controlling
the introduction of plants to California and funding research focused on
crop pests.[65]

Although multiple pest control methods, including the introduction
of both resistant plants and "beneficial" insects, achieved some spectacu-
lar successes in California, most orchardists turned to chemical sprays for
pest control in the early twentieth century. Steven Stoll suggests that a
preference for chemical controls was linked to their rapid and broad killing
power: ladybugs might be effective in controlling only one or two kinds
of insect herbivores, but early chemical controls tended to eliminate —
temporarily — a wide range of insects. Assisted by both researchers at the
University of California and private chemical manufacturers, fruit growers
turned to lead arsenate and other chemical compounds for pest control
nearly thirty years before United Fruit started applying copper sulfate to
control Sigatoka. A handful of studies in the 1910s raised concerns about
the accumulation of soluble arsenic in orchard soils, but the economic
growth that the fruit industry enjoyed at that time muted such criticisms
in much the same way that United Fruit's profits during the same time
period drowned out criticism of its production practices.[66]

The rapid and massive expansion of single-variety production, combined with an increase in the circulation of plant material, resulted in
epidemics of plant pathogens and outbreaks of herbivores and parasites
in many of the export sectors examined here, including bananas, citrus,
grapes, and sugar.[67] Diseases and pests appear to have played a minor
role in Latin American coffee production, whose history cautions against
adopting explanatory models that assume a direct relationship between
expanding monovarietal production and crop plant disease epidemics.
Governments, growers' associations, and corporations responded to the
threats posed by pathogens and pests in a broadly similar fashion that
included sponsoring scientific research focused on reducing economic
losses. Although much attention has been given to the development and
use of synthetic pesticides, the breeding and distribution of crop plant

varieties has played an equally important role in the history of the commodities examined here.

Given the contemporary debates over bioprospecting in the tropics, understanding how different actors valued crop plant germplasm (e.g., seeds) in the past is an important, if largely unexamined question. Warren Dean's environmental history of rubber demonstrates the tremendous strategic value that both Brazilians and Britains placed on controlling *Hevea brasiliense,* but the intrigue-filled history of rubber may be more the exception than the rule. Brazilian nationalists apparently did not protest the removal of mutant navel orange and Cavendish banana cultivars that subsequently generated profits for U.S. agribusinesses in California and Central America. Also, Stuart McCook found that nineteenth-century Asian and Caribbean growers freely exchanged sugar cane varieties. My research on bananas is somewhat less conclusive: varieties seem to have circulated freely in the early twentieth century when both British and United Fruit–sponsored collectors in Asia and the Pacific acquired *Musa* specimens via purchase, barter, and as gifts. However, by the 1960s, exchanges between British breeders and their United Fruit counterparts seem to have diminished. Interestingly, the dynamism of the plants themselves have complicated attempts to establish propietary rights: in all of the industries considered here, important commercial varieties have arisen from field mutations. The role played by Latin American states, growers' associations, and scientific institutions in promoting and/or regulating the movement of plant material is another important topic in need of additional study.[68]

Monovarietal production systems created problems for farmers beyond pathogens and herbivores. Because continuous cropping depleted soil of nutrients, farmers had to invest additional capital, labor, or both over time in order to maintain or increase yields. Banana and sugar producers in Central America and Cuba responded to this problem by shifting production in order to capture rents from forested soils. In some parts of nineteenth-century Brazil, coffee growers remedied falling yields by ordering their laborers (slave and otherwise) to clear forested hillsides. However, in coffee zones dominated by smallholders, abandoning lands was not always a viable option. Furthermore, the lengthy delay — up to five years — between planting coffee and reaping large harvests may have discouraged shifting production. Similarly, the large investments required to establish orchards and vineyards in California, along with a dependency on irrigation, discouraged the shifting of production locations. However, generalizations about yields and the productive life spans of farms are ex-

tremely difficult to make precisely because ecological conditions and cultivation practices tend to vary greatly and are seldom recorded in the census
data and probate records frequently consulted by historians.[69]

In the second half of the twentieth century, small- and large-scale
farmers turned increasingly to synthetic fertilizers to boost yields. Although "Green Revolution" technologies are popularly associated with
basic grain production, plant breeding and synthetic fertilizers came to
play a dominant role in all of the export sectors examined here during the 1950s and 1960s. Although banana plant breeders failed to develop marketable plants with resistance to plant pathogens, they succeeded in significantly reducing the physical size of Cavendish plants. This
enabled unprecedented planting densities, which, along with large inputs of fertilizers and fewer wind-related losses, resulted in record-setting
yields. Dwarf varieties of *arabica* coffee began to gain favor among Latin
American growers in the 1960s; by the 1980s, they dominated production
in Costa Rica, where coffee growers further boosted yields by applying
government-subsidized fertilizers and reducing shade trees.[70]

The use of fertilizers and high-yielding plant varieties lowered unit
production costs, but sharply rising yields coincided with a period of
slow-growing or even declining rates of per capita consumption of bananas, coffee, and sugar in the United States. Cultivators possessing sufficient capital often responded to declining commodity prices by trying to
"rationalize" production through increasing yields, further exacerbating
problems of overproduction. In some places, the use of synthetic fertilizers
strengthened the dominant position of comparatively well off farmers.[71]
The singular focus on boosting yields represents an overlooked (or at best
narrowly interpreted) agroecological context in which late-twentieth-
century conflicts over access to markets—including the so-called banana
wars between the United States and the European Union, and the latest
coffee price crisis—have taken place. Finally, if intensification reduced the
amount of land dedicated to export crop production, it heightened rates
of agrochemical use (particularly herbicides) and created new occupational health hazards for farmworkers and people living in close proximity
to the fields.[72] Fertilizers and pesticides are leading sources of water pol-
lution in the world's agricultural regions. Intensification is often equated
with "modernization," but there is mounting evidence that production
processes oriented toward boosting yields extract enormous environmental, economic, and social costs.[73]

The dynamics of mass production and mass consumption, then, ex-
erted pressures that drastically restricted the varietal diversity of cash

crops. However, they did not necessarily produce homogeneous agrarian landscapes at local levels. For example, some export crops, notably coffee, have historically been intercropped with shade trees (in parts of Central America, Colombia, and Venezuela) and/or food crops for local consumption (in parts of Brazil and Colombia). Intercropping came about in part because of the opportunities and constraints posed by coffee plants. A forest "understory" species, many coffee varieties thrive in heavy shade—a sharp contrast to sugarcane, most bananas, and deciduous fruits. Small-scale growers and contract laborers often planted species of trees and/or bananas and plantains that simultaneously created a favorable environment for coffee while producing food and firewood. Intercropping also offered advantages to coffee planters and investors who could compensate workers with land for cultivation, rather than wages, during periods when coffee prices fell and also during the years between planting and first harvest, when coffee farms did not generate revenues.[74] Intercropping was much less common on sugar, banana, and deciduous fruit farms, but soils judged to be less than ideal for these cash crops were often dedicated to other uses, including pasture, food crops, and firewood collection. In addition, squatters quickly moved onto lands abandoned by export banana growers in Costa Rica and Honduras during the first half of the twentieth century; one suspects that similar dynamics existed elsewhere, including the coffee regions outside of Rio de Janeiro and São Paulo.[75] A commodity chain therefore might be more accurately envisioned as a "commodity web" in order to account for the existence of "horizontal" agroecological and social linkages.

Comparing the environmental contexts in which commodity production occurs brings new actors to the foreground and provides novel ways to appreciate the complexities of older ones. The different shapes, sizes, and life cycles of crop plants gave rise to different cultivation practices and work rhythms: cane cutting meant swinging a machete for an entire day; harvesting bananas involved shouldering 50–100 pound bunches of fruit; citrus was plucked by harvesters perched on ladders; picking tiny coffee berries required fast yet light fingers. The common element in all of these labor processes is, of course, the human worker; during the past century, mechanization had only minimal impacts on harvesting operations for the crops in question. This has required farmers to mobilize labor forces on a seasonal basis. For example, in early-twentieth-century Californian orchards, harvesting operations could require ten times the amount of labor needed during the rest of the season. Twentieth-century coffee farms had similar spikes in labor demand during harvests. In Caribbean cane-growing regions, the extreme variation in labor needs was captured by the use of the phrase *tiempo muerto,* or "dead season," to refer to the months between harvests. Even bananas, harvested throughout the calendar year, displayed variation in labor demand as a result of grower efforts to time their biggest harvests in conjunction with periods of peak market prices.[76]

One historical outcome of seasonal variations in labor demand has been a widespread and enduring dependency on migrant field workers. Post-emancipation sugar and coffee production in Brazil and the Caribbean; export banana farms in Central America; and fruit growers in California relied on regional and transnational flows of migrant laborers throughout much of the twentieth century. In the second half of the twentieth century, even smallholder coffee production relied increasingly on migrant labor for harvesting operations. The preponderance of migrant labor is all the more striking in light of the xenophobia and racism that migrants frequently confronted. The economic and social status of most field hands improved significantly during the twentieth century when workers' movements succeeded in unionizing some commodity sectors. Working people also gained voting rights and greater access to government services. However, by the late twentieth century, both union membership and the political power of farmworkers were in decline in many parts of the Americas. Harvesting operations continued to rely upon migrant field workers who often lacked the rights of full citizens and therefore seldom enjoyed equal access to educational, medical, and financial institutions. The political marginalization of farmworkers cannot be explained — much less justified — by the harvesting cycles of crop plants. Instead, an awareness of production processes sheds light on the particular ways that individual farmers and agribusinesses have historically overcome obstacles to capital accumulation by shifting the risks resulting from environmental processes onto the backs of field workers. Additional research is needed to understand how workers understood and responded to these risks.

A heightened sensitivity to environmental contexts also helps historians to lend content to the lives of people categorized by census takers as *"jornaleros," "colonatos,"* and *"esposas."* By following the movements of actors through space we might discover that they spent a few months harvesting sugarcane or coffee while intermittently tending to a home garden, in addition to hunting, fishing, and collecting plants, water, or firewood from nearby forests, rivers, and wetlands. Acknowledging the importance of the interstitial times and spaces inhabited by farmworkers also opens up new possibilities for understanding political projects.[77] For example, my research in local archives along the North Coast turned up examples of rural working people forging "place-based" identities. These local affinities are somewhat paradoxical given the near constant flow of migrants through the region, but the very tenuousness of their livelihoods may help to explain working peoples' desires to identify with and make claims to local and regional places. I found little evidence that conservation of resources *per se* was a primary concern of working people. This is not to imply that the North Coast's inhabitants were "too poor" to be concerned about the fates of forests, wetlands, and rivers, but rather that they derived their understandings of changes in the land largely through work, not leisure. Environmental historians of Latin America (and beyond), therefore, should pay close attention to workplaces not only because they are often crucial sites of environmental change but also because production ultimately cannot be isolated from consumption, nor can work be separated from leisure.[78]

During his distinguished career William Roseberry called for studies of working people that went beyond typologies. Environmental historians of Latin America should similarly aim to write histories of commodity production that convey the heterogeneity and historical dynamism of organisms and processes that tend to get lumped together as "resources," "land," or simply "space." By breathing life into these and other categories, we can avoid falling into the trap of environmental determinism while demonstrating the dynamic interplay between economies and ecologies, landscapes and livelihoods, and cultural and biological diversity. However, I would caution against analyses that stress diverse outcomes at the expense of comparing similar dynamics. Despite the profoundly different experiences of Chinese cane cutters in mid-nineteenth-century Cuba, Jamaican banana farmers in early-twentieth-century Costa Rica, and late-twentieth-century Mayan coffee pickers in Guatemala, their lives were similarly caught up in commodity webs spun by agroecological, cultural, economic, political, and social processes that in turn gave rise to a common set of production/consumption dynamics.

The export banana trade was unique in a number of important ways including the degree of vertical integration achieved by the U.S. fruit companies in the early twentieth century, the long-term importance of fungal pathogens, and the enduring yet narrow place that the fruit occupied in U.S. foodways. At the same time, banana production/consumption dynamics were rather similar to those of coffee, citrus, grapes, and sugar — crops that at first glance appear to be very different from one another. Production processes for the commodities compared evolved in response to tensions between the standardizing tendencies of mass markets and the diversifying tendencies of environmental processes. These tensions materialized in the forms of the crop plants themselves and the work of cultivation. Investors, corporate managers, and planters went to great lengths to manage both human and non-human components of agroecosystems. Over the course of the twentieth century, all of these industries turned to university-trained scientists and other experts for help with classifying, controlling, and manipulating environmental processes. "Fresh" fruit trades, which were structured around highly perishable commodities sold in markets that placed a high value on visual aesthetics, tended to use greater quantities of insecticides, fungicides, and nematicides than the coffee and sugar industries, whose products were highly processed prior to reaching retail markets. Significantly, all of these industries turned to fertilizers and plant breeding in the twentieth century in order to boost yields and/or reduce losses caused by environmental forces.

Finally, although the export booms of the mid- and late-nineteenth centuries provided opportunities for small-scale farmers throughout much of Latin America to forge respectable livelihoods, capital consolidations and environmental transformations during the twentieth century imposed constraints that have made the lives of smallholders and farmworkers increasingly tenuous. Indeed, the historical record provides little reason to believe that increasing the volume of agroexports will diminish poverty. This can be explained in part by the tendency of power and capital to consolidate in the places that lay in between production and consumption and where much value was added: processors, distributors, and marketers were key players in shaping prices and creating quality standards that became increasingly important as per capita consumption rates leveled off and markets began to segment. Determining the extent to which prices and quality standards were imposed on consumers by middlemen requires more research, but the key point is that ideas about quality emerge and change in specific historical contexts conditioned by culture, politics, and social power.

Agricultural production tended to become more geographically stable over the course of the twentieth century, but the people, plants, and pathogens that inhabited the fields continued to circulate. Indeed, determining just who or what was "local" or "national" in export zones has been, and continues to be, far from straightforward. The significance of all of this motion in the system is not limited to understanding how "global" forces shape "local" places; the movements themselves have conditioned production/consumption dynamics. This is a compelling argument for not limiting studies of commodities to nationalist frameworks.

There is also a need to experiment with new periodizations. Historical studies of Caribbean and Latin American commodities often span
the "boom" years between 1870 and 1930, a periodization largely derived
from theoretical frameworks that matter-of-factly privilege capital, exchange, and labor as the engines of history while using the nation-state
as their primary unit of analysis.[79] While I do not deny the importance
of economic and state institutions, evidence strongly suggests that both
short- and long-term environmental processes have played an equally or
more important role in changing rural landscapes and livelihoods in Latin
America. However, because environmental processes seldom move in sync
with economic cycles or political movements, historians would be wise to
reconsider accepted chronologies and timescales.

The motivations behind researching and writing this book have not
been limited to my scholarly interests. Understanding the export banana's
past is important for plotting its future role in tropical agroecosystems
throughout the world. The relationship between people, plants, and pathogens continues to evolve: Black Sigatoka has spread to most of the major
banana- and plantain-growing areas in the world. Although Panama disease is not presently a factor in Caribbean and Latin American export
banana production centers, strains of *fusaria* capable of infecting Cavendish varieties are spreading in other parts of the world. The historical
record strongly suggests that the pathogen will likely reach the Americas in the foreseeable future. Unfortunately, many scholarly and popular
scientific sources fail to account for the historical (human) dimensions
of interactions between bananas and fungal pathogens. Popular media
sources have recently reported that bananas are on the brink of "extinction" due to diseases implicitly constructed as forces of nature.[80]
Such stories are problematic because they fail to situate crop plant
pathogens in a historical context and unwittingly set the stage for future
"development vs. conservation" dilemmas that pit wealthy, often urban-
based conservationists against the interests of rural working people. However, by viewing crop plant disease epidemics as the outcomes of produc-
tion/consumption dynamics, we can envision a less gloomy, albeit more
complex, future based on the possibilities of refashioning both agriculture
and commodity markets to value the agro-biodiversity and human labor
upon which agricultural production has depended.
Entering the twenty-first century, there are some reasons for optimism. In many industrial and postindustrial societies, new social movements have called attention to the relationship between food production,

eating, environmental sustainability, and human health. The push to liberalize trade has been accompanied by varied and sometimes creative critiques of "globalization" that have exposed the limitations and injustices of U.S. agribusiness production systems that rely on heavy inputs of agrochemicals, irrigation, and government subsidies. In Latin America, new rural-based resistance movements have emerged to challenge the power of nation-states and elites to control access to resources. In short, opportunities for debate, confrontation, and experimentation exist on local and international levels. The challenge is to ensure that alternative models of agricultural production acknowledge the dynamic connections between places of production and consumption, and between social and environmental transformations.

Notes

INTRODUCTION

1. See contributions in Striffler and Moberg, eds., *Banana Wars;* Marquardt, "'Green Havoc'"; and by the same author, "Pesticides, Parakeets, and Unions." For an anecdotal history of banana consumption, see Jenkins, *Bananas.*

2. See Karnes, *Tropical Enterprise;* and May and Plaza, *The United Fruit Company in Latin America.*

3. The foundational dependency text is Cardoso and Faletto, *Dependency and Development in Latin America.* In the Central American context, see Torres Rivas, *Interpretación del desarrollo social centroamericano.* (Also see the English-language version, *History and Society in Central America,* trans. Sullivan-González.) Important analyses of the export banana industry utilizing dependency frameworks include Posas, "La Plantación Bananera en Centroamérica"; Pérez-Brignoli, *A Brief History of Central America;* Laínez and Meza, "El enclave bananero en la Historia de Honduras"; and Frassinetti, *Enclave y sociedad en Honduras.* For an insightful review of dependency perspectives on Honduras, see Euraque, "El Imperialismo y Honduras como 'república bananera.'"

4. LeGrand, "Living in Macondo." For critiques of dependency and world systems theories, see Cooper et al., *Confronting Historical Paradigms.*

5. Euraque, *Reinterpreting the Banana Republic.* Also see LeGrand, *Frontier Expansion and Peasant Protest in Colombia;* Putnam, *The Company They Kept;* Striffler, *In the Shadows of State and Capital;* Forster, "Reforging National Revolution"; Bourgois, *Ethnicity at Work;* and Chomsky, *West Indian Workers and the United Fruit Company.* An unpublished work that devotes considerable attention to non-company banana growers in Honduras is Brand, "The Background of Capitalistic Underdevelopment."

6. On the difficulties of separating culture and nature, see the essays in Cronon, ed., *Uncommon Ground.* On agroecology, see Carroll, Vandermeer, and Rosset, eds., *Agroecology.*

7. Geographer Carl Sauer argued that Native Americans cultivated the banana well prior to contact with Europeans and Africans. Banana expert Norman W. Simmonds disagreed, contending that the first banana arrived from the Canary Islands via the Spanish friar Tomás de Berlanga. For an assessment of the evidence, see Langdon, "The Banana as a Key to Early American and Polynesian History."

8. See essays by Marshall and Tomich in *Cultivation and Culture.* Also see the

collection of primary sources on Brazilian slavery compiled by Conrad, *Children of God's Fire.*

9. Gilbert and Hubbell, "Plant Diseases and the Conservation of Tropical Forests," 104. Note that the relationship between disease incidence and monocultures is not directly linked to levels of biodiversity, but rather to host density. Mundt, "Disease Dynamics in Agroecosystems."

10. See the otherwise impressive works by Bulmer-Thomas, *The Political Economy of Central America Since 1920;* and Wells and Topik, *The Second Conquest of Latin America.*

11. Among the first scholars to note the connection between Panama disease and the preference for Gros Michel bananas in U.S. markets was Kepner, *Social Aspects of the Banana Industry,* 19–21 and 89–91. Three more recent works have also noted the link: Chomsky, *West Indian Workers,* 66; Marquardt, "Green Havoc," 52–58; and Ellis, *Las transnacionales del banano en Centroamerica,* 77–99.

12. On the region's pre-Columbian history, see Newson, *The Cost of Conquest.*

13. Euraque, *Reinterpreting the Banana Republic.* Also see articles in the theme issue edited by Euraque in *Mesoamérica* 42 (December 2001); Echeverri-Gent, "Forgotten Workers"; O'Brien, *The Revolutionary Mission;* Langley and Schoonover, *The Banana Men;* and Karnes, *Tropical Enterprise.*

14. Argueta, *Bananos y política;* Barahona, *El silencio quedó atrás;* García Buchard, *Poder político, interés bananero, e identidad nacional en centroamérica;* and Frasinetti, *Enclave y sociedad en Honduras.*

15. Data on banana exports are neither complete nor entirely reliable for the period of time covered in this study. Sources tend to vary on specific figures, but there is agreement on broad trends: Jamaica was the leading exporter in the early twentieth century until production in Honduras expanded during the 1920s. From the early 1950s to the present, Ecuador has been the leading exporter of bananas. See Kepner and Soothill, *The Banana Empire;* Ellis, *Las transnacionales del banano en Centroamerica,* 53–55, 400; and Bucheli, "United Fruit Company in Latin America," 92.

16. See Karnes, *Tropical Enterprise;* and García Buchard, *Poder político, interés bananero, e identidad nacional en Centroamérica.* There are exceptions to this tendency in the scholarship. Euraque ("Modernity, Economic Power and the Foreign Banana Companies in Honduras") found that 28 of 35 mayors to hold office between 1884 and 1920 were banana growers. Also see Kepner and Soothill, *The Banana Empire,* 95–100 and 256–285; and Brand, "The Background of Capitalistic Underdevelopment," 157–167.

17. In this genre, see Meza and Laínez, "El enclave bananero en la historia de Honduras," 115–156; and Frassinetti, *Enclave y sociedad.*

18. On Zemurray, see Argueta, *Bananos y política;* and Langley and Schoonover, *The Banana Men,* 115–166.

19. Meza, *Historia del movimiento obrero hondureño,* 49–53; and Argueta, *Historia de los sin historia,* 91–98.

20. On the 1954 strike and aftermath, see Argueta, *La gran huelga bananera;* Barahona, *El silencio quedó atrás;* and Posas, *Lucha ideológica y organización sindical en Honduras.* On the role of organized labor in Honduran politics, see Euraque, *Reinterpreting the Banana Republic;* MacCameron, *Bananas, Labor and Politics in Honduras;* and Echeverri-Gent, "Labor, Class and Political Representation."

21. On late-twentieth-century banana contract farming in the Caribbean, see Grossman, *The Political Ecology of Bananas*. In Ecuador, see Striffler, *In the Shadows of State and Capital.*

22. John H. Coatsworth, *Central America and the United States,* 34–35.

23. On U.S.-Honduran relations, see Coatsworth, *Central America and the United States;* and Barahona, *La hegemonía de los Estados Unidos en Honduras.*

24. A similar process occurred on the Atlantic coast of Costa Rica. See Chomsky, *West Indian Workers,* 64–68.

25. Amaya Amador, *Prisión verde.* Amaya Amador was not the only mid-twentieth-century Honduran author to set a novel on the North Coast. See Paca Navas de Miralda, *Barro* (1951); Argentina Díaz Lozano, *Peregrinaje* (1944); and Marcos Carías Reyes, *Trópico* (1948). A celebrated novel set in the banana zones of Costa Rica is Carlos Luis Fallas's *Mamita Yunai* (1941).

26. On women living on the fringes of the plantations, see Putnam, *The Company They Kept.*

CHAPTER 1

1. Young, *Narrative of a Residence on the Mosquito Shore,* 95.

2. Froebel, *Seven Years' Travel,* 183–188.

3. For descriptions of the region's nineteenth-century economy, see Guevara Escudero, "Nineteenth Century Honduras," 35–62; Naylor, *Penny Ante Imperialism;* Dawson, "William Pitt's Settlement," 677–706; Davidson, *Historical Geography of the Bay Islands of Honduras;* and the report of William McKee on the New York and Honduras Fibre Company enclosed in William Burchard to Porter, 10 Sept. 1886, U.S. Department of State, Despatches from U.S. Consuls in Omoa, Trujillo, and Roatán 1831–1893 (mf. T-477), roll 4.

4. Marco A. Soto quoted in Frassinetti, *Enclave y sociedad en Honduras,* 21.

5. See enclosures in R. H. Rousseau to Secretary of State William Seward, Tegucigalpa, 12 Sept. 1866; and Seward to Rouseau, Washington, 10 Oct. 1866, *Foreign Relations of the United States 1866,* part 2, 536–537.

6. William Burchard to William Hunter, Dec. 4, 1884, Despatches from U.S. Consuls in Omoa, Trujillo, and Roatán, roll 5.

7. William C. Burchard to W. Hunter, Roatán, 1 Aug. 1879; and 27 Sept. 1879, Despatches from U.S. Consuls in Omoa, Trujillo, and Roatán, roll 4.

8. Cevallos, *Reseña histórica de las Islas de la Bahía,* 76–83.

9. Frank E. Frye to Secy. of State, San Pedro Sula, 10 Mar. 1875, U.S. Department of State, Despatches from U.S. Consuls in Omoa, Trujillo, and Roatán, 1831–1893, roll 4.

10. William C. Burchard to W. Hunter, 18 Nov. 1880, U.S. Department of State, Despatches from U.S. Consuls in Omoa, Trujillo, and Roatán, 1831–1893, roll 4.

11. J. Hernández to Ministro de Gobernación, 30 Nov. 1880, Archivo Nacional de Honduras (hereafter, ANH), leg. 1881/19.

12. F. Hernández to Hacienda, Roatán, 1 Mar. 1881, ANH, leg. 1881/21.

13. F. Hernández to Hacienda, Roatán, 28 Mar. 1881, ANH, leg. 1881/21.

14. This estimate was hypothetical since production costs, yields, and earnings

varied due to changes in labor costs, weather conditions, and international markets. Burchard to Hunter, 18 Nov. 1880.

15. Burchard to Hunter, 18 Nov. 1880; and Frank E. Frye to William Hunter, Utila, 30 Sept. 1875, U.S. Department of State, Despatches from U.S. Consuls in Omoa, Trujillo, and Roatán, roll 4. These two descriptions are remarkably similar to those described by U.S. consular officials in Jamaica during the late nineteenth century. See Hoskinson, "A Report on the Fruit Trade of the Island of Jamaica," 24 July 1884, U.S. Department of State, *U.S. Consular Papers,* v. 28, 7.

16. Burchard to Hunter, 18 Nov. 1880.

17. C. R. Follin to U.S. Secretary of State, Omoa, 11 Jan. 1845 and 17 Sept. 1853; U.S. Department of State, Despatches from U.S. Consuls in Omoa, Trujillo, and Roatán, 1831–1893 (mf T-477), roll 1.

18. In 1883, 16 of 51 vessels arriving in Roatán were steamships. Burchard to Hunter, 4 Dec. 1884, U.S. Department of State, Despatches from U.S. Consuls in Omoa, Trujillo, and Roatán, 1831–1893, roll 5.

19. F. Hernández to Ministro de Hacienda, 18 Mar. 1881.

20. "Carta de señor Don Guillermo Melhado, Trujillo," *Honduras Industrial,* 1 July 1884, 85.

21. *La Gaceta* no. 582 (9 Sept. 1889).

22. "Return of trade with the U.S. Statement showing declared exports between Puerto Cortés and the U.S. for fiscal year ending 30 June 1887," U.S. National Archives, Consular Post Records (RG 84), v. 1. For La Ceiba, see "Comunicaciones oficiales," *La Gaceta* no. 587 (28 Sept. 1889).

23. William Burchard to Alvey A. Adee, 23 Aug. 1892, U.S. Department of State, Despatches from U.S. Consuls in Omoa, Trujillo, and Roatán, 1831–1893, roll 6.

24. The survey covered four municipalities in the department of Cortés (Puerto Cortés, Omoa, San Pedro Sula, and El Paraíso [Choloma]), and three in the department of Colón (El Porvenir, La Ceiba, and San Luís [Balfate]). The total area planted to export bananas must have been greater than the amount recorded by the survey because at least one important banana-growing municipality (Tela) was excluded. Honduras, Junta Registradora, "Datos relativos a las fincas de bananos," July 1899, ANH, uncatalogued manuscript. I have a photocopy of the manuscript.

25. La Ceiba (26%), El Porvenir (21%), and San Pedro Sula (19%) also had the largest percentages of farms with more than 14 hectares of export banana production.

26. The 1899 report provided monthly yields for each municipality. I computed the 3.3 million figure by summing average monthly yields. The number of bunches exported from these farms would have been smaller due to losses resulting from wind damage and rejections by shippers. On the other hand, the survey's anonymous authors estimated that an additional 10 percent should be added to production figures to compensate for underreporting on the part of tax-fearing farmers. An estimate of 2.5 to 3.0 million exports for 1899 falls within the range (2.0 to 4.7 million) provided by other authors for total exports from Honduras in 1900. See Kepner and Soothill, *Banana Empire,* 37; and Ellis, *Las transnacionales del banano en Centroamerica,* 53.

27. Tela Municipal Acts, v. 3 (31 Jan. 1887).

28. Tela Municipal Acts, v. 12 (1 Aug. 1895).

29. Euraque, "San Pedro Sula, actual capital industrial de Honduras," *Mesoamérica* 26 (Dec. 1993): 228–229; and El Progreso Municipal Acts v. 1 (17 Sept. 1894), 90–92.

30. See William C. Burchard to James Porter, 4 Aug. 1886; and Burchard to Porter, 10 Sept. 1886, Despatches from U.S. Consuls in Omoa, Trujillo, and Roatán, 1831–1893, roll 6.

31. Howard Reed to Ministro de Fomento, Tegucigalpa, 9 Sept. 1902, ANH, leg. 1889–90/3. For additional evidence of labor shortages, see Gobernador Político to Ministro de Gobernación, Roatán, 23 Feb. 1892, ANH, leg. 1892/18; and C. C. Padilla to Ministro de Gobernación, "Anexo N," 12 Oct. 1903, ANH, loose document.

32. Charles, *Honduras*, 114–120. Also see Lombard, *The New Honduras*, 24; and Euraque, "The Threat of Blackness," 229–249.

33. Unfortunately, the role of family structures in shaping early Caribbean banana cultivation has yet to be researched. For a historical account of women banana workers in Jamaica, see Chalmers, "The Romance of the Banana," 20–27. On contemporary women growers in the Caribbean, see Grossman, *The Political Ecology of Bananas*.

34. "Comunicaciones oficiales," *La Gaceta* no. 621 (31 Jan. 1890). See also Rose, *Utilla*, 106–112.

35. Petition signed by 200 residents of Roatán requesting that the national government establish a duty-free port on the island, 30 Nov. 1894, ANH Carpeta, Documentos de 1893.

36. John Richardson to Francis B. Loomis, Utila, 14 Feb. 1905, U.S. Department of State, Dispatches from U.S. Consuls in Utila, 1899–1906, (mf T-701), roll 1.

37. On competition with the mainland, see Rose, *Utilla*, 109; and Davidson, *Historical Geography of the Bay Islands of Honduras*, 93–97.

38. Banana exports for the years 1901 and 1902 did not exceed 15,000 bunches. John Richardson to David Hill, Utila, 17 Feb. 1903, U.S. Department of State, Dispatches from U.S. Consuls in Utila, 1899–1906, roll 1.

39. Ministerio de Fomento, "Memoria de fomento, informe de agricultura" *La Gaceta*, no. 1994 (25 Jan. 1901).

40. Francisco Altschul, "Memoria de fomento y obras públicas," *La Gaceta* no. 2254 (30 Jan. 1903).

41. C. Córdoba, La Ceiba, "Anexo I: Informe de Atlántida," 19 Oct. 1903, ANH, loose document.

42. Ministro de Fomento y Obras Publícas, "Memoria," 1905–1906, ANH, loose document.

43. A 1911 report recorded some 6,100 hectares in Cortés, but the data excluded San Pedro Sula. See General Andrés Leiva, "Departamento de Cortés: sus terrenos, industrias, producciones, etc.," *Boletín de Fomento*, 1, no. 1 (Aug.–Dec. 1911): 132–135; and Governor of Cortés to Ministro de Fomento, San Pedro Sula, 16 Oct. 1912, ANH, leg. 1912.

44. Honduras, Junta Registradora, "Datos relativos a las fincas de bananos."

45. Signers included Salvador Oteri, E. M. Stella, Phil R. Rice, J. B. Camors, E. J. Hart, Jean Laffite, Alfredo Boesch, and J. T. Glynn. Solicitud a Presidente Luis Bográn, 13 Aug. 1891, ANH, leg. 1880/10.

46. Estado en el despacho de justicia, 25 Oct. 1891, ANH, leg. 1880/10.

47. Henry R. Campbell, "Aviso," 13 Jun. 1881, ANH Carpeta, 1881.

48. For an early case on the Bay Islands, see U.S. consul to Governor Tiburcio Hernández, 2 Jul. 1881, U.S. Department of State, Despatches from U.S. Consuls in Omoa, Trujillo and Roatán, roll 5.

49. Honduras, "Comunicaciones oficiales," *La Gaceta* no. 615 (9 Jan. 1890). Similar complaints were recorded in Jamaica. See Soluri, "Development as Ideology."

50. Tela Municipal Acts, v. 12 (15 Oct. 1892).

51. Tela Municipal Acts, v. 12 (5 Feb. 1893).

52. *La Gaceta* (17 Oct. 1893).

53. Tela Municipal Acts, v. 12 (1 Jun. 1894).

54. Tela Municipal Acts, v. 12 (5 Aug. 1894).

55. Nolasco L. to Ministro de Fomento, San Pedro Sula, 3 Jun. 1896, ANH, leg. Notas varias del departamento de Cortés.

56. José Ruiz to Ministro de Fomento, Omoa, 8 Jan. 1901, ANH, leg. Departamento de Cortés, Notas varias, años 1894–1912.

57. José Ruiz to Ministro de Fomento, 8 Jan. 1901.

58. Cruz Cáceres, *En las selvas Hondureñas,* 69.

59. Ibid., 70.

60. "Estatutos de la Sociedad Bananera," Tegucigalpa, 27 Dec. 1894, ANH, loose document. Also see *La Gaceta* no. 1 (6 Mar. 1894), 145.

61. The 1899 survey recorded the holdings of 39 founding members of the association. The size of the farms ranged from 1.4 to 84 hectares; more than half did not exceed seven hectares, and only 4 of the 39 members recorded in 1899 cultivated more than 30 hectares of bananas, suggesting that large-scale growers did not dominate the organization.

62. "Informe del departamento de Cortés al Ministro de Fomento," 17 Oct. 1900, ANH, leg. Notas varias, 1894–1912.

63. Brand, "The Background to Capitalist Underdevelopment," 161–162.

64. "Informe del departamento de Cortés al Ministro de Fomento," 17 Oct. 1900.

65. A growers' association based in El Paraíso (Choloma) expressed concern over the fact that many of its members did not own the land on which they farmed: "Se declara persona juridica a la sociedad agrícola Asociación Bananera de Choloma." *La Gaceta* no. 2493 (1 Nov. 1904).

66. *La Gaceta* no. 1187 (31 May 1895).

67. Members agreed to harvest at least 25 bunches of fruit every fifteen days, a yield likely attainable from a farm as small as 2 hectares.

68. José L. Ruíz, President, Sociedad Bananera Gremio Agrario de Omoa, "Circular a las compañias fruteras," 1 Jan. 1901, ANH, leg. Notas varias del departamento de Cortés.

69. Monthly harvests (in bunches) were as follows: Jan.: 4,940; Feb.: 8,400; Mar.: 12,454; Apr.: 12,342; May: 21,181; June: 20,959; July: 26,019; Aug.: 19,646; Sept.: 16,490; Oct.: 18,154; Nov.: 8,398; Dec: 11,787; total: 180,770.

70. Ruíz, "Circular a las compañias fruteras," 1 Jan. 1901.

71. Felix J. J. Johnson to Assistant Secretary of State, Puerto Cortés, 30 Apr. 1906, USNA, Consular Post Records, Puerto Cortés, v. 12, 429; and Cruz Cáceres, *En las selvas hondureñas,* 68.

72. "Texto del contrato celebrado entre el gobierno de Honduras y Vaccaro-D'Antoni" (Decree 45 1904), reproduced in Sánchez, "En el prisma de la historia," 6. This company later incorporated as the Standard Fruit and Steamship Company. SFSC operated a number of subsidiaries in Honduras, including the Aguan Valley Company, which held most of the land on which the company established farms.

73. Honduras, *La nueva política bananera de Honduras,* 43–50.

74. Ministro de Fomento, "Memoria de fomento," *La Gaceta* no. 3471 (25 Jan. 1910).

75. von Humboldt and Bonpland, *Personal Narratives,* 206.

76. "The Banana, or Plantain," *The Penny Magazine* (29 Sept. 1832), 253. Note that Humboldt's description of plantains linked their cultivation to "mestizo" and "Castilian" cultures.

77. Ibid.

78. Sedgwick, "The Big Banana" (New York: Happy House Co., 1875), Harvard University, Lamont Library, microfiche w 2652.

79. Gordon, "Researches in the Uloa Valley, Honduras," 8.

80. Ibid., 17.

81. Bartlett, "Lorenzo D. Baker and the Development of the Banana Trade."

82. Juan B. Narváez to Ministro de Fomento, Iriona, 19 May 1897, ANH, loose document.

83. Rodriquez, "Bananas," 25.

84. Alejandro García, Professor of History, University of Havana, Cuba, personal communication, Nov. 1999.

85. David Miller, Professor of History, Carnegie Mellon University, personal communication, Feb. 1999.

86. See Jenkins, *Bananas: An American History.*

87. Humphrey, "Where Bananas Grow," 487–488.

88. "The Banana Supply of New York," 422.

89. Ibid.

90. Jenkins, *Bananas: An American History,* 80.

91. Poole, *Fruits and How to Use Them,* 10.

92. For recipes, see *The Boston Cooking School Magazine* (June/July 1897): 47–48; Lincoln, *Boston Cookbook,* 391; Moritz and Kahn, *The Twentieth Century Cookbook,* 10th ed.; and Berry, *Fruit Recipes,* 250–259.

93. *The Boston School of Cooking Magazine* 2, no. 5 (Feb./Mar. 1898): 299.

94. See "The Banana Supply of New York," 422.

95. *The Cook: A Weekly Handbook of Domestic Culinary Art for All Housekeepers* (8 Jun. 1885), quoted in Jenkins, *Bananas: An American History,* 14.

96. "Subjects on Cooking, No. 26," 1889, National Museum of American History (NMAH), Warshaw Collection, Food, box 1, folder "Arbuckles coffee."

97. Hannaford Bros. Co. (Portland, Maine), Price Sheets, 1903–1905, NMAH, Warshaw Collection, Food, box 8, folder "Hannaford Bros. Co."

98. See Higgins, "The Banana in Hawaii," 42; Fawcett, "La industria bananera en Jamaica"; and "The Banana Supply of New York," 423.

99. Andrew Preston to Loren Baker, Boston, 19 Dec. 1891, Lorenzo Dow Baker Papers, box VI, folder "AW Preston, 1891," W. B. Nickerson Memorial Room, Cape Cod Community College, Barnstable, Mass.

100. Andrew Preston to Loren Baker, Boston, 3 June 1892, Lorenzo Dow Baker Papers, box VI, folder "AW Preston, 1892–1898."

CHAPTER 2

1. The treaty represented part of Dávila's attempt to secure a large loan from an international banking group led by J. P. Morgan.

2. The Vacarro Brothers and Company received five concessions during Manuel Bonilla's first presidency (1903-1907). Taracena Arriola, "Liberalismo y poder político," 209-210.

3. For an account of the political maneuvering that brought Bonilla to the presidency, see Argueta, *Bananos y política*, 24-37. On the U.S. military and diplomatic presence in the region, see Coatsworth, *Central America and the United States*, 33-41; and Barahona, *La hegemonía de los Estados Unidos en Honduras*.

4. Dosal, *Doing Business with the Dictators*, 75-94; and Kepner and Soothill, *The Banana Empire*, 107-116.

5. See, for example, the 1906 contract between the first Bonilla administration and the Vacarro Brothers, Decree 121 in *La Gaceta* no. 2 (9 May 1906), 697.

6. Honduras, National Congress, Decree No. 113 in *La Gaceta* no. 3 (29 July 1912), 998.

7. On railroad concessions see Argueta, *Bananos y política;* Flores Valeriano, *La explotación bananera en Honduras;* Karnes, *Tropical Enterprise;* and Kepner and Soothill, *The Banana Empire*.

8. Honduras, Procuraduría General de la República, *Truxillo con X*, 166.

9. William Streich, Puerto Cortés, 6 Feb. 1905, ANH, leg. Notas, año 1905, departamento de Colón, Gobernadores Políticos, Folio 40.

10. Héctor Medina to Ministro de Fomento, General M. B. Rosales, La Ceiba, 17 Aug. 1912, ANH, leg. Ministerio de Gobernación, 1886-1915.

11. Ulises Meza Calix to Ministro de Fomento, Tela, 11 Feb. 1918, ANH, leg. Correspondencia telegráfica, 1918.

12. Jesús A. Ballestrosa to Ministro de Fomento, San Francisco, 7 Mar. 1918, ANH, leg. Correspondencia telegráfica, Atlántida, 1918.

13. Robert L. Keiser to State Department, Tegucigalpa, 26 Feb. 1923, U.S. State Department, Internal Affairs of Honduras, 1910-1929 microfilm roll 41, 815.52/10.

14. Melecio Zelaya to Ministro de Fomento, La Ceiba, 10 Sept. 1925, ANH, leg. Telegramas (this *legajo* did not have a cover).

15. Melecio Zelaya to Ministro de Gobernación, La Ceiba, 27 Sept. 1925, ANH, leg. Telegramas de Atlántida, July-Sept. 1925.

16. Sabiro Tinoco to Ministro de Fomento, Yoro, 6 Apr. 1925, ANH, leg. Correspondencia telegráfica de Yoro 1925.

17. Sabiro Tinoco to Ministro de Fomento, Yoro, 11 Apr. 1925, ANH, leg. Correspondencia telegráfica de Yoro 1925.

18. Rafael Barahona M. to Ministro de Fomento, Agricultura, Obras Publícas y Trabajo, Tela, 9 Feb. 1930, ANH, leg. Notas varias, correspondencia del departamento de Atlántida.

19. Gobernador Político de Atlántida, "Informe del año económico del departamento de Atlántida 1913," 17 Oct. 1913, 6, ANH, leg. Informes al Ministro de Gobernación, 1913.

20. Gobernador Político de Atlántida, "Informe del año económico, 1914-15," Sept. 1915, 8-10, ANH, leg. 1914.

21. My description of the landscape is based on data pertaining to 26 farms included in a United Fruit soil survey. Prescott, "Report on the Examination of Tropical Soils," 342-411. The Robert H. Stover Library (FHIA) holds a copy of this unpublished report. Also see the following maps: Zanonni, 1935; Tela Railroad Company, "General Division Map," 17 Mar. 1948; and Tela Railroad Company, "Map of Railroad Lines: Tela and Cortés Divisions," 10 Aug. 1950, U.S. Library of Congress Map and Geography Division.

22. Prescott, "Report on the Examination of Tropical Soils," 354-378.

23. This was the process used by Tela Railroad Company workers during the 1940s and 1950s, as described by José María Lara and José Almendares, interviews, Aug.-Sept. 1995. For photographic evidence from the 1920s, see United Fruit Company Photograph Collection, Harvard University, Baker Library, Historical Collections.

24. Standard Fruit shipped more than 4,400 mahogany logs to New Orleans in 1925 and 1926. James B. Stewart, 16 Mar. 1927, National Archives at College Park, Md. (hereafter, USNA), Records of the Foreign Agricultural Service (Record Group 166), "Forestry Reports," folder Consular Reports—Honduras.

25. S. L. Wilkinson, "Banana Industry and General Review of Tela District," 5 Jun. 1921, USNA, Foreign Agricultural Service, "Narrative Reports, 1904-1939," box 343, folder Fruits.

26. Wilkinson, "Banana Industry and General Review of Tela District."

27. J. B. Castro Banegas, "Informe del año económico, 1927-8," 18 Sept. 1928, 1, ANH, leg. Ferrocarril Nacional, July 1928-Aug. 1929.

28. The company had more than 14,000 hectares planted in bananas along with nearly 3,000 hectares of seeded pasture. Ministro de Fomento, *Memoria de Fomento,* Appendix "Report of the Tela Railroad Company" (15 Aug. 1930), 55. A 1928 report listed the Tela Railroad Company's holdings in the department of Yoro as 19,878 hectares. See José B. Macedon, "Cuadro que demuestra el número de agricultores y ganaderos matriculados 1927 a 1928," 31 July 1928, ANH, leg. Ferrocarril Nacional, July 1928-Aug. 1929. See also "Informe de la Tela Railroad Company" in Ministro de Fomento, Memoria de Fomento, Obras Públicas, Agricultura, y Trabajo 1927-8, 111-119.

29. J. B. Castro Banegas, "Informe del año económico, 1927-8," 18 Sept. 1928, Appendix 1, ANH, leg. Ferrocarril Nacional, julio 1928-agosto 1929.

30. Standley, "The Flora of Lancetilla," 8-49.

31. Ibid., 18. The secondary growth consisted of "aggressive" herbaceous plants not found in mature forests. Woody plants included the pale garuma (*Cecropia*), balsa (*Ochroma*), and zarzahueca (*Byttneria*), a prickly shrub described by Standley as one of the worst pests of bananas.

32. In the heavily wooded swamps, *Pterocarpus belizensis* predominated among trees. *Bactris minor,* a spiny palm, formed "impenetrable thickets." The prickly-stemmed sarsaparilla (*Smilax ornata*) was also common. In sunlit openings *Montricharida* or *Heliconia Mariae* grew. Swamp trees included large numbers of *Erythrina glauca, Licania hypoleuca,* and *L. platypus;* in grassy marshlands, aquatic vegetation included cattails (*Typha*) and coarse grasses such as wild rice (*Oryza latifolia*) *Panicum grande* and reeds (*Phragmites*). Papyrus-like sedges (*Cyperus giganteus*), Hibiscus, and "vast colonies" of Thalia also inhabited the marshes. Floating plants included water lettuce (*Pistia*), Salvinia, Azolla, duckweed (*Lemna* and *spirodela*), and waterlilies (*Nymphaea*). Cohune palms were "everywhere." Standley, "The Flora of Lancetilla," 12.

33. Peters, "An Ornithological Survey in the Caribbean Lowlands of Honduras," 397–399.

34. Ibid., 398–399.

35. A decade earlier, the expansion of banana farms near Limón, Costa Rica, provoked similar comments from naturalists: "Very few of the forest birds frequent the banana plantations, and with the destruction of the forest they recede or disappear altogether." See *Biologia Centrali-Americana,* 38.

36. Maps dating from the mid-1920s and 1933 depict Toloa Lagoon as being about half the size of nearby Micos Lagoon, but considerably larger than Tinta Lagoon (located east of the Ulúa's mouth). However, a company map from 1948 shows a much-reduced Toloa Lagoon occupying about a quarter of the area taken up by Tinta lagoon. The Tinto-Martínez canal is shown as connecting Toloa Lagoon with the sea. Contemporary maps of Atlántida and Yoro do not depict Toloa Lagoon. See Anon., "Honduras"; Instituto Panamericano de Geografía e Historia, "Honduras" 1933; Tela Railroad Company, "General Division Map," 17 Mar. 1948, and "Map of Railroad Lines: Tela and Cortés Divisions," 10 Aug. 1950; and Instituto Geográfico Nacional, "Departamento de Atlántida" and "Departamento de Yoro," 1985.

37. Salvador Crespo, "Departamento de Colón: Importante reseña del Señor Gobernador Político," *Boletín de Fomento* 1, no. 2 (Jan. 1912): 317.

38. Gobernador Político de Colón, "Informe del año económico," 20 Sept. 1915, ANH, leg. 1914.

39. Winfield H. Scott, 11 Sept. 1926, USNA, Foreign Agricultural Service, Narrative Reports, 1904–1939, folder Fruits.

40. Branch lines connected Puerto Castilla with Trujillo and the village of Aguán. Gregorio Aguilar, "Informe," 15 Oct. 1920, ANH, leg. Informes de las gobernadores políticos, varios departamentos, 1919–1920.

41. E. Evans, 27 Aug. 1925, USNA, Foreign Agricultural Service, Narrative Reports, 1904–1939, Honduras, folder Fruits.

42. *Diario del Norte,* 13 Oct. 1927, 6.

43. Winfield H. Scott, "The Use and Methods of Irrigation in the Puerto Castilla Consular District," 26 July 1926, USNA, Foreign Agricultural Service, Narrative Reports, 1904–1939, Honduras, folder Land.

44. Winfield H. Scott, "Review of Commerce and Industries," 11 Oct. 1926, USNA, Foreign Agricultural Service, Narrative Reports, 1904–1939, Honduras, folder Fruits. A geographer who explored the region in the 1950s wrote that banana plantations did away with "immense forests" both for agricultural purposes and timber products. See Helbig, *Areas y paisajes del noreste de Honduras,* 84.

45. Winfield H. Scott, "Review of Commerce and Industries for the calendar year 1926," 14 Mar. 1927, 16, USNA, Foreign Agricultural Service, Narrative Reports, 1904–1939, Honduras, folder Fruits.

46. I derived this number from a 1933 map that did not indicate how many of these farms were planted in bananas at the time. See "Honduras: North Coast, Truxillo Railroad 42 inch gauge." The map was "traced" by the U.S. Marine Corps, 9 Oct. 1933. U.S. Library of Congress, Geography and Map Division.

47. This total included approximately 43,000 hectares acquired via the terms of the 1912 railroad concession, and an additional 26,500 hectares that were purchased from private owners. Honduras, *Truxillo con X,* 63, 69.

48. Marbut and Bennett, "Informe de los terrenos."

49. Hardwoods included the Santa María, tamarindo, naranjo, higuero, guayabo, chichipote, San Juan, jocote de mico, chino, manaca palm, guaruma, and ceiba. As is often the case, the forest edges along riverbanks featured dense vegetation including epiphytes and lianas such as the *bejuco de agua, bejuco colorado,* and *Borbasco* in addition to several varieties of sarsaparilla. Marbut and Bennett, "Informe de los terrenos," 156.

50. United States Military Intelligence Division, Geographic Section 1928, "Sketch of Territory Showing Clashing Interests of the United and Cuyamel Fruit Companies, Guatemala-Honduras," USNA Cartography Division, War Department Map Collection, 91 Guatemala; and Gobernador Político de Cortés, "Informe del año económico," 14 Oct. 1913, ANH, leg. Informes a Ministro de Gobernación, 1913.

51. Luis Caballero, "Ramo de Agricultura: Cuadro númerico que demuestra las manzanas cultivadas en el departamento de Cortés, de las plantas que se expresan en las casillas siguientes," 5 Nov. 1920, ANH, leg. Informes de las gobernaciones políticas, varios departamentos, 1919–1920.

52. The contract to manage the National Railroad was first granted to the Compañia Agrícola de Sula and later transferred to the Cortés Development Company. Samuel Zemurray controlled both companies; several San Pedro Sula–based entrepreneurs held shares in these subsidiaries. See Euraque, *Reinterpreting the Banana Republic,* 25–26; Argueta, *Bananos y política: Samuel Zemurray y la Cuyamel Fruit Company en Honduras,* 43–45 and 103–116; and Kepner and Soothill, *The Banana Empire,* 123–130.

53. Albert H. Gerberich, "New Sugar Industry in Honduras," 25 May 1920, USNA, Foreign Agricultural Service, Narrative Reports, 1904–1939, Honduras, folder Sugar; and F. C. Zalazar and P. H. Meyers, "Plano general de los Ferrocarril Nacional y Mata de Guineo y los subramales de Santiago, Travesia y Bufalo" (1:80,000), 1923, ANH, loose map.

54. Raymond Fox, "Review of Commerce and Industries for the Year and Quarter ending 1925," 10 Feb. 1926, USNA, Foreign Agricultural Service, Narrative Reports, 1904–1939, box 343, folder Fruits.

55. Raymond Fox, "Excerpt from Commerce and Industries for Quarter ended 3-31-26," 16 Apr. 1926, USNA, Foreign Agricultural Service, Narrative Reports, 1904–1939, Honduras, folder Fruits.

56. See "Agreement of 29 July 1927 between the government of Honduras and the Cuyamel Fruit Company," Tegucigalpa, ANH, leg. Notas varias, 1920–1930; "Informe de la Cuyamel Fruit Company y Cortés Development Company, 1930," in Ministro de Fomento, *Memoria 1930,* 77–78; and Raymond Fox, "Report on Commerce and Industries," 13 Oct. 1927, USNA, Foreign Agricultural Service, Narrative Reports, 1904–1939, Honduras, folder Fruits.

57. Gobernador de Atlántida, "Informe del año económico del departamento de Atlántida, 1913," 6; and "Informe del año económico 1914–15."

58. Gobernador Político de Atlántida, "Informe del año económico del departamento de Atlántida," 6.

59. "Annual Report on the Commerce and Industries of the Ceiba Consular District," 4 Apr. 1919, USNA, Foreign Agricultural Service, Narrative Reports, 1904–1939, Honduras, folder Fruits.

60. Gobernador Ramón Rosa Figueroa and Abelardo R. Fortín, "Cuadro de agri-cultores del departamento de Atlántida durante el año de 1928," June 1928, ANH, leg. 1922–1933.

61. Kepner and Soothill, *The Banana Empire*, 37.

62. For estimated landholdings, see United Fruit Company, *Annual Reports* (1912–1930); "Informe de la Cuyamel Fruit Company y Cortés Development Company, 1930," 77–78; and Figueroa and Fortín, "Cuadro de agricultores."

63. This is the sum of population growth for the departments of Atlántida, Colón, Cortés, and Yoro. For the same period, the population of Honduras nearly doubled, increasing from 553,446 to 962,000. Dirección General de Estadísticas y Censos, *Honduras en cifras 1964* (Tegucigalpa: Tipografía Nacional, 1965).

64. McKenney, "The Central American Banana Blight," 750.

65. Prescott, "Report on the Examination of Tropical Soils," 380–385.

66. "Annual report on the Commerce and Industries of the Ceiba consular dis-trict, 1919."

67. B. Nitkiowicz, "Observations on Panama Disease Conditions in Cultivated Areas, Truxillo, Honduras," *United Fruit Company Research Bulletin* 38 (Aug. 1931).

68. The disease's popular English- and Spanish-language names included "ba-nana blight," "banana wilt," "droop," "tired bananas," *la enfermedad de plátano, la enfermedad,* and *enfermedad Panamá.* See Brandes, "Banana Wilt."

69. Ashby, "Banana Diseases in Jamaica"; Claude Wardlaw, *Diseases of the Ba-nana,* 15.

70. Stover, *Fusarial Wilt,* 3.

71. Erwin F. Smith, "A Cuban Banana Disease," 755.

72. McKenney, "The Central American Banana Blight," 750.

73. Prescott, "Diseases of the Banana." On the importance of Brandes's research, see Stover, *Fusarial Wilt,* 12; and Wardlaw, *Diseases of the Banana,* 16–17. On United Fruit's experiments, see Mark Alfred Carleton, "Note on the Fusarium Wilt Disease of Bananas," 663–664.

74. The first published account of the disease is from Australia in 1876. Ploetz and Pegg, "Fungal Diseases of the Root, Corm, and Pseudostem," 143–158.

75. Stover, *Fusarial Wilt,* 8–9.

76. Ashby, "Banana Diseases in Jamaica," 107.

77. Stover, *Fusarial Wilt,* 11, 40.

78. Philip R. White, "A Disease and Evolution," *Scientific Monthly* 31 (Oct. 1930), 307.

79. Stover, *Fusarial Wilt,* 42.

80. Fungal diseases capable of multiple cycles of infection in a single cropping season frequently reveal a positive correlation between plant density and disease inci-dence. See Mundt, "Disease Dynamics in Agroecosystems," 277.

81. British officials enacted a quarantine in Jamaica around 1912. See Ashby, "Ba-nana Diseases in Jamaica," 111; and Stover, *Fusarial Wilt,* 86–87.

82. Johnston, *Mosaic Disease of Sugar Cane in 1923; Diseases and Pests of the Ba-nana,* 14; and Stover, *Fusarial Wilt,* 88.

83. Winfield Scott, 10 Sept. 1926, U.S. State Department, Internal Affairs of Hon-duras, 1910–1929, National Archives Microfilm 647, roll 42.

84. The survey recorded the soil type, texture, organic matter, total nitrogen,

potash (K2O), phosphoric acid (P2O5), lime (CaO), magnesia (MgO), iron (Fe2O3), alumina (AL2O3), and silica (SIO2); Prescott, "Report on the Examination of Tropical Soils."

85. The soil disinfection experiments were done in pots. Prescott, *United Fruit Company Research Bulletin* 2: 20.

86. Johnston, *Mosaic Disease of Sugar Cane in 1923,* 9, 16–17, and 26. For other early control efforts, see N. J. Volk, "Progress Report: The Apparent Relation of Active Calcium and Magnesium on the Activity of Panama Disease of Gros Michel Bananas," *United Fruit Company Research Department Bulletin* no. 30 (Oct. 1930): 1; and "Preliminary Summary: The Relation of Various Soil Characteristics to the Activity of Panama Disease," *United Fruit Company Research Bulletin* no. 27 (Aug. 1930): 1.

87. McKenney, "The Central American Banana Blight," 750.

88. Fawcett, *The Banana,* 230–234.

89. In 1922, the British founded the West Indian Agricultural College (later renamed Imperial College of Tropical Agriculture) in Trinidad. They established a second research center in Jamaica in 1924.

90. Shepherd, "Banana Research at ICTA," *Tropical Agriculture* 51 (1974): 482.

91. Wardlaw, *Diseases of the Banana,* 116.

92. Rowe and Richardson, "Breeding Bananas for Disease Resistance, Fruit Quality, and Yield" (La Lima, Honduras: Tropical Agriculture Research Services, 1975), 7–8.

93. Permar, "Banana Breeding," *United Fruit Company Research Department Bulletin* 21 (14 Oct. 1929): 2–13.

94. Rowe and Richardson, "Breeding Bananas for Disease Resistance, Fruit Quality, and Yield," 7.

95. Wilson, *Empire in Green and Gold* (New York: Henry Holt and Company, 1947), 184.

96. Silent films included *Banana Skins* (1908) and *The Passing of a Grouch* (1910). For a list of other films, songs, and pop culture expressions centered on bananas, see Jenkins, *Bananas: An American History,* 142–171.

97. Edith Wharton to Sara Norton, 19 Aug. 1904, in *The Letters of Edith Wharton,* ed. R. W. B. Lewis and Nancy Lewis (New York: Charles Scribner's Sons, 1988), 92–93.

98. On the meanings of coffee drinking, see Jiménez, "From Plantation to Cup"; on sugar, see Mintz, *Sweetness and Power.*

99. Wallace Stevens, "Floral Decoration for Bananas," in *The Palm at the End of the Mind,* ed. Holly Stevens (New York: Vintage Books, 1972), 81–82.

100. Dudziak, "Josephine Baker, Racial Protest, and the Cold War," 545–570.

101. Faulkner, *As I Lay Dying,* 240, 249.

102. Willis, "Learning from the Banana," 587–592.

103. For example, see the United Fruit Company publications "The Story of the Banana" [5th ed.] (Boston: 1929) and "About Bananas" (Boston: 1931). For an interesting example of how children's literature romanticized the banana trade, see Lee, *Children of Banana Lands.* I am grateful to Scott Sandage for giving me a copy of this book.

104. Palmer, "The Banana in Caribbean Trade," 271.

105. For examples of this genre, see Adams, *Conquest of the Tropics;* Crowther, *The Romance and Rise of the American Tropics;* Thompson, *Rainbow Republics of Central America;* and Cutter, "Caribbean Tropics in Commercial Transition," 494–507.

106. Banana consumption was rising concurrently in Europe, but the volume of imports paled in comparison to that of the United States: England, the largest European market for bananas in 1914, imported some 6 million bunches. Wilhelm Bitter, "Al margen de la industria bananera," 650–656.

107. United States Department of Agriculture, Bureau of Agricultural Economics, *Consumption of Food in the United States, 1909-1952* (Washington D.C.: 1957), 16; Harvard University Graduate School of Business Administration, Exhibits Presented for the Harvard Advertising Awards, vol. 8, pt. 1, "Report and Recommendations on Field Survey for the Fruit Dispatch Company" [Hereafter, "Field Survey for Fruit Dispatch"], Harvard University, Baker Historical Collections, Ms. Div. SPGD H339a. I thank Catherine LeGrand for bringing this fascinating study to my attention.

108. Palmer, "The Banana in Caribbean Trade," 266.

109. Field Survey for Fruit Dispatch, vol. 8, pt. 1, 15.

110. For market share, see Dosal, *Doing Business with the Dictators,* 155. On regional monopolies, see Field Survey for Fruit Dispatch, "Summary of Jobbers' Reports for Fruit Dispatch Company," vol. 8, pt. 2, 14–15. For the Fruit Dispatch Company's role in price-fixing, see Kepner, *Social Aspects of the Banana Industry,* 42–44.

111. Fruit Dispatch Company, "Conference Report," Chicago, 11–12 Nov. 1925, FHIA, Stover Library.

112. Fruit Dispatch Company, "Conference Report," 4.

113. Fruit Dispatch Company, "Conference Report," 130.

114. "Analysis of Weekly Market Reports," 24 Sept. 1928, USNA, General Records of the Department of Justice, 60-166-56 (United States v. United Fruit Company), Binder: Analysis of Weekly Market Reports, Fruit Dispatch Company, 1927–1934 [hereafter, DOJ File 60-166-56].

115. For Standard Fruit's problems with marketing the Lacatan, see *Revista del archivo y de la biblioteca nacional de Honduras* 12 (Jun. 1931): 434; and Federico Ordóñez P., to Sub-secretario de Fomento, Obras Públicas, Agricultura y Trabajo, 3 July 1926, La Ceiba, Archivo de la Gobernación de Atlántida, Libro copiador de cartas 1926; and Hord, "The Conversion of Standard Fruit Company Banana Plantations," 269–275. For Cuyamel Fruit, see Fox, "Report on Commerce and Industry for the year and quarter ended December, 1925."

116. Researchers interviewed 8,500 consumers in Georgia, Iowa, Massachusetts, Ohio, and Tennessee. The study also incorporated the opinions of more than 1,700 retailers and nearly 100 wholesalers or fruit jobbers. Field Survey for Fruit Dispatch, v. 1.

117. Ibid.

118. Ibid., pt. 3, 49.

119. Ibid., 52.

120. Ibid., 21.

121. Ibid., 18.

122. Retailers reported different preferences for bunch sizes during the 1925 Fruit Dispatch Company conference. See Fruit Dispatch Company, "Conference Report," 5–26.

123. Field Survey for Fruit Dispatch, pt. 3, 54.

124. Ibid., pt. 1, 34. On the persistence of independent grocers in the Chicago area during the 1920s, see Cohen, "Encountering Mass Culture at the Grassroots," 6–33.

125. Bitter, "Al margen de la industria bananera," 651.

126. Analysis of Weekly Market Reports, 6 May 1929 and 20 May 1929, USNA, DOJ File 60-166-56.

127. Nelson R. Park, "Review of Commerce and Industries, La Ceiba, for Quarter Ending Dec. 31, 1928." USNA, Foreign Agricultural Service, Narrative Reports 1904–1939, Honduras, folder Fruits.

128. Honduras, Congreso Nacional, Decree 117 (28 Mar. 1919), mimeograph copy. Tulane University, Howard-Tilton Memorial Library, Standard Fruit and Steamship Company (hereafter, SFSC Papers), box 7, folder 6.

129. E. E. Evans, "Review of Commerce and Industries for Quarter ending June 30, 1926," 16 Aug. 1926, USNA, Foreign Agricultural Service, Narrative reports 1904-1939, Honduras, folder Fruits; and Aguan Valley Company, "Honduras Division," 5 Mar. 1941, SFSC Papers, box 8, folder 12.

130. Some farms to the east of La Ceiba also had been abandoned. *Revista del Archivo Nacional* no. 12 (June 1930): 433; "Cuadro de agricultores del departamento de Atlántida durante el año de 1928," ANH, leg. 1922–1933; and Archivo de la Gobernación de Atlántida, Libro de matrícula de agricultores y ganaderos (1928–1935), 29–33, 49–52, 57, 72, 80–82, 87, 109, 138, 149, and 164–166.

131. "Conocimiento: Fruta embarcada por la Standard Fruit Company, March, Abril, Mayo 1932," Archivo de la Gobernación de Atlántida, loose document.

132. "Informe emitido por el Gobernador Político de Atlántida, año económico 1935–6," ANH, leg. 1936 Informes departamentales de los gobernadores políticos.

133. The text of the 1932 agreement made reference to the "banana disease that has greatly affected its [Standard Fruit's] plantations." The company agreed to pay a $50,000 fine and turn over the rights to 4,000 hectares of land. In 1935, Standard Fruit returned 34 properties totaling 21,396 hectares of land. See Congreso Nacional, Decree 77 (1932); and Decree 83 (1935); and Camilo Gómez to Governor of Atlántida, La Ceiba, 23 Nov. 1936, ANH, leg. Gobernación 1936.

134. Gobernador de Atlántida, Libro de matrícula de agricultores y ganaderos (1933), 109.

135. J. H. Wilson, "Informe de la Truxillo Railroad Company," 29 Sept. 1928, in Ministro de Fomento, *Memoria del Fomento,* 1927–1928, Appendices, 98–99; and Volk, "The Apparent Relation of Active Calcium and Magnesium on the Activity of Panama Disease of Gros Michel Bananas," 8–9.

136. Gobernador de Colón, "Informe del año económico, 1927–8," 16 Nov. 1928, ANH, leg. Ferrocarril Nacional, July 1928–Aug. 1929.

137. Procuraduría General de la República, *Truxillo con X,* 71–72.

138. One observer described the secondary vegetation as follows: ". . . tierra llena de matorrales, madera virgen, enredaderas que cubren hasta grupos de árboles, caña de azúcar silvestre y zacate mucho más alto que el tamaño de un caballo." Helbig, *Areas y paisaje del noreste de Honduras,* 87.

139. Raymond Fox, "Excerpt from review of commerce and industry for the year 1926," 9 Feb. 1927, USNA, Foreign Agricultural Service, Narrative Reports, 1904-1939, Honduras, folder Fruits.

140. Alonzo Valenzuela, "Informe de la inspección de Omoa y Cuyamel," 29 Jul. 1933, ANH, leg. Ministro de Fomento, informes a varias secciones y departamentos de ministro, 1931–1932.

141. "Informe de la Cuyamel Fruit Company y Cortés Development Company, 1930," 77–78.

142. Wardlaw and fellow scientist Laurence P. McGuire visited Costa Rica, Guatemala, British Honduras, Jamaica, Colombia, Panamá, St. Lucia, and Barbados. They did not visit Honduras. See Wardlaw, "Panama Disease of Bananas," 53–54.

143. Wardlaw, "Virgin Soil Deterioration," 244.

144. Ibid.

145. Ibid., 247.

146. Standard Fruit Company of Honduras, "Staff Meeting Proceedings," 8 Nov. 1924, SFSC Papers, box 7, folder 17.

147. The best account of the "battle for Motagua" is found in Dosal, *Doing Business with the Dictators,* 75–94.

148. "Informe de la Cuyamel Fruit Company y Cortés Development Company, 1930," 77–78.

149. Dosal, *Doing Business with the Dictators,* 141–159.

CHAPTER 3

1. Víctor Medina Romero to Ministro de Fomento, Jutiapa, 8 Oct. 1932, ANH, leg. Notas varias, 1932.

2. Ángela Coto-Moreno, author interview, El Progreso, Aug. 1995.

3. The data on yearly production were based on figures provided by the Tela Railroad Company as reported by Robert E. Whedbee, "A Brief, Basic Banana Industry Report," 1941, U.S. Diplomatic Post Records 1930–1945, Honduras, microfilm roll 28. Also see T. Monroe Fisher, "Review of Commerce and Industries for Quarter Ending 30 Sept. 1930, Tela, Honduras," 19 Dec. 1930, USNA, Foreign Agricultural Service, Narrative Reports, 1904–1939, Honduras, folder Fruits. Note that Kepner and Soothill (*The Banana Empire,* 273) provided a much lower figure (19 percent) for the percentage of fruit purchased by the Tela Railroad Company in 1929. On the problems with historical data on banana exports, see Ellis, *Las transnacionales del banano en Centroamérica,* 373–382.

4. During the Depression, total banana imports to the United States fell nearly 40 percent, from 65.1 million bunches to 39.6 million bunches. Kepner, *Social Aspects of the Banana Industry,* 69.

5. Non-company banana production in Colón was considerably less important than in Cortés. The area in bananas, excluding the holdings of the Truxillo Railroad Company, was around 900 hectares in 1926. Between 1929 and 1933, purchased fruit represented no more than 11 percent of the company's total exports. See Ministro de Fomento to R. Barrientos, Tegucigalpa, 14 Dec. 1931; and Truxillo Railroad Company to Ministro de Fomento, 9 Jan. 1929, ANH, leg. Truxillo Railroad Company, Correspondencia, 1920. Also see Ministro de Fomento to Truxillo Railroad Co., 15 Dec. 1931, ANH, leg. Secretaria de Fomento: Libro copiador de correspondencia oficial, Dec. 1931; Gobernador de Colón, "Informe de Colón para el año económico 1935-6," 13, ANH, leg. Informes departamentales de las Gobernaciones Políticas, 1936; and "Datos estadísticos del departamento de Colón, año de 1926," ANH, loose document.

6. Aguan Valley Company, "Detail of Fruit Shipments for Years 1920 to 1930 Inclusive," 5 Mar. 1941, SFSC Papers, box 8, folder 12.

7. "Conocimiento: Fruta Embarcada por la Standard Fruit Company, marzo, abril y mayo," Archivo de la Gobernación de Atlántida (La Ceiba), loose document.

8. Aguan Valley Company, "Detail of Fruit Shipments for Years 1920 to 1930 Inclusive," 5 Mar. 1941.

9. García Buchard, *Poder político, interés bananero, e identidad nacional en centro-américa,* 152–153.

10. I compiled the data that follow from an incomplete agricultural census for the department of Cortés. The survey included a total of 368 farmers and ranchers, a perplexingly small number that excluded both the Tela Railroad and Cuyamel Fruit companies. "Datos estadísticos del departamento de Cortés, año de 1926," ANH, loose document.

11. "Datos estadísticos del departamento de Colón, año de 1926."

12. A 1931 newspaper stated that there were 800 banana farmers in the Sula valley. See *El Pueblo* (San Pedro Sula), 26 Oct. 1931. Two years later, a U.S. consul reported that "several hundred" farmers sold bananas to the company. Kenneth S. Stout, "Review of Commerce and Industry for calendar year 1932," 17 Jan. 1933, USNA, Foreign Agricultural Service, Narrative Reports 1904–39, Honduras, folder Fruits.

13. *El Atlántico,* 21 Feb. 1931.

14. Alejandro Irías, "El día del banano," *El Pueblo,* 8 Feb. 1932. Luís Caballero was recorded in a 1920 list of "Registered Cultivators" in the department of Cortés as the owner of a 35-hectare farm in the municipality of Villanueva (Choloma).

15. In September, United Fruit paid $ .50 for a nine-handed bunch; $ .37 for an eight-handed; $ .25 for a seven-handed; and $ .12 for a six-handed bunch. Two months later the prices had fallen to $ .44, .33, .21, and .09, respectively.

16. The reprinted contract appeared in consecutive editions of *El Pueblo* (21–22 Sept. 1931), a newspaper with close ties to the Liberal Party.

17. Growers assumed all costs associated with getting their fruit loaded.

18. United Fruit did not obligate itself to buy fruit when unable to export on account of "epidemics, quarantines, wars, revolutions, riots, strikes, dangerous seas, or wartime restriction in ship movements."

19. *El Pueblo,* 12 Sept. 1931 and 21 Oct. 1931.

20. *El Pueblo,* 28 Sept. 1931.

21. The paper claimed that a majority of those who had signed the contract were "Cuyamel Fruit Company" employees or persons who farmed on leased lands. *El Pueblo,* 26 Oct. 1931.

22. *El Pueblo,* 14 Dec. 1931.

23. *El Pueblo,* 2 Jan. 1932. In 1932, United Fruit lowered its purchase prices in Costa Rica by approximately the same amount. See Walter W. Hoffman, 16 Jul. 1932, USNA, Foreign Agricultural Service, Narrative Reports 1920–1941, Costa Rica, folder Fruits 1929–1941.

24. *El Pueblo,* 2 Jan. 1932.

25. Kepner and Soothill, *The Banana Empire,* 137–138.

26. *El Pueblo,* 13 Jan. 1932.

27. *El Pueblo,* 19 Apr. 1932.

28. "Contra propuesta a la contrata de Mr. English," San Pedro Sula, 17 Apr. 1932, ANH, leg. Correspondencia del departamento de Cortés, 1932.

29. United Fruit paid even lower prices to *poquiteros* who did not sign contracts. Thus, for growers unable or unwilling to sign a contract with one of United's subsidiaries, the prices set out in the counterproposal may have been competitive. See J. Antonio Reyes to Ministro de Fomento, Tocoa, 16 Oct. 1931. ANH, leg. Correspondencia del departamento de Cortés, 1931.

30. "Contra propuesta a la contrata de Mr. English," San Pedro Sula, 17 Abr. 1932, ANH, leg. Correspondencia del departamento de Cortés, 1932.

31. *El Pueblo,* 26 Apr. 1932.

32. Ibid., 2 May 1932.

33. Ibid., 12 Feb. 1932.

34. Ibid., 19 Feb. 1932.

35. Ibid., 17 Feb. 1932.

36. Although efforts to quantify the benefits of irrigation on banana weights were not undertaken until sometime later, observers in the late 1920s linked irrigation with high-quality bananas. See, for example, Archer Woodford, "Review of Commerce and Industries for Quarter Ended Sept. 30, 1929," 22 Oct. 1929, USNA, Foreign Agricultural Service, Narrative Reports, 1904–1939, Honduras, folder Fruits.

37. *El Pueblo,* 19 Feb. 1932, 1 Mar. 1932, and 14 Mar. 1932.

38. Fred K. Salter, "Irrigation Projects in Honduras," 2 Sept. 1938, Confidential U.S. Diplomatic Post Records, 1930–1945, roll 17.

39. In 1932, the National Congress approved a contract for the use of irrigation waters by the Tela Railroad Company. The contract stipulated that a retroactive payment of US $4,300 be paid for irrigation waters used between 1927 and 1930, suggesting that the company was in arrears. See Congressional Decree No. 115 (12 Mar. 1932), reprinted in "Contratas de las compañías en Honduras: Colección de contratas y acuerdos de la Tela RR Co." (1936), photocopy, Universidad Nacional Autónoma de Honduras, Colección hondureña.

40. A 1932 U.S. consular report from Costa Rica indicated that small-scale growers there had both limited production costs and earnings. Walter W. Hoffman, Port Limón, 16 July 1932.

41. Mayor Samuel E. García et al. to Dr. Colindres Mejía, 31 May 1931, ANH, leg. Correspondencia del departamento de Cortés.

42. Ibid.

43. S. Orellano Rodríguez to Ministro de Fomento, Tela, 2 Jun. 1932, ANH, leg. Notas varias, 1932; and *El Pueblo,* 7 May 1932.

44. *El Pueblo,* 2 May 1932 and 7 May 1932.

45. Rodríguez was a grower of some means: in 1926 he cultivated more than 28 hectares of land in bananas and pasture. Rodríguez to Ministro de Fomento, 2 June 1932; and "Censo de agricultores, Departamento de Cortés, 1926," ANH, manuscript.

46. Rodríguez to Ministro de Fomento, 2 June 1932.

47. Alonso Valenzuela, "Informe de la inspección de Omoa y Cuyamel," 29 July 1933, ANH, leg. Ministro de Fomento, Informes al varias secciones y departamentos de ministerio, 1931–1932.

48. Pascual Torres to Abraham Williams, San Pedro Sula, 24 July 1933, ANH, leg.

Correspondencia de las gobernaciones políticas de la república (julio, agosto y septiembre, 1933).

49. Valenzuela estimated that restoring rail service between Omoa and Cuyamel would cost more than $100,000. He proposed a less costly transportation system that combined canoes, tram lines, and roads. Alonso Valenzuela to Ministro de Fomento, 29 July 1933.

50. The rent was $2 for 10 hectares of land. Cruz Calix to President Tiburcio Carías, 24 July 1933, ANH, leg. Secretaria de Fomento, Agricultura y Trabajo, correspondencia de juntas de fomento.

51. The Tela Railroad Company also adopted a policy of leasing land. In 1935, Honduran families reportedly were growing rice (with seed provided by the company), corn, beans, vegetables, plantains, and other crops on company-owned land. Cornelio Mejía, Informe de la Gobernador Política del departamento de Atlántida, 1934–1935, 29, ANH, loose manuscript.

52. Cruz Calix to President Tiburcio Carías, 24 July 1933.

53. Manuel Paniagua to Ministro de Fomento, Cuyamel, 10 Dec. 1934, ANH, leg. Alcaldías municipales, 1934.

54. Gustavo Castañeda to Ministro de Gobernación, Justicia y Bienestar, San Pedro Sula, 20 Sept. 1937, ANH, leg. Correspondencia de las gobernaciones políticas de la república, septiembre y octubre 1937.

55. See correspondence between Castañeda and the Ministro de Gobernación, 15 Oct. 1937 and 16 Nov. 1937, ANH, leg. Correspondencia de las gobernaciones políticas de la república, septiembre y octubre 1937.

56. This was not the first time that community members from Mezapa had challenged the Tela Railroad Company. In 1928, Mezapans hired a lawyer to represent them in a legal challenge concerning the company's alleged encroachment on the community's *ejido* lands and the subsequent destruction of crops. Julio Guerra, 15 July 1928, Santa Rosa del Norte (Mezapa), ANH, leg. 1923 Notas varias.

57. Unless otherwise noted, my version of events at La Mezapa come from Adolfo Miralda, "Certificación: Asunto de Mesapa-Tela Railroad Co," 30 Aug. 1931, ANH, leg. Correspondencia de la Gobernación de Atlántida, 1931.

58. Modesto Orellano, Tela, 24 Aug. 1931, ANH, leg. Correspondencia telegráfica, Atlántida, 1931.

59. Ciriaco Torres to Governor of Atlántida, Santa Rosa del Norte (Mezapa), 28 Aug. 1931, transcribed in Adolfo Miralda to Ministerio de Gobernación, La Ceiba, 30 Aug. 1931, ANH, leg. Correspondencia recibida de las gobernaciones políticas de la república, 1931.

60. Miralda to Ministerio de Gobernación, La Ceiba, 30 Aug. 1931.

61. Salvador Aguirre to Señor representante de la Standard Fruit Company, Tegucigalpa, 5 July 1933, ANH, leg. Ministro de Fomento, Copias de correspondencia oficial, julio–ago. 1933.

62. Gobernador Político, La Ceiba, 7 March 1929, ANH, leg. Correspondencia recibida de los gobernadores políticos, enero a junio 1929.

63. Jacobo P. Munguía to Presidente Miguel Paz Barahona, Esparta, 16 May 1927, ANH, leg. Correspondencia particular, 1921.

64. On problems with marketing the Lacatan, see *Revista del archivo y de la biblio-*

teca nacional de Honduras 12 (June 1931): 434; and Ordóñez P. to Ministro de Fomento, Obras Públicas, Agricultura y Trabajo, La Ceiba, 3 July 1926, Archivo de la Gobernación de Atlántida, Libro copiador de cartas, 1926.

65. Zoroastro Montes de Oca to Ministro de Fomento, Obras Públicas, Agricultura y Trabajo, La Ceiba, 1 Sept. 1927, ANH, leg. Notas varias, 1927.

66. Urbano Rodríguez et al. to Presidente Vicente Mejía Colindres, La Ceiba, 19 Jan. 1931, ANH, leg. Correspondencia del departamento de Atlántida, 1931.

67. Acuerdo de 1 julio 1932, Archivo de la Gobernación de Atlántida, *Libro de acuerdos del Gobernador Polític*, 1927–1933, 151.

68. Camilio Gómez to Gobernador de Atlántida, La Ceiba, 23 Nov. 1936, ANH, leg. Gobernación, 1936.

69. Meza, *Historia del movimiento obrero hondureño*, 11.

70. Arlington Francisco and Elías Pacheco, Sociedad Lucha Obrera to Ministro de Fomento, Descombros, Atlántida, 13 Jul. 1926, ANH, leg. Correspondencia particular, año 1921.

71. Eduardo Boves, Sociedad de Artesanos El Progreso to Ministro de Fomento, La Ceiba, 5 Sept. 1926; ANH, leg. Correspondencia particular, año 1921.

72. *Diario del Norte*, 27 Jul. 1927 and 31 Dec. 1927.

73. Zoroastro Montes de Oca, 24 Feb. 1927, ANH leg. Notas varias, 1927.

74. J. Amado Flores to Encarnación Martínez, Juticalpa, 31 Jan. 1929, ANH, leg. Truxillo Railroad Company, Correspondencia 1920.

75. Amado Flores to Martínez, 31 Jan. 1929.

76. *El Olanchano* (Juticalpa), 26 Jan. 1929.

77. Amado Flores to Martínez, 31 Jan. 1929.

78. According to Amado Flores, wages in the region were "two pesos plus food per day," a rate that would have equaled or exceeded prevailing wages for field hands on banana plantations.

79. On *mestizaje* and Honduran national identity, see Euraque, "The Threat of Blackness."

80. Libros de las Actas de la Municipalidad de Sonaguera [hereafter, LAMS], 30 Jun. 1907, vol. Jan. 1907–July 1910, Municipio de Sonaguera (Sonaguera, Colón).

81. LAMS, 23 June 1918, vol. 1917–1921, 69.

82. LAMS, 13 July 1920, vol. 1917–1921, 150.

83. LAMS, 28 Oct. 1921, vol. Apr. 1921–Dec. 1923, 29.

84. LAMS, 15 Mar. 1923, vol. Apr. 1921–Dec. 1923, 162.

85. LAMS, 15 Nov. 1924, vol. 1924–1925, 42.

86. LAMS, 21 Sept. 1925, vol. 1924–1925, 132.

87. LAMS, 21 Sept. 1925, vol. 1924–1925, 133.

88. LAMS, 1 Mar. 1926, vol. 1926–1927, 38–41.

89. Nicolás M. Robles, Petrona Ocampo, et al. to Ministro de Fomento, Sonaguera, 15 Feb. 1927, ANH, leg. 1927 Notas varias.

90. Ministro de Fomento to Robles, Ocampo, Ramos, and others, Tegucigalpa, 17 Feb. 1927, ANH, leg. 1927, Notas varias.

91. LAMS, 1 Oct. 1928, vol. 1928–1929, 130; 1 Dec. 1928, vol. 1928–1929, 160; and 15 Dec. 1928, vol. 1928–1929, 167.

92. LAMS, 1 Feb. 1930, vol. 1930, 18.

93. LAMS, 1 Mar. 1930, vol. 1930, 36.

94. In 1930, Sonaguera accounted for about 70 percent of Standard Fruit's banana exports. The following year, local officials anticipated 68,500 dollars in revenue of which export taxes were projected to generate nearly fifty percent, a major increase over previous years. LAMS, 15 Jan. 1931, vol. 1930-1931, 225.

95. The petitioners' banana farms ranged in size from 1 to 35 hectares; the total area amounted to some 175 hectares of cultivated land. See Residents of La Paz village to Ministro de Fomento, 20 Jul. 1929, ANH, leg. Correspondencia particular, June–Dec. 1929.

96. J. J. Zelaya to Ministro de Fomento, Sonaguera, 2 Aug. 1929, ANH, leg. Correspondencia particular, June–Dec. 1929.

97. Ministro de Fomento to Romualdo López, Trujillo, 27 Nov. 1929, ANH, leg. Correspondencia particular, June–Dec. 1929.

98. E. E. Thomas to Governor of Colón, Puerto Castilla, 25 Jul. 1930, ANH, leg. Asuntos de la costa norte, 1927.

99. Apparently, Truxillo Railroad Company management did not receive notice of the agreement until July 1930. Acuerdo 1191 (24 Jan. 1930) had not been printed in *La Gaceta* as of July 1930. See Thomas to Governor of Colón, 25 July 1930.

100. The Standard Fruit Company received access to the land via a legal arrangement (*contrato de permuta*) with the Truxillo Railroad Company.

101. Thomas to Governor of Colón, 25 July 1930.

102. Ibid.

103. LAMS, 1 Sept. 1931, 25; and 1 Oct. 1931, 35.

104. LAMS, 2 Apr. 1934 (1931-1934), 419.

105. The La Paz growers complained that they had to haul their fruit three or four kilometers over roads that were impassable during the rainy season. LAMS, 1 Mar. 1933.

106. A surveyor accompanied them to demarcate the line between lots 18 and 19. Gobernador R. Romero to Ministro de Gobernación, 15 Mar. 1934, ANH, leg. Correspondencia telegráfica, Colón 1934; and Gobernador R. Romero to Ministro de Gobernación, Trujillo, 22 Mar. 1934, ANH, leg. Gobernadores Políticas, Jan.–Apr. 1934.

107. Romero reproduced Myrick's statement in a communication sent to the Ministro de Gobernación. G. A. Myrick to Governor of Colón, Trujillo, 21 Mar. 1934, ANH, leg. Gobernadores Políticas, Jan.–Apr. 1934.

108. Ibid.

109. This lends support to the company's contention that La Paz "village" did not exist in a legal sense prior to this time. See LAMS, 2 Apr. 1934.

110. N. Montiel to Ministro de Gobernación, 12 Apr. 1934, ANH, leg. Correspondencia telegráfica, Colón 1934.

111. R. Romero to Ministro de Gobernación, Trujillo, 23 Apr. 1934, ANH, leg. Correspondencia telegráfica, Colón, 1934.

112. Camilo Gómez to Ministro de Gobernación, Trujillo, 3 May 1934, ANH, leg. Correspondencia telegráfica, Colón, 1934.

113. R. Romero to Ministro de Gobernación, Trujillo, 3 May 1934, ANH, leg. Correspondencia telegráfica, Colón, 1934.

114. R. Romero to Ministro de Gobernación, Trujillo, 1 Jun. 1934, ANH, leg. Correspondencia telegráfica, Colón, 1934.

115. In an unrelated correspondence, a municipal official referred to the area as "las fincas de La Paz de la Truxillo." See Ramón R. Galvez to Ministro de Fomento, Tocoa, 18 Nov. 1935, ANH, leg. Alcaldías municipales, 1934–1937.

CHAPTER 4

1. José Almendares, author interview, El Progreso, Yoro, Aug. 1995. Also see G. Oury-Jackson to Secretary of State, Tela, 29 Nov. 1935, USNA, Records of the Foreign Agricultural Service, Narrative Reports, Honduras, folder Diseases—Plant, 1935–37.

2. One long-term resident of the Sula valley told me that some of the "independent growers" believed that Sigatoka was brought by the hurricane. Pancho Urbina, author interview, El Progreso, Aug. 1995. Other individuals who connected the hurricane and Sigatoka disease included Ángela Coto-Moreno, José Almendares, and Victor Reyes. Author interviews, El Progreso, Yoro, Aug.–Sept., 1995.

3. Lewis Knudson, "Report on the Cercospora Disease of Banana in Honduras with Special Reference to Soil as a Factor," typescript (17 Aug. 1936), unpublished report [hereafter, "Report on the Cercospora Disease"].

4. Vining Dunlap, "Reports on Investigation of Sigatoka Disease Control in the Tela and Cortes Divisions, Nov. 1935–Nov. 1936," 1–2 [hereafter, "Investigation of Sigatoka control"]. I am grateful to Dr. Robert Stover, who provided me with access to this unpublished report.

5. Julian L. Nugent, "The Banana industry in the Puerto Cortés Consular District," Puerto Cortés, 1 Jun. 1942, Confidential U.S. Diplomatic Post Records, 1930–1945, Honduras, microfilm roll 28.

6. Gerald A. Drew to Secretary of State, Tegucigalpa, "Banana Blight in North Coast of Honduras, etc." 22 May 1937, Confidential U.S. Diplomatic Post Records, 1930–45, Honduras, microfilm roll 17.

7. Roberto Fasquelle to Governor of Cortés, San Pedro Sula, 9 Oct. 1936, ANH, leg. Correspondencia recibida de las gobernaciones, 1936 (Tomo II); and G. Oury-Jackson to Secretary of State, Tela, 16 July 1936, USNA, Foreign Agricultural Service Narrative Reports 1920–1941, Honduras, folder Diseases—Plant, 1935–37.

8. In August 1936, a scientist hired by United Fruit to study the pathogen described non-company farms along the Chamelecón River as "badly diseased." Knudson, "Report on the Cercospora Disease."

9. J. A. Milla to Ministro de Gobernación, San Pedro Sula, 7 Dec. 1936, ANH, leg. Gobernación, 1936.

10. Milla to Ministro de Gobernación, 7 Dec. 1936.

11. J. A. Milla to Ministro de Gobernación, San Pedro Sula, 10 Feb. 1937, ANH, leg. Apuntes de 1934, Gobernación Política, v. 1.

12. Myron Schraud, "*Cercospora Musae:* A Plant Disease Affecting the Banana Industry of Honduras," Puerto Cortés, 17 Apr. 1937, USNA, Foreign Agricultural Service Narrative Reports 1920–1941, Honduras, folder Diseases—Plant, 1937–1941.

13. In 1932, after watching the value of United Fruit stock (and his personal fortune) fall sharply, Zemurray came out of retirement to become the "managing director in charge of operations" of United Fruit. See Dosal, *Doing Business With the Dictators,* 183–184.

14. Jesse E. Hobson, "Research in the United Fruit Company," typescript, 4 Nov. 1959. I thank Eugene Ostmark for providing me with a copy of this unpublished document.

15. Claude Wardlaw's 1935 monograph *Diseases of the Banana and of the Manila Hemp Plant* included a brief discussion of leaf spot disease. On the movement of the pathogen, see Meredith, *Banana Leaf Spot Disease,* 22–23.

16. On the global circulation of Sigatoka, see Jones, "Sigatoka," 79–81; and Stover, "Intercontinental Spread of Banana Leaf Spot," 327–338.

17. The name *Mycosphaerella musicola* Leach dates from 1941. Prior to that year, scientific publications identified the fungus as *Cercospora musae.* See Leach, "Banana leaf spot," 91–95.

18. An export banana plant was considered healthy if it had six or more functioning leaves when the fruit bunch emerged.

19. Governor Milla to Ministro de Gobernación, San Pedro Sula, 28 July 1936, ANH, leg. Correspondencia telegráfica, Cortés, 1936 (tomo II).

20. The fungicidal properties of copper were known well prior to the Sigatoka epidemic; Bordeaux spray took its name from the region in France where it was developed around 1885 for use in vineyards.

21. Meredith, *Banana Leaf Spot Disease,* 87–88.

22. The Bordeaux mixture was a 5:5:50 copper sulfate, lime, and water solution. Dunlap, "Investigation of Sigatoka Control," 5.

23. Spraying provided both better sticking (of the fungicide to the leaf) and coverage than dusting. UFCo. Division of Tropical Research, *Annual Report* (1937), 2–6.

24. UFCo. Division of Tropical Research, *Annual Report* (1937), 1

25. UFCo. Division of Tropical Research, *Annual Report* (1939), 3.

26. On Sigatoka control and workers in Costa Rica, see Marquardt, "Pesticides, Parakeets, and Unions," 3–36.

27. Gerald A. Drew to Secretary of State, Tegucigalpa, 22 May 1937, Confidential Diplomatic Post Records, Honduras 1930–1945, microfilm roll 17.

28. G. Oury-Jackson, "Cooperation of American Fruit Company with Independent Planters," 18 May 1938, USNA Foreign Agricultural Service Narrative Reports 1920–1941, Honduras, folder Diseases—Plant, 1937–41.

29. Wardlaw, *Banana Diseases.*

30. Ángela Coto-Moreno, author interview, El Progreso, Yoro, Sept. 1995.

31. John Erwin to Secretary of State, Tegucigalpa, 17 Dec. 1937, USNA Foreign Agricultural Service Narrative Reports 1920–1941, Honduras, folder Fruits 1937–41.

32. Julian L. Nugent, "The Banana Industry in the Puerto Cortés Consular District," Puerto Cortés, 1 Jun. 1942, Confidential U.S. Diplomatic Post Records, Honduras, 1930–1945, roll 28.

33. Schraud, "*Cercospora Musae,*" 2–3.

34. Governor J. Antonio Milla to Ministro de Gobernación, San Pedro Sula, undated 1936, ANH, leg. Correspondencia recibida de las gobernaciones, vol. 2 (1936). Leaf removal was a labor-intensive task that worked best where banana farms were scattered. See Meredith, *Banana Leaf Spot Disease,* 80.

35. Milla to Ministro de Gobernación, 10 Feb. 1937.

36. Milla to Ministro de Gobernación, 10 Feb. 1937.

37. UFCo. Div. of Tropical Research, *Annual Report* (1937), 2.

38. Governor J. Antonio Milla to Ministro de Gobernación, 8 Oct. 1936, ANH, leg. Correspondencia recibida de las gobernaciones, vol. 2 (1936).

39. G. A. Castañeda to Ministro de Gobernación, San Pedro Sula, 1 Mar. 1938, ANH, leg. Correspondencia recibida de los gobernadores, 1938.

40. In late 1937, U.S. diplomat John Erwin traveled with Dr. Antonio C. Rivera, president of the Honduran Congress, and Juan Manuel Gálvez, Minister of War, to the North Coast. Erwin claimed that the trip was evidence of the national government's recognition of the severity of Sigatoka. On tensions between Carías and Liberals in San Pedro Sula, see Euraque, *Reinterpreting the Banana Republic,* 42–75.

41. G. Oury-Jackson, "Cooperation of American Fruit Company with Independent Banana Planters," 18 May 1938, "Enclosure No 1: La Compañía Frutera proyecta curar las fincas de los agricultores que poseen buenas tierras," USNA Foreign Agricultural Service Narrative Reports 1920–1941, Honduras, folder Diseases—Plant, 1937–1941.

42. Oury-Jackson, "Cooperation of American Fruit Company with Independent Banana Planters," 18 May 1938.

43. Ibid.

44. Ibid. Oury-Jackson's description of the plan differed from that published in *El Comercio* in its estimations of the annual per-acre installation costs of the spray system. Oury-Jackson put the figure at $350.00 per acre ($300 for materials and $50 for labor costs), which was exactly one-half of the *El Comercio* figure of 1,400 lempiras (which at the prevailing 2:1 exchange rates was the equivalent of $700.00).

45. The cash loan would be made at 6 percent interest payable by discounting 20 percent of the value of fruit sales.

46. In 1939 officials in San Pedro Sula, citing losses suffered by "national growers" on account of Sigatoka, lowered the municipal tax on banana exports from 2 cents per bunch to 1 cent per bunch. Gustavo A. Castañeda to Ministro de Gobernación, San Pedro Sula, 17 July 1939, ANH, leg. Correspondencia recibida de los gobernadores, 1938.

47. Julian L. Nugent, Puerto Cortés, 1 June 1942, Confidential U.S. Diplomatic Post Records, 1930–1945, Honduras, microfilm roll 28.

48. Nugent, Puerto Cortés, 1 June 1942.

49. Standard had 1,755 hectares of land under irrigation in 1938. See Fred K. Salter, "Irrigation Projects in Honduras," Tegucigalpa, 2 Sept. 1938, Confidential U.S. Diplomatic Post Records, 1930–1945, Honduras, microfilm roll 17.

50. Application rates of copper sulfate between 1938 and 1942 ranged from 988 pounds to 1,457 pounds per hectare. A. J. Chute to John Erwin, Tegucigalpa, 19 May 1943 [copy], Enclosure 3, in John Faust to Secretary of State, 21 May 1943, USNA Foreign Agricultural Service Narrative Reports 1941–1945, Honduras, folder Fruits—marketing policies.

51. Wymberley Der Coerr, "Basic Report on Banana Industry," La Ceiba, 7 May 1942. Also see Der Coerr's reports dated 31 Mar. 1942 and 30 Jun. 1942, Confidential U.S. Diplomatic Post Records, 1930–1945, microfilm roll 28.

52. Der Coerr, "Basic Report on Banana Industry," 30 June 1942.

53. For example, between May and June 1942, non-company growers who sold their fruit to Standard Fruit lost 36 percent of their produce due to irregular steamer schedules.

54. United Fruit, Division of Tropical Research, *Annual Report* (1940), 3.

55. Ibid.

56. United Fruit, Division of Tropical Research, *Annual Reports* (1941–1952).

57. Stahel, "Notes on Cercospora Leaf Spot of Bananas," 262–263.

58. Studies by Simmonds (1939) and Calpouzos (1955) showed a correlation between the presence of dew and infection. For a review, see Meredith, *Banana Leaf Spot Disease*, 33.

59. Leach, "Banana Leaf Spot Investigations," 454–462; 499–502.

60. Leach, "Banana Leaf Spot Investigations," 500. By 1941, Leach was also experimenting with Bordeaux spray. See Alfred F. Butler, Cedar Grove Experiment Station, Jamaica, 26 Aug. 1941 [copy], Hunt Institute for Botanical Documentation, Wilson Popenoe Papers, box 32, folder 2.

61. Prior to the mid-1930s, cultivators in Trinidad often grew bananas as a shade plant for cacao. In 1934 the Canadian Banana Company began exporting fruit from the island, prompting planters to replace old stands of cacao and species of *Erythrina* trees with Gros Michel monocultures. See Thorold, "Cultivation of Bananas under Shade," 213–214.

62. Ibid., 213.

63. Vining Dunlap, "Sigatoka Disease," United Fruit Company Tropical Research Department Bulletin (Sept. 1950), 6; Luis Calpouzos, "Studies on the Sigatoka Disease of Bananas and Its Fungus Pathogen" (Cuba: Atkins Garden and Research Laboratory, 1955); Guyot and Cuillé, "Les traitements fongicides des bananeraies," 101–107; and Meredith, *Banana Leaf Spot Disease*, 80–1. Standard Fruit briefly grew a Cavendish cultivar variety under shade in Honduras, but the outcome of this experiment is unknown. See Muery, "Historical Overview," 6. I sincerely thank J. P. Sánchez, of La Ceiba, for providing me with a copy of this unpublished report.

64. Cheesman and Wardlaw, "Specific and Varietal Susceptibility," 335.

65. Ibid., 336.

66. Muery, "Historical Overview," 5–6.

67. John D. Erwin, Tegucigalpa, 17 Dec. 1937, USNA Foreign Agricultural Service Narrative Reports 1920–1941, Honduras, folder Fruits 1937–41.

68. One historian estimates that during the 1940s, Sigatoka control work employed more than one-quarter of United Fruit's field hands. See Marquardt, "Pesticides, Parakeets, and Unions," 7–8; and Dunlap, "Sigatoka Disease," 19.

69. Dunlap, "Sigatoka Disease," 19.

70. Ibid.

71. UFCo. Division of Tropical Research, *Annual Report* (1944), 9.

72. By 1952, the average labor cost of one spray cycle was around 90 cents per acre. Assuming that the company was spraying at least 40,000 acres in Honduras in 1952, one cycle would have incurred approximately $36,000 in labor costs. If each acre received an average of 15 cycles annually, labor costs for Sigatoka control would have exceeded $500,000. See UFCo. Division of Tropical Research, *Annual Report* (1951), 17–18; and *Annual Report* (1952), 17.

73. UFCo. Division of Tropical Research, *Annual Report* (1952), 20.

74. Amaya Amador, *Prisión verde*, 30.

75. Ibid., 60.

76. Ibid., 61–2.

77. Ibid., 62.

78. Ibid., 149–154.

79. Cantalisio Andino, author interview, Calpules Aldea, Yoro, Sept. 1995.

80. Bricio Fajardo, author interview, Olanchito, Yoro, Sept. 1995.

81. Ibid.

82. Neche Martínez, author interview, El Ocote, Yoro, 1995.

83. Feliciano Núñez, author interview, El Progreso, Yoro, Aug. 1995.

84. Ibid.

85. Ibid.

86. José Almendares Ortiz, author interview, El Progreso, Yoro, Aug. 1995.

87. Feliciano Núñez, interview, El Progreso, Yoro, Aug. 1995.

88. One worker who applied Bordeaux spray for two years during the 1950s recalled experiencing loss of appetite and weight loss. Andrés Alvarado, author interview, Campo Limones (La Lima), Cortés, Sept. 1995.

89. Víctor Reyes, author interview, El Progreso, Yoro, Aug. 1995.

90. José María Lara, author interview, La Lima, Cortés, Aug. 1995.

91. Camilo Rivera Girón, author interview, San Pedro Sula, Cortés, Aug. 1995.

92. Congreso Nacional, *Informe de la comisión especial sobre la verdadera situación de los trabajadores en Honduras* (Tegucigalpa: Talleres Tipo-Lito Ariston, 1950), 13. UNAH, Colección hondureña, Rare Books Shelves.

93. Marquardt, "Pesticides, Parakeets, and Unions," 10–16.

94. Lourdes Mejía [pseudonym], author interview, San Pedro Sula, Cortés, Aug. 1995. Our conversation was not tape-recorded at her request.

95. Historically, the primary risk for contracting tuberculosis has been breathing infected air. Transmission is believed to occur exclusively in "enclosed environments." Although often associated with urban areas, tuberculosis in migrant farmworker populations has been documented in the United States. See Smith and Moss, "The Epidemiology of Tuberculosis"; and Hibbs and Yeager, "Tuberculosis among migrant farm workers," 1775; and in the same journal, Ciesielski et al., "The Epidemiology of Tuberculosis," 1715–1719.

96. The human body possesses several mechanisms that help to prevent the absorption of excess copper into the blood stream. In the United States, most reported cases of copper toxicity involve ingestion of contaminated water or suicide attempts with copper sulfate. U.S. Department of Health and Human Services, Agency for Toxic Substances and Disease Registry, *Toxicological Profile for Copper* (Dec. 1990), 37–42.

97. Cortez Pimentel and Marqués, " 'Vineyard sprayer's lung,' " 678–688.

98. Pimentel and Marqués, " 'Vineyard sprayer's lung,' " 685.

99. The researchers also carried out controlled trials that exposed guinea pigs to Bordeaux spray. The guinea pigs developed lesions similar to those observed in the two farmworkers. Pimentel and Marqués, " 'Vineyard sprayer's lung,' " 681.

100. Villar, "Vineyard Sprayer's Lung," 545–555.

101. Ibid. Only 3 of the 15 cases studied had been clinically diagnosed with vineyard sprayer's lung.

102. Exceedingly few studies exist on vineyard sprayer's lung. See Peixoto de Menezes, "Novos aspectos." A more recent study that potentially qualifies the earlier findings is Romeu-Moreno et al., "Respiratory Toxicity of Copper," 339–340.

103. The vineyard workers studied had used backpack sprayers to apply a 1–2.5

percent solution of copper sulfate anywhere from 2–12 times per year. In contrast, banana workers used high-pressure hoses to apply a 10 percent solution of copper sulfate 13–26 times per year. These differences make it difficult to assume that rates and routes of exposure were the same for vineyard and banana plantation workers.

104. Bricio Fajardo (interview) recalled that workers often smoked cigarettes while spraying.

105. Marquardt, "Pesticides, Parakeets, and Unions" 16–17.

CHAPTER 5

1. The sketch is based on the author's interviews with 24 men and women who lived on company farms.

2. Euraque, *Reinterpreting the Banana Republic,* 42–43.

3. *El Olanchano* (Juticalpa), 3 Mar. 1928. The ad ran every week in March and continued to appear on a regular basis through September.

4. *El Olanchano,* 1 Dec. 1928.

5. For United Fruit employment figures, see Tela Railroad Company to Ministro de Fomento, 31 Dec. 1929, ANH, leg. 1923, Notas varias; and Ministerio de Fomento, *Memoria del Fomento* (1927–1928), 99. For Standard Fruit payrolls, see E. Pineda to Ministro de Fomento, La Ceiba, 28 Jan. 1931, ANH, leg. Correspondencia del departamento de Cortés, 1931.

6. Francis S. Newton to State Department, San Pedro Sula, 11 Mar. 1949, USNA Foreign Agricultural Service, Narrative Reports 1946–1949, Honduras, folder Fruits—Fresh; U.S. Consul to State Department, San Pedro Sula, 24 Aug. 1950, USNA Foreign Agricultural Service Narrative Reports, 1950–1954, Honduras, folder Fruits—Insects; Ministerio de Fomento, Agricultura y Trabajo, *Informe 1951–1952* (Tegucigalpa: Tipografía Nacional, 1952), 157; Albert K. Ludy Jr., to State Department, Tegucigalpa, 21 Nov. 1947, USNA Foreign Agricultural Service Narrative Reports, 1946–1949, Honduras, folder Fruit; Cornelio Mejía, "Informe rendido por el Gobernador Político de Atlántida, año económico 1938-9," 38, ANH, leg. Informes de los Gobernadores Políticos, 1938–1939; and Byron E. Blankinship to Secretary of State, Tegucigalpa, 21 Apr. 1950, USNA Foreign Agricultural Service Narrative Reports 1950–1954, Honduras, folder Labor-Legislation.

7. Blankinship to Secretary of State, 21 Apr. 1950.

8. For the case of Guatemala, see Forster, "Reforging National Revolution," 196–226.

9. Truxillo Railroad Company to Ministro de Fomento, Puerto Castilla, 16 Apr. 1929, ANH, leg. Truxillo Railroad Company, Correspondencia 1920.

10. Historians continue to debate the scale and significance of West Indian migration to the North Coast. For a recent assessment of the evidence, see Euraque, "The Threat of Blackness."

11. The fruit company–provided figures probably undercounted the number of blacks due to government pressure to give preference to non-black "Hondurans." Mejía, "Informe rendido," 38.

12. Pastor Martínez, author interview, Coyoles Central, Yoro, 1995.

13. Francisco Portillo, author interview, La Lima, 1995.

14. Ángela Coto-Moreno, author interview; and Gladys Nieves, author interview, Camp Tacamiche, Cortés, 1995.

15. The under-40 population for Cortés broke down as follows: persons under 5: 12,116; persons between 5 and 14: 16,276; persons between 15 and 25: 16,217; and persons between 25 and 40: 18,417. In Atlántida, the under-40 population broke down as follows: persons under 5: 6207; persons between 5 and 14: 10,949; persons between 15 and 24: 8,726; and persons between 24 and 40: 9,969. See respectively, "Resumen del censo general de población, departamento de Cortés levantado el 30 de junio de 1935," ANH, leg. Informe del año económico de gobernadores y alcaldes municipales de Cortés, 1933–1934; and "Resumen del censo general de población del departamento de Atlántida, levantado el 30 de junio de 1940," ANH, leg. Correspondencia recibida de las gobernaciones políticas, ago.–nov. 1940.

16. The fruit companies directly employed most non-field laborers, including railroad workers, carpenters, machinists, clerics, and medical care providers.

17. Blankinship to Secretary of State, 21 Apr. 1950.

18. On wage rates, see Warren C. Stewart to State Department, La Ceiba, 1 Nov. 1931, Confidential U.S. Diplomatic Post Records, Honduras, 1930–1945, microfilm roll 3.

19. Francisco Portillo, author interview, La Lima, Cortés, 1995.

20. Bricio Fajardo, author interview, Olanchito, Yoro, 1995.

21. Víctor Reyes, author interview, El Progreso, Yoro, 1995.

22. Juan Gavilán, author interview, Coyoles Central, Yoro, 1995.

23. This was probably during the late 1920s and early 1930s. Gladys Nieves, author interview, Camp Tacamiche, Cortés, 1995.

24. Ángela Coto-Moreno, author interview.

25. Isabel Mangandí de Duarte, author interview, La Ceiba, Atlántida, Aug. 1995.

26. Kepner, *Social Aspects of the Banana Industry,* 128.

27. Blankinship to Secretary of State, 21 Apr. 1950.

28. Pastor Martínez, author interview.

29. Neche Martínez, author interview, El Ocote, Yoro, 1995.

30. Juan Gavilán, author interview.

31. Cantalisio Andino, author interview, Calpules aldea, Olanchito, 1995.

32. Manuel Canales, author interview, La Lima, Cortés, 1995.

33. Pastor Martínez, author interview.

34. José María Lara, author interview, La Lima, Cortés, Aug. 1995.

35. Cantalisio Andino, author interview.

36. R. Romero to Ministro de Gobernación, Trujillo, 14 Feb. 1934, ANH, leg. Correspondencia telegráfica de Colon, vol. 1 (Jan.–Apr. 1934).

37. Feliciano Núñez, author interview, El Progreso, Yoro, 1995.

38. Ibid.

39. I have told this story primarily from Feliciano's perspective; Margarita declined to be interviewed.

40. E. V. Siracusa, "Annual Economic Review," 21 Feb. 1944, 5–6, USNA Foreign Agricultural Service Narrative Reports 1942–1945, Honduras, folder Fruits—marketing policies.

41. Robert E. Whedbee, "Monthly Economic Report, Oct. 1942," USNA Foreign Agricultural Service Narrative Reports 1942–1945, Honduras, folder Labor.

42. Ibid.

43. Siracusa, "Annual Economic Review," 21 Feb. 1944.

44. Ibid.

45. This memory is circa 1930. Ángela Coto-Moreno, author interview.

46. On United Fruit's malaria control programs, see Chomsky, *West Indian Workers*, 96–104; and Kepner, *Social Aspects of the Banana Industry*, 109–123.

47. Chomsky, *West Indian Workers*, 101–104.

48. Gobernador político de Atlántida, "Informe emitido por el gobernador político de Atlántida, año económico, 1935–6," ANH, leg. 1936 Informes departamentales de la gobernación política, 30.

49. Ibid., 19.

50. R. K. Thomas to Ministro de Fomento, Puerto Castillo, 31 Aug. 1936, ANH, leg. Informes departamentales de la gobernación política, 1936.

51. Chomsky, *West Indian Workers*, 114–121.

52. Deeks, "Some Aspects of Malaria Control," 185.

53. Some workers tried their own methods of mosquito control; popular repellents used prior to the availability of DDT included the smoke from burning cohune palms and termite nests. Gavilán, author interview.

54. Amaral, "The Snake-bite Problem," 31.

55. March, "Field Notes on Barba Amarilla," 92–97; and Ditmars, "A Reptile Reconnaissance in Honduras," 25–29.

56. Amaya Amador, *Prisión verde*, 143.

57. In author interviews, José María Lara and Francisco Portillo both recalled "difficult times" for workers due to heavy rainy seasons.

58. Francis S. Newton to State Department, San Pedro Sula, 26 Aug. 1949, 3; USNA Foreign Agricultural Service Narrative Reports 1946–1949, Honduras, folder Fruits.

59. Most ex-farmworkers indicated that there had been a minimum wage which they consistently remembered as being around 2.25 lempiras ($US1.10) per day. However, many ex-workers, including harvesters and ditch diggers, expressed their pay in terms of piece rates. For a discussion of wage rates in the late 1920s, see Kepner, *Social Aspects of the Banana Industry*, 124–142.

60. José Almendares Ortiz, author interview.

61. In an author interview José Almendares Ortiz stated that a *palero* could excavate a thirty-yard section in two days. At prevailing wage rates of 18 cents per cubic yard, a ditch digger earned about $US5.40 for the two days. Also see *El Combate*, 19 Feb. 1932; and J. B. Canales et al. to J. F. Aycock, "Tabla especial para el aumento de salarios de los trabajadores del departamento de agricultura," 11 May 1954, in "Aspectos fundamentales de la mediación en el conflicto laboral de la Tela RR Company" (San Pedro Sula, 1954), Universidad Nacional Autónoma de Honduras, Colección hondureña, Rare Books shelves.

62. Hutchings, "Luck and Itching Feet," 62.

63. José María Lara, author interview.

64. Neche Martínez and Cantalisio Andino, author interviews; and Canales et al. to Aycock, "Tabla especial para el aumento de salarios de los trabajadores del departamento de agricultura." Kepner and Soothill (*The Banana Empire*, 317) reported higher piece rates for weeding in Costa Rica ($1.40–$1.60).

65. This example comes from Costa Rica, but Soothill claimed that overseers

throughout United Fruit's Central American plantations resorted to similar ploys. See Kepner and Soothill, *The Banana Empire,* 318.

66. Hutchings, "Luck and Itching Feet," 71.

67. Ibid, 71.

68. Graham S. Quate, "Agricultural Program of the Tela Railroad Company," 17 Sept. 1947, USNA Foreign Agricultural Service Narrative Reports 1946–49, Honduras, folder Agriculture — Coffee.

69. Francisco Portillo, author interview.

70. Pastor Martínez, author interview.

71. Bricio Fajardo, author interview.

72. Francisco Portillo and José Almendares, author interviews. By the late 1940s, the Tela Railroad Company had built "hundreds of miles" of paved trails through particularly humid plantations to facilitate mule transport. Quate, 17 Sept. 1947, 11.

73. Hutchinson, "Luck and Itching Feet," 66–67.

74. Among the demands made by striking Standard Fruit workers in 1932 was the creation of a two-tiered wage rate for harvesters based on the distance that fruit bunches had to be hauled. See *El Combate,* 19 Feb. 1932, 1.

75. Amaya Amador, *Prisión verde,* 62–63.

76. Ibid., 63.

77. Hutchinson, "Luck and Itching Feet," 37.

78. José María Lara, author interview. Also see Hutchinson, "Luck and Itching Feet," 37–40.

79. Amaya Amador, *Prisión verde,* 101–102, 112.

80. José María Lara, Francisco Portillo, Pastor Martínez, Neche Martínez, and Ramón Vallecillo were offered positions as *capataces.* Author interviews.

81. Ramón Vallecillo, author interview, El Ocote, 1995.

82. Ibid.

83. José Maria Lara, author interview.

84. Ibid.

85. Juan Gavilán and José María Lara, author interviews. Also see Hutchings, "Luck and Itching Feet," 38.

86. A couple of different oral sources recounted a story about a *mandador* killed on a farm of the Truxillo Railroad Company in the lower Aguán valley, but I found no evidence that violence against either foremen or overseers was common. Juan Gavilán, author interview; and Woodrow Wilson Patterson, author interview, Sonaguera, Colón, 1995.

87. José María Lara, author interview.

88. Blankinship to Secretary of State, 21 Apr. 1950.

89. José Maria Lara, author interview.

90. Miguel Antonio Fiallos to Sanitation Commissioner, Trujillo, 27 Aug. 1925, 6, ANH, leg. Correspondencia de la Dirección General de Sanidad, vol. 2 (Jun.–Dec. 1925).

91. José Maria Lara, author interview.

92. Chomsky, *West Indian Workers,* 96–100; and 130–137. For data on Honduras, see "United Fruit Company Consolidated Table I," Harvard Medical School, Countway Library of Medicine, Rare Books Department, Papers of Dr. Richard Pearson Strong (1911–1945).

93. Blankinship to Secretary of State, 21 Apr. 1950.

94. Lourdes Mejia, author interview, San Pedro Sula, 1995.

95. Blankinship to Secretary of State, 21 Apr. 1950.

96. José María Lara, author interview.

97. Francisco Portillo, author interview.

98. Bricio Fajardo, author interview.

99. Blankinship to Secretary of State, 21 Apr. 1950.

100. José María Lara, author interview.

101. Most camps had dispensaries where medicines could be obtained.

102. Blankinship to Secretary of State, 21 Apr. 1950.

103. Víctor Reyes, author interview.

104. Quate, "Agricultural Program of the Tela Railroad Company."

105. McCann, *An American Company,* 40.

106. Pastor Martínez, author interview, Coyoles, 1995.

107. Between paydays, workers could receive small advances every ten or fifteen days. Thus, the *pago general* was equal to a laborer's monthly earnings, less any advances received over the course of that month.

108. Truxillo Railroad Company to Ministro de Fomento, Tegucigalpa, 8 Sept. 1930, ANH, leg. Truxillo Railroad Company, correspondencia, 1920. Also see Corleta to Truxillo Railroad Company, 13 Aug. 1930, ANH, leg. Copias de notas, 1930.

109. Ángela Coto-Moreno, author interview.

110. Bricio Fajardo, author interview.

111. Neche Martínez, author interview.

CHAPTER 6

1. "Miss Chiquita Returns," 1.

2. USDA, Agricultural Marketing Service, *Consumption of Food in the United States, 1909–1952* (Washington D.C.: 1957), 16; and "Banana Giant That Has to Shrink," *Business Week,* 15 Feb. 1958, 110.

3. My discussion of Miranda is based on the following sources: Enloe, *Bananas, Beaches, and Bases,* ch. 6; Shari Roberts, "The Lady in the Tutti-Frutti Hat," 3–23; and *Carmen Miranda: Bananas Is My Business,* VHS, written and produced by Helena Solberg and David Meyer (International Cinema Inc., 1994).

4. Shari Roberts, "The Lady in the Tutti-Frutti Hat," 5.

5. Ibid.

6. This is not to suggest that Miranda was a dupe for Hollywood producers and the U.S. State Department. Working within the constraints imposed by Hollywood's view of Latin American women, Miranda became one of the wealthiest film stars of her day while retaining some artistic control over the productions in which she appeared. However, Miranda seldom made public comments on political matters. Here, the contrast between Miranda and Josephine Baker is instructive. After fleeing the Nazi occupation in France, Baker became an outspoken critic of U.S. racism and a civil rights advocate. She eventually returned to perform in the United States, where she spent many years under the scrutiny of the U.S. government. Dudziak, "Josephine Baker, Racial Protest, and the Cold War," 545–570.

7. Jobbers apparently had to meet certain criteria before being permitted to use the Chiquita label. United Fruit Company, *Annual Report* (1951), 26; and *Annual Report* (1954), 16.

8. UFCo., Division of Tropical Research, *Annual Reports* (1939–1953).

9. Quate, "Agricultural Program of the Tela Railroad Company," 6.

10. United Fruit engineers began experimenting with swamp drainage and flood control as early as 1925. United Fruit, *Annual Report* (1949), 20.

11. Quate, "Agricultural Program of the Tela Railroad Company," 6–8.

12. Francis S. Newton, "Bananas—Honduras," 11 Mar. 1949.

13. UFCo., Division of Tropical Research, *Annual Report* (1939), 2.

14. Ibid. (1942), 9.

15. Ibid. (1949), 1.

16. Charles Leftwich to Salvador D'Antoni, 20 Feb. 1942, SFSC Papers, box 8, folder 13.

17. A. J. Chute to P. C. Rose, La Ceiba, 21 Feb. 1941, 3, SFSC Papers, box 8, folder 12.

18. P. C. Rose to C. D'Antoni, New Orleans, 25 Feb. 1946; P. C. Rose to C. D'Antoni, 7 Mar. 1946; and P. C. Rose to R. C. Lally, 5 Feb. 1947, SFSC Papers, box 8, folders 19, 20, and 27, respectively.

19. John Miceli to C. D'Antoni, La Ceiba, 29 Sept. 1945, SFSC Papers, box 8, folder 17.

20. John Miceli to Salvador D'Antoni, La Ceiba, 20 Oct. 1945, SFSC Papers, box 8, folder 18.

21. Chute to Rose, La Ceiba, 21 Feb. 1941.

22. P. C. Rose to C. D'Antoni, New Orleans, 14 June 1946, SFSC Papers, box 8, folder 21.

23. Depending on soil conditions, the company used a combination of surface and overhead irrigation systems. Rose to D'Antoni, 14 Jun. 1946.

24. Woodrow Wilson Patterson, author interview.

25. Muery, "History of Standard Research."

26. One source reported that the Tela Railroad Company used an average of 32 props per acre. Quate, "Agricultural Program of Tela Railroad Company."

27. Standard Fruit Company, "Memorandum of Conference held in the board room on the afternoon of January 3, 1947, for discussion of various matters concerning our Honduras and Nicaragua Divisions," SFSC Papers, box 8, folder 26.

28. August P. Miceli to Salvador D'Antoni, New Orleans, 16 Dec. 1947, SFSC Papers, box 8, folder 33.

29. Miceli to D'Antoni, New Orleans, 16 Dec. 1947.

30. Francis S. Newton to State Department, San Pedro Sula, 26 Aug. 1949.

31. Muery, "History of Standard Research," 1.

32. Euraque, *Reinterpreting the Banana Republic,* 41–43.

33. Ibid., 142–143.

34. Francisco Portillo, author interview.

35. Euraque, *Reinterpreting the Banana Republic,* 92–93.

36. The CCO published *Voz Obrera;* the PDHR's paper was the *Vanguardia Revolucionaria.* See Barahona, *El silencio quedó atrás,* 55–62.

37. For narrative accounts of the strike, see Barahona, *El silencio quedó atrás,* 55–118; and Argueta, *La gran huelga bananera,* 65–108.

38. On events in Guatemala, see Dosal, *Doing Business with the Dictators;* Immerman, *The CIA in Guatemala;* and Gleijeses, *Shattered Hope.* On Honduran politics during this period, see Euraque, *Reinterpreting the Banana Republic,* 71–72.

39. Meza, *Historia del movimiento obrero hondureño,* 96–97.

40. Norman E. Warner to State Department, Tegucigalpa, 26 Nov. 1954, USNA, Foreign Agricultural Service Narrative Reports 1950–1954, Honduras, folder Fruits-Insects. Also see Barahona, *El silencio quedó atrás,* 362.

41. Warner to State Department, 26 Nov. 1954, 3.

42. Tela Railroad Company, "Un recorrido aéreo y por tren para conocer parte del programa de rehabilitación iniciado por la Tela RR Company después del desastre de Septiembre de 1954," 18 Mar. 1956 (mimeograph), FHIA, Stover Library.

43. For employment figures, see *Correo del Norte,* 28 May 1958, 8–9. For acreage, see United Fruit Company *Annual Reports* (1953) and (1959).

44. Ellis, "The Banana Export Activity in Central America," 321.

45. *Correo de Norte,* 31 May 1958 and 9 July 1958; Camilo Rivera Girón, author interview, San Pedro Sula, Cortés, 1995; and Ellis, "The Banana Export Activity in Central America," 102.

46. Camilo Rivera Girón, author interview.

47. *El Sindicalista,* 16 May 1959, 4.

48. *Ibid.,* 17 Apr. 1958, 8.

49. *Correo del Norte,* 31 May 1958, 15.

50. *Ibid.;* and Tela Railroad Company, "Datos de 1962," 2, FHIA, Stover Library.

51. United Fruit Company, *Annual Report* (1960), 2.

52. Each of these farms exceeded 100 hectares. Tela Railroad Company, "Datos de 1962," 2.

53. James Cunningham to State Department, 19 Oct. 1960, USNA, Department of State, Central Decimal File, Honduras 1955–1959, 815.2376/10-1960.

54. In 1960, José del Carmen Licona, president of the newly created Banana Industry Workers' Union (SITRAINBA), authorized SITRATERCO to lobby the Villeda Morales administration to extend the contract between the Tela Railroad Company and SITRATERCO to SITRAINBA, which represented the employees of associate growers. *El Sindicalista,* 31 July 1960, 5; and 30 June 1962, 3.

55. *El Sindicalista,* 30 Sept. 1963, 1; 15 Mar. 1965, 8; and 17 Apr. 1958, 8.

56. Camilo Rivera Girón, author interview; and Edward R. O'Connor to State Department, 24 Apr. 1959, USNA, Department of State, Central Decimal File, Honduras 1955–1959, 815.2376/4-2459.

57. Camilo Rivera Girón, author interview.

58. Robert S. Ashford to State Department, 26 Nov. 1962, USNA, Department of State, Central Decimal File, Honduras, 1960–1963, 815.2376/11-2662.

59. Ellis, "The Banana Export Activity in Central America," 331.

60. The two companies merged in 1968. See Castle and Cook Corporation, *Annual Reports* (1965) and (1969).

61. Robert E. White to State Department, 30 Dec. 1965, USNA, Foreign Agricultural Service Narrative Reports 1962–1965, Honduras, folder Declassified foodstuffs — tobacco.

62. White to Department of State, 30 Dec. 1965.

63. Ellis, "The Banana Export Activity in Central America," and Muery, "History of Standard Research."

64. The Cavendish group consisted of five varieties related to each other by somatic mutation. Simmonds, "A Survey of the Cavendish Group of Bananas," 126–130.

65. Muery, "History of Standard Research," 5–6.

66. P. C. Rose to S. D'Antoni, New Orleans, 24 Sept. 1943; and A. J. Chute to P. C. Rose, La Ceiba, 6 May 1944, SFSC Papers, box 8, folder 15.

67. Chute to Rose, La Ceiba, 6 May 1944.

68. Hord, "The Conversion of Standard Fruit Company Banana Plantations," 272.

69. May and Plaza, *The United Fruit Company in Latin America*, 56.

70. Arthur, Houck, and Beckford, *Tropical Agribusiness*, 155.

71. *Correo del Norte*, 12 Feb. 1958, 8–9.

72. Ibid., 11 Jul. 1958, 9.

73. Joseph S. D'Antoni to All Employees, 20 Apr. 1960 [copy], Harvard University, Baker Library, Henry B. Arthur Papers, "Retailing and Demand, 1964–65."

74. May and Plaza, *The United Fruit Company in Latin America*, 60.

75. Charles C. Armbruster, "Events Leading up to the Development of Standard's Boxing Program," 20 Apr. 1960 [copy], Harvard University, Baker Library, Henry B. Arthur Papers, "Retailing and Demand, 1964–65."

76. United Fruit Company, "Summary of discussions and reports," Research Meetings, Palo Alto, Calif., 29–31 Aug. 1957, [copy] FHIA, Stover Library.

77. United Fruit Company, "Summary of Discussions and Reports," 4.

78. United Fruit Company, Division of Tropical Research, *Research Extension Newsletter*, Nov. 1959, 10.

79. Edward O'Connor to State Department, 12 Dec. 1959, USNA Department of State, Central Decimal File, Honduras, 1955–1959, 815.2376/12-1259.

80. Hobson, "Research in the United Fruit Company," 2–3; and United Fruit Company, *Annual Report* (1951), 5; and *Annual Report* (1957), 2.

81. McCann, *An American Company*, 72. Also see American Consulate to State Department, San Pedro Sula, 12 Dec. 1959, USNA, Central Decimal File, Honduras, 1955–1959, 815.2376/12-1259.

82. Between 1949 and 1959, U.S. banana imports from Ecuador rose from 4 million bunches to 22 million bunches. Simmonds, *Bananas*, 324.

83. The average annual retail price for bananas in the United States fluctuated between 16 and 17 cents per pound during the 1950s, before dropping by about one cent per pound in the 1960s. See Arthur, Houck, and Beckford, *Tropical Agribusiness*, 148.

84. Dosal, *Doing Business with the Dictators*, 225–231.

85. McCann, *An American Company*, 64; and Arthur, Houck, and Beckford, *Tropical Agribusiness*, 146.

86. Arthur, Houck, and Beckford, *Tropical Agribusiness*, 150.

87. UFCo., Division of Tropical Research, *Annual Report* (1959).

88. Ibid. (1960), and *Research Extension Newsletter*, Nov. 1959: 11.

89. Ortiz, Ferris, and Vuylsteke, "Banana and Plantain Breeding."

90. For a more detailed discussion of banana breeding, see Soluri, "Banana Breeding, Biodiversity, and the Paradoxes of Commodification."

91. UFCo., Division of Tropical Research, *Annual Report* (1962), vii.

92. Arthur, Houck, and Beckford, *Tropical Agribusiness*, 151.

93. Tela Railroad Company, "Datos de 1962," 12; and "Datos de 1963," 2, FHIA, Stover Library.

94. Tela Railroad Company, "Datos de 1963," 1.

95. Thomas Sunderland, quoted in Arthur, Houck, and Beckford, *Tropical Agribusiness*, 151. Original emphasis.

96. Arthur, Houck, and Beckford, *Tropical Agribusiness*, 152–153.

97. "United Fruit Adopts Chiquita as Brand Name," *Advertising Age*, 13 May 1963, 3.

98. United Fruit Sales Corporation, "Branded P.O.P. Material Makes Variety of Displays," Harvard University, Baker Library, Henry B. Arthur Papers, "Banana Study, Unifruitco info/pamphlets, 1916–1968."

99. "Yes, they sell more bananas," 92.

100. Jenkins, *Bananas: An American History*, 165–166.

101. United Fruit Company, *Unifruitco*, 30 May 1969.

102. United Brands, *Unibranco*, June 1972.

103. Ibid.

104. Ibid., United Brands, *Annual Report* (1972), 7.

105. The list of defects included fruit blossoms adhering to the ends of fingers (i.e., individual bananas); pitting disease; bruises; malformed fingers, including "wild" fingers on cluster; fused fingers; mutilated fingers, including cuts and split peel; rots and molds, and ripe and turning finger. United Brands, *Banana Operations Manual*, V1-6, FHIA, Stover Library.

106. Muery, "History of Standard Research," 46.

107. Ibid.

108. Olivia Zaldívar, author interview, La Lima, Cortés, 2002; and Esperanza Rivera Nájera, author interview, El Ocote, Yoro, 1995. For photographic evidence, see Tela Railroad Company, "Datos de 1962," and "Datos de 1963."

109. Yaya, author interview, Coyoles, Yoro, 2002; and Juana Meléndez, author interview, Olanchito, Yoro, 2002.

110. Esperanza Rivera Nájera, author interview.

111. Olivia Zaldívar, author interview.

112. Ibid.

113. Omar González, author interview, Olanchito, Yoro, 2002.

114. Juana Meléndez, author interview.

115. Pepe Puerta (pseudonym), author interview, Calpules Aldea, Yoro, 1995.

116. UFCo., Division of Tropical Research, *Annual Report* (1960).

117. UFCo., Division of Tropical Research, *Annual Report* (1968), iii. On early chlorine treatments, *Annual Report* (1963), iii; and *Annual Report* (1965), 35.

118. Esperanza Rivera Nájera, author interview.

119. "Contrato colectivo de trabajo celebrado entre la Standard Fruit Company y el Sindicato Unificado de Trabajadores de la Standard Fruit Company (SUTRASFCO)," La Ceiba, July 1974, 26–27.

120. "How United Fruit Was Plucked," *Business Week*, 22 Feb. 1969, 122–124; Arthur, Houck, and Beckford, *Tropical Agribusiness*, 156; and McCann, *An American Company*, 6–13.

CHAPTER 7

1. Jorge Romero, author interview, La Lima, Cortés, 1995.
2. UFCo., Division of Tropical Research, *Annual Report* (1952).
3. Thorton, "The Use of Fungicides in Central and South America."
4. UFCo., Division of Tropical Research, *Annual Report* (1949) and (1951).
5. Ibid. (1949).
6. Ibid. (1951).
7. Following World War II, United Fruit's research infrastructure included two laboratories in the United States and field stations in Colombia, Costa Rica, Cuba, and Panama. UFCo., Department of Research, *Problems and Progress in Banana Disease Research* (Boston: 1958); UFCo., Division of Tropical Research, *Annual Report* (1958) and ibid. (1953), 14.
8. On the rise of pesticide production in the United States, see Russell, *War and Nature;* and Dunlap, *DDT.*
9. United States Department of Agriculture, "African Oil Palm in Central America," (Aug. 1952), 2. On United Fruit forestry projects, see Chable, "Reforestation in the Republic of Honduras, Central America."
10. According to one source, reforestation projects served both as long-term investments and to demonstrate an active use of the land "in resistance to squatters and nationalization by local governments." Paul J. Shank, "General Report of Results of Previous Reforestation Work and Recommendations for Future Planting," unpublished manuscript, 12 Nov. 1958, FHIA Stover Library. For crop acreage figures, see UFCo., Division of Tropical Research, *Annual Report* (1951), 65.
11. One company official in Honduras claimed that United Fruit made more money in 1959 from African oil palm production than from bananas! Harry E. Bergold Jr. to State Department, Tegucigalpa, 28 Mar. 1960, USNA Department of State, Central Decimal Files, 1960–1963, 815.2376/3-2860.
12. United Fruit Company, *Research Extension Newsletter* (July 1958).
13. Hobson, "Research in the United Fruit Company," 7. The company also awarded fellowships and grants to scientists affiliated with the Rockefeller Institute and Cornell, Harvard, Purdue, and Stanford universities. United Fruit Company, *Jobber and Dealer Service Conference Proceedings,* 18–20 Oct. 1954, FHIA, Stover Library.
14. On the connections between warfare and agricultural pesticides, see Russell, *War and Nature.*
15. Percentage derived from data in the following sources: United Fruit Company, *Research Extension Newsletter* (Apr. 1955); Arthur, Houck, and Beckford, *Tropical Agribusiness,* 146; and Cox, "Our Research Program," in *Jobber and Dealer Service Conference Proceedings,* 2.
16. Dunlap, "Sigatoka Disease," 12.
17. Meredith, "Banana Leaf Spot Disease," 92–96.
18. UFCo., Division of Tropical Research, *Annual Report* (1957) 19; and *Research Extension Newsletter* (Nov. 1959), 1–2.
19. *El Sindicalista,* 15 Nov. 1957, 6.
20. Ibid., 1.
21. Ibid., 31 Dec. 1957, 3.
22. Magee, "Banana Leaf Spot," 3.

23. *El Sindicalista,* 15 Nov. 1957, 6. In Costa Rica, banana unions were similarly preoccupied first and foremost with preventing the loss of Sigatoka spray jobs. Marquardt, "Pesticides, Parakeets, and Unions," 24.

24. UFCo., Division of Tropical Research, *Annual Report* (1959).

25. United Fruit Company, *Research Extension Newsletter,* Nov. 1959, 7.

26. Barney B. Taylor to State Department, Tegucigalpa, 6 Oct. 1959, U.S. State Department Central Decimal File, 1955–1959, 815.2376/10-659.

27. Emilio Funes, author interview, La Lima, Cortés 1995.

28. United Fruit Company, *Annual Report* (1960). Dithiocarbamate fungicides include the metallic dimethyldithiocarbamates and ethylene bisdithiocarbamate salts based on dithiocarbamic acid. *Farm Chemical Handbook,* C 131.

29. Soluble copper is toxic to plants. A 1960 study found that one company farm in Honduras that had been treated with Bordeaux spray for 20 years had concentrations of copper that ranged from 4 to nearly 30 times the levels found in non-treated soils. UFCo., Division of Tropical Research, *Annual Report* (1960), 221–222. In the Golfito region of Costa Rica, high concentrations of copper in several thousand hectares of soils limited the range of crops that were cultivated on former banana farms. Marquardt, "Pesticides, Parakeets, and Unions," 28.

30. These costs are not adjusted for inflation. UFCo., Division of Tropical Research, *Annual Report* (1952) and (1966).

31. Muery, "History of Standard Research," 20; and Bricio Fajardo, author interview.

32. Víctor Reyes, author interview.

33. Ellis, "The Banana Export Activity in Central America," 321; and *Correo del Norte,* 28 May 1958, 8–9.

34. United Brands, Division of Tropical Research, *Annual Report* (1973), 3.

35. United Brands, Division of Tropical Research, *Annual Report* (1973), 3. Also see Meredith, "Banana Leaf Spot Disease," 117; and Simmonds and Stover, *Bananas,* 281–283.

36. United Brands Company, Division of Tropical Research, *Annual Report* (1974), 1; Simmonds and Stover, *Bananas,* 282; and Marquardt, "Pesticides, Parakeets, and Unions," 27.

37. Benlate, or 1- (butylcarbamoyl)-2-benzimidazole carbamic acid methyl ester, was developed by DuPont. United Fruit tested Benlate in 1967, and found it to be an effective but expensive control for Sigatoka. By 1973, the U.S. Food and Drug Administration had approved Benlate for agricultural uses. United Fruit Company, Division of Tropical Research, *Annual Reports* (1967), (1968), and (1973).

38. United Brands, Division of Tropical Research, *Annual Report* (1974), 7; and Simmonds and Stover, *Bananas,* 293.

39. Muery, "History of Standard Research," 20.

40. David Pimentel et al., "Environmental and Economic Costs of Pesticide Use," 750–650; and Pimentel and Lehman, eds., *The Pesticide Question.*

41. Hobson, "Research in the United Fruit Company," 5; and United Fruit Company, *Problems and Progress in Banana Disease Research,* 16–23.

42. Meredith, "Major Banana Diseases," 541–542; Buddenhagen and Kelman, "Biological and Physiological Aspects of Bacterial Wilt," 203–205; and United Fruit Company, *Problems and Progress in Banana Disease Research,* 16.

43. UFCo., Division of Tropical Research, *Annual Report* (1960), 43; and *Annual Report* (1961), ii.

44. UFCo., Division of Tropical Research, *Annual Report* (1961) and (1963); Meredith, "Major Banana Diseases," 542; and Buddenhagen and Kelman, "Biological and Physiological Aspects of Bacterial Wilt," 213.

45. United Fruit Company, Division of Tropical Research, *Annual Report* (1963), 53.

46. UFCo., Research Department, Monthly Letter, 30 May 1963, 2, FHIA, "Guarumas Files." I am very grateful to Dr. Adolfo Martínez for providing me with access to these documents.

47. UFCo., Division of Tropical Research, *Annual Report* (1965), 53.

48. American Embassy to State Department, Tegucigalpa, 30 Dec. 1965, USNA, Foreign Agricultural Service, Declassified Narrative Reports, 1962–1965, Honduras, folder Foodstuffs—Tobacco. According to Muery ("History of Standard Research," 40) Moko first appeared on Standard Fruit farms in the late 1950s and became a "serious menace" to Gros Michel farms prior to the conversion to Giant Cavendish. However, D. S. Meredith ("Major Banana Diseases," 541), citing his own unpublished report written for Standard Fruit, stated that Moko first appeared in the Aguán valley in 1963.

49. United Fruit Company, Division of Tropical Research, *Annual Report* (1965), 57.

50. UFCo., Division of Tropical Research, *Annual Report* (1968), ii; *Annual Report* (1971), 3–7; and Muery, "History of Standard Research."

51. Ramón Vallecillo, author interview.

52. Abel Posas, author interview.

53. United Brands, *Banana Operations Manual* (Mar. 1972), VIII 18–20.

54. UFCo., Division of Tropical Research, *Annual Report* (1973), 49.

55. UFCo., Division of Tropical Research, *Annual Report* (1971), 6.

56. United Fruit Company, *Research Extension Newsletter,* July 1955, 8; and Apr. 1959, 14.

57. United Fruit Company, "Ayude a erradicar la enfermedad Moko del banano" (Jan. 1957), FHIA, Stover Library.

58. United Brands, *Banana Operations Manual* (Aug. 1970), III-2. Standard Fruit implemented a similar measure. Abel Posas, author interview.

59. Abel Posas, author interview.

60. Ramón Vallecillo, author interview. Formaldehyde is classified as "moderately toxic" in the case of dermal exposure. Both the U.S. Environmental Protection Agency and the International Agency for Research on Cancer consider formaldehyde to be a carcinogen.

61. Muery, "History of Standard Research," 30. When interviewed, Ramón Vallecillo also said that the change to Beloran was due to workers' dislike of formulina.

62. UFCo., Division of Tropical Research, *Annual Report* (1967).

63. Lewis Knudson, "The Palomas Nitrate Experiment," *United Fruit Company Research Bulletin* (1930), FHIA, Stover Library.

64. In 1946 United Fruit imported 16.5 million pounds of sodium nitrate into Honduras. Standard Fruit imported more than 5 million pounds of fertilizers that year. Neither company paid import duties on fertilizers. Albert K. Ludy Jr., 11 Sept. 1946,

USNA, Foreign Agricultural Service Narrative Reports 1946–1949, Honduras, folder Finance—Fruits.

65. Quate, "Agricultural Program of the Tela Railroad Company."

66. United Fruit planted 450–500 Valery rhizomes/acre. By comparison, Gros Michel was typically planted at densities of 360/acre. UFCo., Division of Tropical Research, *Annual Report* (1967), v; Thorton, "Production Management of Gros Michel Bananas," 3, paper presented at the First FAO/CCTA International Meeting on Banana Production, Abidjan, Ivory Coast, 12–19 Nov. 1960. FHIA, Stover Library; and United Brands, *Banana Operations Manual,* III-9.

67. United Brands, *Banana Operations Manual,* I-3.

68. Muery, "History of Standard Research" 31.

69. Pepe Puerta, author interview. On the work of applying fertilizers in Caribbean Costa Rica, see Bourgois, *Ethnicity at Work,* 128.

70. No cautions were given about Diuron, a carcinogen capable of damaging reproductive processes. United Brands, *Banana Operations Manual,* III-6 and III-7.

71. Approximately 50 pages of the 330-page annual report for 1966 were devoted to post-harvest problems. UFCo., Division of Tropical Research, *Annual Report* (1966).

72. United Fruit Company, *Banana Operations Manual,* IV-1, 2.

73. United Brands, *Banana Operations Manual,* VII-16; UFCo., Division of Tropical Research, *Annual Report* (1967), iv.

74. United Brands, Division of Tropical Research, *Annual Report* (1971).

75. UFCo., Division of Tropical Research, *Annual Report* (1969), iv.

76. For example, see guidelines for handling gramoxone in United Brands, *Banana Operations Manual,* III-7 and VII-10.

77. Neche Martínez, interview.

78. Thorton, "Pesticides in Banana Culture," 73; and Meredith, "Major Banana Diseases," 543.

79. Thorton, "Control of Insects of the Banana," 2–3.

80. UFCo., Division of Tropical Research, *Annual Report* (1957), 11; *Research Extension Newsletter* (Oct. 1955), 3–6; and *Annual Report* (1953), 52.

81. United Fruit Company, *Research Extension Newsletter* (Oct. 1956), 6; and UFCo., Division of Tropical Research, *Annual Report* (1957), 12.

82. Thorton, "Control of Insect Pests of the Banana," 2.

83. UFCo., Division of Tropical Research, *Research Extension Newsletter* (Jan. 1956), 6; and *Research Extension Newsletter* (Oct. 1955), 3.

84. United Fruit Company *Research Extension Newsletter* (Apr. 1956), 14.

85. Furber S. Roberts, "Insects Affecting Banana Production in Central America," 414.

86. UFCo., Division of Tropical Research, *Annual Report* (1957), 12.

87. UFCo., Division of Tropical Research, *Annual Report* (1961), ii. See also Stephens, "Ecological Upset," 101–105.

88. United Fruit Company, *Banana Operations Manual,* VII-10.

89. UFCo., Division of Tropical Research, *Annual Report* (1970), 6–8. Allied Chemical stopped manufacturing Kepone in 1977 after the U.S. government banned its use. U.S. Environmental Protection Agency, "Suspended, Cancelled and Restricted Pesticides," (Jan. 1985), 13.

90. Stephens, "Ecological Upset," 103; and Thrupp, "Entrapment and Escape from Fruitless Insecticide Use," 173–189.

91. UFCo., Division of Tropical Research, *Annual Report* (1957), 26.

92. Shell Oil Company, "El Banano: Sus plagas, enfermedades y malezas" (1959?). Dow Chemical also produced and sold DBCP under the name Fumazone. See Vilardebo, "First Tests."

93. United Fruit Company, *Problems and Progress in Banana Disease Research,* 32; Division of Tropical Research, *Annual Report* (1960), 49; and "Report on the Nematode Survey of the Honduras Division, Tela RR Company," 1959, 12, FHIA, Stover Library.

94. UFCo., Division of Tropical Research, *Annual Report* (1961), 41; *Annual Report* (1963), 77; and *Annual Report* (1965), 61.

95. The experiments applied 6 gallons per acre of DBCP semi-annually. United Brands, Division of Tropical Research, *Annual Report* (1970), ii; *Annual Report* (1971), 13–30; *Annual Report* (1972), 32; *Annual Report* (1973), 7 and 31; *Annual Report* (1974), 15; and *Banana Operations Manual,* VIII-59.

96. Muery, "History of Standard Research," 24.

97. Bricio Fajardo and Juan Gavilán, author interviews.

98. Perryman and Twyford, "Banana Growing in Central America," 3; Muery, "History of Standard Research," 24; and author interviews with Bricio Fajardo, Ramón Vallecillo, and Juan Gavilán.

99. Cantalisio Andino, author interview.

100. Ramón Vallecillo, author interview.

101. Bricio Fajardo, author interview.

102. Neche Martínez, author interview.

103. Juan Gavilán and Neche Martínez, author interviews.

104. Juan Gavilán, author interview.

105. Thrupp, "Sterilization of Workers from Pesticide Exposure," 731–757.

106. See, for example, Wright, *The Death of Ramón Gonzales;* and Murray, *Cultivating Crisis.*

107. Rowe, "Breeding Bananas and Plantains," 139; and Simmonds and Stover, *Bananas,* 172–173.

108. Gowen, "Pests," in *Bananas and Plantains,* ed. Gowen, 383.

109. Muery, "History of Standard Research," 21.

110. On Cesar Chavez and U.S. environmentalism, see Pulido, *Environmentalism and Economic Justice;* and Gottlieb, *Forcing the Spring,* 240–244. On Rachel Carson, see Gottlieb, *Forcing the Spring,* 81–86; and Lear, *Rachel Carson: Witness for Nature.*

CHAPTER 8

1. Alan Riding, "Honduran Army Ousts Leader Named in Bribery Case in U.S." *New York Times,* 23 Apr. 1975.

2. Robert Cole, "S.E.C. Suit Links A Honduras Bribe to United Brands," *New York Times,* 10 Apr. 1975.

3. Cole, "S.E.C. Suit."

4. No other charges were brought against the company. "Business Briefs," *New York Times,* 28 Jan. 1976.

5. The author of a recently published study of worker-cultivators in Ecuador has made a similar point, noting that the fruit companies' power was exercised through "real agents that occupy particular places." See Striffler, *In the Shadows of State and Capital*, 207.

6. Roseberry, "Introduction," in *Coffee, Society, and Power in Latin America*, 7–8.

7. On U.S. sugar consumption, see César Ayala, *American Sugar Kingdom*, 17 and 28; and Galloway, *The Sugar Cane Industry*, 1–10. For data on coffee, see Steven Topik, "The Integration of the World Coffee Market." Coffee was not the only stimulant whose consumption increased. Imports of cacao beans (cocoa) rose by fifteen times between 1885 and 1914. Coca leaf imports also surged during this period, driven by both novel medical applications for cocaine and the popularity of Coca-Cola. See, respectively, Clarence-Smith, *Cocoa and Chocolate;* and Gootenberg, "Between Coca and Cocaine," 126.

8. Steinberg, *Down to Earth*, 181. Steinberg's discussion of California citrus drew heavily on a manuscript version of Sackman, *Orange Empire.*

9. Strasser, *Satisfaction Guaranteed.*

10. Mintz, *Sweetness and Power;* Jiménez, "From Plantation to Cup"; McNeill, *Something New Under the Sun;* and Chandler, *Scale and Scope* and *The Visible Hand.* On technological changes in processing, see Hounshell, *From the American System to Mass Production.* On judicial decisions expanding the power of corporations, see Strasser, *Satisfaction Guaranteed*, 25–26.

11. On European sugar consumption, see Mintz, *Sweetness and Power*, 74–150; and Galloway, *The Sugar Cane Industry*, 5–8. On sugar and empire, see Ayala, *American Sugar Kingdom.*

12. John Arbuckle, one of the first entrepreneurs to mass market coffee in consumer-sized packages, coated his roasted beans with a sugar glaze. He engaged the Havemeyer-led sugar trust in a cutthroat competition for several years. See Ayala, *American Sugar Kingdom*, 42–44.

13. Brenner, *The Emperors of Chocolate.* The Charles Hire Company (of root beer fame) also purchased sugar mills in Cuba. Galloway, *The Sugar Cane Industry*, 168.

14. On orange juice consumption, see Sackman, *Orange Empire*, chapter 3. I am grateful to the author for providing me with this chapter prior to publication.

15. Strasser, *Satisfaction Guaranteed*, 29–57.

16. Sunkist utilized many of the same media forms and exploited similar tropes (of nature, science, health, and sex) as the fruit companies. Sackman, *Orange Empire*, chapter 3.

17. On the rapid growth of advertising agencies in the 1920s, see Marchand, *Advertising the American Dream.*

18. Stoll, *The Fruits of Natural Advantage*, 81–88; and Jiménez, "From Plantation to Cup," 48–52. Topik ("The Integration of the World's Coffee Market," 38–39) does not discuss advertising, but he notes that as coffee's status as a luxury good declined in the early twentieth century, consumers became less likely to alter their purchase habits in response to price changes (and presumably marketing campaigns). However, one author credits mass advertising with helping to boost per capita consumption of coffee during the 1920s. Pendergrast, *Uncommon Grounds*, 155–158.

19. Quoted in Marchand, *Advertising the American Dream*, 162–163.

20. Mintz, *Tasting Food, Tasting Freedom.*

21. On women in California packing plants, see Ruiz, *Cannery Women, Cannery Lives;* and Sackman, "Nature's Workshop," 27–53.

22. Jímenez, "From Plantation to Cup," 50–51.

23. Progressive-era campaigns against non-medicinal uses of narcotics and alcohol played a hand in leading to the criminalization of cocaine consumption. By 1922, both local and federal governments had placed strict controls over the importation and consumption of coca and cocaine. See Gootenberg, "Between Coca and Cocaine," 128–129. On anti-coffee campaigns, see Pendergrast, *Uncommon Grounds,* 95–112.

24. Unless otherwise indicated, data on per capita consumption drawn from United States Department of Agriculture, Agricultural Marketing Service, *Consumption of Food in the United States, 1909–1952* (Washington DC: 1957), 16; and Putnam and Allshouse, *Food Consumption, Prices, and Expenditures, 1970–97.*

25. Some fruits, including grapes, were also consumed in processed forms. See Charlet and Rastegaria Henneberry, "A Profile of Food Market Trends"; and Pillsbury, *No Foreign Food,* 187–208.

26. Charlet and Rastegaria Henneberry, "A Profile of Food Market Trends." The rise of chain "specialty retailers" (e.g. Starbucks) and small-scale roasters in the 1990s halted the slide in U.S. per capita coffee consumption. A handful of corporate roasters/marketers, including Nestlé and Procter & Gamble, dominate the industry. See Dicum and Luttinger, *The Coffee Book.*

27. See, for example, the website of the Brooklyn, New York–based Cumberland Packing Corporation (http://www.sugarintheraw.com). I am grateful to Lowell Gudmundson for calling my attention this product.

28. Topik, "Coffee Anyone?", 245. A considerable amount of variation existed in the percentage of profits captured by coffee growers. See Gudmundson, "On Paths Not Taken."

29. Dye, *Cuban Sugar in the Age of Mass Production,* 72.

30. Stoll, *The Fruits of Natural Advantage,* 63–78.

31. Sackman, "Nature's Workshop," 27–53.

32. Ayala, *American Sugar Kingdom,* 33.

33. Dye, *Cuban Sugar in the Age of Mass Production,* 78–84.

34. On different kinds of processed sugar, including those for domestic markets, see Galloway, *The Sugar Cane Industry.*

35. On the politics of regulated food, see Strasser, 252–285.

36. See, Topik, "The Integration of the World Coffee Market," 21–49; Jiménez, "From Plantation to Cup," 45–48; Tucker, *Insatiable Appetite,* 188–195; and Pendergrast, *Uncommon Grounds.*

37. Sackman, " 'Nature's Workshop,' " 39–44.

38. Samper "The Historical Construction of Quality and Competitiveness."

39. This tendency is by no means limited to crop plants. For a fascinating discussion of beef cattle preferences in twentieth-century Brazil, see Wilcox, "Zebu's Elbows."

40. Note that Marchand's research (*Advertising the American Dream,* introduction and chapter 3) did not address marketing campaigns directed toward businesses.

41. The post-1950s decline in the number of wholesalers and jobbers in food distribution and marketing also needs to be explored in order to understand its impact on constructions of quality. In a world dominated by a handful of producers, distributors,

and retailers, mass advertising may become more important. However, middle links in commodity chains continue to be important in Caribbean and Central American "non-traditional" agroexport industries. Murray, *Cultivating Crisis.*

42. On the impact of British policies on banana producers, see Grossman, *The Political Ecology of Bananas.* The French government adopted similar policies in their Caribbean colonies. Raynolds, "The Global Banana Trade." On British banana breeding programs, see Soluri, "Bananas, Biodiversity, and the Paradox of Commodification."

43. On the role of forest rents in Brazilian coffee, see Brannstrom, "Coffee Labor Regimes and Deforestation on a Brazilian Frontier"; Topik, "Coffee"; Dean, *With Broad-ax and Firebrand;* and Stein, *Vassouras.* In the case of Cuban sugar production, see Funes Monzote, "Deforestation and Sugar in Cuba's Centre-East"; Mark Smith, "The Political Economy of Sugar Production and the Environment of Eastern Cuba"; and Galloway, *The Sugar Cane Industry,* 162–64.

44. The classic work is Crosby, *The Columbian Exchange.*

45. For a summary of arguments and evidence, see Whitmore and Turner, *Cultivated Landscapes of Middle America on the Eve of Conquest;* and Denevan, "The Pristine Myth: The Landscape of the Americas in 1492." At least one United Fruit Company scientist was aware of the region's pre-Columbian settlement history and its implications for forest cover. See Raup, "Notes on Reforestation in Tropical America III," unpublished manuscript (Apr. 1951), FHIA, Stover Library.

46. The literature on race, ethnicity, and nation in modern Latin America is extensive. For a recent survey, see Appelbaum, Macpherson, and Rosenblatt, eds., *Race and Nation in Modern Latin America.* For examples of territorial expropriations linked to expanding agro-commodity production, see Gallini, "A Maya-Mam Agroecosystem in Guatemala's Coffee Revolution: Costa Cuca, 1830s–1880s"; and Clarence-Smith, *Cocoa and Chocolate, 1765–1914,* 150–151.

47. On Latin American perceptions of "vastness," see Mires, *El discurso de la naturaleza.* On the creation of "neo-European landscapes," see Crosby, *Ecological Imperialism.* For a fascinating (and disturbing) example of forest clearing that seemingly defied economic rationality, see Fernando Ramírez Morales, "La guerra contra los "montes," y la extracción de los "palos": una aproximación histórico-ecológica a los procesos de degradación de los bosques nativos del sur de Chile," paper presented at the I Simposio de Historia Ambiental Americana, Santiago, Chile, 14–18 Jul. 2003.

48. Roseberry, "Introduction," in *Coffee, Society, and Power in Latin America,* 30. For a recent assessment of research on coffee production scales, see Topik, "Coffee Anyone?", 242–244. Recent regional studies that highlight variation in coffee systems include Charlip, *Cultivating Coffee;* Lauria-Santiago, *An Agrarian Republic;* David McCreery, *Rural Guatemala, 1760–1940;* and Gudmundson, "Peasant, Farmer, Proletarian," 136–138.

49. On the historical and contemporary participation of small-scale banana producers beyond Honduras, see Marquardt, "Green Havoc"; Putnam, *The Company They Kept,* 35–75; Chomsky, *West Indian Workers,* 28–32; LeGrand, "Living in Macondo;" Striffler, *In the Shadows of State and Capital;* and Grossman, *The Political Ecology of Bananas.*

50. Ayala, *American Sugar Kingdom,* 121–147. Also see Galloway, *The Sugar Cane Industry,* 162–182; and Scott, *Slave Emancipation in Cuba.*

51. Stoll, *The Fruits of Natural Advantage,* 162–173.

52. Other commodities in which small-scale producers have been crucial include cacao and coca. See, respectively, Clarence-Smith, *Cocoa and Chocolate,* 146–152; and Gootenberg, "Between Coca and Cocaine."

53. Important export crops native to the Americas include cacao, henequen, rubber (*Hevea brasiliensis*), and chinchona (quinine). All of these crops excepting henequen would eventually become important export commodities in tropical Africa and Asia. On henequen, see Allen Wells, "Henequen," in *The Second Conquest of Latin America: Coffee, Henequen, and Oil during the Export Boom, 1850–1930,* edited by Topik and Wells. On chinchona, see Brockway, *Science and Colonial Expansion.* On rubber, see Dean, *Brazil and the Struggle for Rubber.*

54. Galloway, *The Sugar Cane Industry,* 11–12.

55. McCook, *States of Nature,* 79–81; and Galloway, *The Sugar Cane Industry,* 96–99.

56. Galloway, *The Sugar Cane Industry,* 142.

57. The story was different in Puerto Rico, where cane growers swiftly adopted disease-resistant varieties. McCook, *States of Nature,* 90–104.

58. Robusta beans have enjoyed popularity in both France and Italy, a reminder of the degree to which taste is socially constructed. See Pendergrast, *Uncommon Grounds.*

59. Samper, "The Historical Construction of Quality and Competitiveness," 136–142.

60. There is a temptation to attribute the historical absence of leaf rust epidemics to the prevalence of fragmented, small-scale coffee systems in parts of Central and South America, but this explanation is weakened by the historical absence of epidemics in southern Brazil, where large-scale coffee plantations resembled the shifting plantation agriculture of export banana zones. On the epidemic in Brazil, see Wrigley, *Coffee,* 316–317. On the intricate ecological relationship between leaf rust and shade in coffee systems, see Soto-Pinto, Perfecto, and Caballero-Nieto, "Shade over Coffee."

61. Perfecto, Rice, Greenberg, and Van der Voort, "Shade Coffee."

62. Coffee Research Institute website, www.coffeeresearch.org.

63. Sackman, "Nature's Workshop."

64. On the history of plant acclimatization in California, see Tyrell, *True Gardens of the Gods.*

65. Stoll, *The Fruits of Natural Advantage,* 99–102.

66. Ibid., 102–123.

67. Plant disease epidemics also affected rubber and cacao industries in Brazil and Ecuador. See, respectively Dean, *Brazil and the Struggle for Rubber;* and McCook, "The Flight of the Witches' Broom." I am extremely grateful to the author for sharing this unpublished manuscript.

68. Writing crop plant histories faces some formidable challenges. Firstly, archival sources on the movement of plants are rare. Secondly, interpreting available evidence is far from straightforward due to the difficulty of reconciling historical popular names with those used by contemporary taxonomists. Plant species, not unlike human racial categories, are social constructs with particular histories and uncertain futures. On the role of Latin American states in supporting agricultural research, see Dean, *Brazil and the Struggle for Rubber;* McCook, *States of Nature;* and Eakin, "The Origins of Modern Science in Costa Rica."

69. Detailed studies of contemporary "shade" coffee farms reveal significant agro-ecological variation. See Soto-Pinto, Perfecto, Castillo-Hernández, and Caballero-Nieto, "Shade Effect on Coffee Production."

70. The availability of new technologies did not single-handedly determine the timing of the shift toward maximizing yields. During the 1960s and 1970s, a wave of U.S.-supported land reform movements combined with increasingly organized labor forces and grower cooperatives contributed to a rise in fertilizers and other inputs (*paquetes técnicos*).

71. Gudmundson, "Peasant, Farmer, Proletarian," 136–38.

72. Herbicide use in nearly every sector of commercial agriculture skyrocketed in the late twentieth century. See Murray, *Cultivating Crisis;* and Roberts and Thanos, *Trouble in Paradise*, 65–93.

73. On the loss of biodiversity linked to coffee cropping systems, see Perfecto and Armbrecht, "The Coffee Agroecosystem in the Neotropics."

74. On intercropping and wage flexibility in the context of Brazil, see Stolcke, "The Labors of Coffee in Latin America." Also see Brannstrom, "Coffee Labor Regimes and Deforestation."

75. On the movement of *colonos* in Brazilian coffee zones, see Topik, "Coffee," 50.

76. On labor needs in California orchards and Costa Rican coffee farms, see, respectively, Stoll, *The Fruits of Natural Advantage,* 126–133; and Gudmundson, "Class Formation in a Smallholder Coffee Economy," 135–36. On migrant labor in Cuban sugar-producing regions, see Carr, " 'Omnipotent and Omnipresent'?." For a classic portrait of cane worker life during harvests and "dead seasons," see Mintz, *Worker in the Cane.*

77. In this context, Emiliano Zapata's rallying cry "land, woods, and water" takes on new meanings. On environmental transformations in Porfirian Mexico, see Tortolero Villaseñor, "Transforming the Central Mexican Waterscape." On the importance of "marginal" environments in sugarcane growing regions, see Gould, *To Lead as Equals;* and Friedrich, *Agrarian Revolt in a Mexican Village.*

78. On the value of integrating labor and environmental histories, see Richard White, "Are You an Environmentalist or Do You Work for a Living?"; and Taylor, "Unnatural Inequalities."

79. Fernando Coronil has criticized both liberal and Marxist social theories for their failure to appreciate the importance of "land" (i.e., nature) in favor of a historical dynamic driven almost exclusively by a capital-labor dialectic. Building on the writings of Henry Lefebvre, Coronil argues that the international division of labor is simultaneously a "global division" of nature. His model of an interactive capital-labor-nature triad is a welcome intervention in social theory, but the concept of a global division of nature potentially reinforces problematic "North-South" dichotomies by ignoring the extent to which modernity has been accompanied by a jumbling of the world's people and biota. See Coronil, *The Magical State,* 21–66.

80. For a recent example of a widely circulated science story on banana pathogens as "natural disasters," see "Last Days of the Banana." For a scholarly account by prominent ecologists that falls into a similar trap, see Gilbert and Hubbell, "Plant Diseases and the Conservation of Tropical Forests."

Bibliography

ARCHIVAL SOURCES

ARCHIVO NACIONAL DE HONDURAS, TEGUCIGALPA, HONDURAS

Official Correspondence

Correspondencia de las juntas de fomento.
Correspondencia de la Dirección General de Sanidad, vol. 2.
Correspondencia de la gobernación política (1931) (June–Dec. 1925).
Correspondencia de las gobernaciones políticas de la república (July–Sept. 1933).
Correspondencia de las gobernaciones políticas de la república (Sept./Oct. 1937).
Correspondencia de los gobernadores políticos.
Correspondencia de los gobernadores políticos (Jan.–Apr. 1934).
Correspondencia del departamento de Atlántida (1931).
Correspondencia del departamento de Cortés (1931).
Correspondencia del departamento de Cortés (1932).
Correspondencia particular (1921).
Correspondencia particular (June–Dec. 1929).
Correspondencia recibida de las gobernaciones políticas de la república (1931).
Correspondencia recibida de las gobernaciones, vol. 2 (1936).
Correspondencia recibida de las gobernadores (1938).
Correspondencia, Truxillo Railroad Company (1920).
Gobernación Política (1886–1912).
Gobernación Política, Choluteca y Roatán (April 1894–July 1903).
Secretaria de Fomento, libro copiador de correspondencia (Dec. 1931).

Telegrams

Correspondencia telegráfica (1918).
Correspondencia telegráfica, Atlántida (1918).
Correspondencia telegráfica, Atlántida (July–Sept. 1925).
Correspondencia telegráfica, Atlántida (1931).
Correspondencia telegráfica, Colón (Jan.–Apr. 1934).
Correspondencia telegráfica, Cortés (May–Aug. 1936).

Correspondencia telegráfica, Yoro (1925).
Telegramas (no date).

Government Ministry Reports

Gobernación (1936).
Informes a Ministro de Gobernación (1913).
Informes a varias secciones y departamentos de ministerio (1931–1932).
Informes de los gobernadores políticos, varios departamentos (1919–1920).
Informes de los gobernadores políticos (1938–1939).
Informe del gobernador político, Atlántida (1934–1935).
Informes departamentales de los gobernadores políticos (1936).

Miscellaneous Documents

Alcaldías municipales (1934–1937).
Apuntes, gobernador político, vol. 1 (1934).
Copias de notas (1930).
Datos estadísticos, Colón (1926).
Datos estadísticos, Cortés (1926).
Documentos de 1893.
Honduras, Junta Registradora. "Datos relativos a las fincas de bananos" (July 1899).
Legajo 1881.
Notas varias (1884–1893).
Notas varias (1894–1912).
Notas varias (1920–1930).
Notas varias (1927).
Notas varias (1932).
Notas varias, correspondencia, Atlántida.
Notas varias, Cortés.
Notas varias, Cortés (1894–1912).
Zalazar, F. C., and P. H. Meyers, "Plano general de los Ferrocarril Nacional y Mata de Guineo y los subramales de Santiago, Travesia, y Bufalo" [map]. 1923.

ARCHIVO DE LA GOBERNACIÓN DE ATLÁNTIDA, LA CEIBA, HONDURAS

Conocimiento: Fruta embarcada por la Standard Fruit Company (Mar.–May, 1932) [loose document].
Libro copiador de cartas (1926).
Libro de acuerdos del gobernador político (1927–1933).
Libro de matrícula de agricultores y ganaderos (1928–1935).
Registro de la Propiedad, vol. 1 (1926).

ARCHIVOS MUNICIPALES, HONDURAS

La Ceiba. *Libros de actas,* vols. 17–19 (20 Oct. 1920–1 Mar. 1929).
El Progreso. *Libros de actas,* vols. 1–10 (1893–1926) and vols. 13–15 (1935–39).

Sonaguera. *Libros de actas* (Jan. 1907–1 July 1910; and 1917–1934).
Tela. *Libros de actas* (3 Jan. 1887–5 Jan. 1888); (12 Jan. 1892–1 Nov. 1896); and (1 Sept. 1911–1 Feb. 1915).

FUNDACIÓN HONDUREÑA DE INVESTIGACIÓN
AGRÍCOLA (FHIA), LA LIMA, CORTÉS

Fruit Dispatch Company. "Conference Report." Chicago, Nov. 11–12, 1925.
"Guarumas Files." United Fruit Company, Division of Tropical Research. Documents pertaining primarily to banana breeding experiments.
Knudson, Lewis. "Report on the Cercospora Disease of Banana in Honduras with Special Reference to Soil as a Factor." Unpublished manuscript (Aug. 17, 1936).
Prescott, Samuel C. "Diseases of the Banana." *Research Lab Bulletin* no 2. United Fruit Company, Jan. 1917.
———. "Report on the Examination of Tropical Soils." Report submitted to the United Fruit Company, 1 July 1918.
Vilardebo, A. "First Tests of the Fight against Nematodes of Bananas in French New Guinea." Paper presented at 4th International Congress on Control of Enemies of Plants. Hamburg, 1957.

PRIVATE PAPERS OF DR. ROBERT H. STOVER,
LA LIMA, HONDURAS

United Fruit Company, Division of Tropical Research. *Annual Reports* (1935–1953 and 1957–1974).
———. *Research Extension Newsletter* (Oct. 1954–Feb. 1960).

BAKER LIBRARY, HARVARD BUSINESS SCHOOL,
CAMBRIDGE, MASSACHUSETTS

Graduate School of Business Administration, exhibits presented for the Harvard Advertising Awards, vol. 8 (Ms. Div. SPGD H339a).
Henry B. Arthur Papers, ca. 1960–1973.
United Fruit Company Photograph Collection.

COUNTWAY LIBRARY OF MEDICINE,
HARVARD MEDICAL SCHOOL, BOSTON

Papers of Dr. Richard Pearson Strong (1911–1945).

HOWARD-TILTON MEMORIAL LIBRARY, TULANE UNIVERSITY,
NEW ORLEANS, LOUISIANA

Standard Fruit and Steamship Company Papers, 1901–1963.

UNITED STATES, LIBRARY OF CONGRESS, GEOGRAPHY AND
MAP DIVISION, WASHINGTON, D.C.

Anon. Honduras (1:120,000). 1926.
Instituto Panamericano de Geografía e Historia. Honduras. 1933.
Tela RR Company. General Division Map. 17 Mar. 1948.
Tela RR Company. Map of Railroad Lines: Tela and Cortés Divisions. 10 Aug. 1950.
U.S. Marine Corp. Honduras: North Coast, Truxillo Railroad 42 inch gauge. 9 Oct. 1933.
Zannoni, E. G. Map of North Coast of Honduras between Tela and Truxillo Showing Standard Fruit Company Railroad and Connections. Oct. 1935.

UNITED STATES NATIONAL ARCHIVES,
COLLEGE PARK, MARYLAND

Textual Sources

Foreign Service Post Records (Record Group 84). Honduras. Puerto Cortés, 1886–1946.
General Records of the Department of Justice (Record Group 60). *United States v. United Fruit Company,* File 60-166-56.
General Records of the Department of State (Record Group 59). Central Decimal File. Honduras, 1955–1959 and 1960–1963.
Records of the Foreign Agricultural Service (Record Group 166). Narrative Reports, 1904–1965.

Microfilmed Sources

Confidential U.S. Diplomatic Post Records. Honduras, 1930–1945. University Publications of America (42 rolls).
Confidential U.S. State Department Central Files. Honduras. Internal Affairs and Foreign Affairs, 1945–1949. University Publications of America (11 rolls).
U.S. Department of State. Dispatches from U.S. Consuls in Utila, 1899–1906. National Archives microfilm publication T-701 (2 rolls).
Despatches from U.S. Consuls in Omoa, Trujillo, and Roatán, 1831–1893. National Archives microfilm publication T-477 (6 rolls).
Records of the Department of State Relating to the Internal Affairs of Honduras, 1910–1929. National Archives microfilm publication M 647 (49 rolls).

Non-textual Sources

Cartographic Division. War Department Map Collection (Record Group 77).

NATIONAL MUSEUM OF AMERICAN HISTORY,
WASHINGTON, D.C.

Warshaw Collection

HUNT INSTITUTE FOR BOTANICAL DOCUMENTATION,
PITTSBURGH, PA.

Wilson Popenoe Papers

NEWSPAPERS

El Atlántico, 1929, 1931.
El Combate, 1932.
Correo del Norte, 1958.
Diario del Norte, 1927.
El Ferrocarril Interoceánico, 1870.
Honduras Industrial (Tegucigalpa), 1 July 1884.
New York Times.
El Olanchano, 1927–1929.
El Pueblo, 1931, 1932.
El Sindicalista, 1957–1963.

AUTHOR INTERVIEWS
(Unless noted otherwise, I tape-recorded all interviews between June
and September 1995.)

Almendares, Pancho. Olanchito, Yoro.
Alvarado, A. Campo Limónes (La Lima), Atlántida.
Andino, Cantalisio. Calpules aldea (Olanchito), Yoro.
Canales, Manuel. La Lima, Cortés.
Cano, Ruben. Olanchito, Yoro.
Coto Moreno, Ángela. El Progreso, Yoro.
Fajardo, Bricio. Olanchito, Yoro.
Funes, Emilio. La Lima, Atlántida.
Gavilán, Juan. Coyoles Central (Olanchito), Yoro.
González, Omar. Olanchito, Yoro. July 2002.
Lara, José Maria. La Lima, Cortés.
Mejía, Lourdes. San Pedro Sula, Cortés. Interview not tape-recorded.
Mangandí de Duarte, Isabel. La Ceiba, Atlántida.
Martínez, Francisca. Coyoles Central (Olanchito), Yoro.
Martínez, Neche. El Ocote (Olanchito), Yoro.
Martínez, Pastor. Coyoles Central (Olanchito), Yoro.
Melendez, Juana. Olanchito, Yoro. July 2002.
Nieves, Gladys [pseudonym]. Tacamiche (La Lima), Cortés.
Nuñez, Feliciano. El Progreso, Yoro.
Portillo, Francisco. La Lima, Cortés.
Posas, Abel. Calpules aldea (Olanchito), Yoro.
Reyes, Víctor. El Progreso, Yoro.
Rivera Girón, Camilo. San Pedro Sula, Cortés.

Rivera Nájera, Esperanza. El Ocote, Yoro.
Romero, Jorge. La Lima, Cortés.
Vallecillo, Ramón. El Ocote (Olanchito), Yoro.
Wilson, Woodrow. Sonaguera, Colón.
Yaya. Coyoles, Yoro. July 2002.
Zaldívar, Olivia. La Lima, Cortés. July 2002.

PUBLISHED SOURCES

Adams, Frederick Upham. *Conquest of the Tropics.* New York: Doubleday, Page and Company, 1914.

Altieri, Miguel, ed. *Agroecology: The Scientific Basis of Alternative Agriculture.* Boulder: Westview, 1987.

Amarel, Afranio do. "The Snake-bite Problem in the United States and in Central America." *Bulletin of the Antivenin Institute of America* 1, no. 2 (July 1927): 31–35.

Amaya Amador, Ramón. *Prisión verde.* Tegucigalpa: Editorial Universitaria, 1990.

Appelbaum, Nancy P., Anne S. MacPherson, Karin Alejandra Rosemblatt, eds. *Race and Nation in Modern Latin America.* Chapel Hill: University of North Carolina Press, 2003.

Argueta, Mario. *Bananos y Política: Samuel Zemurray y la Cuyamel Fruit Company.* Tegucigalpa: Editorial Universitaria, 1989.

———. *La gran huelga bananera: Los 69 días que estremecieron a Honduras.* Tegucigalpa: Editorial Universitaria, 1996.

———. *Historia de los sin historia.* Tegucigalpa: Editorial Guaymuras, 1992.

Arthur, Henry B., James P. Houck, and George L. Beckford. *Tropical Agribusiness Structures and Adjustments—Bananas.* Boston: Harvard Business School, 1968.

Ashby, S. F. "Banana Diseases in Jamaica." *Bulletin of the Department of Agriculture, Jamaica* 2, no. 6 (1913): 95–128.

———. "Bananas Resistant to Wilt (Panama Disease)." *Tropical Agriculture* 1 (1924): 172–173.

Ayala, César. *American Sugar Kingdom: The Plantation Economy of the Spanish Caribbean, 1898–1934.* Chapel Hill: University of North Carolina Press, 1999.

"Banana Giant That Has to Shrink." *Business Week* (15 Feb. 1958), 110.

"The Banana, or Plantain." *The Penny Magazine* (29 Sept. 1832), 253.

"The Banana Supply of New York." *Garden and Forest* (11 Oct. 1893), 422–423.

Barahona, Marvin. *La hegemonía de los Estados Unidos en Honduras (1907–1932).* Tegucigalpa: Centro de Documentación de Honduras, 1989.

———. *El silencio quedó atrás: Testimonios de la huelga bananera de 1954.* Tegucigalpa: Editorial Guaymuras, 1994.

Berry, Riley M. Fletcher. *Fruit Recipes.* New York: Doubleday, Page and Company, 1911.

Biologia Centrali-Americana. Zoology, botany, and archaeology. Ed. Frederick Ducane Godman and Osbert Salvin. Introductory vol. by Frederick Ducane Godman. London: published for the editors by R. H. Porter, 1915.

Bitter, Wilhelm. "Al margen de la industria bananera." *Revista Económica* 9, no. 10 (1922): 650–656.

Boston Cooking School Magazine (June/July 1897): 47–48.

Boston School of Cooking Magazine 2 no. 5 (Feb./Mar. 1898): 299.

Bourgois, Phillippe. *Ethnicity at Work: Divided Labor on a Central American Banana Plantation.* Baltimore: John Hopkins University Press, 1989.

Brandes, E. W. "Banana Wilt." *Phytopathology* 9 (1919): 339–389.

Brannstrom, Christian. "Coffee Labor Regimes and Deforestation on a Brazilian Frontier, 1915–1965." *Economic Geography* 76 (2000): 326–346.

———, ed. *Territories, Commodities, and Knowledges: Latin American Environmental Histories in the Nineteenth and Twentieth Centuries.* London: Institute for the Study of the Americas, 2004.

Brenner, Joël Glenn. *The Emperors of Chocolate: Inside the Secret World of Hershey and Mars.* New York: Random House, 1999.

Brockway, Lucile H. *Science and Colonial Expansion: The Role of the Royal British Botanical Gardens.* New York: Academic Press, 1979.

Bucheli, Marcelo. "United Fruit Company in Latin America." In *Banana Wars: Power, Production, and History in the Americas,* ed. Steve Striffler and Mark Moberg, 80–100. Durham: Duke University Press, 2003.

Buddenhagen, Ivan, and Arthur Kelman. "Biological and Physiological Aspects of Bacterial Wilt Caused by Pseudomonas Solanacearum." *Annual Review of Phytopathology* 2, (1964): 203–230.

Bulmer-Thomas, Victor. *The Political Economy of Central America since 1920.* Cambridge: Cambridge University Press, 1987.

Cáceres Lara, Victor. *Astillas de Historia.* Tegucigalpa: Banco Atlántida, 1992.

Cardoso, Henrique, and E. Faletto. *Dependency and Development in Latin America.* Trans. Marjory Mattingly Urquidi. Berkeley: University of California Press, 1979.

Carías Reyes, Marcos. *Trópico.* 2d ed. Tegucigalpa: Editorial Universitaria, 1990.

Carleton, Mark Alfred. "Note on the Fusarium Wilt Disease of Bananas." *Science* 56 (1922): 663–664.

Carr, Barry " 'Omnipotent and Omnipresent'? Labor Shortages, Worker Mobility, and Employer Control in the Cuban Sugar Industry." In *Identity and Struggle at the Margins of the Nation-State,* ed. Aviva Chomsky and Aldo Lauria-Santiago, 260–291. Durham: Duke University Press, 1998.

Carroll, C. R., J. V. Vandermeer, and P. Rosset, eds. *Agroecology.* New York: McGraw-Hill, 1990.

Castro, Agapito Robleda. *40 años después: La verdad de la huelga de 1954 y de la formación del SITRATERCO.* Tegucigalpa: SEDAL, 1995.

Cevallos, Fernando P. *Reseña histórica de las Islas de la Bahía.* Tegucigalpa: Tipografía Nacional, 1919.

Chable, A. C. "Reforestation in the Republic of Honduras, Central America." *Ceiba* 13 (1967): 1–56.

Chalmers, Stephen. "The Romance of the Banana." *The Anglo-American Magazine* 8 (1902): 20–27.

Chandler, Alfred. *Scale and Scope: The Dynamics of Industrial Capitalism.* Cambridge, Massachusetts: Harvard University Press, 1990.

———. *The Visible Hand: The Managerial Revolution in American Business.* Cambridge, Mass.: Harvard University Press, 1977.

Charles, Cecil. *Honduras: The Land of Great Depths.* Chicago: Rand, McNally and Company, 1890.

Charlet, Barbara, and Shida Rastegaria Henneberry. "A Profile of Food Market Trends and Changing Market Institutions." PDF file, Oklahoma State Cooperative Extension website, www.osuextra.com, 21 Jun. 2004.

Charlip, Julie. *Cultivating Coffee: The farmers of Carazo, Nicaragua, 1880–1930*. Athens, Ohio: Ohio University Press, 2003.

Cheesman, E. E., and Claude Wardlaw. "Specific and Varietal Susceptibility of Bananas to Cercospora Leaf Spot." *Tropical Agriculture* 14, no. 12 (1937): 335–336.

Chomsky, Aviva. *West Indian Workers and the United Fruit Company in Costa Rica, 1870–1940*. Baton Rouge: Louisiana State University Press, 1996.

Chomsky, Aviva, and Aldo Lauria-Santiago, eds. *Identity and Struggle at the Margins of the Nation-State*. Durham: Duke University Press, 1998.

Ciesielski, S. D. et al. "The Epidemiology of Tuberculosis among North Carolina Migrant Farm Workers." *Journal of the American Medical Association* 265, no. 13 (3 Apr. 1991): 1715–1719.

Clarence-Smith, William Gervase. *Cocoa and Chocolate, 1765–1914*. London: Routledge, 2000.

Coatsworth, John H. *Central America and the United States*. New York: Twayne Publishers, 1994.

Cohen, Lizabeth. "Encountering Mass Culture at the Grassroots: The Experience of Chicago Workers in the 1920s." *American Quarterly* 41, no. 1 (1989): 6–33.

Conrad, Robert. *Children of God's Fire*. State College, Penn.: Pennsylvania State University Press, 1984.

Cooper, Frederick, et al. *Confronting Historical Paradigms: Peasants, Labor and the Capitalist World System in Latin America and Africa*. Madison: University of Wisconsin Press, 1993.

Coronil, Fernando. *The Magical State: Nature, Money, and Modernity in Venezuela*. Chicago: University of Chicago, 1997.

Cronon, William, ed. *Uncommon Ground: Rethinking the Human Place in Nature*. New York: Norton, 1996.

Crosby, Alfred. *The Columbian Exchange: Biological and Cultural Consequences of 1492*. Westport, Conn.: Greenwood Press, 1972.

―――. "Metamorphosis of the Americas." In *Seeds of Change: A Quincentennial Commemoration*, ed. Herman J. Viola and Carolyn Margolis, 70–89. Washington, D.C.: Smithsonian Press, 1991.

Crowther, Samuel. *The Romance and Rise of the American Tropics*. Garden City, N.Y.: Doubleday, Doran and Company, 1929.

Cruz Cáceres, Francisco. *En las selvas hondureñas*. Tegucigalpa: Tipografía Nacional, 1955.

Cutter, Victor. "Caribbean Tropics in Commercial Transition." *Economic Geography* 2 (1926): 494–507.

Dawson, Frank Griffith. "William Pitt's Settlement at Black River on the Mosquito Shore: A Challenge to Spain in Central America, 1732–87." *Hispanic American Historical Review* 63, no. 4 (1983): 677–706.

Davidson, William V. *Historical Geography of the Bay Islands of Honduras*. Birmingham: University of Alabama Press, 1979.

Dean, Warren. *Brazil and the Struggle for Rubber*. Cambridge: Cambridge University Press, 1987.

————. *With Broadax and Firebrand*. Berkeley: University of California Press, 1995.

Deeks, William E. "Some Aspects of Malaria Control." *Journal of Tropical Medicine and Hygiene* 29 (1926): 185.

Denevan, William M. "The Pristine Myth: The Landscape of the Americas in 1492." *Annals of the Association of American Geographers* 83 (1992): 369–385.

Díaz Lozano, Argentina. *Peregrinaje*. 9th ed. Tegucigalpa: Alin Editora, 1993 [1944].

Dicum, Gregory, and Nina Luttinger. *The Coffee Book: Anatomy of an Industry from Crop to the Last Drop*. New York: New Press, 1999.

Ditmars, Raymond L. "A Reptile Reconnaissance in Honduras." *Bulletin of the Antivenin Institute of America* 2 (1928): 25–29.

Dosal, Paul J. *Doing Business with the Dictators: A Political History of the United Fruit Company in Guatemala*. Wilmington, Del.: Scholarly Resources, 1993.

Drost, A. W. "The Surinam Panama Disease of the Gros Michel Banana." Trans. S. F. Ashby. *Bulletin of the Jamaica Department of Agriculture* 26 (March 1912): 128–149.

Dudziak, Mary L. "Josephine Baker, Racial Protest, and the Cold War." *Journal of American History* 81, no. 2 (1994): 545–570.

Dunlap, Thomas R. *DDT: Scientists, Citizens, and Public Policy*. Princeton: Princeton University Press, 1981.

Dye, Alan. *Cuban Sugar in the Age of Mass Production*. Stanford: Stanford University Press, 1998.

Eakin, Marshall. "The Origins of Modern Science in Costa Rica: The Instituto Físico-Geográfico Nacional, 1887–1904." *Latin American Research Review* 34, no. 1 (1999): 123–150.

Echeverri-Gent, Elisavinda. "Forgotten Workers: British West Indians and the Early Days of the Banana Industry in Costa Rica and Honduras." *Journal of Latin American Studies* 24 (1992): 275–308.

Ellis, Frank. *Las transnacionales del banano en Centroamérica*. Trans. Juan Mario Castellanos. San José, Costa Rica: Editorial Universitaria Centroamericana, 1983.

Enloe, Cynthia. *Bananas, Beaches, and Bases: Making Feminist Sense of International Politics*. Berkeley: University of California Press, 1989.

Escobar, Arturo. *Encountering Development: The Making and Unmaking of the Third World*. Princeton: Princeton University Press, 1995.

Euraque, Darío. "Modernity, Economic Power and the Foreign Banana Companies in Honduras: San Pedro Sula as a Case Study, 1880s–1945." In *Essays in Economic and Business History*, vol. 11, ed. Edwin J. Perkins, 49–65. Los Angeles: University of Southern California, 1993.

————. *Reinterpreting the Banana Republic: Region and State in Honduras, 1870–1972*. Chapel Hill: University of North Carolina Press, 1996.

————. "San Pedro Sula, actual capital industrial de Honduras: Su trajectoría entre villorrío colonial y emporio bananero, 1536–1936." *Mesoamérica* 26 (1993): 217–252.

————. "The Threat of Blackness to the Mestizo Nation: Race and Ethnicity in the Honduran Banana Economy." In *Banana Wars: Power, Production, and History in the Americas*, ed. Steve Striffler and Mark Moberg, 229–249. Durham: Duke University Press, 2003.

Fallas, Carlos Luis. *Mamita Yunai*. San José, Costa Rica: Editorial Costa Rica, 1986.

Farm Chemical Handbook. Ohio: Meister Publishing Company, 1994.

Faulkner, William. *As I Lay Dying.* New York: Vintage Books, 1964.

Fawcett, William. *The Banana: Its Cultivation, Distribution, and Commercial Uses.* 2d ed. London: Duckworth and Company, 1921.

———. "La industria bananera en Jamaica." *Boletín del Instituto Físico-Geográfico de Costa Rica* 2, no. 23 (30 Nov. 1902): 267–286.

Flores Valeriano, Enrique. *La Explotación Bananera en Honduras.* 2d ed. Tegucigalpa: Editorial Universitaria, 1987.

Forster, Cindy. "Reforging National Revolution: Campesino Labor Struggles in Guatemala, 1944–1954." In *Identity and Struggle at the Margins of the Nation-State,* ed. Aviva Chomsky and Aldo Lauria-Santiago, 196–226. Durham: Duke University Press, 1998.

Frassinetti, Antonio Murga. *Enclave y sociedad en Honduras.* Tegucigalpa: Editorial Universitaria, 1978.

Friedrich, Paul. *Agrarian Revolt in a Mexican Village.* Englewood Cliffs, N.J.: Prentice-Hall, 1970.

Froebel, Julius. *Seven Years' Travel in Central America, Northern Mexico, and the Far West of the United States.* London: Richard Bentley, 1859.

Funes Monzote, Reinaldo. "Deforestation and Sugar in Cuba's Centre-East: The Case of Camagüey, 1898–1926." In *Territories, Commodities, and Knowledges: Latin American Environmental Histories in the Nineteenth and Twentieth Centuries,* ed. Christian Brannstrom, 148–170. London: Institute for the Study of the Americas, 2004.

Gallini, Stefania. "Maya-Mam Agroecosystem in Guatemala's Coffee Revolution: Costa Cuca, 1830s–1880s." In *Territories, Commodities, and Knowledges: Latin American Environmental History in the Nineteenth and Twentieth Centuries,* ed. Christian Brannstrom, 23–49. London: Institute for the Study of the Americas, 2004.

Galloway, J. H. *The Sugar Cane Industry.* Cambridge: Cambridge University Press, 1989.

García Buchard, Ethel. *Poder político, interés bananero, e identidad nacional en Centro América.* Tegucigalpa: Editorial Universitaria, 1997.

Gilbert, Gregory S., and Stephen P. Hubbell. "Plant Diseases and the Conservation of Tropical Forests." *BioScience* 46, no. 2 (1996): 98–106.

Gleijeses, Piero. *Shattered Hope: The Guatemalan Revolution and the United States, 1944–1954.* Princeton, N.J.: Princeton University Press, 1991.

Gliessman, Stephen R. "Agroecology: Researching the Ecological Basis for Sustainable Agriculture." In *Agroecology,* edited by Stephen R. Gliessman, 3–10. New York: Springer-Verlag, 1990.

Gootenberg, Paul. "Between Coca and Cocaine: A Century or More of U.S.-Peruvian Drug Paradoxes, 1860–1980." *Hispanic American Historical Review* 83, no. 1 (2003): 119–150.

Gordon, George Byron. "Researches in the Uloa Valley, Honduras." *Memoirs of the Peabody Museum,* v. 4–5. Cambridge, Mass.: Harvard University, 1898. Reprint New York: Krause Reprint Company, 1970.

Gottlieb, Robert. *Forcing the Spring: The Transformation of the American Environmental Movement.* Washington, D.C.: Island Press, 1993.

Gould, Jeffrey. *To Lead as Equals: Rural Protest and Political Consciousness in Chinandega, Nicaragua, 1912–1979.* Chapel Hill: University of North Carolina Press, 1990.

Gowen, Simon R. "Pests." In *Bananas and Plantains,* edited by Simon R. Gowen, 382–402. London: Chapman and Hall, 1995.

Green, James N. *Beyond Carnival: Male Homosexuality in Twentieth-Century Brazil.* Chicago: University of Chicago Press, 1999.

Grossman, Lawrence S. *The Political Ecology of Bananas: Contract Farming, Peasants, and Agrarian Change in the Eastern Caribbean.* Chapel Hill: University of North Carolina Press, 1998.

Gudmundson, Lowell W. "On Paths Not Taken: Commercial Capital and Coffee Production in Costa Rica." In *The Global Coffee Economy in Africa, Asia, and Latin America, 1500–1989,* ed. Steven Topik and William Gervase Clarence-Smith, 335–359. New York: Cambridge University Press, 2003.

———. "Peasant, Farmer, Proletarian: Class Formation in a Smallholder Coffee Economy, 1850–1950." In *Coffee, Society, and Power in Latin America,* ed. William Roseberry, Lowell Gudmundson, and Mario Samper Kutschbach, 112–150. Baltimore: Johns Hopkins University Press, 1995.

Guyot, H., and J. Cuillé. "Les traitements fongicides des bananeraies. Efficacités des différents modes de traitements. Role de l'huile." *Fruits d'outre mer* 10 (1955): 101–107.

Hall, Carolyn. *Costa Rica: Una interpretación geográfica con perspectiva histórica.* San José: Editorial Costa Rica, 1984

Helbig, Karl. *Areas y paisajes del noreste de Honduras.* Trans. Guillermo Cano. Tegucigalpa: Banco Central de Honduras, 1953.

Hibbs, J., S. Yeager, and J. Cochran. "Tuberculosis among Migrant Farm Workers." *Journal of the American Medical Association* 262, no. 13 (6 Oct. 1989): 1775.

Higgins, J. E. "The Banana in Hawaii." *Hawaii Agricultural Experiment Station Bulletin No. 7.* Honolulu: Hawaiian Gazette Company, Inc., 1904.

Honduras. *Boletín de Fomento,* Aug.–Dec. 1911; 1 Jan. 1912; and May 1 1912.

———. Congreso Nacional. *Informe de la Comisión Especial sobre la verdadera situación de los trabajadores en Honduras.* Tegucigalpa: Talleres Tipo-Lito Ariston, 1950.

———. Dirección General de Estadísticas y Censos. *Honduras en cifras 1964.* Tegucigalpa, 1965.

———. *Informe de Fomento, Agricultura, y Trabajo, 1951–1952.* Tegucigalpa: Tipo. Nac. 1953.

———. *Memoria de Fomento, Agricultura, y Trabajo.* Tegucigalpa: Tipo. Nac. 1931.

———. Ministerio de Fomento. *Memoria de Fomento, Obras Públicas, Agricultura, y Trabajo.* Tegucigalpa: Tipo. Nac. 1929.

———. *La Nueva Política Bananera de Honduras 1903–1975.* Tegucigalpa: Secretaria de Cultura, Turismo e Información, 1975.

———. *Revista del Archivo y de la Biblioteca Nacional de Honduras.*

———. Procuraduría General de la República. *Truxillo con X.* Tegucigalpa: CETTNA, 1979.

Hord, H. H. V. "The Conversion of Standard Fruit Company Banana Plantations in Honduras from the Gros Michel to the Giant Cavendish Variety." *Tropical Agriculture* 43, no. 4 (1966): 269–275.

Hounshell, David. *From the American System to Mass Production, 1800–1932: The Devel-*

opment of Manufacturing Technology in the United States. Baltimore: Johns Hopkins University Press, 1984.

"How United Fruit Was Plucked." *Business Week* (22 Feb. 1969): 122–124.

Humphrey, James Ellis. "Where Bananas Grow." *Popular Science Monthly* (Feb. 1894): 487–488.

Hutchings, Harry Hinson Sr. "Luck and Itching Feet." In *Bananeros in Central America,* ed. Clyde S. Stephens, 33–80. Fort Meyers, Fla.: Press Printing Company, 1989.

Immerman, Richard H. *The CIA in Guatemala: The Foreign Policy of Intervention.* Austin: University of Texas Press, 1982.

Jenkins, Virgina Scott. *Bananas: An American History.* Washington, D.C.: Smithsonian Institution, 2000.

Jiménez, Michael F. " 'From Plantation to Cup': Coffee and Capitalism in the United States." In *Coffee, Society and Power in Latin America,* ed. William Roseberry, Lowell Gudmundson, and Mario Samper Kutschbach, 38–64. Baltimore: Johns Hopkins University Press, 1995.

Johnston, John R. *Mosaic Disease of Sugar Cane in 1923; Diseases and Pests of the Banana.* Boston: United Fruit Company, 1923.

Jones, David R. "Sigatoka." In *Diseases of Banana, Abaca, and Enset,* ed. David R. Jones, 79–92. New York: CAB International, 2000.

Karnes, Thomas L. *Tropical Enterprise: The Standard Fruit and Steamship Company in Latin America.* Baton Rouge: Louisiana State University Press, 1978.

Kepner, Charles. *Social Aspects of the Banana Industry.* New York: Columbia University Press, 1936.

Kepner, Charles, and Jay Henry Soothill. *The Banana Empire: A Case Study in Economic Imperialism.* New York: Russell and Russell, 1967.

Laínez, Vilma, and Víctor Meza. "El enclave bananero en la historia de Honduras." *Estudios Sociales Centroamericanos II* (1973): 115–156.

Langdon, Robert. "The Banana as a Key to Early American and Polynesian History." *Journal of Pacific History* 28 (1993): 15–35.

Langley, Lester, and Thomas Schoonover. *The Banana Men.* Lexington: University of Kentucky Press, 1995.

"Last Days of the Banana." *New Scientist* 18 (2003): 26–29.

Lauria-Santiago, Aldo. *An Agrarian Republic: Commercial Agriculture and the Politics of Peasant Communities in El Salvador, 1823–1918.* Pittsburgh: University of Pittsburgh Press, 1999.

Leach, R. "Banana Leaf Spot Investigations: The Basis of Control." *Journal of the Jamaica Agricultural Society* 44 (Nov.–Dec. 1940): 454–462, 499–502.

———. "Banana Leaf Spot, *Mycosphaerella musicola,* the Perfect Stage of *Cercopora musae* Zim." *Tropical Agriculture* 18 (1941): 91–95.

Lear, Linda J. *Rachel Carson: Witness for Nature.* New York: Henry Holt, 1997.

Lee, Melicent Humason. *Children of Banana Lands.* New York: Thomas Crowell Company, 1936.

LeGrand, Catherine. *Frontier Expansion and Peasant Protest in Colombia, 1850–1936.* Albuquerque: University of New Mexico, 1986.

———. "Living in Macondo: Economy and Culture in a United Fruit Company Banana Enclave in Colombia." In *Close Encounters of Empire: Writing the Cultural History of U.S.–Latin American Relations,* ed. Gilbert M. Joseph, Catherine

LeGrand, and Ricardo D. Salvatore, 333–368. Durham: Duke University Press, 1998.

Lincoln, Mary J. *Boston Cookbook*. Boston: Little, Brown and Company, 1900.

MacCameron, Robert. *Bananas, Labor and Politics in Honduras, 1954–1963*. Syracuse, N.Y.: Syracuse University Press, 1983.

Magee, C. J. "Banana Leaf Spot: Spraying and Dusting Trials, 1939–1940." New South Wales, Department of Agriculture, Miscellaneous publication no. 3,203 (Oct. 1940).

Mandala, Elías. *Work and Control in a Peasant Economy*. Madison: University of Wisconsin Press, 1990.

March, Douglas D. II. "Field Notes on Barba Amarilla (*Bothrops atrox*)." *Bulletin of the Antivenin Institute of America* 1 (1928): 92–97.

Marchand, Roland. *Advertising the American Dream*. Berkeley: University of California Press, 1985.

Marquardt, Steve. " 'Green Havoc': Panama Disease, Environmental Change and Labor Process in the Central American Banana Industry." *American Historical Review* 106, no. 1 (2001): 49–80.

———. "Pesticides, Parakeets, and Unions in the Costa Rican Banana Industry, 1938–1962." *Latin American Research Review* 37, no. 2 (2002): 3–36.

Marshall, Woodville K. "Provision Ground and Plantation Labor in Four Windward Islands: Competition for Resources during Slavery." In *Cultivation and Culture: Labor and the Shaping of Black Life in the Americas*, ed. Ira Berlin and Philip Morgan, 203–220. Charlottesville: University of Virginia, 1993.

May, Stacy, and Galo Plaza. *The United Fruit Company in Latin America*. Washington, D.C.: National Planning Association, 1958.

McCann, Thomas P. *An American Company: The Tragedy of United Fruit*. New York: Crown Publishers, 1976.

McCook, Stuart. *States of Nature: Science, Agriculture, and Environment in the Spanish Caribbean, 1760–1940*. Austin: University of Texas Press, 2002.

McCreery, David. *Rural Guatemala, 1760–1940*. Stanford: Stanford University Press, 1994.

McGuire, Laurence. "Panama Disease of Bananas, Reports on the Banana Growing Countries of the West Indies, Central and South America." London: HMSO, July 1929.

McKenney, R. E. B. "The Central American Banana Blight." *Science* 31 (13 May 1910): 750–751.

McNeill, John R. *Something New Under the Sun: An Environmental History of the Twentieth-Century World*. New York: W. W. Norton, 2000.

Melville, Elinor. *A Plague of Sheep*. Cambridge: Cambridge University Press, 1994.

Meredith, D. S. "Banana Leaf Spot Disease (Sigatoka) Caused by *Mycosphaerella Musicola* Leach." *Phytopathological Papers*, no. 11. Kew, England: Commonwealth Mycological Society, April 1970.

———. "Major Banana Diseases: Past and Present Status." *Review of Plant Pathology* 49 (1970): 539–554.

Meza, Victor. *Historia del movimiento obrero hondureño*. Tegucigalpa: Centro de documentación de Honduras, 1991.

Mintz, Sidney. *Sweetness and Power*. New York: Penguin Books, 1986.

————. *Tasting Food, Tasting Freedom: Excursions into Eating, Culture, and the Past.* Boston: Beacon Press, 1996.

————. *Worker in the Cane: A Puerto Rican Life History.* New York: W. W. Norton, 1974.

Miralda, Paca Navas de. *Barro.* Tegucigalpa: Editorial Guaymuras, 1992.

Mires, Fernando. *El discurso de la naturaleza en América Latina.* Santiago, Chile: Editorial Amerinda, 1990.

"Miss Chiquita Returns." *Unibranco,* June 1972, 1.

Moritz, C. F., and Adele Kahn, eds. *The Twentieth Century Cookbook.* 10th ed. New York: M. A. Donohue and Company, 1898.

Mundt, Christopher C. "Disease Dynamics in Agroecosystems." In *Agroecology,* ed. C. R. Carroll, John Vandermeer, and Peter Rosset, 263–299. New York: McGraw-Hill, 1990.

Murga Frassinetti, Antonio. *Enclave y sociedad en Honduras.* Tegucigalpa: Editorial Universitaria, 1978.

Murray, Douglas. *Cultivating Crisis: The Human Cost of Pesticides in Latin America.* Austin: University of Texas Press, 1994.

Naylor, Robert A. *Penny Ante Imperialism: The Mosquito Shore and the Bay of Honduras, 1600–1914.* Toronto: Associated University Presses, 1989.

Newson, Linda. *The Cost of Conquest: Indian Decline in Honduras Under Spanish Rule.* Boulder, Colo.: Westview Press, 1986.

O'Brien, Thomas. *The Revolutionary Mission: American Enterprise in Latin America, 1900–1945.* Cambridge: Cambridge University Press, 1999.

Offen, Karl. "The Geographical Imagination, Resource Economies, and Nicaraguan Incorporation of the Mosquitia, 1838–1909." In *Territories, Commodities, and Knowledges: Latin American Environmental Histories in the Nineteenth and Twentieth Centuries,* ed. Christian Brannstrom, 50–89. London: Institute for the Study of the Americas, 2004.

Ortiz, R., R. S. B. Ferris, and D. R. Vuylsteke. "Banana and Plantain Breeding." In *Bananas and Plantains,* ed. Simon Gowan, 110–146. London: Chapman and Hall, 1994.

Painter, Michael, and William Durham, eds. *The Social Causes of Environmental Destruction in Latin America.* Ann Arbor: University of Michigan, 1995.

Palmer, Jesse T. "The Banana in Caribbean Trade." *Economic Geography* 8 (1932): 262–273.

Pendergrast, Mark. *Uncommon Grounds: The History of Coffee and How It Transformed Our World.* New York: Basic Books, 1999.

Pérez-Brignoli, Héctor. *A Brief History of Central America.* Berkeley: University of California Press, 1989.

Perfecto, Ivette, and Inge Armbrecht. "The Coffee Agroecosystem in the Neotropics: Combining Ecological and Economic Goals." In *Tropical Agroecosystems,* ed. John Vandermeer, 157–192. New York: CRC Press, 2003.

Perfecto, Ivette, Robert A. Rice, Russell Greenberg, and Martha E. Van der Voort. "Shade Coffee: A Disappearing Refuge for Biodiversity." *BioScience* 46 (1996): 598–608.

Perryman, D. A., and I. T. Twyford. "Banana Growing in Central America." Supplement to *WINBAN News* (1967), Windward Island Banana Association.

Peters, James L. "An Ornithological Survey in the Caribbean Lowlands of Honduras." *Bulletin of the Museum of Comparative Zoology* 69, no. 12 (1929): 397–478.

Pillsbury, Richard. *No Foreign Food.* Boulder, Colo.: Westview Press, 1998.

Pimentel, David, and Hugh Lehman, eds. *The Pesticide Question: Environment, Economics, and Ethics.* New York: Chapman Hill, 1993.

Pimentel, David, et al. "Environmental and Economic Costs of Pesticide Use." *BioScience* 42, no. 10 (1992): 750–760.

Pimentel, J. Cortez, and Fernando Marqués. " 'Vineyard sprayer's lung': A New Occupational Disease." *Thorax* 24 (1969): 678–688.

Pimentel, J. Cortez, and A. Peixoto Menezes. "Liver Granulomas Containing Copper in Vineyard Sprayer's Lung." *American Review of Respiratory Disease* 8 (1975): 189–195.

Ploetz, R. C., and K. G. Pegg. "Fungal Diseases of the Root, Corm, and Pseudostem." In *Diseases of Banana, Abacá, and Enset,* edited by David R. Jones, 143–158. New York: CAB International, 2000.

Poole, Hester M. *Fruits and How to Use Them.* New York: Fowler & Wells, 1890.

Posas, Mario. *Lucha ideológica y organización sindical en Honduras, 1954–1965.* Tegucigalpa: Editorial Universitaria, 1980.

———. "La Plantación bananera en Centroamérica (1870–1929)." In *Las repúblicas agroexportadoras,* edited by Víctor Hugo Acuña Ortega, 111–166. Vol. 4 of *Historia General de Centroamérica,* coordinated by Edelberto Torres Rivas. Madrid: Sociedad Estatal Quinto Centenario and FLACSO, 1993.

Pulido, Laura. *Environmentalism and Economic Justice: Two Chicano Struggles in the Southwest.* Tucson: University of Arizona Press, 1996.

Putnam, Judith Jones, and Jane E. Allshouse. *Food Consumption, Prices, and Expenditures, 1970–97.* Food and Rural Economics Division, Economic Research Service, USDA Statistical Bulletin 965. Washington, D.C.: Apr. 1999 (PDF file available at http://www.ers.usda.gov/publications/sb965/).

Putnam, Lara. *The Company They Kept: Migrants and the Politics of Gender in Caribbean Costa Rica, 1870–1960.* Chapel Hill: University of North Carolina Press, 2002.

Raynolds, Laura. "The Global Banana Trade." In *Banana Wars: Power, Production, and History in the Americas,* ed. Steve Striffler and Mark Moberg, 23–47. Durham: Duke University Press, 2003.

Roberts, Furber S. "Insects Affecting Banana Production in Central America." In *Proceedings of the Tenth International Congress of Entomology,* vol. 3 (1956): 411–415.

Roberts, J. Timmons, and Nikki Demetria Thanos. *Trouble in Paradise: Globalization and Environmental Crises in Latin America.* New York: Routledge, 2003.

Roberts, Shari. " 'The Lady in the Tutti-Frutti Hat': Carmen Miranda, a Spectacle of Ethnicity." *Cinema Journal* 32, no. 3 (1993): 3–23.

Rodriquez, D. W. "Bananas: An Outline of the Economic History of Production and Trade with Special Reference to Jamaica." Kingston: Government Printer, 1955.

Romeu-Moreno, A., et al. "Respiratory Toxicity of Copper." *Environmental Health Perspectives* 102 (1994): Supplement 3, 339–340.

Rose, Richard H. *Utilla: Past and Present.* Danville, N.Y.: F. A. Owen Publishing, 1904.

Roseberry, William. "Introduction." In *Coffee, Society, and Power in Latin America,* edited by William Roseberry, Lowell Gudmundson, and Mario Samper Kutschbach, 1–37. Baltimore: Johns Hopkins University Press, 1995.

Roseberry, William, Lowell Gudmundson, and Mario Samper Kutschbach, eds. *Coffee, Society, and Power in Latin America*. Baltimore: Johns Hopkins University Press, 1995.

Rowe, Phillip. "Breeding Bananas and Plantains." *Plant Breeding Reviews* 2 (1984): 135–155.

Rowe, Phillip R., and D. L. Richardson. *Breeding Bananas for Disease Resistance, Fruit Quality, and Yield*. La Lima, Honduras: Tropical Agriculture Research Services, 1975.

Ruiz, Vicki. *Cannery Women, Cannery Lives: Mexican Women, Unionization, and the California Food Processing Industry, 1930–1950*. Albuquerque: University of New Mexico Press, 1987.

Russell, Edmund. *War and Nature: Fighting Humans and Insects from World War I to Silent Spring*. New York: Cambridge University Press, 2001.

Sackman, Douglas C. " 'Nature's Workshop': The Work Environment and Workers' Bodies in California's Citrus Industry, 1900–1940." *Environmental History* 5 (2000): 27–53.

———. *Orange Empire: California and the Fruits of Eden*. Berkeley: University of California Press, 2004.

Samper, Mario. "The Historical Construction of Quality and Competitiveness: A Preliminary Discussion of Coffee Commodity Chains." In *The Global Coffee Economy in Africa, Asia, and Latin America, 1500–1989*, edited by Steve Topik and William Clarence Gervase-Smith, 120–153. New York: Cambridge University Press, 2003.

Scott, Rebecca. *Slave Emancipation in Cuba: The Transition to Free Labor, 1860–1899*. Princeton: Princeton University Press, 1985.

Sedgwick, Alfred B. "The Big Banana" New York: Happy House Co., 1875.

Sequeira, Luis. "Influence of Organic Amendments on Survival of *Fusarium oxysporum* f. *cubense* in the Soil." *Phytopathology* 52 (Oct. 1962): 976–982.

Shell Oil Company. "El Banano: Sus plagas, enfermedades y malezas." 1959?

Shepherd, K. "Banana Research at ICTA." *Tropical Agriculture* 51, no. 4 (1974): 482–490.

Silver, Frank, and Irving Cohn. "Yes, We Have No Bananas." In *Songs of the Twenties*. Milwaukee: Hal Leonard Corporation, 1989.

Simmonds, Norman W. *Bananas*. 1st ed. London: Longman, 1959.

———. "A Survey of the Cavendish Group of Bananas." *Tropical Agriculture* 31 (1954): 126–130.

Simmonds Norman W., and Robert H. Stover. *Bananas*. 3d ed. London: Longman, 1987.

Slutsky, Daniel, and Esther Alonso. *Empresas transnacionales y agricultura: El caso del enclave bananero en Honduras*. Tegucigalpa: Editorial Universitaria, 1982.

Smith, Erwin F. "A Cuban Banana Disease." *Science* 31 (13 May 1910): 755.

Smith, Mark. "The Political Economy of Sugar Production and the Environment of Eastern Cuba, 1898–1923." *Environmental History Review* 19, no. 4 (1995): 31–48.

Smith, P. G., and A. R. Moss. "The Epidemiology of Tuberculosis." In *Tuberculosis: Pathogenesis, Protection and Control*, ed. Barry R. Bloom, 47–59. Washington, D.C.: American Society of Microbiology, 1994.

Soluri, John. "Bananas, Biodiversity, and the Paradox of Commodification." In *Territories, Commodities, and Knowledges: Latin American Environmental Histories in the Nineteenth and Twentieth Centuries,* ed. Christian Brannstrom, 195–217. London: Institute for the Study of the Americas, 2004.

Soto-Pinto, L., I. Perfecto, and J. Caballero-Nieto. "Shade Over Coffee: Its Effects on Berry Borer, Leaf Rust, and Spontaneous Herbs in Chiapas, Mexico." *Agroforestry Systems* 55 (2002): 37–45.

Soto-Pinto, L., I. Perfecto, J. Castillo-Hernandez, and J. Caballero-Nieto. "Shade effect on coffee production at the northern Tzeltal zone of the state of Chiapas, Mexico." *Agriculture, Ecosystems, and Environment* 80 (2000): 61–69.

Stahel, Gerold. "Notes on Cercospora Leaf Spot of Bananas." *Tropical Agriculture* 14, no. 12 (1937): 257–264.

Standley, Paul C. "The Flora of Lancetilla." *Field Museum of Natural History Botany* 10 (1931): 8–49.

Stein, Stanley J. *Vassouras: A Brazilian Coffee County, 1850–1900.* Princeton: Princeton University Press, 1985 [1958].

Steinberg, Theodore. *Down to Earth: Nature's Role in American History.* New York: Oxford University Press, 2002.

Stephens, Clyde S. "Ecological Upset and Recuperation of Natural Control of Insect Pests in Some Costa Rican Banana Plantations." *Turrialba* 34, no. 1 (1984): 101–105.

Stevens, Wallace. "Floral Decoration for Bananas." In *The Palm at the End of the Mind,* edited by Holly Stevens, 81–82. New York: Vintage Books, 1972.

Stolcke, Verena. "The Labors of Coffee in Latin America: The Hidden Charm of Family Labor and Self-Provisioning." In *Coffee, Society, and Power in Latin America,* edited by William Roseberry, Lowell Gudmundson, and Mario Samper Kutschbach, 65–93. Baltimore: Johns Hopkins University Press, 1995.

Stoll, Steven. *The Fruits of Natural Advantage: Making the Industrial Countryside in California.* Berkeley: University of California Press, 1998.

Stouse, Pierre. "Instability of Tropical Agriculture: The Atlantic Lowlands of Costa Rica." *Economic Geography* 46 (1970): 78–97.

Stover, Robert Harry. "Fusarial Wilt (Panama Disease) of the Banana and other Musa Species." Commonwealth Mycological Institute: *Phytopathological Paper* no. 4 (18 Apr. 1962).

———. "Intercontinental Spread of Banana Leaf Spot (*Mycosphaerella musicola* Leach)." *Tropical Agriculture* 39, no. 4 (Oct. 1962): 327–338.

———. "The Use of Organic Amendments and Green Manures in the Control of Soilborne Phytopathogens." *Recent Progress in Microbiology* 8 (1963): 267–275.

Strasser, Susan. *Satisfaction Guaranteed: The Making of the American Mass Market.* Washington, D.C.: Smithsonian Institution Press, 1989.

Striffler, Steve. *In the Shadows of State and Capital: The United Fruit Company, Popular Struggle, and Agrarian Restructuring in Ecuador, 1900–1995.* Durham: Duke University Press, 2002.

Striffler, Steve, and Mark Moberg, eds. *Banana Wars: Power, Production, and History in the Americas.* Durham: Duke University Press, 2003.

Taracena Arriola, Arturo. "Liberalismo y poder político en Centroamérica, 1870–1929." In *Las repúblicas agroexportadoras,* ed. Víctor Hugo Acuña Ortega, 167–254. Vol. 4 of *Historia general de Centroamérica,* coord. Edelberto Torres Rivas. Madrid: Sociedad Estatal Quinto Centenario and FLACSO, 1993.

Taylor, Alan. "Unnatural Inequalities: Social and Environmental History." *Environmental History* 1 (1996): 6–19.

Thompson, Wallace. *Rainbow Countries of Central America.* Chautauqua, N.Y.: Chautauqua Press, 1927.

Thorold, C. A. "Cultivation of Bananas Under Shade for the Control of Leaf Spot Disease." *Tropical Agriculture* 17, no. 11 (1940): 213–214.

Thorton, Norwood C. "Pesticides in Banana Culture." In *Pesticides in Tropical Agriculture,* ed. Thorton, 71–75. Washington, D.C.: American Chemical Society, 1954.

———. "The Use of Fungicides in Central and South America." In *Proceedings of the American Phytopathological Society Meeting.* Ithaca, N.Y., Sept. 9, 1952.

Thrupp, Lori Ann. "Entrapment and Escape from Fruitless Insecticide Use: Lessons from the Banana Sector of Costa Rica." *International Journal of Environmental Studies* 36, no. 3 (1990): 173–189.

———. "Sterilization of Workers from Pesticide Exposure: The Causes and Consequences of DBCP-induced Damage in Costa Rica and Beyond." *International Journal of Health Services* 21 (1991): 731–757.

Tomich, Dale. "*Une Petite Guinée:* Provision Ground and Plantation in Martinique, 1830–1848." In *Cultivation and Culture: labor and the shaping of black life in the Americas,* eds. Ira Berlin and Philip Morgan, 221–242. Charlottesville: University of Virginia, 1993.

Topik, Steven C. "Coffee." In *The Second Conquest of Latin America: Coffee, Henequen, and Oil during the Export Boom, 1850–1930,* edited by Steven C. Topik and Allen Wells, 37–84. Austin: University of Texas Press, 1998.

———. "Coffee Anyone?" *Hispanic American Historical Review* 80, no. 2 (May 2000): 225–266.

———. "The Integration of the World Coffee Market." In *The Global Coffee Economy in Africa, Asia, and Latin America, 1500–1989,* edited by Steven Topik and William Gervase Clarence-Smith, 21–49. New York: Cambridge University Press, 2003.

Topik, Steven, and William Gervase Clarence-Smith, eds. *The Global Coffee Economy in Africa, Asia, and Latin America, 1500–1989.* New York: Cambridge University Press, 2003.

Torres Rivas, Edelberto. *History and Society in Central America.* Trans. Douglass Sullivan-González. Austin: University of Texas Press, 1993.

———. *Interpretación del desarrollo social centroamericano.* San José, Costa Rica: EDUCA, 1971.

Tortolero Villaseñor, Alejandro. "Transforming the Central Mexican Waterscape: Lake Drainage and its Consequences during the Porfiriato (1877–1911)." In *Territories, Commodities, and Knowledges: Latin American Environmental History in the Nineteenth and Twentieth Centuries,* ed. Christian Brannstrom, 121–147. London: Institute for the Study of the Americas, 2004.

Tucker, Richard. *Insatiable Appetite: The United States and the Ecological Degradation of the Tropical World.* Berkeley: University of California Press, 2000.

Tyrell, Ian. *True Gardens of the Gods: California-Australian Environmental Reform, 1860–1930.* Berkeley: University of California Press, 1999.

"United Fruit Adapts Chiquita as Brand Name." *Advertising Age* 13, May 1963, 3.

United Fruit Company. Department of Research. *Problems and Progress in Banana Disease Research* (Boston: 1958).

U.S. Department of Agriculture, Bureau of Agricultural Economics. *Consumption of Food in the United States, 1909–1952.* Washington, D.C.: USDA, 1957.

U.S. Department of Agriculture, Office of Foreign Agricultural Relations. "African Oil Palm in Central America." *Foreign Agricultural Report* no. 52 (Washington: Aug. 1950).

U.S. Department of Health and Human Services, Agency for Toxic Substances and Disease Registry, *Toxicological Profile for Copper* (Dec. 1990).

U.S. Department of State. *Foreign Relations of the United States* (1866), part 2.

U.S. Environmental Protection Agency. "Suspended, Cancelled and Restricted Pesticides." (Jan. 1985.)

van der Laat, J. E. "Las enfermedades del banano." *Boletín de Fomento de Costa Rica* no. 5 (1911–1914): 294–8.

Villar, T. G. "Vineyard Sprayer's Lung." *American Review of Respiratory Disease* 110 (1974): 545–555.

von Humboldt, Alexander, and Aimé Bonpland. *Personal Narratives of the Travels to the Equinoctial Regions of America during the Years 1799–1804,* vol. 1, ed. and trans. Thomasina Ross. London: Henry G. Bohn, 1852.

Wardlaw, Claude W. *Banana Diseases Including Plantains and Abaca.* London: Longmans, 1961.

———. *Diseases of the Banana and of the Manila Hemp Plant.* London: MacMillan, 1935.

———. "Panama Disease of Bananas: Reports on the Banana Growing Countries of the West Indies, Central and South America." London: HMSO, July 1929.

———. "Virgin Soil Deterioration." *Tropical Agriculture* 6, no. 9 (1929): 243–249.

Wells, Allen, and Steve Topik. *The Second Conquest of Latin America.* Austin: University of Texas Press, 1998.

White, Philip R. "A Disease and Evolution." *Scientific Monthly* 31 (1930): 306–318.

White, Richard. " 'Are You an Environmentalist or Do You Work for a Living?': Work and Nature." In *Uncommon Ground: Rethinking the Human Place in Nature,* edited by William Cronon, 171–185. New York: W. W. Norton, 1996.

Whitmore, Thomas M., and B. L. Turner. *Cultivated Landscapes of Middle America on the Eve of Conquest.* New York: Oxford University Press, 2001.

Wilcox, Robert W. "Zebu's Elbows: Cattle Breeding and the Environment in Central Brazil, 1890–1960." In *Territories, Commodities, and Knowledges: Latin American Environmental Histories in the Nineteenth and Twentieth Centuries,* ed. Christian Brannstrom, 218–246. London: Institute for the Study of the Americas, 2004.

Williams, Raymond. *Keywords.* New York: Oxford University Press, 1976.

Willis, Susan. "Learning from the Banana." *American Quarterly* 39, no. 4 (Winter 1987): 586–600.

Wilson, Charles Morrow. *Empire in Green and Gold.* New York: Henry Holt and Company, 1947.

Wright, Angus. *The Death of Ramón Gonzales: The Modern Agricultural Dilemma.* Austin: University of Texas Press, 1990.

Wrigley, Gordon. *Coffee.* London: Longman, 1988.

"Yes, They Sell More Bananas." *Business Week,* 8 July 1967, 90–94.

Young, Thomas. *Narrative of a Residence on the Mosquito Shore; with an Account of*

Truxillo and the Adjacent Islands of Bonacca and Roatan. New York: Krause Reprint Company, 1971 [1847].

UNPUBLISHED SOURCES

Bartlett, Wilson Randolph Jr. "Lorenzo D. Baker and the Development of the Banana Trade between Jamaica and the United States, 1881–1890." Ph.D. diss., American University, 1977.

Brand, Charles A. "The Background of Capitalistic Underdevelopment: Honduras to 1913." Ph.D. diss., University of Pittsburgh, 1972.

Calpouzos, Luis. "Studies on the Sigatoka Disease of Bananas and Its Fungus Pathogen." Typescript dated 1955.

Dunlap, Vining. "Sigatoka Disease." *United Fruit Company Tropical Research Department Bulletin* (Sept. 1950).

Echeverri-Gent, Elisavinda. "Labor, Class and Political Representation: A Comparative Analysis of Honduras and Costa Rica." Ph.D. diss., University of Chicago, 1988.

Ellis, Frank. "The Banana Export Activity in Central America, 1947–1976." Ph.D. diss., University of Sussex, 1978.

Euraque, Darío. "El imperialismo y Honduras como 'república bananera': Hacia una nueva historiografía." Paper presented at the Latin American Studies Conference, Guadalajara, Mexico, April 17–19, 1997.

Fruit Dispatch Company. "Conference Report." Chicago, 11–12 Nov. 1925.

Guevara Escudero, José. "Nineteenth Century Honduras: A Regional Approach to the Economic History of Central America, 1839–1914." Ph.D. diss., New York University, 1983.

Hobson, Jesse E. "Research in the United Fruit Company." Typescript dated 4 Nov. 1959.

Knudson, Lewis. "Report of Cercospora Disease of Banana in Honduras with Special Reference to Soil as a Factor." Typescript dated 17 Aug. 1936.

———. "The Palomas Nitrate Experiment." *United Fruit Company Research Department Bulletin* (1930).

LaBarge, Richard Allen. "A Study of United Fruit Company Operations in Isthmian America, 1946–1956." Ph.D. diss., Duke University, 1959.

Marbut, C. F., and Hugh H. Bennett. "Informe de los terrenos y la agricultura de la región cubierta por el estudio económico de la expedición guatemalteco-hondureña." In *Estudio económico de la zona fronteriza entre Guatemala y Honduras practicado durante los meses de mayo y junio de 1919 bajo la superintendencia de la Sociedad Geográfica Americana, para el departamento de Estado de los Estados Unidos de América.* Trans. J. E. M. Alonso. Unpublished manuscript.

McCook, Stuart. "The Flight of the Witches' Broom": Liberalism, Neoliberalism, and Epidemic Crop Diseases in Tropical Latin America, 1900–2000." Unpublished manuscript.

Muery, Henry O. "History of Standard Fruit Company Research, 1950–1980." Typescript dated 17 May 1984.

Nitkiowicz, B. "Observations on Panama Disease Conditions in Cultivated Areas,

Truxillo, Honduras." *United Fruit Company Research Department Bulletin* no. 38 (Aug. 1931).

Permar, J. H. "Banana Breeding." *United Fruit Company Research Department Bulletin* no. 21 (14 Oct. 1929).

Prescott, Samuel C. "Report on the Examination of Tropical Soils." Report submitted to the United Fruit Company, 1 Jul. 1918.

Ramírez Morales, Fernando. "La guerra contra los 'montes,' y la extracción de los 'palos': una aproximación histórico-ecológica a los procesos de degradación de los bosques nativos del sur de Chile." Paper presented at I Simposio de Historia Ambiental Americana, Santiago, Chile, 14–18 Jul. 2003.

Raup, Hugh M. "Notes on Reforestation in Tropical America III." Typescript dated Apr. 1951.

Shank, Paul J. "General Report of Results of Previous Reforestation Work and Recommendations for Future Planting." Typescript dated 12 Nov. 1958.

Soluri, John. "Development as Ideology: Small-settlers, Banana Plantations and Environmental Change in Jamaica, 1880–1906." Master's thesis, School of Natural Resources and Environment, University of Michigan, 1994.

Tela Railroad Company. "Un recorrido aéreo y por tren para conocer parte del programa de rehabilitación iniciado por la Tela RR Company después del desastre de septiembre de 1954." Mimeograph dated 18 Mar. 1956.

Thorton, Norwood C. "Control of Insects of the Banana." Paper presented at the First FAO/CCTA International Meeting on Banana Production, Abidjan, Ivory Coast, Oct. 12–19, 1960.

———. "Production Management of Gros Michel Bananas." Paper presented at the First FAO/CCTA International Meeting on Banana Production, Abidjan, Ivory Coast, 12–19 Oct. 1960.

United Brands. "Banana Operations Manual." 1970–1972.

United Fruit Company. "Report on the Nematode Survey of the Honduran Division, Tela Railroad Company." Report dated 1959.

———. "Summary of Discussions and Reports." Research Meetings, Palo Alto, California, 29–31 Aug. 1957.

———. "Jobber and Dealer Service Conference Proceedings." 18–20 Oct. 1954.

Volk, N. J. "Progress Report: The Apparent Relation of Active Calcium and Magnesium on the Activity of Panama Disease of Gros Michel Bananas." *United Fruit Company Research Department Bulletin* no. 30 (Oct. 1930).

———. "Preliminary Summary: The Relation of Various Soil Characteristics to the Activity of Panama Disease." *United Fruit Company Research Department Bulletin* no. 27 (Aug. 1930).

Index